Third Edition

THEATRE
Brief Version

· ·

ALSO BY ROBERT COHEN

Giraudoux: Three Faces of Destiny
Acting Power
Creative Play Direction, SECOND EDITION
    (WITH JOHN HARROP)
Eight Plays for Theatre
Acting Professionally, FOURTH EDITION
Acting in Shakespeare
Acting One, SECOND EDITION
Twelve Plays for Theatre
Theatre: THIRD EDITION

Third Edition

• •

THEATRE
Brief Version

R O B E R T   C O H E N

University of California, Irvine

MAYFIELD PUBLISHING COMPANY

Mountain View, California
London • Toronto

Copyright © 1994, 1988, 1983 by Robert Cohen

Library of Congress Cataloging-in-Publication Data

Cohen, Robert
   Theatre : brief version / Robert Cohen. — 3rd ed.
     p. cm.
   Includes bibliographical references and index.
   ISBN 1-55934-143-2
   1. Theater. I. Title.
PN2101.C632 1993
792 — dc20   92-46051
                          CIP

Manufactured in the United States of America
10 9 8 7 6 5 4 3 2

Mayfield Publishing Company
1240 Villa Street
Mountain View, California 94041

Sponsoring editor, C. Lansing Hays; production editor, Lynn Rabin Bauer; manuscript editor, Joan Pendleton; text and cover designer, Anna George; art director, Jeanne Schreiber; art editor, Robin Mouat; manufacturing manager, Martha Branch. The text was set in 10/12 Galliard by Thompson Type and printed on 50# Somerset Matte by Arcata Graphics.

TO WHITNEY COHEN

PREFACE

I am sitting in a darkened theatre correcting the galley sheets for the book you are about to read. A technical rehearsal for a play I am directing is in progress; I am seated at a makeshift desk in the back of the house, my reading illuminated by a tiny covered gooseneck lamp. On stage stand several actors, silent and motionless, as light plays over their faces and bodies. Above me, unseen and unheard, technicians operate, adjust, and record the settings for another of the play's hundred and fifty light cues. To the outside observer, it is the dullest situation imaginable; nothing observable happens for twenty or thirty minutes at a stretch. A pool of light intensifies and then recedes, muffled conversation crackles over headsets, footsteps clang on steel catwalks lacing the ceiling, and a spotlight is carefully repositioned. This has been going on now since eight in the morning, and it is already past dinnertime.

And yet my eye is continually pulled from these pages to the dance of light upon the stage. The violet and amber hues are rich with color, and the sharp shafts of incandescence dazzle with brilliance. I am fascinated by the patient weariness of the actors, alternately glowing in and then shadowed by the lights, endlessly holding the positions that, in performance, they will occupy for only a few transitory seconds. I gaze with admiration at the followspot operator, his hands gloved, as he handles his instrument with the precision and sensitivity of a surgeon.

The silence, the stasis, is hypnotic. All is quiet but profound with held-back beats, incipient torrents of passion and exhilaration. The potential is riveting — I am alive with excitement — and I look back to these cold galley sheets with alarm.

How can I have thought to express the thrill of the theatre in these pages? How can I have hoped to make recognizable the joy and awe I feel in theatrical involvement?

The theatre is not merely a collection of crafts, a branch of literature, a collaboration of technique, or even an all-encompassing art form. It is a life. It is people. It is people making art out of themselves. Its full reality transcends by light years anything that could be said or written about it.

What I have tried to do in these pages is not so much to introduce the theatre or to survey it as to *present* the theatre with its liveliness and humanness intact, with its incipient passion and exhilaration always present, with its potential for joy, awe, wisdom, and excitement as clear to the reader as they have been made clear to me.

WHAT'S NEW?

This is a brief version of a larger book that is being published simultaneously; both are third editions of volumes that first appeared in 1981 (*Theatre*) and 1983 (*Theatre: Brief Edition*). The larger volume includes four chapters on theatrical history that do not appear here and three chapters (instead of two) on the modern theatre. The third editions of both versions have been substantially revised and expanded, particularly in their coverage of modern theatrical activity.

The brief third edition continues the goal of the first and second: it is intended to provide students surveying theatrical theory and practice — but not dramatic history — with a comprehensive text in the dramatic arts as they exist today. The expanded section on modern theatre and the full-color photographs of current professional productions should help to amplify the successful realization of that goal.

No study of the theatre can be truly comprehensive, however, without seeing and reading plays. It is my hope that regular playgoing and playreading, supported by the discussions in these pages (and, if you choose, in the companion anthologies *Eight Plays for Theatre* and *Twelve Plays for Theatre*), will provide a foundation for the reader to develop an informed and critical enthusiasm for the art of drama, to which goal this book is dedicated.

ACKNOWLEDGMENTS

I again thank the people who contributed their help and concern in the preparation of the earlier editions of this book. I also am grateful to the many reviewers who made hundreds of suggestions for the three editions, all of which helped to sharpen my writing and improve my understanding of many fine points: Mary Jo Beresford, Northern Kentucky University; William Brasmer, Denison University; Bill G. Cook, Baylor University; Kenneth Cox, Oklahoma State University; Jerry L. Crawford, University of Nevada, Las Vegas; Al Cyrus, University of Maine; John Ford, Foothill College; Bob Hetherington, Wright State University; Robert Jenkins, San Jose State University; Joseph Karioth, Florida State University; Briant Hamor Lee, Bowling Green State University; Helen Manfull, Pennsylvania State University; W. Colin McKay, East Los Angeles College; James Norwood, University of Minnesota; Thomas Pallen, Austin Peay State University; Gordon Rogoff, Brooklyn College; Carl White, American River College; Joan-lee Woehler, Santa Rosa Junior College; Stephen Wyman, University of Texas; and James Yeater, Arizona State University.

During my photo research, I have been deeply indebted to Peter Roberts at *Plays International*, Christopher Gross at the South Coast Repertory Theatre, Achim Kuensebeck at the German Information Center, Michael Bigelow Dixon at the Actors Theatre of Louisville, Kent Thompson at the Alabama Shakespeare Festival, Scott Phillips and Bruce Lee at the Utah Shakespearean Festival, Daniel Y. Bauer at the McCarter Theater, Lara Rindfleisch at the Guthrie Theatre, Isaac Schambelain at the Theatre by the Blind, Katalin Mitchell and Manfred Kuhnert at the American Repertory Theatre, Carrie Jack at the Goodman Theatre, Sheryl Berger at the Alley Theatre, Teusa Masuda at the Japan America Theatre, Carol Fineman with Richard Kornberg and Associates, Scottie Hinckey and Mark Zufelt at the University of California, Irvine, and to the dozens of outstanding photographers whose work is featured in this text.

. . . .

CONTENTS

Third Edition

THEATRE
Brief Version

• •

It is evening in Manhattan. On Broadway and the streets that cross it—44th, 45th, 46th, 47th, 50th, 52nd—marquees light up, "Performance Tonight" signs materialize in front of double doors, and beneath a few box office windows placards announce "This Performance Completely Sold Out." At Grand Central Station three long blocks to the east and at Pennsylvania Station ten shorter blocks to the south, trains disgorge suburbanites from Greenwich, Larchmont, and Trenton, students from New Haven and Philadelphia, daytrippers from Boston and Washington. Up from the Seventh and Eighth Avenue subway stations of Times Square troop denizens of the island city and the neighboring boroughs. At the Times Square "TKTS" Booth, hundreds line up in the deepening chill to buy the half-price tickets that go on sale a few hours before curtain time for undersold shows. Now, converging on these few midtown blocks of America's largest city, come limousines, restaurant buses, private cars, and taxis, whose drivers search for a curbside slot to deposit their riders among the thousands of pedestrians who already throng the streets. Financiers and dowagers, bearded intellectuals, bedraggled bohemians, sleek executives, hip Harlemites, arm-in-arm widows, conventioneers, Japanese tourists, honeymooners, out-

INTRODUCTION

1

of-work actors, celebrities, pushers, the pre-cocious young—all commingle in this bizarre aggregation that is the Broadway audience. It is as bright, bold, and varied a crowd as is likely to assemble at any one place in America.

It is eight o'clock. In thirty or forty theatres houselights dim, curtains rise, spotlights pick out performers whose lives center on this moment. Here a new musical, here a star-studded revival of an American classic, here a contemporary English comedy from London's West End, here a new play fresh from its electrifying Seattle or San Diego premiere, here a one-woman show, here an off-Broadway hit moving to larger quarters, here a new avant-garde dance-drama, here a touring production from Eastern Europe, and here the new play everyone expects will capture this year's coveted Pulitzer Prize. The hours pass.

Eleven o'clock. Pandemonium. All the double doors open as at a signal, and once again the thousands pour out into the night. At nearby restaurants, waiters stand by to receive the after-theatre onslaught. In Sardi's private upstairs room, an opening-night cast party gets under way; downstairs, the patrons rehash the evening's entertainment and sneak covert glances at the celebrities around them and at the actors heading for the upstairs sanctuary to await the reviews that will determine whether they will be employed next week or back on the street.

Now turn back the clock.

It is dawn in Athens, the thirteenth day of the month of Elaphebolion in the year 458 B.C. From thousands of low mud-bricked homes in the city, from the central agora, from temples and agricultural outposts, streams of Athenians and visitors converge upon the south slope of the Acropolis. Bundled against the early damp, carrying with them breakfast figs and flagons of wine, they pay their tokens at the entrance to the great Theatre of Dionysus and take their places in the seating spaces allotted them. Each tribe occupies a separate area. They gather for the Festival of the Great Dionysia, celebrating the greening of the land, the rebirth of vegetation, and the long sunny days that stretch ahead. It is a time for revelry, a time for rejoicing at fertility and its fruits. And it is above all a time for the ultimate form of Dionysian worship: the theatre.

The open stone seats carved into the hillside fill up quickly. The crowd of 17,000 people here today comprises not only the majority of Athenian citizens, but thousands of non-citizens as well: women, slaves, tradesmen, foreign visitors, and resident aliens. Even the paupers are in attendance, thanks to the two obols meted out to each of them from a state fund so they can purchase entry; they sit with the foreigners and latecomers on the extremities of the *theatron*, as this first of theatres is called.

Now as the eastern sky grows pale, a masked and costumed actor appears atop a squat building set in full view of every spectator. A hush falls over the crowd, and the actor, his voice magnified by the wooden mask from which it emanates, booms out this text:

> I ask the gods some respite from the
>   weariness
> of this watchtime measured by years I lie
>   awake . . .

And the entranced crowd settles in, secure in the knowledge that today they are in good hands. Today they will hear and see a new version of a familiar story—the story of Agamemnon's homecoming and his murder, the revenge of that murder by his son Orestes, and the final disposition of justice in the case of Orestes' act—as told in the three tragedies that constitute *The Oresteia*. This magnificent trilogy will last from dawn to midafternoon and will be followed by a bawdy, hilarious, and mocking satyr play on the same theme by the same author. It is a story of astounding

The Broadway theatre district. About three dozen theatres line the streets of a mere ten blocks in midtown Manhattan; four of them — the Royale, the Golden, the Imperial (Les Misérables), and the Martin Beck (Guys and Dolls) — are shown here in a single half-block of 45th street. Broadway was largely developed at the turn of the century as theatres replaced aging apartment buildings in what was originally a quiet residential district known as Longacre Square. The theatres — mostly designed by one man, Herbert J. Krapp — are relatively intimate (most seat 1,000 or less), and are closely situated, making for a bustling concentration of theatres unknown in most other cities.

familiarity; but today it will take on a new complexity owing to the dramatic intrigue, suspense, spectacle, and rhetorical magnificence, as well as the complicated interpretations of character, motivation, and moral ramifications supplied by the playwright Aeschylus, Athens' leading dramatist for more than forty years. The spectators watch closely, admiring but critical. Tomorrow they or their representatives will have to decide by vote whether the festival prize should go to this group of plays or to one of those shown yesterday or the day before, whether Aeschylus still reigns supreme or the young Sophocles has better sensed the true pulse of the time.

Night falls, the plays are over. Back to the agora, to the baths, to the establishments of the courtesans, and finally to their homes go the Athenians to discuss what they have seen. Even forty years later the comic playwright Aristophanes will be arguing the merits and demerits of this day's work.

It is noon in London, and the first Queen Elizabeth sits on the throne. Flags fly boldly atop three of the taller buildings in Bankside, on the other side of the Thames, announcing performance day at The Globe, The Rose, and The Swan. Boatmen have already begun ferrying theatre-bound Londoners across the broad river. Meanwhile, north of town, other flocks of Londoners are headed by foot and by carriage up to Finsbury Fields and the theatres of Shoreditch: The Fortune and The Curtain. Public theatres have been banned in the city for some time now by action of the Lords Aldermen; however, an ensemble of trained schoolboys is rehearsing for a private candlelight performance before the Queen.

Now, as the morning sermon concludes at St. Paul's Cathedral, the traffic across the river increases; London Bridge fills with pedestrians hurrying to Bankside, where The Globe players will present a new tragedy by Shakespeare (something called *Hamlet,* supposedly after an old play by Thomas Kyd), and The

Rose promises a revival of the late Christopher Marlowe's *Dr. Faustus.* The noisy crowds swarm into the theatres, where the price of admission is a penny; another penny is needed for a pint of beer, and those who wish to go upstairs and take a seat on one of the benches in the gallery—the best place to see the action, both on stage and off—must plunk down yet more pennies.

At The Globe, 2,000 spectators are on hand for the premiere. A trumpet sounds, sounds again, and then builds into a full fanfare. The members of the audience exchange a few last winks with friends old and new, covert and overt invitations to postperformance intimacies of various kinds, and then turn their attention to the pillared, trestled, naked stage. Through one giant door Bernardo bursts forth. "Who's there?" he cries. Then through another door, a voice: "Nay, answer me: stand and unfold yourself," and Francisco enters with lighted lantern in hand. In 2,000 imaginations, the bright afternoon turns to midnight, the Bankside gives way to the outskirts of Elsinore. A shiver from the actors on stage sets up an answering chill among the audience as Francisco proclaims, "'Tis bitter cold, and I am sick at heart." The audience strains forward. The tragedy has begun.

It is evening at Versailles, 1664. King Louis XIV nods graciously as the celebrated actor-playwright bows before him. Jean Baptiste Poquelin, known throughout France as Molière, has just presented his *Tartuffe,* with its scathingly witty denunciation of the powerful Church extremists. The courtiers, taking Louis's nod, applaud vigorously; in one corner of the glittering hall, however, a bishop glares coldly at the actor. The Archbishop of Paris will hear of this.

It is 5 A.M. in Moscow, 1898. At a café in the shadow of the Kremlin wall, Konstantin Stanislavski and Vladimir Nemirovich-Danchenko hotly discuss the wretched state of the current

Russian theatre. It is too declamatory, they agree; it is also too insensitive, too shallow, too inartistic. Out of this all-night session the Moscow Art Theatre will be formed, bringing to the last days of czarist society the complex, gently ironic masterpieces of Chekhov and an acting style so natural as to astonish the world.

It is midnight in a coffeehouse in the East Village, or on the Left Bank, or in the campus rehearsal room. Across one end of the room, a curtain has been drawn across a pole suspended by wires. It has been a long evening, but a play yet remains to be seen. The author is unknown, but rumor says that this new work is brutal, shocking, poetic, strange. The audience, by turns skeptics and enthusiasts, look for the tenth time at their programs. The lights dim. Performers, backed by crudely painted packing crates, begin to act.

There is a common denominator in all these scenes: they are all theatre.

Theatre is the most natural of the arts. There is no culture that has not had a theatre in some form, for theatre, quite simply, is the art of people acting out—and giving witness to—their most pressing, most illuminating, and most inspiring concerns. Theatre is at once a showcase and a forum, a medium through which a society's ideas, fashions, moralities, and entertainments can be displayed and its conflicts, dilemmas, and struggles can be debated. Theatre has provided a stage for political revolution, for social propaganda, for civil debate, for artistic expression, for religious conversions, for mass education, and even for its own self-criticism. It has been a performance ground for witch doctors and priests, intellectuals, poets, painters, technologists, militarists, philosophers, reformers, evangelists, prime ministers, jugglers, peasants, children, and kings. It has taken place in caves, in fields and forests, in circus tents, in inns and in castles, on street corners, and in public buildings grand and squalid all over the world. And it goes on incessantly in the minds of its authors, its actors, its producers, its designers, and its audiences.

For theatre is, above all, a *living* art form—a *process,* an *event* that is fluid in time, feeling, and experience. It is not simply a matter of "plays," but also of "playing"; and a play is composed not simply of "acts," but also of "acting." As "play" and "act" are both noun and verb, so theatre is both a "thing" and a "happening." It is continually forming, continually present in time. In fact, that very quality of "presentness" (or, in the actor's term, "stage presence") defines great theatrical performance.

Theatre, unlike the more static arts, presents a number of classic paradoxes:

> It is unique to the moment, yet it is repeatable.
> It is spontaneous, yet it is rehearsed.
> It is participatory, yet it is presented.
> It is real, yet it is simulated.
> It is understandable, yet it is obscure.
> The actors are themselves, yet they are characters.
> The audience believes, yet it does not believe.
> The audience is involved, yet it remains apart.

These paradoxes stem not from any flaw or weakness in the logic of theatrical construction, but from the theatre's essential strength, which resides in its kinship and concern with the ambiguity and irony of human life—our life. It is *we* who are at the same time unique yet conventional, spontaneous yet premeditating, involved yet isolated, candid yet contriving, comprehensible yet fundamentally unknown and unknowable. Theorists of dramatic literature and of dramatic practice often ignore these paradoxes in their attempts to "explain" a play or the art of the stage; in this they do a grave disservice to art as well as to scholarship, for to "explain" the theatre without reference to its ambiguities is to remove its dynamic tension — in other words, to kill it. And although much valuable information can certainly be discovered at an autopsy table, it is information pertinent only to the appearance and behavior of a corpse.

In this book we shall not be overly concerned with corpses. Our task will be the harder one — to discover the theatre in being, *alive* and with all its paradoxes and ambiguities intact. From time to time it will be necessary for us to make some separations — between product and process, for example — but we must bear in mind at all times that these separations are conveniences, not representations or fact. In the end we shall be looking at the theatre as part of the human environment and at the ways in which we fit into that environment — as participants and observers, artists and art critics, role models and role players, actors and persons. So this book about the theatre is also about ourselves.

$\mathbf{W}$ •

hat is the theatre?

The word comes from the Greek *theatron,* or "seeing place." It is "a place where something is seen."

And the companion term *drama* comes from the Greek *dran,* "to do." It is "something done."

Theatre: Something is seen, something is done.

We now use the word *theatre* in many ways.

We use it often to describe the *building* where plays are put on: the architecture, the structure, the *space* for dramatic performance—the place where "something is seen." In popular parlance, we also use the term to indicate where films are shown, as in "movie theatre." And we use it metaphorically to refer to where wars and surgeries take place: the theatre of operations and the operating theatre.

But that's just the "hardware" definition of theatre, the merely physical layout. The "software" definition—the theatre *activity* that goes into a theatre—is far more important.

For *theatre* also refers to the *company of players* (and owners, and managers, and technicians) that perform in such a space and to the body of plays that such a company will tend to produce. This is the "something that is done." When we say "the Guthrie Theatre,"

CHAPTER 1

WHAT IS THE THEATRE?

THEATRE AND DRAMA

The words *theatre* and *drama* are often used interchangeably, yet they can also have distinct meanings.

While both are very general terms, *theatre* often denotes the elements of the whole theatrical production (architecture, scenery, acting) and *drama,* a more limited term, tends to refer mainly to the plays that are produced in such a "theatrical" environment. To use a modern metaphor, theatre is the "hardware" of play production, and drama is the "software." This reflects back on the words' separate etymologies: theatre is that which "is seen," and drama is that which "is done."

"Theatre" can mean a building; "drama" cannot. "Theatre" is used to include all the theatrical arts — architecture, design, acting, scenery construction, advertising, marketing, and so on — while "drama" is often used in a more limited sense to refer to plays and to dramatic texts (or dramatic literature). Therefore drama-derived terms like *dramatic* and *dramaturgy* are often used to refer to the verbal aspects of theatre; "theatrical" tends to suggest visual aspects, as well as "effects" that generate audience impact. (Detractors of the theatre sometimes use the word *theatrical* in a pejorative sense, implying gaudiness and sensationalism, as in "mere theatricality.")

In some parts of North America, particularly in Canada, a further distinction is made, where *theatre* is used more to denote staged plays (the product), and *drama* refers more to the acting and improvising of situations (the process).

we are referring not merely to a building on Vineland Place in Minneapolis, but also to the group of stage artists and administrators that work in this building and to the body of plays that are produced there. We are also referring to a body of ideas — a vision — that animates the artists and integrates them with the body of plays. "Theatre," in this sense, is a combination of people, ideas, and the works of art that emanate from their collaboration.

And, finally, we also use the word *theatre* to summon up an *occupation* that is the professional activity — and often the passion — of thousands of men and women all over the world. It is a vocation, and sometimes a lifetime devotion. *A Life in the Theatre* is the title of one theatre artist's autobiography (Tyrone Guthrie, in fact, for whom the Guthrie Theatre is named), but it is also the informal title for the unwritten biographies of all theatre artists who have dedicated their professional lives to perfecting the special arts of acting, directing, designing, managing, and writing for "the theatre" in *all* of the above senses.

A building, a company, an occupation: we should look at all three of these more closely.

THE THEATRE BUILDING

Sometimes it's not a building at all, but merely, in Peter Brook's term, an empty space. The most ancient Greek *theatron* was probably nothing but a flat circle where performers chanted and danced before a hillside where people sat watching them. The minimal requirement for a theatre "building" is nothing but a place to act and a place to watch.

And when there is a text for the performance, it is a place to *hear* as well as to watch. Hence the word *audience,* from the Latin "those who hear."

The empty space needs some definition, then. This includes some attention to a large number of people seeing the performers, hence the hillside presenting a bank of seats, each with a good view. It also includes some attention to *acoustics* (from the Greek *acoustos,* "heard") so that the sound is protected from the wind and directed (or reflected) toward the hearers.

Often these "places"—for performing and for seeing and hearing—can be casually defined: the audience up there, the actors down there. Occasionally, the spaces are even merged together, with the actors mingling with—and sometimes interacting with—the watchers and listeners. When tickets began to be sold and actors began to be paid (both practices are more than twenty-five hundred years old), rigid physical separation of the spaces began to be employed.

Theatre buildings may also be very elaborate structures. Greek theatres of the fourth century B.C.—the period immediately follow-ing the "Golden Age" of Greek playwrights—were gigantic stone edifices, capable of holding upwards of 17,000 spectators at a time. Magnificent, three-story Roman theatres, complete with gilded columns, canvas awnings, and intricate marble carvings, were often erected for dramatic festivals in the time of Nero and Caligula—only to be dismantled when the festivities ended. Grandly free-standing Elizabethan theatres utterly dominated the London skyline in the illustrated sixteenth-century pictorial maps of the town. Opulent proscenium theatres were built throughout Europe and in the major cities of the United States in the eighteenth and nineteenth centuries, and many are in full operation today—where they compete with

The audience surrounds the action in Tyrone Guthrie's 1963 production of The Three Sisters *at the Guthrie Theatre in Minneapolis. (Photo: Courtesy the Guthrie Theatre.)*

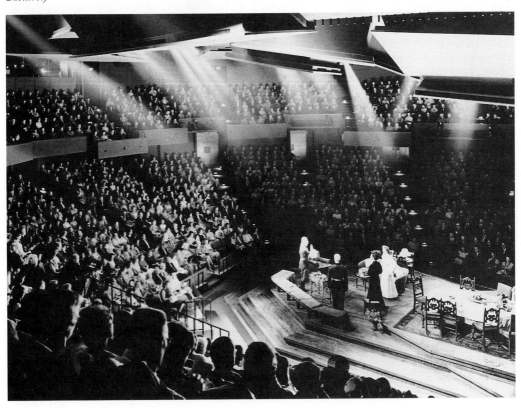

A play's action may be staged wherever an audience can see it. In this "open" environmental staging, actors surround — and are surrounded by — the audience. (Photo: Martha Swope.)

splendid new stagehouses of every description, serving as the urban focus for metropolitan areas around the world. Theatres (the buildings) are central to modern urban architecture, just as theatre (the art) is central to contemporary life.

THE COMPANY OR "TROUPE" OF PLAYERS

Theatre is a collaborative art, usually involving dozens, even hundreds, of people for a single performance. Historically, therefore, theatre practitioners have worked together in long-standing companies or "troupes" of such theatre artists. Since the third century B.C.,

companies or troupes of "players" (actors or, more generally, play-makers) have toured the countrysides and settled in cities to present a repertory (or repertoire) of plays as a means of earning their livelihood. Generally these players have included actor-playwrights and actor-technicians as well, so that the company becomes a self-contained production unit, capable of writing, preparing, and presenting whole theatrical works that tend to define the "theatre" named after it. Some of these troupes — and the works spawned by them — have become legendary: the Lord Chamberlain's Men of London, which counted actor-playwright William Shakespeare as a member; the Kabuki Theatre of Edo (now Tokyo), which was the artistic home of the great Japanese writer Chikamatsu; various *commedia dell'arte* troupes that toured Italy during the Renaissance; and the "Illustrious Theatre" of Paris, founded and headed by the great actor-writer Molière. These companies and their works will be remembered as long as civilization endures. And mid-twentieth-century American theatre troupes, such as the Living Theatre of Julian Beck and Judith Malina, the Open Theatre headed by Joseph Chaikin, and the Story Theatre ensemble gathered around Paul Sills, have enjoyed a vibrant history in relatively recent times, with, in many cases, the company members sharing living quarters as well as theatrical duties. A theatre troupe is something more than a purely professional association; it inevitably includes at least a notion of an artistic "family."

These "theatres"—these companies of players—have proven more long-lasting than the buildings that in some cases survived them; they represent the genius and creativity of theatre in a way that stone and steel alone cannot.

In a more general sense, we may also treat theatre practitioners as theatre "families" linked by geography, era, aesthetics, or ideology. In this way, the term *theatre* may also be used to indicate a category of associated works, such as the American theatre, the Elizabethan theatre, dance theatre, musical theatre, the theatre of the absurd, the theatre of Neil Simon, and black theatre: any or all of these terms may serve to represent a specifically defined grouping of plays, players, authors, and buildings that form a broad identity in the minds of theatre students, critics, and enthusiasts.

Improvisational theatre is sheer performance—performance without script. Here the Paul Sills company is seen in a presentation of "Story Theatre," which consists of children's stories improvised and acted out by versatile adult performers. Originally produced at the Mark Taper Forum Theatre in Los Angeles, Sills's Story Theatre proved immensely popular and subsequently enjoyed a considerable run on Broadway. (Photo: Courtesy Mark Taper Forum.)

THE OCCUPATION OF THEATRE

And, finally, theatre is a principal occupation of its practitioners — a vocation for professionals, an avocation for amateurs. In either case, theatre is *work*. Specifically, it is that body of artistic work in which actors impersonate characters in a live performance of a play. Each one of these terms deserve some attention in this chapter designed to address the question, What is theatre?

Work

The "work" of the theatre is indeed hard work. An original play — as distinct from a revival — usually takes about one year to produce and often five years or more from conception to actual presentation. Rehearsal alone accounts for a minimum of four weeks, and for most effective productions it goes on a good deal longer. The labors of theatre artists in the final weeks before an opening are legendary: the ninety-hour week becomes commonplace, expenditures of money and spirit are intense, and even the unions relax their regulations to allow for an almost unbridled invasion of the hours the ordinary world spends sleeping, eating, and unwinding. The theatre enterprise may involve hundreds of people in scores of different efforts — many more backstage than onstage — and the mobilization and coordination of these efforts is in itself a giant task. So when we think of the "work" embodied in the plays of Shakespeare or Neil Simon, for example, we must think of work in the sense of physical toil as well as in the loftier sense of *oeuvre,* by which the French designate the sum of an artist's creative endeavor.

The work of the theatre is generally divisible into a number of crafts:

Acting, in which actors perform the roles of characters in a play

Designing, in which designers map out the visual and audio elements of a production, including the scenery, properties, costumes and wigs, make-up, lighting, sound concepts, programs, advertising, and general ambience of the premises

Building, in which carpenters, costumers, wigmakers, electricians, make-up artists, recording and sound engineers, painters, and a host of other specially designated craftspeople translate the design into reality by constructing and finishing in detail the "hardware" of a show

Running, in which technicians execute in proper sequence, and with carefully rehearsed timing, the light and sound cues, the shifting of scenery, the placement and return of properties, and the assignment, laundering, repair, and changes of costumes

Producing, which includes securing all necessary personnel, space, and financing, supervising all production and promotion efforts, fielding all legal matters, and distributing all proceeds derived from receipts

Directing, which includes controlling and developing the artistic product and providing it with a unified vision, coordinating all its components, and supervising all rehearsals

Stage managing, which includes the responsibility for "running" a play production in all its complexity in performance after performance

House managing, which includes the responsibility for admitting, seating, and providing for the general comfort of the audience

And finally, there is *playwriting,* which is in a class by itself. It is the one craft of the theatre that is usually executed away from the theatre building and its associated shops—that may indeed take place continents and centuries away from the production it inspires.

Of course, the work of the theatre need not be apportioned precisely as the preceding list indicates. In any production, some people will perform more than one kind of work; for example, many of the "builders" will also be "runners." Moreover, many a play has been produced with the actors directing themselves, or the director handling production duties, or the dialogue improvised by the actors and director. On occasion most, if not all, of the craft functions have been performed by the same person: Aeschylus not only wrote, directed, and designed his Greek tragedies, but he probably also performed the leading parts. Although there is nothing inevitable or necessary about the allocation of craft functions of the theatre's work, the functions themselves have remained fairly constant over the theatre's history. In virtually every era we can look back and see the same sorts of work going on—and the same kinds of efforts being expended—as we see in the work of the theatre today, be it professional or amateur, American or European, commercial or academic. Later on in this book we shall take a closer look at the various craft and managerial functions that go into the creation of a theatrical event.

Theatre is also work in the sense that it is not "play." This is a more subtle distinction than we might at once imagine. First, of course, recall that we ordinarily use the word "play" in describing the main product of theatre work. This is not merely a peculiarity of

the English tongue; for we find that the French *jeu,* the German *Spiel,* and the Latin *ludi* all share the double meaning of the English *play,* referring both to plays and playing in the theatrical sense and to sports activities or games. This association points to a relationship that is fundamental to the understanding of theatre: theatre *is* a kind of game, and it is useful for us to see how and why this is so.

The theatre and games have a shared history. Both were developed to a high level of sophistication in Greek festivals: the Dionysian festivals for theatre and the Olympian festivals for sport were the two great cultural events of ancient Greece at which the legendary Greek competition for excellence was most profoundly engaged. The Romans merged sports and theatre in their circuses, where the two were performed side by side and in competition with each other. In much the same fashion, the Elizabethan Londoners built playhouses to accommodate both dramatic productions and animal-baiting spectacles somewhat akin to the modern bullfight; the stage that was set up for the plays was simply removed for "play." Today, sports and dramatizations dominate the television fare that absorbs so much leisure time not only in America but also in most of the Western world. Moreover, professional athletes and entertainers are among the foremost celebrities of the modern age—and many a retired sports hero has found a second career in acting. Thus it is not extraordinary that sports and the theatre still share in the compound use of the word *play.*

For the individual, a link between games and theatre is formed early in life, in "child's play," which usually manifests both gamelike and dramalike aspects. The game of hide-and-seek, for example, is a playful competition between children that can be repeated over and over, a harmless but engrossing activity involving counting, hiding, searching, and at last the triumph of finding. It is also an acting out of one of childhood's greatest fears—the fear of separation from the parent, or "separation anxiety," as psychologists term it. Hide-and-seek affords the child a way of dealing with that fear by confronting it over and over "in play" until it loses much of its power. Play is *often* grounded in serious concerns, and through play the individual gradually develops means of coping with life's challenges and uncertainties.

Drama and sports are different but related adult forms of the same "play." One of the aspects of adult play—in both its forms—is that it attracts a tremendous amateur following; as child's play is engaged in without prompting or reward, so adult sports and theatre commonly yield no remuneration beyond sheer personal satisfaction. Both sports and theatricals offer splendid opportunities for intense physical involvement, competition, self-expression, and emotional engagement—and all within limits set by precise and sensible rules. What is more, both can generate an audience because the energies and passions they project are rarely expressed so openly in daily life beyond the playgrounds of childhood. It is little wonder that people who spend a lifetime in the theatre or in athletics are often regarded as childlike—or, more pejoratively, as immature and irresponsible—for their "playing" evokes memories of youth.

But the theatre must finally be distinguished from child's play, and from sports as well, because theatre is by its nature a calculated act from beginning to end. Unlike adult games, which are open-ended, every theatre performance has a preordained conclusion. The Yankees may not win the World Series this year, but Hamlet definitely will die in the fifth act. The *work* of the theatre, indeed, consists in keeping Hamlet alive up to that point—brilliantly alive—to make of that foreordained end a profoundly moving, ennobling, even surprising climax to the whole experience.

We might say, finally, that *theatre is the art of making play into work; specifically, into a work of art*. It is exhilarating work, to be sure, and it usually inspires and invigorates the energies

and imaginations of all who participate; it transcends more prosaic forms of labor as song transcends grunts and groans. But it is work: that is its challenge, and the great accomplishments of the theatre are always attended by prodigious effort.

Art

As we have suggested, the work of the theatre goes beyond the mere perfecting of skills, which is after all a goal of professionals in every field of endeavor. The theatre is *artistic* work. The word *art* brings to mind a host of intangibles: creativity, imagination, elegance, power, aesthetic harmony, and fineness of form; in addition, we expect a work of art to capture something of the human spirit and to touch upon sensed, but intellectually elusive, meanings in life. Certainly great theatre never fails to bring together many of these intangibles. In great theatre we glimpse not only the physical and emotional exuberance of play, but also the deep yearnings that propel humanity's search for purpose, meaning, and the life well lived.

Art, of course, is one of the most supreme pursuits of humanity, integrating, in a unique fashion, our emotions with our intellects and our aesthetics with our revelations. Art is empowering, to both those who make it and those who appreciate it. Art sharpens thought and focuses feeling; it brings reality up against imagination and presses creativity to the ever-

Audiences are first captivated by the sheer exuberance of August Wilson's characters and then drawn into the tragedies and broken dreams that confront at least some of them. Wilson's plays, such as The Piano Lesson *shown here, provoke laughter and tears, entertainment and profound realizations. The play, under the direction of Lloyd Richards, won the 1990 Pulitzer Prize. The talented ensemble includes, left to right, Lou Myers, Rocky Carroll, Samuel L. Jackson, and Carl Gordon. From the world premiere production at the Yale Repertory Theatre. (Photo: Gerry Goodstein.)*

expanding limits of human potential. Although life may be fragmented, inconclusive, and finally frustrating, art can provide integration, synthesis, and lasting satisfaction. One might, of course, find similar values in religion or philosophy as well; but art, lacking a formal dogma, is accessible without catechism: it is an ecumenical and open-ended response — and a refreshingly civil approach — to life's unending puzzles. It is for this very reason that all great religions — Eastern and Western, ancient and modern — have expansively employed art and artworks (including great exemplars of dramatic art) in their liturgies, structures, and services from the very earliest of times.

The art of the theatre is never "pure" art in the sense that it represents the personal vision of a solitary artist. Indeed, many "pure" artists consider theatrical art a bastard form, combining as it does the several arts of acting, writing, designing, directing, and architecture. It is perhaps significant, however, that such great individual artists as Shelley, Beethoven, Piranesi, Tolstoy, Eliot, Palladio, and Yeats have achieved only moderate success when they turned their efforts to this impure art; the theatre seems to reserve its greatest rewards for those whose artistic lives are first and foremost theatrical. The creative work of the theatre is in its essence collaborative and interdisciplinary, and thus its art can be judged only on its own merits.

Impersonation

The theatrical art involves actors impersonating characters. This feature is unique to the theatre and separates it quite definitively from other art forms such as poetry, painting, sculpture, music, performance art, and the like. Furthermore, impersonation is the single most important aspect of the theatre; it is its very foundation.

Try to imagine what extreme conceptual difficulties the ancient creators of the theatre must have encountered in laying down the ground rules for dramatic impersonation. For how was the audience to distinguish the "real person" from the "character" portrayed, the actor-as-himself from the actor-as-character? And when the playwright was also an actor, how could onlookers distinguish between the

In Jean Genet's The Blacks, *black actors wear white make-up or white masks as shown here in the American premiere of the play directed by Gene Frankel. This bitterly ironic play deals with the social masks an individual wears and with the way racial accommodation is determined by skin color. (Photo: Martha Swope and Associates.)*

thoughts of playwright-as-himself and those of the playwright-as-character? Questions such as these are often asked by children today as they watch a play; and it is inevitable that when a public press conference is arranged by the producer of a television soap opera, some fans will address the actors by the names of the characters they play and ask them questions pertinent only to their stage lives. Given this confusion in what we like to think of as a sophisticated age, it is easy to see why the ancients had to resolve the problem of actor-character separation before the theatre could become a firmly established institution.

The solution the ancient world found was the mask. We might say that Western theatre had its true beginning that day in ancient Greece when an actor first stepped out of the chorus, placed an unpainted mask over his face, and thereby signaled that the lines he was about to speak where "in character." The Noh Drama in Japan and many of the ritual dance-dramas of Africa, Asia, and native America have used the mask to similar effect. Basically, the mask is the tool of impersonation, at once hiding the face of the performer and projecting that of the "character" demanded by the play. Although today the mask is rarely seen in the dramas of the Western world, it remains the symbol of the theatre — usually in the form of the double masks of Comedy and Tragedy that adorn the prosceniums of numerous playhouses and the letterheads of various theatrical organizations.

The mask provides a physical as well as symbolic separation between the impersonator and the impersonated, thus aiding the literal-minded onlooker to suspend awareness of the real world of the former and to accept in its place the stage world of the latter. In a play, it must be the "characters" who have apparent life; the actors themselves are expected to disappear into the shadows, along with their personal preoccupations, anxieties, and career ambitions. This convention gives rise to one of the great paradoxes of the theatre, what the eighteenth-century French en-

The opulent interior of Booth's Theatre, New York, at its 1869 opening. This grand "temple of theatre" was built by America's finest actor of the time, Edwin Booth (the brother of Lincoln's assassin). Booth staged and performed in a classical repertory of Shakespearean plays at his theatre for four years. The side "boxes," similar to those that still exist in older Broadway theatres today, had poor sight lines: spectators electing to sit there were more interested in being seen than in seeing the play. The luxurious seating in the orchestra made this a particularly comfortable as well as an elegant way to see classic theatre. This watercolor was painted by Charles Witham, Booth's original stage designer; part of Witham's scenery (a street scene) is shown on stage. (Courtesy Museum of the City of New York. Photo: Judy Davis.)

Exciting theatre today is not always comfortable; audiences often have to "work" as well. Here, at dawn in Central Park, producer Joseph Papp addresses the audience after the New York Shakespeare Festival's all-night production of the "Wars of the Roses" (the three parts of Shakespeare's Henry VI plus Richard III). Papp, who founded the Festival and headed it until his death in 1991, continually challenged—as well as entertained—a vast public. (Photo: George Joseph.)

Kabuki is a traditional and enormously popular musical dance-drama, performed in Japan for more than 500 years. Employing highly stylized costumes, props, and make-up, the Kabuki actors (all are male) perform with dazzling virtuosity. Most actors are members of historic Kabuki families, as is Ichikawa Danjuro XII, pictured, performing with the Royal Kabuki Theatre. (Photo: Courtesy Japanese-American Cultural and Community Center.)

cyclopedist Denis Diderot called "the paradox of the actor": when the actor has perfected his or her art it is the *simulated* character, the mask, which seems to live before our eyes, while the *real* person has no apparent life at all. The strength of such an illusion still echoes in our use of the word *person*, which derives from the Latin word for mask.

But of course we know that the actor does not die behind the mask, and herein lies perhaps an even greater paradox. We believe in the character, but at the end of the play we

applaud the actor. Not only that—but as we watch good theatre we are always, somewhere in the back of our mind, applauding the actor. Our appreciation of theatre rests largely on our dual awareness of actor and character and our understanding that they live inside the same skin.

Actors, of course, are aware of the same duality. For them, the art of acting is a sublime combination of the freedom that comes with anonymity (since they are hidden in their roles) and the ego gratification that comes with exhibitionism. Thus actors commonly report that they both "lose themselves" and "find themselves" in theatrical performances and indeed that these phenomena sometimes happen simultaneously. The sense of liberation and heightened self-awareness that comes with an intense, creative effort within a standardized, formalized structure is one of the functions of all play, including sport.

The act of impersonation, with or without an actual mask, depends on an implicit agreement or set of agreements between actor and audience. In essence, the agreement is that the actor will pretend to "be" a character and the audience will pretend to "see" him or her as that character. This agreement does not at all mean that the actor must perform the role in a lifelike manner. On the contrary, the agreement concerning mutual pretense allows the acceptance on both sides of certain conditions, such as that the character will wear a mask, or speak into a microphone, or perform a dance when angered, or employ any of the scores of other devices and actions that have found acceptance in the theatre over time. In this century, particularly since the rise of motion pictures and television, much attention has been paid to the desirability of the actor's "use of self" in creating the characters he or she plays; this emphasis reflects a trend, but not a fundamental shift, in the art of theatrical impersonation. Remember that impersonation itself remains a constant in the theatre despite changing modes and styles of theatrical presentation.

Throughout history actors have often been accused of flirting with a suspect morality in impersonating characters. Audiences too have been castigated for applauding this impiety. The Greek word for actor was *hypokrites,* a term that originally meant "answerer" (the actor "answered" the odes of a chorus), but it came to mean "pretender" as well. The more negative connotation has come down to us as "one who dissembles." Indeed, the oldest recorded anecdote in theatrical history portrays the ancient lawmaker Solon chiding Thespis,

the first actor, for "telling so many lies before such a number of people." When Thespis replies that there is no harm in lying "in play," Solon answers, "Ah, if we honor and commend such 'play' as this, we shall find it some day in our business." At least since Solon's day, actors have had to contend with varying degrees of social skepticism, and the same notoriety that has given them celebrity status has occasioned intense and often disapproving curiosity about their private affairs.

The impersonation that underlies the acting art is not, however, aimed at imposture; its goal is artistic. The actor does not pretend to "be someone else," for a dramatic character is not a person but an abstraction, no more human than paint on a canvas or words on a page. It is true that the dramatic character is represented by a living person who goes through the motions of the character's acts and in many cases experiences them fully as well. It is also true that some characters are drawn from life, and their dialogue may be taken from the actual transcripts of a historical event. Nonetheless, the character is not a "somebody else"; it is an artistic fabrication — a shaped presence — that gains acceptance as a real person only by virtue of the implicit agreement of actors and audience alike. Actors deserve no moral disgrace for engaging in impersonation, nor should they feel hypocritical about engaging in impersonated acts and feelings; they are "honest hypocrites," in William Hazlitt's words, and their pretending is simply part of the artistic work of an old and endlessly creative profession.

Nowadays, as we have seen, the art of impersonation rarely calls for use of a mask that conceals the actor's face; instead, costume, make-up, dialogue, accent, movement, gesture, and a variety of acting methods and techniques support the delineation of character formerly expressed by mask and voice alone. Owing to a twentieth-century emphasis on verisimilitude, most American and European actors favor, in whole or in part, the concepts of Konstantin Stanislavski, the Russian actor-director and acting teacher who proclaimed that the actor should "live the life of the character onstage." This view has fostered the development of a number of techniques and training methods to aid the actor not only in performing a character's actions in minute physiological detail, but also in experiencing the character's feelings to such a degree that occasionally even the presence of the audience is forgotten. If this movement of modern times has its fervent supporters, however, it also has its equally aroused critics. It is probably fairest to say that the question of the proper relationship between the actor and the role—or of the degree to which the actor ought to "identify with" the part—remains as perplexing today as it was two hundred years ago when Diderot defined the paradox of acting.

Performance

Theatre is performance; but what, exactly, does "performance" mean? Simply stated, performance is an action or series of actions taken for the ultimate benefit (attention, entertainment, enlightenment, or involvement) of someone else. We call that someone else the audience.

If two people engage in a strictly private conversation, that is a simple communication between them. If, however, their conversation is undertaken in order to impress or involve a third person who they know is in a position to overhear it, the "communication" becomes a performance and the third person becomes its audience.

Obviously, performance is a part of everyday life; indeed, it has been analyzed as such in a number of recently published psychological and sociological works. When two teenage boys wrestle on the schoolground, they may well be "performing" their physical prowess for the benefit of their peers. The student who asks a question in the lecture hall is frequently "performing" for the other students—

and the professor "performs" for the same audience in providing a response. Trial lawyers examining witnesses invariably "perform," often drawing on a considerable repertoire of grunts, snorts, shrugs, raised eyebrows, and disbelieving sighs for the benefit of that ultimate courtroom audience, the jury. Politicians kiss babies for the benefit of parents (and others) in search of a kindly candidate. Even stony silence can be a performance—if, for example, it is the treatment a woman metes out to an offensive admirer. We are all performers, and the theatre only makes an art out of something we all do every day.

The theatre reflects our everyday performances and expands those performances into a formal mode of artistic expression.

The theatre makes use of two general modes of performance: direct and indirect. Direct performance is the basic nightclub mode. Nightclub performers continuously acknowledge the presence of the audience: they sing to them, dance for them, joke at them, and respond overtly to their applause, laughter, requests, and heckling. Dramatic forms of all ages have employed these techniques and a variety of other direct presentational methods as well, including asides, soliloquies, direct address, plays-within-plays, and curtain calls.

Indirect performance, however, is probably the more fundamental mode in drama; it is certainly the one that makes drama "dramatic" as opposed to simply "theatrical." For indirect performance is the mode whereby the audience watches interactions that are staged as if no audience were present at all. As a result the audience is encouraged to concentrate on the events that are being staged, not on their presentation. In other words, the members of the audience "believe in" the play and allow themselves to forget that the characters are really actors and that the apparently spontaneous events taking place before their eyes are really a series of scripted scenes. This belief—or, to borrow Coleridge's famous double negative, this "suspension of disbelief"—engenders

Direct performance: the cast of the 1991 off-Broadway musical comedy, Song of Singapore, *performs directly to the audience. Directed by the late A. J. Antoon. (Photo: Martha Swope and Associates.)*

audience participation via the psychological mechanism of *empathy.* In other words, the audience is likely to feel kinship with certain (or all) of the characters, to identify with their aspirations, sympathize with their plights, exult in their victories — to care deeply about what happens to them. When that happens, the audience experiences the "magic" of the theatre. Well-written and well-staged dramas make people *feel;* they draw in the spectator emotionally and leave him or her in some measure a changed person. This is as much magic as the modern world provides anywhere, and its effect is the same all over the world.

Occasionally either the direct or the indirect mode of performance is taken to an extreme. For examples of the former, look at the plays of Bertolt Brecht, the twentieth-century German author who deliberately set out to repudiate the "magic" of the theatre by direct appeals to the audience on a variety of social and political issues. Brecht's plays featured songs, signs, chalk talks, arguments addressed directly to the house, and slide projections; he specifically avoided use of concealed stage trickery or "effects." Brecht wanted his audience distanced from the story of the play; he also wanted them to consider his actors as performer-illustrators rather than as specific

Indirect performance: three businessmen have lunch in Howard Korder's 1990
Search and Destroy. *As the characters try to impress ("perform for") each other, the*
actors playing them are also performing for the audience. From the world premiere
production at South Coast Repertory Theatre. (Photo: Christopher Gross.)

characters with specific involvements, so that the political and social themes of the play would dominate the viewer's awareness.

In this effort, Brecht was specifically attacking the realist movement of the turn of the century, a movement that afforded many cases of the other extreme. It propounded a style of performance in which the actors behaved exactly as they did in life, in settings made as lifelike as possible (in one notable example, a celebrated New York restaurant was disassembled and reconstructed on stage, complete with its original moldings, wallpaper, furniture, silverware, and linens). At times the indirect mode so dominated in the realist productions that actors spoke with their backs to audiences, directors allowed interminable pauses and inaudible whispers, playwrights culled their dialogue from random fragments of overheard conversations, and house managers timed intermissions to the presumed time elapsing in the play's story. The realistic theatre of that time was sometimes called "the theatre of the fourth wall removed" because its goal typically was to re-create life inside a room, and the sole departure from complete verisimilitude that was allowed was the removal of one wall to let the audience peer in—much as the lab scientist peers at a slide through a microscope.

The two modes of performance, however, can never be entirely separated. The fact is that the Brechtian theatre, despite all the best efforts of Brecht himself and all the resources he had at his disposal, never managed to eliminate audience empathy with the leading characters; and even the most resolutely realistic theatres have never escaped the ultimate audience recognition that the actors are, indeed, performing. As it turns out, theatrical performance is always *both* direct and indirect, and it is always both simultaneously.

What is more, the audience inevitably demands two things of a theatrical performance: it demands characters it can care about and it demands actors it can admire. In other words, the audience wants to see the characters struggle and the actors sweat. In watching a performance, therefore, the members of an audience intuitively look for two things. They look for a well-crafted dramatic story that holds implications for their own lives, and they look for extraordinary individual acting performances. One of these elements may predominate—as when a cast of brilliant actors submerge themselves in a masterpiece by Chekhov or, con-

The masked chorus cringes in awe, in a modern (1992) production of Euripides' Iphigeneia at Aulis, *directed by Garland Wright, with costumes and masks by Susan Hilfterty. (Photo: Courtesy the Guthrie Theatre, Minneapolis.)*

versely, when a relatively trivial script becomes the vehicle for a "star's" bravura performance. Both elements are always present in a successful production; and when they are, the viewer experiences a complex and deeply satisfying sense of inner expansion.

There are two other aspects of performance that distinguish theatre from certain other forms: theatre is *live* performance, and it is in most cases a *scripted* and *rehearsed* event.

Live Performance Unlike video and cinema (although sometimes employing elements of them), the theatre is fundamentally a living, real-time event, with performers and audience mutually interacting in the same space and at the same time, each fully aware of the other's immediate presence.

This turns out to be an extremely important distinction. Actors who are accomplished in both "live" and filmed performance invariably report a strong preference for the former, despite the usually greater financial rewards of the latter. In explaining this preference, they often mention the applause of the crowd, the sensation of "presence," and a special tingle of excitement. Beyond question, some fundamental forces are at work in live theatre.

The first of these forces consists of a rapport between actor and audience. Both are breathing, as it were, the same air. Both are involved, at the same time and in the same space, with the stage life depicted by the play, and sometimes their mutual fascination is almost palpable. A collective gasp from the audience at a climactic moment in a play can be the spark that evokes a transcendent performance from an actor. Every actor's performance is affected in some measure, for better or for worse, by the way in which the audience yields up or withholds

The medieval trestle stage — a few planks on trestles — was a standard performance space for more than a thousand years. Portable, serviceable, and inexpensive, it could be set up almost anywhere and could be dismantled in an instant if the actors chanced to be chased out of town — as they often were. Such trestle stages may still be seen at many summertime European festivals. (Drawing: John von Szeliski.)

Live performance: one of the excitements of theatregoing is seeing plays of the past come vividly to life in our own times. The job of the contemporary theatre artist is to make the genius of the past speak persuasively in the present. In Andrei Serban's radically contemporized production of Shakespeare's Twelfth Night, *the Duke Orsino arrives, with his bodyguards, by helicopter. (Photo: Richard Feldman.)*

its responses—its laughter, its sighs, its applause, its silences. Thus live theatrical performance is always a two-way communication between stage and "house."

A second major element in live theatre has to do with the relationship between the members of the audience who, having arrived at the theatre locked inside their own personalities and predilections, quickly find themselves fused into a common enterprise with total strangers. This particular sort of intra-audience relationship is never developed by television drama, which is directed chiefly to solitary watchers or to small audiences of viewers known to each other—two to four people in each of a million different living rooms. Nor is it likely to happen in motion picture houses, where audiences find themselves in essentially

a one-to-one relationship with the screen and rarely break out in any *collective* response. Live theatrical presentations foster the kinds of audience behaviors that are demonstrably *social* in nature: everyone arrives at the theatre at about the same time and all depart together; intermissions allow for an exchange of ideas; theatre programs afford material for conversation. Further, audience responses to the entertainment are social in nature. Laughter and applause build upon themselves and gain strength from the recognition that others are laughing and applauding. The ovation—unique to live performance—inevitably involves the audience applauding itself, as well as the performers, for its own understanding and appreciation of theatrical excellence. Plays with social themes can be particularly effective sublime. The actors' constant striving toward self-transcendence gives the theatre a vitality that is missing from performances fixed unalterably on tape or celluloid. But perhaps most appropriately, the immediacy of live performance creates a "present-ness" or "presence" that embodies the fundamental uncertainty of life itself. One prime function of theatre is to address the uncertainties of human existence, and the very format of live performance presents a certain moment-to-moment uncertainty right before our eyes. Ultimately this "immediate theatre" helps us to define the questions and confusions of our lives and lets us grapple, in the present, with their implications.

in creating a feeling of audience participation and oneness. In a celebrated example in the 1930s, the American play *Waiting for Lefty* was set up to treat the audience as a group of union members at a meeting, and by the play's end the whole audience was yelling "Strike! Strike!" Obviously, only a live performance could evoke such a response.

Finally, live performance inevitably has the quality of immediacy. The action of the play is taking place *right now* as it is being watched, and anything can happen. Although in most professional productions the changes that occur in performance from one night to another are so subtle that only an expert would notice, the fact is that each night's presentation is unique and everyone present—in the audience, in the cast, and behind the scenes—knows it. This awareness lends an excitement that simply is not present in theatrical events that are wholly "in the can." One reason for the excitement, of course, is that in live performance mistakes can happen; this possibility occasions a certain abiding tension, perhaps even an edge of stage fright, which some people say creates the ultimate thrill of the theatre. But if disaster can come without warning, so can splendor. On any given night, each actor is trying to better his or her previous performance, and no one knows when this collective effort will coalesce into something

Scripted and Rehearsed Performance
Theatre events ordinarily differ from certain "happenings" and other forms of performance art by the fact that they are largely derived from written and rehearsed texts, or, in theatrical parlance, scripts. While improvisation and ad-libbing may play a role in the preparation process, and even in certain actual performances, most theatre events proceed according to a set "plan" that is established before—and modified during—the play's rehearsal period. Most plays are then rehearsed and polished to such a de-

THEATRE: EAST AND WEST

The English word *theatre* is of European origin; and through the latter part of the twentieth century, the vast majority — at least 98 percent — of plays produced in the United States have been European or North American in origin, as have been the main traditions of acting, theatre architecture, stage production, and design.

However, dramatic performance has a worldwide history. Dramatic productions have been recorded in Egypt and the Middle East from the time of deepest antiquity: before 3000 B.C. Masterpieces of non-European theatre predate the birth of Christ. In India, written Sanskrit drama reached a very high literary level by 300 B.C., and formal Chinese drama was written and produced in the Han dynasty from at least 200 B.C. T'ang Emperor Ming Huang created the world's first formal drama school, the "Pear Garden," in 20 A.D. By the time of Europe's Middle Ages, the Japanese had developed an enormously sophisticated classical theatre (the Noh Drama); Native Americans (Anasazi) were producing ritual dramas in the pueblo *kivas,* and troupes of dramatic performers were touring the great Mali Empire from Senegal to Nigeria with dances and dramatic presentations. During the current century, the Western world — and the Northern Hemisphere — has increasingly begun to appreciate and incorporate the discoveries, the artistries, and the creative genius of these and other non-European theatre artists. Touring theatre companies, such as the Grand Kabuki, the Chinese Opera, and the (South African) Market Theatre have brought Asian and African theatres to major European and American cities. At the same time, exchanges between theatre troupes and individual theatre artists, proliferating international theatre festivals, mass tourism and East-West population migration, and the universal denominator of global television have brought the theatres of the world to previously isolated countries and communities. The study of the "history of the theatre," which in the United States has heretofore largely meant the history of European and American theatre, is presently being expanded to include a history of *all* theatre and all theatre-making the world over.

pendable level of regularity as the actors and staff can sustain. Mainstream professional play productions, therefore, appear virtually the same night after night: barring major cast changes, the Broadway production of *Miss Saigon* that you see on Thursday will be almost identical to the show your friend saw on Wednesday or that your mother saw last fall. And when you read the published text, you will see on the page the same words you heard spoken or sung on the stage.

But the text of a play is not, by any means, the play itself. The play fully exists only in its performance: the script is merely the record the play leaves behind after the audience has gone home. The script, therefore, is to the play it represents only what a shadowpainting is to the face it silhouettes: it outlines the principal features, but conveys only the outer margins of the spirit, the complexity, the color, the smell, and the nuance of the living actuality.

Let us now take a closer look at the relations between playscript and play production. First, we should be aware that the finished playscript does not necessarily precede the finished performance. In fact, virtually all important playscripts available to us today were published *following* their initial performance, and the versions we read reflect not only the staging decisions of a director and the portrayal choices of many actors, but also the changes in dialogue that took place during the play's rehearsal period and frequently in its performance period as well. While most original play productions are begun with a script in hand (usually it is called the "working script"), that script is rarely treated as a sacred document. The evolution and "doctoring" of new playscripts during rehearsal is a process that took place in past times as well as in the present, as historical accounts amply attest. For revivals, of course, a "fixed" script generally dictates the dialogue in fairly strict manner, but that script was itself fixed by the one or more productions which intervened between the play's first drafting and its eventual publication.

Second, let us bear in mind that even a fixed script is in some ways as notable for what it lacks as for what it contains. Apart from the odd stage-set description or acting note (for example, "through her tears," "crossing to the bannister," or "softly"), a written playscript usually tells almost nothing about a play's nonverbal components. For how can it describe the degrees of expression within the range of even the beginning actor? How can it capture the bead of sweat that forms on Hamlet's brow as he stabs Polonius or Romeo's nervous laugh as he tries to part dueling adversaries? Written stage descriptions (which in any case hardly ever appear in playscripts that antedate the present century) serve mainly to delineate the outer form of a play and do little to convey its inner life. As for the words of dialogue, although they are probably the most important single element of a play,

they are not in any way the whole experience. Words on a page do not resound in the mind in the same way as do words spoken aloud; and even spoken words do not encompass the facial expressions, the color and sweep of costumes, the play of light, the movement of form in space — and the audience response — that conspire to support a living production.

The chief value of playscripts, then, is that they generate theatrical production and they provide an invaluable, albeit imperfect, record of performances past. Two and a half millennia of play productions have left us a repository of thousands upon thousands of scripts, some awful, many ordinary, a few magnificent. This rich store puts us in touch with theatre history in the making and allows us to glimpse the nature of the originals in production. It also suggests ways in which the plays of yesterday can serve as blueprints for vital theatre today.

This, then, is the theatre: buildings, companies, and plays; work, art, impersonation, and performance; living performers and written, rehearsed scripts.

It is a production, an assemblage of actions, sights, sounds, ideas, feelings, words, light, and, above all, people.

It consists of playing and — of course — plays.

But what is a play? That question deserves a separate chapter.

A play is, essentially, the basic unit of theatre. It is not a "thing" but an event, taking place in real time and occupying real space. It is a "drama" — remember its origin from the Greek *dran,* "something done." It is *action;* not just words in a book.

Action is not merely movement, of course: it is argument, struggle, persuasion, threats, seduction, sound, music, dance, speech, and passion. It comprises all forms of human energy, including language, spatial dynamics, light, color, sonic shocks, aesthetic harmonies, and "remarkable things happening" from moment to moment. It is *live* action, ordinarily unmediated by video electronics or cinematic celluloid.

And yet a play does not merely produce (or reproduce) live action, but also frames and focuses it. Life may be, as Shakespeare's Macbeth says, "a tale told by an idiot, full of sound and fury, signifying nothing"; but drama, which is also full of sound and fury, signifies all sorts of things: if not answers, then at least perspectives, vocabularies, and aesthetic illuminations. Plays give us stories against which we can judge our own struggles; they present characters that can serve us as positive and negative role models; they offer up themes, ideas, and revelations that we can accept, scorn, or store away for further contemplation. A play is a piece of life — animated,

CHAPTER **2**

WHAT IS A PLAY?

shaped and framed to become a work of art. It provides a structured synthesis — sometimes a critique and sometimes a celebration — of both life's glories and life's confusions.

Of course, a play is also a piece of literature. There has been a reading audience for plays at least since the time of the ancient Greeks, and play collections — such as Shakespeare's works — have been published since the Renaissance. Today, plays are often printed in literary anthologies, intermixed with poems, short stories, and even novels. But drama should not be thought of as merely a "branch" or "genre" of literature; it is a live performance, some of whose repeatable aspects (chiefly, the words) may be captured in a written and published text.[1]

Finally, "a play" is "playing" and those who create plays are "players." The theatrical play contains root notions of "child's play" in its acting-out and adventurism, of "dressing up" in its costumes and props, and of the thrill of sportive competition in its energy and abandon. Like all play, drama is an exhibition, and its players are, in a real sense, willingly exhibitionistic. These are not fundamentally literary characteristics.

CLASSIFYING PLAYS

Plays may be volatile, but they are also contained. They are framed, with a beginning and an end, and, no matter how original or unique, they can be seen to fall into a variety of classifications. Two of these are duration and genre. Although these classifications have been emphasized more in the past than they are today, they still play a part in our understanding of drama.

Duration

"How long is a play?" American playwright Arthur Miller admitted that when he first thought of writing for the theatre, "How long should it be?" was his most pressing question. The answer is far from obvious.

Historically, in Western drama, a "full-length" play has usually lasted somewhere between two and four hours. This is not an entirely arbitrary period of time; it represents roughly the hours between lunch and dinner (for a matinee), or between dinner and bedtime. The Jacobean playwright John Webster wrote that the actor "entertains us in the best leisure of our life, that is between meals, the most unfit time either for study or bodily exercise." Webster was thinking of the afternoon performances in the outdoor theatres of his day (c. 1615). A few years earlier, speaking of candlelit evening performances at court, Shakespeare's Theseus (*A Midsummer Night's Dream*) asks for a play "to wear away this long age of three hours between our after-supper and bed-time." Inasmuch as eating and sleeping habits have remained fairly constant over the millennia, we should not be too surprised that the two- to four-hour standard has been common to the drama since ancient times.

But plays may be much shorter or longer. "One-act" plays of an hour or less, often combined in a "bill" with other short works, are often presented as full theatre programs; on other occasions such short plays are presented in nontraditional settings, such as lunchtime theatres, dramatic festivals, school assemblies, social gatherings, street entertainments, or cabaret performances. Very short plays are known from ancient times; the Greek satyr plays, for example, could be performed in a half-hour and were presented following a day-

---

[1] If the arboreal metaphor is insisted upon, drama would have to be considered the "trunk" of the literary tree, not merely a branch. Certainly no other literary form — the novel, the epic poem, the lyric poem, the short story — has the sustained level of literary excellence over twenty-five centuries as does the written dramatic work of Aeschylus, Sophocles, Euripides, Aristophanes, Marlowe, Shakespeare, Jonson, Chikamatsu, Webster, Racine, Corneille, Lope de Vega, Calderón, Molière, Congreve, Dryden, Farquhar, Fielding, Goethe, Schiller, Ibsen, Wilde, Yeats, Chekhov, Shaw, O'Casey, O'Neill, Pirandello, Giraudoux, Sartre, Brecht, Beckett, Williams, Churchill, Wilson, etc.

The basic action of many plays is a seemingly ordinary conversation, in which, however, the stakes turn out to be much higher than usual. An ordinary bench in New York's Central Park is the setting for many recent American plays, including Richard Greenberg's The Extra Man, *shown here in its 1992 South Coast Repertory Theatre premiere. (Photo: Christopher Gross.)*

long series of three tragedies. Nobel Prize winner Samuel Beckett probably holds the minimalist record in drama, with his sixty-second play, *Breath,* initially presented in a fanciful "erotic entertainment" (*O, Calcutta!*) that consisted of more than a dozen short works, some written by celebrities (like John Lennon), as compiled by critic Kenneth Tynan in 1969.

The very long play has also been a recurring anomaly and, in the Eastern world, a

Tuck Mulligan, Charles Hallahan (standing), and Ronald Hippe in The Kentucky Cycle, *by Robert Schenkkan. The cycle, which won the 1992 Pulitzer Prize for Drama, consists of nine interrelated "plays" performed over a six-and-a-half-hour period. From the Mark Taper Forum Theatre (Los Angeles) production, which was coproduced by the Intiman Theatre (Seattle) and directed by Warner Shook. (Photo: Jay Thompson.)*

"It will have blood," Macbeth cries, and blood-soaked violence is common at the climax of tragedy. Illustrated is Julius Caesar, *directed by Gavin Cameron-Webb at the Alabama Shakespeare Festival, 1990.*

Peter Brook's *The Mahabharata* in Paris and Los Angeles, Peter Stein's *Oresteia* in Berlin, and Ariane Mnouchkine's *Les Atrides* (which includes the *Oresteia* and then some) in Paris, Montreal, and New York. In 1992, the Pulitzer Prize for Drama was awarded to Robert Schenkkan's nine-play, six-hour cycle, *The Kentucky Cycle,* which was performed in Seattle and Los Angeles, requiring viewing on two successive nights or during one long afternoon and evening "marathon" divided by dinner. The same schedule was employed for Tony Kushner's extraordinary *Angels in America,* which was commissioned by the Eureka Theatre of San Francisco, and was subsequently performed in Los Angeles and New York in 1992–93.

The American actor-director Robert Wilson probably holds the absolute duration record, however, first with his twelve-hour, overnight, *The Life and Times of Joseph Stalin,* and subsequently with his *Ka Mountain,* which has been performed for anywhere between 24 and 168 continuous hours. These extremes, however, demand such drastic accommodation on the part of audiences, actors, and behind-the-scenes personnel that it is highly doubtful they will be commonplace in the future.

Genre

Genre is a more subjective means of classifying plays than is duration, and the term brings with it certain critical perspectives. *Genre* is directly derived from the Old French word for "kind" (this is also our root word for "gender"); thus to define a play's genre is to categorize it—to say "what kind of play" it is. Editors and publishers of playtexts have often sought to identify genres as a shorthand description: early publications of Shakespeare's plays bore generic classifications on the title pages (for example, *The Most Excellent Conceited Tragedy of Romeo and Juliet*); and when the first collection of his plays was published

standard. Chinese theatre usually lasts all day (spectators bring their meals), as did the Japanese Kabuki in its classical seventeenth-century period (modern Kabuki is somewhat more contained). In English-language theatre of the 1920s, Eugene O'Neill's *Strange Interlude* and George Bernard Shaw's *Back to Methuselah* were each performed with dinner breaks between two sessions of more than three hours, and in the 1980s and 1990s a number of six- to nine-hour dramatic epics were celebrated internationally: Trevor Nunn's *Nicholas Nickleby* in London and New York, (the First Folio of 1623), his plays were divided into three genre classifications: "Comedies," "Tragedies," and "Histories."

Considerations of genre in some periods, however, degenerated into a pseudoscientific taxonomy, with absolute rules defining what would constitute, say, a "tragedy." Because of this, many critics, and even more authors, ridicule the notion of genre altogether (see box). But an identification of genres can generate useful distinctions — not only for the student but also for the practitioner. The great Russian playwright Anton Chekhov certainly guided the principal director of his works, Konstantin Stanislavski, by pointing out that his plays were intended as "comedies," thereby agreeably blunting what he thought was Stanislavski's excess of directorial naturalism. And many an actor, hamstrung by considerations of psychological realism, has been freed to find a more vigorous theatricality when given to understand that the author meant the play as "farce," thereby encouraging a rampaging and "over-the-top" comic style.

Two genres have dominated dramatic criticism since ancient times: *tragedy* and *comedy.* To Aristotle, the Greek philosopher generally recognized as the father of dramatic criticism, tragedy and comedy were not genres, but wholly separate art forms, derived from entirely unrelated sources. Tragedy, to Aristotle, was an outgrowth of certain prehistoric religious rituals, whereas comedy was a secular entertainment developed out of bawdy skits and popular revels. Aristotle strove to create a poetics (poetic theory) that would define these dramatic forms and that would create standards for their perfection. Unfortunately, only his poetics for tragedy has survived.

Today, aestheticians and scholars recognize a number of generic classifications. In addition to the original tragedy and comedy (now more narrowly defined than in Aristotle's day), the interlude, cycle play, history play, tragicomedy, dark comedy, melodrama, farce, documentary, and the musical have been identified as major genres into which modern

GENRE-LY SPEAKING

Shakespeare has brightly parodied the division of plays into genres, a practice which in his time was already becoming almost an affectation. In *Hamlet,* he has Polonius describe an acting company as "The best actors in the world, either for tragedy, comedy, history, pastoral, pastoral-comical, historical-pastoral, tragical-historical, tragical-comical-historical-pastoral, scene individable, or poem unlimited."

plays (and, retroactively, older plays) can be classified.

A *tragedy* is a serious play (although not necessarily devoid of humorous episodes) which a topic of universal human import as its theme. Traditionally, the central character, often called the *protagonist,* is a person of high rank or stature. During the play, the protagonist undergoes a decline of fortune, leading to suffering and death. Integral to tragedy is the protagonist's period of insightful recognition or understanding. The effect of a tragedy, Aristotle claimed, was to elicit both pity and terror in the audience, which were resolved in a *catharsis,* or purging, of those aroused emotions.

The insightful recognition of the protagonist, his or her struggle against decline, and the consequent catharsis of the audience's aroused feelings are central to the tragic experience, which is not to be confused with a merely sad or pathetic experience. Tragedy is neither pathetic nor sentimental; it describes a bold, aggressive, human attack against huge, perhaps insurmountable odds. Tragic protagonists are often flawed in some way (indeed, classical tragic theory insists that they must be flawed or at least acting in ignorance), but they are leaders, not victims, of the play's events. Indeed, their leadership of the play's action and their discoveries during the course of that action bring the audience to deep emotional and intellectual involvement.

The notion of *protagonist* (Greek: "carrier of the action") is complemented by a notion of *antagonist* ("opposer of the action"), which gives tragedy its fundamental conflict and character struggle. The protagonists of tragedy often go forth against superhuman antagonists: gods, ghosts, "fate," or else the hardest of human realities. Such protagonists are *heroes*—or tragic heroes—because their supreme struggle, although perhaps a doomed effort, takes on larger-than-life proportions. Then, through the heat of supreme conflict, the tragic heroes themselves assume a superhuman force and draw us into the full magnitude of their thoughts and actions. Thus tragedy offers us a link with the divine and puts us at the apex of human destiny.

A tragedy should ennoble, not sadden us. Characters that we admire may fall, but not before heroically challenging the elements, divinity, and death. Tragic heroes carry us to the brink of disaster—but, finally, it is their disaster and not ours, or at least not ours yet. Seeing a tragedy is to contemplate and perhaps rehearse in our minds the great conflicts we may still have ahead of us.

There are only a few universally acknowledged tragedies of this sort. Sophocles' *Oedipus Tyrannos* was Aristotle's model of a great tragedy; most critics also class that author's *Electra* and *Antigone*; Aeschylus' *Oresteia* and *Prometheus Bound*; Euripides' *The Trojan Women, Medea,* and *The Bacchae*; Racine's *Phèdre*; and Shakespeare's *Hamlet, King Lear, Othello,* and *Macbeth* as among a dozen or so true tragic masterpieces. The question is often raised as to whether a modern play can be such a tragedy. Arthur Miller's *Death of a Salesman* (1947) is often the play for which this question is posed, for Miller deliberately challenged the traditional notion of a high-ranking protagonist by naming his principal character "Willy Loman," (that is, low man). Furthermore, the antagonists Willy challenges are faceless bureaucrats, insensitive children, and an impersonal capitalistic economic system—not gods, fates, or ghosts. Most critics today, if they approach this question at all, deny Miller's play the tragic dimension on the grounds that the struggle is human, not superhuman, and that tragedy demands a larger-than-life context. If that is the case, tragedy probably belongs to an earlier world, one where audiences could be expected to accept without dissent the presence of divine forces mixing in with everyday human affairs.

Comedy began, according to Aristotle, as an improvised entertainment that combined satirical skits, bawdy jokes, erotic singing and dancing, and uninhibited revelry. The first known written comedies were those of Aristophanes, a playwright of brilliantly funny wit and savagely penetrating political acumen. Writing in Athens in the late fifth century, Aristophanes set the general pattern, although not the structure, for comedies to come: interpersonal conflicts, topical issues, witty dialogue, physical buffoonery, verbal and sexual playfulness.

Comedy is not a simple amusement, however, nor is comedy simply entertaining; comedy is always about a serious human conflict. The passionate pursuit of love, ambition, social status, and money are age-old comic themes. Indeed, the themes of many comedies are often hard to distinguish from those of tragedies; the plot and the style of comedies, not the theme, assure that the dramatic experience will avoid sustained pity or terror and will elicit more laughter than cathartic shock. The comic plot requires a generally happy ending; the comic style includes characters drawn on human scale, often in an exaggerated manner, who face the kinds of everyday problems we know well in our own lives. Gods, fate, suffering, and death rarely figure significantly in comedies, and the problems of the characters are social rather than cosmic, interpersonal rather than metaphysical.

The best comedies are often those in which characters foolishly overreach themselves and are hilariously shown up for their foolishness. Not only are Aristophanes' plays (*The Birds, The Frogs, The Clouds, The Acharnians,* for

Comedy often involves violence as well, but the bright colors and stylized expressions create a different tone. The passions are largely comic at this point in Libby Appel's 1991 production of All's Well That Ends Well *at the Alabama Shakespeare Festival, with boldly colorful costumes by Elizabeth Novak.*

example) masterpieces of this format, but so are the great comedies of Shakespeare (*As You Like It, Twelfth Night, A Midsummer Night's Dream*) and Molière (*The Miser, The Bourgeois Gentleman, The School for Wives*). In these plays, excesses of romantic love, intellectual pretension, physical braggadocio, or financial greed are wittily shown up, to the delight of the spectators in the audience—who can also recognize the germs of such behaviors in themselves. In this fashion, comedy seeks to advise as well as to entertain. The Roman poet Horace coined the term *utile dulce,* or "sweet instruction," to denote this deeper purpose of the comic drama.

There are many modern authors of dramatic comedy: George Bernard Shaw, George S. Kaufman, Simon Gray, Alan Ayckbourne, and Neil Simon are only a few of the twentieth-century playwrights who have succeeded in this genre. Because they are topical, comedies are usually less long-lasting than tragedies. Because they generally probe less profoundly into the matter of human destiny, they offer less fertile ground to academic scholarship. Hence, relative to tragedies, comedies are usually less frequently published in play anthologies, less frequently examined in critical literature, and less frequently studied in most academic institutions. Nevertheless, comedy's place in the theatre is every bit as secure as is tragedy, and its impact on audiences is no less strong now than it was in Aristophanes' day.

Comedy and tragedy remained the two "official" dramatic genres through the seventeenth century, when neoclassic French critics attempted to formalize them into absolutely rigid classifications. But from the Renaissance onward, playwrights and critics began to develop new dramatic genres or to dispense with genres altogether.

The medieval theatre, for example, brought to the stage *interludes,* comic entertainments presented between courses at state banquets (from *inter* = between and *ludus* = play), and *cycle* plays, short biblical plays performed in a series (cycle), often in procession through a town.

Shakespeare's editors divided his plays into the traditional genres of tragedy and comedy, plus a newly defined genre: the *history,* which is a play purporting to dramatize the key events in the life of a king or head of state. Shakespeare seems to have invented this genre; and his great series of nine history plays, covering English royal history from 1377 to 1547 (inaccurate as they may be as historical documents) provides the bulk of what most people ever remember of the English kings Richard II, Henry IV, Henry V, Henry VI, and Richard III. Shakespeare's histories combine serious scenes, brilliant poetry, battlefield pageants, and hilarious comic moments. None of the plays, however, seeks to attain the classical catharsis of tragedy or the sustained humor of comedy. The history play thus seems to have been a mixed genre whose only successful proponent was its originator, Shakespeare himself.

More long-lived are two other mixed genres, *tragicomedy* and *dark comedy,* which also have both tragic and comic components.

Tragicomedy, as the name implies, is a form that deliberately attempts to bridge the two original genres. It maintains a serious theme throughout but varies the approach from serious to humorous and relaxes tragedy's larger-than-life scale. The problems of tragicomedy

Shakespeare's history plays treat the real personnages—kings, queens, nobles, and peasants—of the late medieval period in England. Eight of these plays treat the Wars of the Roses: the internecine battles between the royal families of York and Lancaster, each struggling for the English crown. Today, the plays are often combined in production, as in the Guthrie Theatre's version of the two parts of Henry IV (1990), directed by Guthrie Artistic Director, Garland Wright. At left, Stephen Yoakham as King Henry IV, and Barton Tinapp as his son, Prince Hal (who becomes Henry V in the next play). Costumes by Ann Hould-Ward, lighting by Marcus Dilliard. (Photo: Michal Daniel.)

are solvable, and the antagonists are not divinely insuperable; tragicomedies, despite their rousing speeches and sentiments, conclude without the violent catharsis that its audience has been led to expect. It has been called "tragedy that ends happily." *Amphitryon,* by the Roman playwright Plautus, is generally considered the first tragicomedy (the play has been revised by subsequent authors into both tragic and comic versions). Many of Shakespeare's tragedies were in fact turned into tragicomedies by rewrite men in the tragicomedy-prone seventeenth century: Nahum Tate's 1687 revision of *King Lear,* for example, concludes with Lear and Gloucester retiring to "calm reflections on our fortunes past" and with Cordelia installed as Queen of England; all are dead at the close of Shakespeare's original.

Dark comedy is the obverse: an often comic but finally disturbing play that ends darkly (or ironically), leaving the impression of an unresolved universe surrounding the play's characters—and perhaps surrounding the audience as well. Dark comedies are usually funny, at least at the beginning, but they don't aim to leave us laughing. There are dark themes and ironic endings to many of Shakespeare's later plays, including *The Tempest, The Winter's Tale,* and *Pericles* (these are also often classed as romances), and to many of the late nineteenth- and early twentieth-century plays of Anton Chekhov, Bertolt Brecht, George Bernard Shaw, Luigi Pirandello, and Jean Giraudoux. In modern (post–World War II) times, the dark comedy has come to dominate the theatre, particularly in the work of playwrights such as Harold Pinter, Samuel Beckett, Edward Albee, Joe Orton, Beth Henley, August Wilson, Wendy Wasserstein, John Guare, Christopher Durang, Terence McNally, and Caryl Churchill.

If histories, tragicomedies, and dark comedies are mixed genres, then *melodramas* and *farces* are pure extremes, carrying the notion of dramatic genre as far as it can be taken.

Melodramas are plays that purport to be serious but that are in fact trivial entertainments, often embellished with spectacular stagings, sententious dialogue, and highly suspenseful—and contrived—plotting. Melodrama presents a simple and finite confrontation between good and evil rather than a complex exposition of universal human aspirations and sufferings. Plays in this genre cannot sustain unpleasant endings or generate catharsis, but can indeed provoke a deeply emotional outpouring of audience sentiment—always a powerful theatrical response. A pure creation of the theatre, melodramas employ every possible theatrical device to generate audience emotion (the name "melo-drama" reveals the function music originally played in the mel-

Melodrama, an exaggerated seriousness, is evident in this moment from the American Conservatory Theatre production of The Tavern, *an early twentieth-century theatrical piece by showman George M. Cohan. (Photo: William Ganslen, ACT.)*

odramatic experience) and tend to reflect reality, or real human issues, only on the most superficial and sentimental level. Melodrama in its pure form rarely exists today—the melodramas that are occasionally produced these days are parodies, played for laughs—but melodramatic elements frequently find their ways into dramas of every sort.

Farces are similarly pure creations of the theatre. In farce, one finds a wildly hilarious treatment of a trivial theme, ordinarily one of the various stock themes—mistaken identity, illicit infatuation, physical dissolution, monetary scheming—that have come down from ancient times. Plot components of farces are also drawn from a set of stock situations and events; identical twins, lovers in closets or under tables, full-stage chases, switched potions, switched costumes (often involving transsexual dressing), misheard instructions, and pear—just as we are beginning to lament the demise of this popular dramatic genre.

Many minor genres have been usefully described in the contemporary theatre; the *documentary* and the *musical* are of particular importance.

The *documentary* is a genre of fairly recent development, in which a great deal of authentic evidence is used as a basis for portraying relatively recent historical events. Trial transcripts, news reports and pictures, personal and official records are marshaled as documentation to bring alive a particular issue and point of view. Famous court trials—those of J. Robert Oppenheimer, John C. Scopes, Adolph Eichmann, the "Zoot Suit" gangs, and Leopold and Loeb, for example—have

Andre Gregory and Joyce Van Patten are dinner guests forced by bizarre circumstances to cook and serve their own meal in Neil Simon's Rumors *(1990), the author's only self-proclaimed farce. The Old Globe Theatre of San Diego produced the world premiere production, shown here, which was directed by Gene Saks. (Photo: Martha Swope and Associates.)*

various disrobings, discoveries, and disappearances characterize this age-old and perennially durable dramatic genre. Elements of farce exist in almost all comedies, but pure farce makes no pretense toward Horace's *utile dulce;* the motto instead is "laugh 'til you cry," and in a well-written, well-staged farce the audience does just that. Michael Frayn's *Noises Off,* a pure farce set in a provincial English theatre, had audiences collapsed in hysteria on both sides of the Atlantic in the 1980s; every couple of years a new "laugh-riot" tends to ap-

The essence of farce is captured in this production photograph from Georges Feydeau's Hotel Paradiso, *as presented by the American Conservatory Theatre. Actors' exaggerated expressions and postures, as well as multiple-door setting, are standard features of farcical plays. The actors, left to right, are Sydney Walker, Raye Birk, Elizabeth Huddle, Michael Winters, and Ruth Kobart. (Photo: William Ganslen, ACT.)*

Jerome Lawrence and Robert E. Lee's Inherit the Wind *(1956) dramatizes the 1925 trial of a young Tennessee biology teacher accused of teaching Darwin's theory of evolution, in violation of state law. This documentary play, which includes portions of the actual court testimony, dissects the scientific and religious conflicts that continue to the present day. Shown here: the 1991 Alabama Shakespeare Festival production, directed by Kent Thompson. Actors, left to right, are Barry Boys, Michael Rudko, and Philip Pleasants.*

been a prime source of material for documentary dramatizations.

The *musical* genre is defined by its extensive musical score, particularly by its vocal score. Operas and operettas are, of course, examples of musical theatre but are generally considered more music than theatre. The musical exists as a dramatic genre, however, in such popular and stage-oriented forms as musical comedy (a comedy with songs and dances, such as *Crazy for You*), musical drama (a serious play with songs and dances, like *Fiddler On The Roof*), musical documentary (such as the World War I-inspired *Oh, What a Lovely War!*), or a musical melodrama (Stephen Sondheim's *Sweeney Todd, the Demon Barber of Fleet Street*). The musical play has often been considered America's greatest contribution to the theatre, particularly owing to the great post-World War II musicals by Cole Porter (*Kiss Me Kate*), Frank Loesser (*Guys and Dolls*), Alan Jay Lerner and Frederick Loewe

Musicals are often dismissed as simply light entertainment, but modern musicals often have serious themes and thought-provoking dramatic action. Grand Hotel, *staged by Tommy Tune on Broadway in 1989, was set in 1930s Germany and convincingly re-created the savagely decadent atmosphere in which fascist mentalities and anti-Semitism could flourish. (Photo: Martha Swope and Associates.)*

(*Cats, Evita, Phantom of the Opera, Aspects of Love*), and Alain Boublil/Claude-Michel Schönberg in France (*Les Misérables, Miss Saigon*). The musical is considered more fully in the discussion of modern theatre.

Potentially, of course, there are as many theatrical genres as the diligent critic wishes to define. No system of classification should obscure the fact that each play is unique, and the grouping of any two or more plays into a common genre is only a convenience for purposes of comparison and analysis. We in the twentieth century have certainly learned that past formulations of tragedy and farce have had little bearing on the long-range assessment of the importance, quality, or worth— on the staying power—of any individual play; and critics who today dwell inordinately on such questions as "Is *Death of a Salesman* a true tragedy?" are doubtless spending too much time deciding what box to put the artistic work in and too little time examining and revealing the work itself.

On the other hand, genre distinctions can be useful if we keep their limitations in mind. They can help us to comprehend the broad spectrum of purposes to which plays may be put and to perceive important similarities and differences. For the theatre artist, an awareness of the possibilities inherent in each genre— together with a knowledge of the achievements that have been made in each—stimulates the imagination and aids in setting work standards and ambitions.

STRUCTURE

(*Brigadoon, My Fair Lady*) and Richard Rodgers and Oscar Hammerstein (*Oklahoma, South Pacific, The Sound of Music, The King and I*). Today, however, the musical is at least a multinational dramatic genre, with much of the newest work originating from Stephen Sondheim in America (*Follies, A Little Night Music, Sunday in the Park with George, Assassins*); Andrew Lloyd Webber in England

Plays can be analyzed structurally in two ways: by their components (that is, plot, character, theme, etc.) and by their order of organization (exposition, development, climax, etc.). Both methods are used by most people who find it worthwhile to analyze dramatic art, and both will be used in this book. However, it must be clear from the outset that a drama which is taken apart in the classroom inevitably loses something. The individual components and the sequential aspects of any given play are never in fact isolated in the theatrical experience, and any truly useful dramatic analysis must end with a resynthesis of the studied portions into a living whole. The complexity of the theatrical experience and its multisensual impact decree that we see it always as greater than the sum of its parts.

The Components of a Play

The division of plays into components is an ancient analytical practice. Aristotle in his *Poetics* (325 B.C.) described the components of a tragedy (by which he meant a serious play) as plot, character, theme, diction, music, and spectacle—in that order. Aristotle's list, with some modification and elaboration, still serves as a pretty fair breakdown of what theatre is all about, although the relative importance of each of the components has been a matter of continuing controversy.

Plot While we may colloquially think of "plot" as synonymous with "story," the two words are quite different: plot refers to the *mechanics* of storytelling: it includes the sequence of comings and goings of the characters; the timetable of the play's events; and the specific order of revelations, reversals, quarrels, discoveries, and actions that take place on stage, as in "furthering the plot." (In London theatres of the sixteenth century, a written "platte" or "plotte" was hung on the wall backstage, reminding the actors of the play's order of major events, entrances, and exits.) Plot is a *structure of actions:* both outer actions (such as Romeo stabbing Tybalt) and inner ones (such as Romeo falling in love with Juliet). The specific sequence and arrangement of these actions is essentially what we take away from the play; it is usually the way we *describe* the play to someone who has not yet seen it. This is undoubtedly why Aris-

Singing and dancing, often allied to romantic themes, are the traditional distinguishing arts of the American musical play. One of the classic American musicals was the 1930 Girl Crazy, *by the late Gershwin Brothers, George (who wrote the music) and Ira (lyrics). With a new script (by Ken Ludwig), a new title—*Crazy for You*—and some additional Gershwin songs, this show became a new Broadway hit in 1992. Pictured are Harry Groener and Jody Benson as the "Embraceable You" romantic leads. (Photo: Joan Marcus.)*

totle describes "plot" first in his list of the elements of tragedy (drama). Creating a dramatically compelling plot is certainly one of the most difficult and demanding tests of a playwright's skill.

Traditionally, the primary demands of plot are logic and suspense. To satisfy the demand for logic, the actions portrayed must be plausible, and events must follow one upon another in an organic rather than arbitrary fashion. To sustain suspense, the actions portrayed must set up expectations for further actions, drawing the audience along in a story that seems to move inexorably toward an ending that may be sensed but is never wholly predictable. Melodramas and farces tend to rely heavily on intricate and suspenseful plots. The "well-made plays" of the late nineteenth century reflect an attempt to elevate plot construction to the highest level of theatrical art; today, murder mysteries and "whodunits" are likely to be the most plot-intensive works to be seen on the stage.

Characters The *characters* of a play are the human figures — the impersonated presences — who undertake the actions of the plot. Their potency in the theatre is measured by our interest in them *as people*. The most brilliant plotting in the world cannot redeem a play if the audience remains indifferent to its characters; therefore, the fundamental demand of a play's characters is that they make the audience *care*. To this end, characters cannot be mere stick figures, no matter how elaborately detailed. The great dramatic characters of the past — Hamlet, Masha, Amanda, Iago, Vladimir, Peer Gynt, Phaedra, to name a few — bring to an experienced theatregoer's or playreader's mind personalities as vivid and memorable as those of good friends (and hated enemies); they are whole images, indelibly human, alive with the attributes, feelings, and expectations of real people. We can identify with them; we can sympathize with them.

Character depth is what gives a play its psychological complexity, its sensuality, and its warmth. Without it, we cannot experience love, hate, fear, joy, hope, despair — any of the emotions we expect to derive from theatre; and a theatre devoid of those emotions that stem from the humanness of the characters portrayed would be a theatre without an audience in a matter of days. For this reason many playwrights have scoffed at the notion of primacy of plot and at the often mechanical contrivances of the well-made play. Indeed, several playwrights have fashioned plays that were quite arbitrarily plotted, with the story line designed simply to show various aspects of a fascinating character.

Theme The *theme* of a play is its abstracted intellectual content. It may be described as the play's overall statement: its topic, central idea, or message, as the case may be. Some plays have obvious themes, such as Euripides' *The Trojan Women* (the horrors of war) or Molière's *The Bourgeois Gentleman* (the foolishness of social pretense). Other plays have less clearly defined themes, and the most provocative of these have given rise to much scholarly controversy. *Hamlet*, *Oedipus Tyrannos*, and *Waiting for Godot* all suggest many themes, and each has spawned

Bertolt Brecht's "distanced" theatre combines bold theatricality, songs, and blatant stage mechanics to promulgate a social/political aesthetic. From a Berlin production of Brecht's cabaret opera, The Rise and Fall of The City of Mahagonny. *(Photo: Arvid Lagenpusch.)*

a great many debates among adherents arguing fiercely about which theme is central.

Nothing demands that a play have a single theme, of course, or even that it be at all reducible to straightforward intellectual generalization. Indeed, plays that are too obviously theme-intensive are usually considered too propagandistic or too somberly academic for theatrical success: "If you want to send a message," one Broadway saying goes, "use a fax machine." What is more, although the themes of plays address the central questions of society and mankind, their theatrical impact hinges always on audience engagement in plot and characterization.

The importance of theme is that a play must have something to say, and that something must seem *pertinent* to the audience. Further, the play must be sufficiently focused and limited to give the audience at least some insight into that something within its two- to four-hour framework. Plays that try to say nothing or, conversely, plays that try to say everything, rarely have

even a modest impact, no matter how entertaining or well plotted they may be. Thus, from the beginning, playwrights working in every genre, be it tragedy, comedy, melodrama, or farce, have recognized the merit of narrowing their field of intellectual investigation when crafting a play.

Diction Aristotle's fourth component, *diction,* relates not only to the pronunciation of spoken dialogue but also to the literary character of a play's text, including its tone, imagery, cadence, and articulation, as well as its use of literary forms and figures such as verse, rhyme, metaphor, apostrophe, jest, and epigram.

The theatrical value of poetry has been well established from the beginning; until fairly recent times, as a matter of fact, most serious plays were written largely in verse. Today, comedies as well as more serious plays still make liberal use of carefully crafted dialogue, although the verse form is relatively rare. Many plays succeed on the basis of brilliant repartee, stunning epigrams, poetic language, witty arguments, and dazzling tirades. Other, quite different, sorts of plays feature a poetry of silences and inarticulate mutterings: these, as fashioned by Anton Chekhov or Harold Pinter, for example, can create a diction no less effective than the more ostentatiously crafted verbal pyrotechnics of a Bernard Shaw or a Tom Stoppard (see the chapters on modern drama).

The diction of a play is by no means the creation of the playwright alone. It is very much the product of the actor as well, and for that reason throughout the history of Western theatre an effective stage voice has been considered the prime asset of the actor. Even today, the study of voice is a primary and continuous obligation at most schools and conservatories of classical acting. The chief aim of these schools is to create an acting voice capable of dealing in quite spectacular fashion with the broad palette of dramatic diction demanded by the works of the world's most noted playwrights.

Music Any discussion of *music,* Aristotle's fifth component of theatre, forces us to remember that in Aristotle's time plays were sung or chanted, not simply spoken. That mode of presentation has all but disappeared, and yet the musical component remains directly present in most plays performed today, indirectly present in the rest.

Music is directly present in the large number of plays that call for actual music in their presentation. This music takes many forms. Songs are common in the plays of Shakespeare, as well as in the works of modern writers, such as Bertolt Brecht, who feature "direct" performance techniques. Many naturalistic writers have found occasion to work familiar songs into their scripts, sometimes by having characters play records on stage. Chekhov and Tennessee Williams both make extensive use in their plays of off-stage music — for example, a military marching band can be heard in Chekhov's *The Three Sisters;* and Williams provides for music from a nearby dance hall in *A Streetcar Named Desire* and from a cantina in *Night of the Iguana.* Directors also frequently add incidental music to play productions — sometimes to set a mood during intermissions or before the play begins, sometimes to underscore the play's action itself. The power of music directly present in the theatre is well known, and its effectiveness in moving an audience to ever-deeper feeling is one that few playwrights or directors wish to ignore.

Indirectly, music is present in every play. It is in the rhythm of sounds that, while not specifically tuneful, combine to create a play's "score," its orchestration of sound. Vocal tones, footsteps, sighs, shouts, offstage railroad whistles, the shrilling of a telephone, muffled drumbeats, gunshots, animal cries, conversations in the next room, and amplified special effects (heartbeats, respiration, otherwordly noises, for instance) are frequently employed by authors and directors to create a symphony of the theatre

What we see complements and underlines what we hear. King Lear (Dudley Knight) standing tall amidst his kneeling knights and daughters, emphasizes Lear's regal authority — just before he loses it — in this 1986 Colorado Shakespeare Festival production of King Lear. *The costumes are by James Berton Harris and the setting by Douglas-Scott Goheen.*

quite apart from, though supportive of, the plot, characters, dialogue, and theme. Moreover, the spoken word creates, in addition to its semantic impact (its meaning and connotation), an aural impact: it is an integer of pure sound, and it can be appreciated as pure musical vibration. Under the guidance of a skilled director, all of a play's sounds can be orchestrated to produce a performance of such dramatic force that it can thrill even persons wholly unacquainted with the language of the dialogue.

Spectacle Aristotle's last component, *spectacle,* encompasses the visual aspects of production: scenery, costumes, lighting, make-up, properties, and the overall *look* of the theatre and stage. It would be wrong to infer that "spectacle" is synonymous with "spectacular," for some productions are quite restrained in their visual artistry. Rather, it is spectacle in the sense that it is something seen. If this point seems obvious, it is also crucial. Theatre is a visual experience every bit as much as it is an aural, emotional, or intellectual one: the ancient Greeks clearly had this in mind when they

chose the name "seeing place" to designate the site of their performances.

Much as the cinema has been called the art of "moving pictures," so the theatre might be called the art of fluid sculpture. This sculpture is fashioned in part from the human body in motion and in part from still or moving scenery and props, natural and manufactured items of both dramatic and decorative importance, all illuminated by natural or artificially modulated light. It is a sculpture that moves in time as well as in space; and although it is generally considered to be primarily a support for the plot, characters, and theme of a play, it has an artistic appeal and an artistic heritage all its own. Certainly some ardent patrons of the theatre pay more attention to settings and costumes than to any other aspect of a play, and in many a successful production dramatic visual effects have virtually carried the play.

Memorable visual elements can be both grand and prosaic, imposing and subtle. Nineteenth-century Romanticism, which survives today primarily in the form of grand opera, tends to favor mammoth stag-

A priest is about to take his designated place in a stone seat in the first row of the ancient theatre of Athens. (Drawing: John von Szeliski.)

ings featuring processions, crowd scenes, palaces, animals, triumphal arches, and lavish costumes. Twentieth-century movements are more likely to go in for domestic environments and archetypal images: Jimmy and Cliff reading newspapers while Alison irons a shirt in John Osborne's *Look Back in Anger* and Laura playing with her glass animals in Tennessee Williams's *The Glass Menagerie;* or Mother Courage pulling her wagon in Brecht's *Mother Courage* and Nagg and Nell in the ashcans of Samuel Beckett's *Endgame.* In the long run, conceptual richness and precision in a play's visual presentation are far more telling than grandeur for its own sake.

Convention   To these six components of every play we should add a seventh that Aristotle apparently never saw reason to consider as a discrete component: theatrical *convention.* The agreement between audience and actor includes a whole set of tacit understandings that form the context of playwatching—conventions that make us understand, for example, that when the stage lights fade out, the play (or the act) has ended. Over the years, other common conventions of the European-American stage have included the following:

- When one actor turns directly from the others and speaks to us, the other charac-

"Spectacle" need not be pretty as much as visually penetrating and evocative. In Henrik Ibsen's play, Peer Gynt, *the author's stage direction merely says "A Madhouse;" in this Berlin production directed by the celebrated Peter Stein, the madhouse is created by hanging and writhing bodies, mostly naked, and an immense sculpture. (Photo: Courtesy German Information Center.)*

ters are presumed not to hear him. This is the convention of the *aside* (to the audience).

- When the actors all leave the stage, and then they or others reenter (particularly when the lights change), time has elapsed, and the locale may be changed.
- When the actors onstage freeze, we are seeing some sort of "dream state" (of one of the characters, presumably), and the words we hear are to be considered his or her thoughts, not anyone's speech.

The conventions of the theatre permit a sort of shorthand communication with the audience, without the encumbrance of extensive physical elaboration or acting out. If the locale can effectively be changed by the convention of a simple light shift, instead of by moving a half ton of scenery, the theatre saves money and the audience saves time. Stage violence is usually executed conventionally (that is, with little physical mayhem) rather than with lifelike (or cinematographic) verisimilitude, since the difficulty in realistically portraying severed torsos, rupturing intestines, and bleeding limbs on stage ordinarily outweighs any dramatic advantage in doing so; and the theatrical convention ("stab, grab, scream, collapse, and die") can be accepted fully if performed with emotional and psychological (although not physical) authenticity.

Many of our stage conventions are so imbedded in the fabric of the theatregoing experience that we tend to forget about them altogether unless something happens that casts them into relief. Our theatre conventions are most visible when we see them from afar — in contrast to the practices of theatres of other cultures. For example, the conventions of the Japanese Noh Drama decree that major characters enter on a gangway, that choruses sing the lines of characters who are dancing, that hand-held fans are used in certain ways to indicate wind, water, rain, or the rising moon. Patrons of the Noh Drama accept these conventions as unquestioningly as

we accept the convention that, when the stage lights dim, we are to ignore the scurrying about of actors and stagehands during a scene change.

Each play sets up its own system of conventions, but in most cases they accord with the traditions of their times and therefore go largely unnoticed (doubtless that is why Aristotle, familiar with no drama other than his own, made no specific mention of them). In modern times, with playwrights and directors becoming increasingly aware of other traditions and possibilities, more and more play productions seek to employ conventions of ancient times or foreign cultures and even to establish new ones. Peter Shaffer's *Black Comedy,* which supposedly takes place in the dark, utilizes a convention that Shaffer attributes to the Chinese: when the lights are on they are "off," and when they are off they are "on." Eugene O'Neill's *Strange Interlude* and Steven Berkoff's *Kvetch* give us to understand that when the actors freeze and speak, we in the audience — but not the other characters in the play — hear their thoughts. Jean Anouilh's *Antigone* uses a variation on the Greek device of the chorus: a single man speaks with the author's voice as the characters on stage freeze in silence. Lanford Wilson, in *The Rimers of Eldritch,* presents a story in more than a hundred tiny scenes that jump back and forth in time, and only at the play's end do we get any real sense of story line. Arthur Miller's *After the Fall* places an imaginary psychiatrist in the midst of the audience, and the play's protagonist repeatedly interrupts the action of the drama to address his analyst in highly theatrical "therapy" sessions. And so it goes. There is no formal requirement for the establishment of theatrical conventions, except that the audience must "agree" (which it does, of course, unconsciously) to accept them.

These seven components of every play — with the seventh more or less framing Aristotle's six — are the raw material of drama. All are important, and certainly the theatre could not afford to dispense with any one. Some plays are intensive in one or more; most great productions show artistry in all. The *balancing* of these components in theatrical presentation is one of the primary challenges facing the director, who on one occasion may be called upon mainly to clarify and elaborate a theme, on another to find the visual mode of presentation that best supports the characters, on another to develop and "flesh out" the characterizations in order to give strength and meaning to the plot, on another to heighten a musical tone in order to enhance sensual effect, on another to develop the precise convention—the relationship between play and audience—that will maximize the play's artistic impact. For as important as each of these components is to the theatrical experience, it is their combination and interaction, not their individual splendor, that is crucial to a production's success.

The Order of a Play

Plays can also be looked at in terms of their temporal (time) structure. Here again, Aristotle affords some help. He tells us that drama has "a beginning, a middle, and an end," and here and there in his *Poetics* he proffers a little detail about the nature of each of these elements. We can expand Aristotle's list somewhat, for by now some fairly consistent features can be distinguished in the orderly sequencing of a theatrical experience. We can divide these individual features into three major groupings: the preplay, the play proper, and the postplay.

The events that take place before the play proper begins are referred to as the *preplay*.

The Gathering of the Audience Dramatic theorists often either ignore the audience in considering the crucial elements of the theatre or else dismiss it as a "paratheatrical" (para meaning "only somewhat") concern. The gathering of the audience is, however, an extremely important consideration in the presentation of a play, and it entails a process that is not without its artistic and cultural significance. The chief concerns in that process have to do with publicity, admission, and seating. Each of these concerns has given theatre producers much food for thought since ancient times.

For how does the theatre attract its audience in the first place? Theatregoing, after all, is not a need of mankind in the same way that eating is a need; the population of a society does not spend half its waking hours trying to supply itself with theatre in the way it strives to secure food, shelter, and physical security. Rather the theatre, if it is to survive, must go out and recruit attention; in every era, theatre has had the responsibility of gathering its audience.

Therefore, the goal of every theatre producer is to make his or her theatre accessible, inviting, and favorably known to the widest possible public—and also, in many eras, to the *richest* possible public—and to make theatre as an art form as thrilling and spiritually *necessary* as it can possibly be.

One of the oldest known ways of publicizing the theatre is by means of a procession. The circus parade, which still takes place in some of the smaller towns of Europe and the United States, is a remnant of a once universal form of advertisement for the performing arts that probably began well in advance of recorded history.

The Greeks of ancient Athens opened their great dramatic festivals with a *proagon* (literally, "pre-action") in which both playwrights and actors were introduced at a huge public meeting and given a chance to speak about the plays they were to present on subsequent days. Today, similar conclaves—usually via television talk shows in this global village of ours—are often used to promote theatrical events to the public at large. The Elizabethans flew flags atop their playhouses on performance days, and the flags could be seen across the Thames in "downtown" London, enticing hundreds away from their commercial and religious activities. The lighted marquees of Broadway theatres around Times Square and of London theatres in the West End are a modern-day equivalent of the flags that waved over those first great English public theatres.

Developments in the printing and broadcast media have spurred the growth of theatre advertising until it is today a major theatrical craft in its own right. Splendid posters, illustrated programs, multicolor subscription brochures, full-page newspaper advertisements, staged media events, articulate press releases, and flashy 30-second television commercials have been employed to summon us out of the comfort of our homes and into the theatre. For premieres or for openings of new playhouses, giant searchlights are often used to beckon the public to the theatrical location. Far from being an inconsequential aspect of theatre, publicity today occupies a place of fundamental importance in the thinking of theatrical producers and commands a major share of the budget for commercial theatrical ventures.

Procedures for admitting and seating the audience are usually straightforward and conventional; however, they can have important—and occasionally decisive—effects on the overall theatrical presentation.

Ordinarily, theatre is supported at least in part by fees charged the audience. These fees make up what is called the "box office revenue." For commercial theatres, box office revenue provides the sole means of meeting production costs and providing a profit to investors. The admission charge dates from ancient Greek days, and since then only a few amateur or civic productions (such as the religious pageants of medieval England or the free Shakespeare performances in contemporary New York City) have managed to survive without it.

Seating is frequently determined by the price of admission: the best seats cost the most. What determines "best" and "poorest" seating, however, depends on many things. In modern Broadway and West End theatres, the most costly seats are in the orchestra (known in the West End as "the stalls"), which is the ground-level seating area; balcony seats ordinarily cost less, and the higher the balcony, the smaller the price. In the public theatres of Elizabethan London, however, the ground level (which was standing room) provided the cheapest space, and the "gentlemen's rooms" in the balcony—where one could be seen and visited—commanded up to twelve times as much. In the Restoration period, seats on the stage itself brought the highest prices of all, assuring their purchasers the widest possible personal recognition (but affording a ridiculously poor view of the play's action).

Seating is not always scaled according to price, however. In the Greek drama festivals of ancient Athens, the front-row seats were reserved for priests, and members of the lay audience sat in sections of the *theatron* reserved for their particular tribe. In many noncommercial theatres today, the best seats go to those patrons willing to wait longest in line to get them. The National Theatre of England has experimented with a seating system designed to reward the most eager of its fans, not the richest; this practice is common in East European countries. In racially divided countries, audiences are segregated according to the color of their skin. This regrettable practice persisted well into the twentieth century in the United States, and indeed in the 1960s was occasionally revived by "Black Theatre" companies. Perhaps the most radical seating experiments occurred in the "New Theatre" movement of the early 1970s, in which audiences were often led one by one to seats determined in an impromptu interview with one or another of the cast members acting as ushers. What is more, patrons were sometimes ordered to leave their assigned seats in midperformance to make room for actors!

The Transition Gathered, admitted, and seated, the audience remains a collection of individuals preoccupied with their daily concerns. Now the theatre must transform them into a community devoted to the concerns of the play and enmeshed in the actions of imaginary characters. The theatre, in other words, must effect in their awareness a transition from real life to stage life, and it must do so in a smooth and agreeable fashion.

The written program is one modern device (modern in the sense that it dates from the eighteenth century) that helps to prepare the audience for the fiction they are about to see. It gives them the locale and time of the action, the names of the characters and of the actors who impersonate them; in these ways it allows the audience to preview the general scope of the play's environment—spatial, temporal, and personal—and to accept the actors as valid impersonators of the play's characters. Having read that Kevin Kline is playing Hamlet, for example, we don't spend playwatching time trying to figure who the lead actor is.

Often music is used, in the contemporary theatre, to set the mood or tone of a play, particularly when the action is set in a certain period in the past. For a musical production, an entire orchestral piece—called the overture—sometimes precedes the action on stage.

Lobby displays are sometimes used to supplement the written programs, featuring either pictures of the actors or other pictures and documents relevant to the play, its period, its author, and its critical reception. Occasionally the seating area is altered to aid in this transition, sometimes by the addition of wall posters, sometimes by other ornamentation. When no curtain is used, the scenery may be "warmed" by preshow lighting that eases the audience into an expectation of the performance to follow—in some productions that "scenery" includes actors sitting, standing, or lying motionless on the set or engaging in quiet, understated movement. Sometimes slide presentations, songs, or improvised activities take place on stage before the play begins, and the patrons may be asked to participate in some way as they find their way to their seats. Many of these methods date from ancient times; all of them have been used to introduce modern plays to an audience and to prepare the audience to enter the world of the stage.

Finally, a swift new transition to stage life occurs: the play proper begins. Most often this is a shared moment. The houselights dim and a curtain rises or stage lights come up to reveal a scene. Occasionally this transition is more subtle, and each member of the audience glides into the play at his or her own moment of discovery; a preshow improvisation begins to take on a more pronounced, attention-demanding character, or perhaps some small but seemingly significant alteration galvanizes the consciousness to full attention. Either way, the transition is complete. The thinking of the audience shifts from workaday concerns to the characters of the play and their story. This, to use a familiar theatrical term, is "magic time."

Almost all plays (as compared to most happenings, improvisations, and performance art pieces) contain a structured sequence of these four identifiable dramatic elements in the *play proper:* exposition, conflict, climax, and denouement. Alternative dramatic structures will be discussed in Chapters 8 and 9.

The Exposition No important play has ever begun with a character dashing onstage and shouting "The house is on fire!" At best, such a beginning could only confuse the audience, and at worst it could cause them to flee in panic. For at that point they would have no way of knowing what house, or why they should care about it. Most plays, whatever their style or genre, begin with dialogue or action calculated to ease us, not shock us, into the concerns of the characters with whom we are to spend the next two hours or so.

Exposition is a word not much in favor now, coming as it does from an age when play structure was considered more scientific than it is today. But it is still a useful term, referring to the background information the audience must have in order to understand "what's going on" in the action of a play.

In the rather mechanical plotting of the "well-made" plays, the exposition is handled with little fanfare, with a few characters, often servants (minor figures in the action to follow), discussing something that is about to happen and enlightening each other (and, of course, the audience) about certain details around which the plot will turn. Consider these lines from the opening scene of Henrik Ibsen's 1884 classic, *The Wild Duck:*

PETTERSEN, *in livery, and* JENSEN, *the hired waiter, in black, are putting the study in order. From the dining room, the hum of conversation and laughter is heard.*

PETTERSEN: Listen to them, Jensen; the old man's got to his feet—he's giving a toast to Mrs. Sorby.

JENSEN: (*pushing forward an armchair*) Do you think it's true, then, what they've been saying, that there's something going on between them?

PETTERSEN: God knows.

JENSEN: He used to be quite the lady's man, I understand.

PETTERSEN: I suppose.

JENSEN: And he's giving this party in honor of his son, they say.

PETTERSEN: That's right. His son came home yesterday.

JENSEN: I never even knew old Werle had a son.

PETTERSEN: Oh, he has a son all right. But he's completely tied up at the Hoidal works. In all the years I've been here he's never come into town.

A WAITER: (*in the doorway of the other room*) Pettersen, there's an old fellow here . . .

The exposition of Lee Blessing's A Walk in the Woods *is complex and comprehensive: the park-bench play (this one set in Geneva, Switzerland) concerns nuclear disarmament and is based on a real-life dialogue between a U.S. and a Soviet diplomat. Here the American, played by Lawrence Pressman, shares scientific data with his Russian counterpart, played by Michael Constantine; we have to understand it, too, in order to make much sense of this highly intelligent, fascinating play. The La Jolla Playhouse production was directed by Playhouse artistic director Des McAnuff, 1986. (Photo: Micha Langer.)*

PETTERSEN: (*mutters*) Damn. Who'd show up at this time of night?

After a few more lines, Pettersen, Jensen, and the waiter make their exits and are seen no more. Their function is purely expository—to pave the way for the principal characters. The conversation they are having is a contrivance intended simply to give us a framework for the action—and the information they impart is presented by means of a conversation among servants only because a convention of realism decrees that words spoken in a play be addressed to characters, not to the audience.

The exposition of nonrealistic plays can be handled more directly. It was the Greek custom to begin a play with a prologue preceding the entrance of the chorus and the major play episodes; the prologue was sometimes a scene and sometimes a simple speech to the audience. Shakespeare also used prologues in some of his plays. In one particularly interesting example, Shakespeare's *Henry V,* each of the five acts begins with a character called Chorus directly addressing the audience and setting the scene for the act:

CHORUS: O for a Muse of fire, that would
    ascend
The brightest heaven of invention!
A kingdom for a stage, princes to act,
And monarchs to behold the swelling
    scene!
Then should the warlike Harry, like
    himself,
Assume the port of Mars, and at his heels
(Leash'd in, like hounds) should famine,
    sword, and fire
Crouch for employment. But pardon,
    gentles all,
The flat unraised spirits that hath dar'd
On this unworthy scaffold to bring forth
So great an object. Can this cockpit hold
The vasty fields of France? Or may we
    cram
Within this wooden O the very casques
That did affright the air at Agincourt?
O, pardon! since a crooked figure may
Attest in little place a million,
And let us, ciphers to this great accompt,
On your imaginary forces work.
Suppose within the girdle of these walls
Are now confin'd two mighty monarchies,
Whose high, upreared, and abutting
    fronts
The perilous narrow ocean parts asunder.
Piece out our imperfections with your
    thoughts;
Into a thousand parts divide one man,
And make imaginary puissance;
Think, when we talk of horses, that you
    see them
Printing their proud hoofs i' th' receiving
    earth;
For 'tis your thoughts that now must deck
    our kings,
Carry them here and there, jumping o'er
    times,
Turning th' accomplishment of many
    years

Into an hour-glass: for the which supply,
Admit me Chorus to this history;
Who, Prologue-like, your humble patience
    pray,
Gently to hear, kindly to judge, our play.

This justly famous prologue establishes setting, characters, and audience expectation of plot in an utterly straightforward manner, and begs the audience's indulgence for the theatrical conventions they will be called upon to entertain.

The Conflict   Now is the time for the character to enter shouting "The house is on fire!"

It is a truism that drama requires conflict; in fact, the very word *drama,* when used in daily life, implies a situation fraught with conflict. No one writes plays about characters who live every day in unimpaired serenity; no one, quite certainly, would ever choose to watch such a play. Conflict and confrontation are the mechanisms by which a situation becomes dramatic.

Why is this so? Why are conflict situations so theatrically interesting? The reasons have to do with plot, theme, and character. Plot can hold suspense only when it involves alternatives and choices: Macbeth has strong reasons to murder King Duncan and strong reasons not to; if he had only the former or only the latter, he would project no real conflict and we should not consider him such an interesting character. We are fascinated by a character's actions largely in light of the actions he rejects and the stresses he has to endure in making his decisions. In other words, plot entails not only the actions of a play but also the inactions — the things that are narrowly rejected and do *not* happen. A character's decision must proceed from powerfully conflicting alternatives if we are to watch his behavior with empathy instead of mere curiosity. In watching a character act, the audience must also watch him *think;* a playwright gets him to think by putting him into conflict.

Conflict can be set up between characters as well as within them; it may be reducible to one central situation or it may evolve out of many. Whatever the case, conflict throws characters into relief and permits the audience to see deeply into the human personality. To see a character at war with himself or in confrontation with another is to see how that character *works,* and this is the key to our caring.

The theme of a play is ordinarily a simple abstraction of its central conflict. In Sophocles' *Antigone,* for example, the theme is the conflict between divine law and civil law; in *Death of a Salesman,* it is the conflict between Willy's reality and his dreams. Conflicts are plentiful in farces and comedies as well—the conflicts inherent in the "eternal triangle," for example, have provided comic material for dramatists for the last two millennia. Many of the more abstract philosophical conflicts—independence versus duty, individuality versus conformity, idealism versus pragmatism, integrity versus efficiency, pleasure versus propriety, progress versus tradition, to name a few—suggest inexhaustible thematic conflicts that appear in various guises in both ancient and contemporary plays.

The playwright introduces conflict early in a play, often by means of an "inciting incident" in which one character poses a conflict or confrontation either to another character or to himself. For example:

Cassius and Brutus begin as allies, but the conflict that emerges between them after they conspire to assassinate Julius Caesar creates much of the dramatic momentum of the play. Here Delroy Lindo plays Cassius, to Dakin Matthews's Brutus, in the 1991 Mark Taper Forum production of Julius Caesar, *directed by Oskar Eustis. (Photo: Jay Thompson.)*

FIRST WITCH: All hail, Macbeth, hail to thee, Thane of Glamis!
SECOND WITCH: All hail, Macbeth, hail to thee, Thane of Cawdor!
THIRD WITCH: All hail, Macbeth, that shalt be King hereafter!
BANQUO: Good sir, why do you start, and seem to fear
Things that do sound so fair?

In this, the inciting incident of Shakespeare's *Macbeth* (which follows two brief expository scenes), a witch confronts Macbeth with the prediction that he will be king, thereby posing an alternative that Macbeth has apparently already considered, judging from the startled response that elicits Banquo's comment.

Once established, conflict is intensified to crisis, usually by a series of incidents, investigations, revelations, and confrontations that the playwright creates. Sometimes even non-events serve to intensify a conflict. Such is certainly the case in the modern classic, *Waiting for Godot,* in which two characters simply wait, through two hour-long acts, for the arrival of a third who never comes. Indeed, with this play, Samuel Beckett virtually rewrote the book on playwriting technique by showing how time alone, when properly managed, can do the job of heightening and developing conflict in a dramatic situation.

The Climax Conflict cannot be intensified indefinitely. In a play, as in life, when conflict becomes insupportable, something has

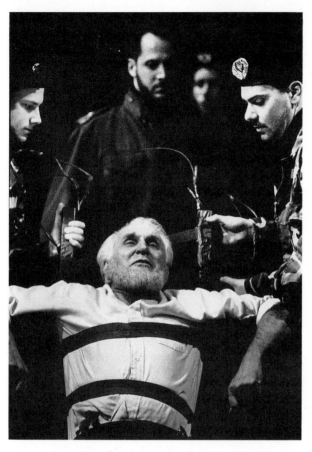

Ray Reinhardt, as Gloucester, waits to be blinded by Cornwall and his thugs in the horrifying third-act climax of Shakespeare's King Lear. *Reinhardt, a veteran professional, was a guest artist in this student production at the University of California at Irvine. (Photo: Philip Channing.)*

to give. Thus every play, be it comic, tragic, farcical, or melodramatic, culminates in some sort of dramatic explosion.

Aristotle described that dramatic explosion, in tragedy, as a *catharsis,* or purification. Aristotle's conception is susceptible to various interpretations, but it has been widely accepted and broadly influential for centuries. According to Aristotle's system, the catharsis is the crucial axis in the structure of tragedy, evolving out of the tragic hero's recognition (*anagnorisis*) of some fundamental truth and his consequent reversal (*peripeteia*) of some former igno-

rance, such as a horrific deed unknowingly performed (*pathos*). The catharsis releases the audience's pity and thereby permits the fullest experience of tragic pleasure, washing away, as it were, the terror that has been mounting steadily during the play's tragic course. Such catharsis as accompanies Oedipus' gouging out his own eyes as he recognizes his true self illustrates the extreme theatrical explosion of which the classical Greek tragic form is capable.

For any dramatic form, the climax is the conflict of a play taken to its most extreme; it is the moment of maximum tension. At the climax, a continuation of the conflict becomes unbearable, impossible: some sort of change is mandated. Climaxes in modern plays do not as a rule involve death or disfiguration (although there are exceptions: Peter Shaffer's celebrated *Equus* reaches its climax with the blinding of six horses, and Edward Albee's *The Zoo Story* climaxes with one character impaling himself on a knife held by another); however, they inevitably contain elements of recognition and reversal if not of catharsis, and usually the major conflicts of the play are resolved by one or more of these.

The Denouement The climax is followed by and the play concluded by a denouement, or resolution, in which a final action or speech or even a single word or gesture indicates that the passions aroused by the play's action are now stilled and a new harmony or understanding has been reached.

The tenor of the denouement tends to change with the times. In the American theatre of the 1950s and 1960s, for example, the sentimental and message-laden denouement was the rule: in Robert Anderson's *Tea and Sympathy,* a teacher's wife prepares to prove to a sensitive boy that he is not homosexual; in Dore Schary's *Sunrise at Campobello,* a future American president makes his way on crippled legs to a convention platform. In the current theatre, in this existential age that looks with suspicion on

The exuberant curtain call for this American Conservatory Theatre production of The Bourgeois Gentleman *presents the entire cast to the audience for a rousing final bow. (Photo: William Ganslen, ACT.)*

tidy virtues and happy endings, more ironic and ambiguous denouements are to be expected. The current theatre also provides less in the way of purgation than do more classical modes; that is doubtless because the conflicts raised by the best of contemporary drama are not amenable to wholesale relief. But a denouement still must provide at least some lucidity concerning the problems raised by the play, some vision or metaphor of a deeper and more permanent understanding. Perhaps the final lines of *Waiting for Godot* best represent the denouement of the current age:

ESTRAGON: Well, shall we go?
VLADIMIR: Yes, let's go.
    They do not move.

Events that take place after the play ends are referred to as the *postplay*.

The Curtain Call The last staged element of a theatrical presentation is the curtain call, in which the actors bow and the audience applauds. This convention, which has been customary in the theatre at least since the time of the Romans, plays an important but often overlooked role in the overall scope of theatrical presentation.

The curtain call is *not* simply a time for the actors to receive congratulations from the audience, although many actors today seem to think it is. Historically, it is a time in which the actors show their respect for the audience that patronizes them. And aesthetically, it is a time in which the audience allows itself to see the other side of the "paradox of acting." The curtain call liberates the audience from the world of the play, and when there is no curtain call audiences are palpably distressed and often disgruntled. For it fulfills the last provision, so to speak, in the mutual agreement that characterizes the theatre itself—the agreement by which the audience agrees to view the actors as the characters the actors have agreed to impersonate. It is at the curtain call that actors and audience can acknowledge their mutual belonging in the human society, can look each other in the eye and say, in effect, "We all know what it is to experience these things we've just seen performed, we must all try to understand life a little better, we have enjoyed coming this far together, we are with you, we like you." In the best theatre, this communication is a powerful experience.

The Aftermath: Criticism What follows the curtain call? The audience disperses, of course; but the individual audience members do not die, and through them the production enjoys an extended afterlife both in talk and in print — in late-night postmortems at the theatre bar; in probing conversations and published reviews over the next few days; and sometimes in formal classroom discussions, television talk shows, letters to the editor in the local newspaper, and scholarly articles and books seen weeks, months, or years later. For the theatre is a place of public stimulation, both intellectual and emotional, and it should be expected that the stimulation provided by a provocative production would generate both animated discussions and illuminating commentaries.

Both of these we may call *dramatic criticism,* which is the audience's contribution to the theatre. Criticism is as ancient as Aristotle and as contemporary as the essays and lectures that are presented daily in newspapers, journals, books, and academies all over the world. But criticism is not solely an expert enterprise; criticism — which combines analysis and evaluation — is everybody's job. We shall look further at this key aspect of the theatre's art in the final chapter of the book.

She stands alone in the darkness, waiting in the wings, listening with one ear to the insistent rhythms of the dialogue played out upon the stage immediately beyond. Her heart races, and she bounces lightly on the balls of her feet, fighting the welling tension, exhilarated by the sense of something rushing toward her, about to engulf her.

The stage ahead of her is ablaze with light; dazzling colors pour on from all possible directions. The energy on stage is almost tangible: it is there in the eyes of the actors, the pace of the dialogue, the smell of the make-up, the sparkle of sweat and saliva glittering in the lights, the bursts of audience laughter and applause, the sudden silence punctuated by a wild cry or a thundering retort.

She glances backward impatiently. Other actors, costumed like herself, wait in the backstage gloom. Some perform kneebends and roll their necks against the tension. Some gaze thoughtfully at the action of the play; some stare at the walls. In one corner a stage manager, his head encased in electronic paraphernalia, his body hunched over a dimly lighted copy of the script, whispers commands into an intercom. The backstage shadows pulse with anticipation.

Suddenly the onstage pace quickens: the lines, all at once, take on a greater urgency

CHAPTER 3

THE ACTOR

and familiarity. It is the cue . . . if only there were time to go to the bathroom . . . it is the cue . . . she takes a deep breath, a deeper breath, a gasp . . . it is *the cue* and she bounds from the dimness into the dazzle: she is on stage, she is an actor!

It is perhaps the world's most bewildering profession.

At the top, it can be extraordinarily rewarding. The thrill of delivering a great performance, the roar of validation from an enraptured audience, the glory of getting inside the skin of the likes of Hamlet, Harpagon, and Hecuba: these are excitements and satisfactions few careers can match. Nor are the rewards purely artistic and intellectual ones: audience appreciation and the producer's eye for profit can catapult some actors to the highest income levels in the world, with salaries in the millions of dollars for actors achieving "star" status in films. And the celebrity that can follow is legendary: the private lives of the most universally admired actors become public property, their innermost thoughts the daily fare of televison talk shows and fan magazines.

And yet, for all the splendor and glamour, the actor's life is more often than not depressingly anxious, beset by demands for sacrifice from every direction: psychological, financial, and even moral. Stage fright—the actor's nemesis—is an ever-present nightmare that often increases with experience and renown. Fear of failure, fear of competition, fear of forgetting lines, fear of losing emotional control, fear of losing one's looks, fear of losing one's audience—this combination is endemic to acting as to no other profession.

Nor are the economic rewards in general particularly enticing. The six- and seven-figure salaries of the stars bear little relation to the scale pay for which most actors work: theirs is the lowest union-negotiated wage in the capitalist economy, and actors as a rule realize less income than the janitors who clean the theatres or the assistant stage managers who bring them coffee. Neither are the working

Acting is a flesh-and-blood art: within the lifeless frame of scenery and proscenium, the actors' bodies, minds, feelings, and fantasies are deeply involved, animating the play with vibrant human passion and imagination. The impersonation we call "acting" takes place on every level: physiological, psychological, and spiritual. From the Peter Brook production of The Mahabharata. *(Photo: Gilles Abegg.)*

conditions of the average actor much to envy: frightfully long hours, drafty and unpainted dressing rooms, tawdry and unheated rehearsal halls, long stretches of idleness, and weeks and months of grueling travel "on the road." And although the stars billed "above the title" may be treated like celebrities or royalty, the common run of actors are freely bullied by directors, bossed about by stage managers, capriciously hired and fired by producers, dangled and deceived by agents, squeezed and corseted by costumers, pinched by wig dressers, poked and powdered by make-up men, and traduced by press agents. Certainly no

All actors were male, in the Greek and Elizabethan theatre, and in traditional Japanese (Noh and Kabuki) theatre as well; men have played women onstage for more than two thousand years. When they do so in modern plays, it is often as an example of a character's cross-dressing or transvestism; the male actor doing so is said to perform "in drag," as in a skirt that drags on the ground. (Male characters played by females are correspondingly known as "pants roles.") Here, actress Cynthia Mace and actor Stephen Spinella (in "drag") have a gabfest about their respective husbands/boyfriends (among other things) in Tony Kushner's Angels in America, *produced at the Mark Taper Forum in Los Angeles in 1992. This brilliant play, called by its author "a gay fantasia on national themes," explores many social, political, sexual, medical, and even comic aspects of gay American life. (Photo: Jay Thompson.)*

The actor Ray Reinhardt as the famous nineteenth-century author Mark Twain. Costumes and make-up are certainly part of Reinhardt's performance, but his research into Twain's mannerisms and behavior and his ability to portray Twain's personality in a theatrically convincing way are also keys to successful performance.

profession in the world entails more numbing uncertainties than acting, none demands more sacrifices, and none measures its rewards in such extreme and contradictory dimensions.

WHAT IS ACTING?

But what is acting? The question is not as simple as it might seem.

It is, of course, the oldest of the theatrical arts. Theatre begins with the actor, who improvised his own dialogue. Thespis, the first known actor (from whence our word *thespian,* meaning "actor"), was also the author of the dramas in which he appeared.

It is also the most public art of theatre, and the average theatregoer today can name many more actors than playwrights, designers, and directors put together.

Essentially, the art of acting involves "playing" dramatic roles. This playing, however, involves two somewhat different processes that must be joined together.

Mimesis: Imitation

Superficially, the actor "imitates" a dramatic character. In more technical terms, we can say that the actor presents a "mimesis," or a simulation, of the sort of behavior that the author has written about. Part of acting is always mimetic, or imitative. Costume, make-up, and mannerisms may be part of this mimetic activity.

In some cases, imitation is of a real-life person—as when the actor Robert Morse, in the production of Jay Presson Allen's *Tru,* imitated the voice, appearance, and mannerisms of the play's well-known title character, Truman Capote. Richard Burbage, although with more historical distance (and without the advantage—or disadvantage—of photos or videotapes), had much the same task in creating Shakespeare's roles of Richard III and Coriolanus, both based on real individuals.

In other cases, the simulation is of an entirely fictional or even a fantasy character, such as Chekhov's Masha or Barrie's Peter Pan.

Mimesis—imitation—is deeply rooted in child's play, which in all cultures includes "pretending" and "dressing up" as ways of exploring adult roles. We all have a history of imitations; we have all been mimetic "actors" in the "play" of our early lives.

That mimesis is central to theatre was specifically noted by Aristotle, drama's first theorist, who defined tragedy as an "imitation of an action." It is not enough, Aristotle implied, to present the blinding of Oedipus, but the actor has to imitate the action fully as well.

Embodiment: Becoming

Nevertheless, external mimesis is not the whole of acting; and from the earliest times, actors have gone well beyond merely imitating their characters: they have "embodied" them and have seemed to actually "become" them. And actors themselves, throughout history, have sought to invest their own real-life person into their roles.

Of course, much of this embodiment is unavoidable. The actress Jessica Lange may play the role of Blanche du Bois, but it is Lange's arms, legs, face, and eyes that we will see; it is Lange's voice we will hear and, indeed, it is Lange's racing pulse and hard breathing that audience members in the first rows can distinctly observe; it is even Lange's perspiration that we may see gathering on her brow. It is Lange, not "Blanche" who sweats. The actor *is* the character in many regards. But how about the actor's personality? Or the actor's feelings?

Most actors, in most eras, have sought to act their role "from the inside" as well as from the "outside." These actors believe they "feel" their role's emotions as much as (or more than) they simply imitate feelings artificially. The "pretending" of acting, therefore, goes very deep into the center of the actor's personality. In embodying a role, the actor embodies (puts into his/her body) the feelings as well as the actions of the character.

This embodiment can be quite literal: one ancient Greek actor, we are told, was so overcome by emotion while playing Atreus that he drew his sword and sliced off the head of an errant stagehand during one performance. Another Greek actor, one Polus by name, when playing the role of Electra, brought the ashes of his dead son onstage with him, so as to generate the requisite feeling for a cry of lamentation. (Jessica Lange, in

a contemporary variation of that practice, wore the scent used by a friend of hers who had died of AIDS when she was performing her Broadway Blanche; the perfume aided her emotional expression in a speech about Blanche's dead husband.) Embodying a character, as opposed to merely imitating one, requires that the actor's self-expression come from the center. This can elicit a performance that seems — or maybe even *is* — "real" in the sense that the actor's whole physiology performs: pulse, respiration, neural systems, and hormones. (Indeed, the etymology of *emotion* refers to the "out-motion" of presumed "humours" that medieval physicians believed ruled passions and personality — the hormones, in other words.)

The theatre, therefore, has provided the stage not only for character and dramaturgic development, but for actor embodiment and self-expression as well and has done so since the earliest of times. The rituals of the earliest Dionysian dithyrambs and tragedies were improvised out of direct, immediate, ecstatic, and intensely personal demands, as much as from a desire to "imitate" anything. Socrates, noting that the rhapsodic poets of his day were overcome by feelings when they recited their work, considered these performances more inspired than rational: "Are you not carried out of yourself, and does not your soul, in ecstasy, seem to be among the persons or the places of which you are speaking?" he

We don't know what the real Mark Antony looked like, and we probably don't care. What the actor has to do in playing the role is to convince us of his grief at the death of Caesar, his fury at Caesar's assassins, and his passionate commitment to avenge Caesar's death and fulfill his own ambitions. This calls for attention to the "internal" aspects of acting; that is, playing the character's feelings and acting with (what seems like) the character's level of intensity. Al Pacino in the 1988 Julius Caesar *at the New York Shakespeare Festival. John McMartin is the dead Caesar. (Photo: George Joseph.)*

asked the poet Ion. Ion agreed that in speaking he was emotionally transported, as was his audience. Horace, in Rome, put this together by stating that orators (and, by implication, actors) could move their audience *only* when, indeed, they were moved themselves; and the vast majority of theatre theorists and critics since — as well as acting teachers — have

agreed. Some have even argued that actors should live out their parts in real life. Sainte Albine (1747) proposed that only actors who were truly in love could effectively play lovers onstage, unless they could develop a "happy insanity" that could persuade them that they were experiencing exactly what their characters seemed to experience; and for the next two centuries great actors were thought to be either promiscuous — or insane.

Not all have held this view of the actor's emotions, however, and later writers applied Apollonian brakes to some of the Dionysian ecstasies. French encyclopedist Denis Diderot, in his *Paradox of the Actor,* written later in the eighteenth century, argued fervently that the actor should be coldly *un*emotional and should reproduce his part with only rational intelligence and sober aesthetic judgement. "At the moment when [the great actor] touches your heart he is listening to his own voice; his talent depends not, as you think, upon feeling, but upon rendering so exactly the outward signs of feeling that you fall into the trap. . . . The broken voice, the half-uttered words, the stifled or prolonged notes [are all just] . . . magnificent apery," said Diderot. Although a radical statement of a view rarely accepted today, Diderot's words illuminate the issue of what the actor is or is not doing during the moments of actual performance.

Virtually all contemporary acting theories and pedagogies (teaching methods) attempt to integrate the imitative and expressive sides of acting — or to consolidate working from the "outside" and from the "inside," as actors tend to describe these apparently paradoxical demands. Obviously, a performance that fails to fulfill, in its outward (imitative) form, the expectations that the text establishes — a performance, for example, that fails to show Prometheus as angry, Falstaff as blustery, or Cleopatra as regally arrogant — will be strikingly unsatisfying. But so will be a performance where the characters' interactions, no matter how boldly or eloquently executed, seem merely flat and mechanical, or where the passions seem shallowly pasted on, or where no sparks fly and no romance kindles between the persons seemingly represented onstage. Imitation without embodiment rings hollow, and embodiment ("being real") without mimetic definition soon grows tiresome. The best acting synthesizes its expressive and its mimetic aspects and its Dionysian and Apollonian roots.

Beyond these two main lines of the actor's art, there are two other aspects one always finds in the greatest performers: *virtuosity* of technique and the ineffable "magic" that defines the greatest artists in any field.

Virtuosity

Greatness in acting, like greatness in almost any endeavor, demands a superb set of skills.

The characters of drama are rarely mundane; they are exemplary and so must be the actors who portray them. Merely to impersonate — to imitate and embody — the genius of Hamlet, for example, one must deliver that genius oneself. Similar personal resources are needed to project the depth of Lear, the lyricism of Juliet, the fervor of St. Joan, the proud passion of Prometheus, the bravura of Mercutio, or the heroics of Hecuba. Outsized characters demand outsized abilities and the capacity to project them.

Moreover, it is ultimately insufficient for an actor merely to fulfill the audience's preconceptions of his or her character; finally it is necessary that the actor strive to transcend those preconceptions and to create the character afresh, transporting the audience to an understanding of — and a compassion for — the character that they would never have achieved on their own.

Both of these demands require of the actor a considerable virtuosity of dramatic technique.

Traditionally, the training of actors has concentrated on dramatic technique. Since Roman times (and probably before then),

Falstaff must be seen as blustery and fat. Actor Lou Zorich creates both characteristics in JoAnne Akalaitis's 1991 production of Henry IV *at the New York Shakespeare Festival. Zorich's grizzled beard and stomach padding (costumes are by Gabriel Berry) help, but the performance finally will be defined by the energy Zorich puts into his depiction. (Photo: George Joseph.)*

actors have spent most of their lifetime perfecting such performing skills as juggling, dancing, singing, versifying, declaiming, clowning, miming, stage fighting, acrobatics, and sleight of hand. Certainly no actor before the present century had any chance of success without several of these skills, and few actors today reach the top of their profession without fully mastering at least a few of them.

Whatever the individual skills required of an actor over time, the sought-after dramatic technique that is common to history and to our own times can be summed up in just two features: a splendidly supple body and a magnificently expressive voice. These are the tools every actor strives to attain, and when brilliantly honed they are valuable beyond measure.

The actor's voice has received the greatest attention through history; Greek tragic actors were awarded prizes for their vocal abilities alone, and many modern actors, such as James Earl Jones, Patrick Stewart, Glenn Close, and Maggie Smith are celebrated for their distinctive use of the voice. The potential of the acting voice as an instrument of great theatre is immense. The voice can be thrilling, resonant, mellow, sharp, musical, stinging, poetic, seductive, compelling, lulling, and dominating; and an actor capable of drawing on many such "voices" clearly can command a spectrum of acting roles and lend them a splendor that the less gifted actor or the untrained amateur could scarcely imagine. A voice that can articulate, that can explain, that can rivet attention, that can convey the subtlest nuance, that can exult, dazzle, thunder with rage and flow with compassion: this, when used in the service of dramatic impersonation, can hold an audience utterly spellbound for as long as its owner cares to recite.

The actor's use of his or her body—the capacity for movement—is the other element of fundamental technique, the second basis for dramatic virtuosity. Most of the best actors are strong and supple; all are capable of great physical self-mastery and are artists of body language. The effects that can be achieved through stage movement are as numerous as those that can be achieved through voice. Subtly expressive movement in particular is the mark of the gifted actor, who can accomplish miracles of communication with an arched eyebrow, a toss of the head, a flick of the wrist, a whirl of the hem, or a shuffle of the feet. But bold movements, too, can produce indelible moments in the theatre: Helene Weigel's

---

A THRILLING VOICE

Mr. [Richard] Burton happens to possess a vocal instrument that . . . is exactly what we expect to hear, and almost never do hear, on going to the theatre. The sounds produced in the living theatre are not meant to be the sounds produced in day-to-day life, though that is what actors have been giving us for years on end. We look for a "liveness" that has been intensified, as it is so often intensified in the control rooms of recording studios. Mr. Burton was his own control room, sending out sounds that swept the walls of the theatre clean with an apparently effortless power, magnifying the "natural" until we were caught up in its gale, left stunned and breathless. And yes, we said to ourselves, this is precisely the penetrating resonance all actors should possess, if the tonalities of the stage are to be differentiated from those of film. Not everyone, to be sure, can be born in Wales. But the sound, with all of its nuances and its pressures, can be acquired, as Irene Worth has acquired it. It is thrilling when heard, and the thrill is what playhouses are for.

Walter Kerr

---

powerful chest-pounding when, as Mother Courage, she loses her son; Laurence Olivier's breathtaking fall from the tower as Coriolanus—these are sublime theatricalizations accomplished through the actors' sheer physical skill, strength, and dramatic audacity.

Virtuosity for its own sake can be appealing in the cabaret or lecture hall as well as in the theatre, but when coupled with the impersonation of character it can create dramatic performances of consummate depth, complexity, and theatrical power. We are always impressed by skill—it is fascinating, for instance, to watch a skilled cobbler at his bench—but great skill in the service of dramatic action can

The actor was called "hypokrites" by the Greeks, and the word has come to mean someone who pretends to be someone he or she isn't. Here, Al Hamacher, a distinguished actor and acting teacher at the Alliance Theatre of Atlanta, performs the role of a deranged derelict in the Alliance's production of High Standards. *Hamacher's skillful and expressive use of his body is remarkable in this portrayal. (Photo: Charles M. Rafshoon.)*

be absolutely transporting. Of course, virtuosity is not easy to acquire, and indeed it will always remain beyond the reach of many people. Each of us possesses natural gifts, but not all are gifted to the same degree; some measure of dramatic talent must assuredly be inborn or at least early learned. But the training beyond one's gifts, the shaping of talent into craft, is an unending process. " You never stop learning it," said actor James Stewart after nearly fifty years of stage and film successes, and virtually all actors would agree with him.

Traditional notions of virtuosity in acting went into a temporary eclipse in the middle of this century, owing mainly to the rise of realism, which required that acting conform to the behaviors of ordinary people leading ordinary lives. The *cinéma vérité* of the post–World War II era in particular fostered an "artless" acting style, to which virtuosity seemed intrusive rather than supportive. It is certainly true that the virtuosity of one age can seem mere affectation in the next and that modern times require modern skills, a contemporary virtuosity that accords with contemporary dramatic material. Yet even the traditional skills of the theatre have made a great comeback in recent decades: circus techniques, dance, and songs are now a part of many of the most experimental of modern stagings; and multiskilled, multitalented performers are in demand as never before. The performer rich in talent and performing skills, capable not merely of depicting everyday life but of fashioning an artful and exciting theatrical expression of it as well, once again commands the central position in contemporary drama.

Magic

Beyond impersonation and virtuosity, though incorporating them, remains a final acting ingredient that has been called "presence," "magnetism," "charisma," and many other terms. We shall call it "magic."

It is a quality that is difficult to define but universally felt, a quality we cannot explain except to say we know it when we are under its spell.

We must always remember that the actor began not as a technician of the theatre, but as a priest—and that he embodied not ordinary men, but gods. We may witness this function directly today in certain tribal dramas, in which a shaman or witch doctor is accepted by cocelebrants as the possessor of divine attributes—or as one possessed by them.

The modern secular actor also conveys at least a hint of this transcendent divinity. Elevated upon a stage and bathed in light for all to see, charged with creating an intensity of feeling, a vivid characterization, and a well-articulated eloquence of verbal and physical mastery, the actor at his or her finest becomes an almost extraterrestrial being, a "star," or, in the French expression, a "sacred monster."

The actor's presence, the ability to project an aura of magic—this does not come about as a direct result of skill at impersonation or technical virtuosity. It does, however, depend on the actor's inner confidence, which in turn can be bred from a mastery of the craft. Therefore, while "magic" cannot be directly acquired or produced, it can be approached, and its fundamental requisites can be established. For gifted individuals it might come quite quickly; for others, despite abundant skills and devoted training, it comes late or not at all and they can never rise above pedestrian performances. It is perhaps frustrating to find that acting greatness depends so heavily on this elusive and inexplicable goal of "magic," but it is also true that every art incorporates elements that must remain as mysteries. The best acting, like any art, ultimately transcends the reach of pure descriptive analysis; it cannot be acquired mechanically. The best acting strikes chords in the nonreasoning

Robert DeNiro is surely one of the most charismatic actors of recent years, and his film credits (Jake LaMotta in Raging Bull *won him an Oscar) have made him internationally known. His stage performances are no less noteworthy, however; DeNiro exudes frightening, riveting intensity. Here, he performs with young Ralph Macchio in Reinaldo Povod's powerful play of contemporary urban life,* Cuba and His Teddy Bear, *at the New York Public Theatre. (Photo: George Joseph.)*

parts of our being; it rings with a resonance we do not fully understand, and it evokes a reality we no longer fully remember. We should extol, not lament, this fact.

BECOMING AN ACTOR

How does one become an actor? Many thousands ask this question every year; many thousands, indeed, *act* in one or more theatrical productions every year. The training of actors is now a major activity in hundreds of colleges, universities, conservatories, and private and commercial schools in the United States; and theories of actor training constitute a major branch of artistic pedagogy.

Essentially, actor training entails two distinct phases: development of the actor's instrument and development of the actor's method of approaching a role. There is no general agreement on the order in which these phases should occur, but there is a widespread understanding that both are necessary and that the two are interrelated.

The Actor's Instrument

The actor's instrument is the actor's self—mind, mettle, and metabolism are the materials of an acting performance. An actor's voice is the Stradivarius to be played; an actor's body is the sculpting clay to be molded. An actor is a portrait artist working from inside the self, creating characters with his or her own organs and physiological systems. It is obvious that a great artist requires first-rate equipment: for the actor this means a responsive *self*, disciplined yet uninhibited, capable of rising to the challenges of great roles.

The training of the actor's instrument is both physiological and psychological; for that reason it must be accomplished under the personal supervision of qualified instructors. In the past, acting instructors were invariably master actors who took on younger apprentices; even today, students of classical French and Japanese acting styles learn their art by relentless imitation of the actors they hope to succeed. In America, however, acting instruction has expanded to include a great many educational specialists who may or may not have had extensive professional acting experience themselves; indeed, some of the most celebrated and effective acting teachers today are play directors, theatrical innovators, and academicians.

No one, however, has yet discovered the art of training an actor's instrument simply by reading books or thinking about problems of craft. This point should be borne in mind in reading the rest of this chapter.

Voice and speech, quite naturally, are the first elements of the actor's physiological instrument to be considered: "Voice, voice, and more voice" was the answer Tommaso Salvini, the famed nineteenth-century Italian tragedian, gave to the question, "What are the three most important attributes of acting?" We have already discussed the importance of vocal skills in the acting profession: voice- and speech-training programs are aimed at acquainting the actor with a variety of means to achieve and enhance these skills.

The basic elements of voice (breathing, phonation, resonance) and of speech (articulation, pronunciation, phrasing)—as well as their final combination (projection)—are all separate areas of the integrated instruction a good vocal training program will provide. Such a program ordinarily takes three years or longer, and many actors continue working on their voice and speech all their lives.

As devoted as teachers and scientists have been to the problems of perfecting voice and speech, however, a certain mystery still surrounds much of their work. Even the fundamental question of how the voice actually works is still a subject of fierce dispute among specialists in anatomy and physiology. Moreover, the processes involved in breathing and speaking have acquired a certain mystique—for example, the dual meaning of "inspiration" as both "inhalation" and "spirit stimulus" has given rise to a number of exotic theoretical dictums that border on religiosity. Some of the fundamental practices of vocal and speech instruction, however, are generalized in the box on the components of voice and speech.

Movement is the other main factor to be considered in training the actor's physiological instrument, and this factor is developed primarily through exercises and instruction designed to create physical relaxation, muscular control, economy of action, and expressive rhythms and movement patterns. Dance, mime, fencing, and acrobatics are traditional training courses for actors; in addition, circus techniques and masked pantomime have become common courses in recent years.

Sheer physical strength is stressed by some actors: the late Laurence Olivier, for example, accorded it the absolutely highest importance because, he contended, it gives the actor the stamina needed to "hold stage" for several hours of performance and the basic resilience to accomplish the physical and psychological work of acting without strain or fatigue.

An actor's control of the body permits him or her to stand, sit, and move on stage with alertness, energy, and seeming ease. Standing tall, walking boldly, turning on a dime at precisely the right moment, extending the limbs joyously, sobbing violently, springing about uproariously, and occupying a major share of stage space are among the capacities of the actor who has mastered body control, and they can be developed through training and confidence. In the late days of the Greek the-

THE COMPONENTS OF VOICE AND SPEECH

Breathing pumps air through the vocal tract, providing a carrier for the voice; "breath support," through expansion of the rib cage and lowering and controlling the diaphragm, is a primary goal, as is natural, deep, free breathing that is sufficient to produce and sustain tone, but not so forced as to create tension or artificial huffing and puffing.

Phonation is the process whereby vocal cord oscillations produce sound, a process that remains something of an anatomical and physiological mystery even today. Vocal warm-ups are essential for the actor to keep his or her vocal cords and other laryngeal (voice box) tissues supple and healthy; they also prevent strain and the growth of "nodes" that may cause raspiness and pain as well as phonic failure (laryngitis).

Resonance is the sympathetic vibration or "resounding" of the voice as it is amplified in the throat, chest, and head. Resonance gives phonation its *timbre* or tonal quality, its particular balance of "bass" and "treble" sounds. Open-throatedness—the actual lowering of the larynx within the neck, as by a yawn—increases the resonance in the pharynx (throat) and is a major goal in voice work. Keeping the mouth open while speaking and raising the soft palate also increase resonance and add to vocal quality.

Articulation is the shaping of vocal sound into recognizable *phonemes,* or language sounds, forty of which are easily distinguishable in the English language. Programs of speech training aim at improving the actor's capacity to articulate these sounds distinctly, naturally, and unaffectedly—that is, without slurring, ambiguous noise, or self-conscious maneuvering of the lip and tongue. A lazy tongue and slovenly speaking habits inhibit articulation and must be overcome with persistent drill and disciplined attention.

Pronunciation makes words both comprehensible and appropriate to the character and style of the play; clear standard pronunciation, unaffected by regional dialect, is a cru-cial part of the actor's instrument, as is the ability to learn regional dialects and foreign accents when required. Occasionally an actor achieves prominence with the aid of a seemingly permanent dialect—Andy Griffith and Sissy Spacek are two examples—but such actors are likely to find their casting opportunities quite limited unless they can expand their speaking range.

Phrasing makes words meaningful and gives them sound patterns that are both rhythmic and logical. The great classical actors are masters of nuance in phrasing, capable of subtly varying their pitch, intensity, and rate of speech seemingly without effort from one syllable to the next. They rarely phrase consciously; rather they apparently develop their phrasing through years of experience with classical works and a sustained awareness of the value of spontaneity, naturalness, and a commitment to the dramatized situation. Training programs in speech phrasing aim at enabling actors to expand the pitch range of their normal speech from the normal half-octave to two octaves or three, to double their clear-speaking capacity from 200 words a minute to 400, and to develop their ability to orchestrate prose and verse into effective and persuasive crescendos, diminuendoes, sostenutos, and adagios just as if they were responding to a musical score.

Projection, which is the final element in the delivery of voice and speech to the audience, is what ultimately creates dramatic communication; it governs the force with which the character's mind is heard through the character's voice, and it determines the impact of all other components of the actor's voice on the audience. Anxiety and physical tension are the great enemies of projection because they cause shallow breathing, shrill resonance, and timid phrasing; therefore, relaxation and the development of self-confidence become crucial at this final stage of voice and speech development.

An extraordinary degree of movement discipline, including dance and mime technique, is required for the actors in Robert Wilson's theatrical experiments. Wilson's staging relies heavily on dream-like images, with actors often moving in extreme slow motion through a variety of hard-to-sustain poses and actions. Pictured here is Wilson's startling performance piece, The Forest, *in its 1988 German premiere; Wilson has subsequently restaged the work in the United States. (Photo: Gerhard Kassner; courtesy German Information Center.)*

atre, known as the Hellenistic period, actors used elevated footwear, giant headdresses, and sweeping robes to take on a larger-than-life appearance; the modern actor has discovered that the same effect can be achieved simply by tapping the residual expansiveness of the body.

Economy of movement, which is taught primarily through the selectivity of mime, permits the conveyance of subtle detail by seemingly inconspicuous movement. The waggle of a finger, the flare of a nostril, the quiver of a lip can communicate volumes in a performance of controlled movement. The beginner is often recognized by uncontrolled behaviors — fidgeting, shuffling, aimless pacing, and fiddling with fingers — which actually draw unwanted audience attention. The pro-

fessional understands the value of physical self-control, and the explosive potential of a simple movement that follows a carefully prepared stillness. *Surprise,* which is one of the actor's greatest weapons, can be achieved only through the actor's mastery of the body.

Imagination, and the willingness and ability to use it in the service of art, is the major *psychological* component of the actor's instrument. At the first level, an actor must use his imagination to make the artifice of the theatre *real enough to himself* to convey that sense of reality to the audience: painted canvas flats must be imagined as brick walls, an offstage jangle must be imagined as a ringing onstage telephone, and an actress no older than the actor himself must be imagined as his mother or grandmother.

The scene between Hamlet and his mother Gertrude is one of the most unsettling in drama, intermixing deep affection and violent rage. There's a killing, a ghost, and tumultuous feelings of guilt and betrayal. Here, Kevin Kline plays Hamlet (he also directed the play) and Dana Ivey plays Gertrude in a 1990 production at the New York Public Theatre. (Photo: George Joseph.)

At the second, far more important level, the actor must *imagine himself in an interpersonal situation created by the play:* in love with Juliet, in awe of Zeus, in despair of his life. This imagination must be broad and all-encompassing: the successful actor is able to imagine himself performing and relishing the often unspeakable acts of his characters, who may be murderers, despots, or monsters; insane or incestuous lovers; racial bigots, atheists, devils, perverts, or prudes. To the actor,

nothing must be unimaginable; the actor's imagination must be a playground for expressive fantasy and darkly compelling motivations.

At the third, deepest level, the actor's imagination must become more active; it must go beyond the mere accommodation of an accepted role pattern to become a *creative* force that makes characterization a high art. For each actor creates his or her role uniquely—each Romeo and Juliet are like no others before them, and each role can be uniquely fashioned with the aid of the actor's imaginative power. The final goal of creating a character is to create it freshly, filling it with the pulse of real blood and the animation of real on-the-spot thinking and doing. The actor's imagination, liberated from stage fright and mechanical worries, is the crucial ingredient in allowing the actor to transcend the pedestrian and soar toward the genuinely original.

The liberation of imagination is a continuing process in actor training; exercises and "theatre games" designed for that purpose are part of most beginning classes in acting, and many directors use the same exercises and games at the beginning of play rehearsal periods. Because the human imagination tends to rigidify in the course of maturation—the child's imagination is usually much richer than that of the adult—veteran professional actors often profit from periodic returns to "mind-expanding" or imagination-freeing exercises and games.

Discipline is the fourth and final aspect of an actor's instrument, and to a certain extent it is the one that rules them all.

The imagination of the actor is by no means unlimited, nor should it be. It is restricted by the requirements of the play, by the director's staging and interpretation, and by certain established working conditions of the theatre. The actor's artistic discipline keeps him or her within these bounds and at the same time ensures artistic agility.

The actor is not an independent artist, like a writer or painter. The actor works in an ensemble and is but one employee (paid or unpaid) in a large enterprise that can succeed only as a collaboration. Therefore, although actors are sometimes thought to be universally temperamental and professionally difficult, the truth is exactly the opposite: actors are among the most disciplined of artists, and the more professional they are, the more disciplined they are.

The actor, after all, leads a vigorous and demanding life. Make-up calls at 5:30 in the morning for film actors, and nightly and back-to-back weekend live performances for stage actors, make for schedules that are difficult to maintain on a regular basis. Furthermore, the physical and emotional demands of the acting process, the need for extreme concentration in rehearsal and performance, the need for physical health and psychological composure, the need for the actor to be both the instrument and the initiator of his or her performance, and the special demands of interacting with fellow performers at a deep level of mutual involvement—these aspects of the actor's life do not permit casual or capricious behavior among the members of a cast or company.

Truly professional actors practice the most rigorous discipline over their work habits. They make all "calls" (for rehearsal, costume fitting, photographs, make-up, audition, and performance) at the stated times, properly warmed up beforehand; they learn lines at or before stipulated deadlines, memorize stage movements as directed, collaborate with the other actors and theatre artists toward a successful and growing performance, and continually study their craft. If they do not do these things, they simply cease to be actors. Professional theatre producers have very little sympathy or forgiveness for undisciplined performers, and this professional attitude now prevails in virtually all community and university theatres as well.

Being a disciplined actor does not mean being a slave, nor does it mean foregone capitulation to the director or the management. The disciplined actor is simply one who works rigorously to develop his or her physiological and psychological instrument, who meets all technical obligations unerringly and without reminder, and who works to the utmost to ensure the success of the entire production and the fruitful association of the whole acting ensemble. The disciplined actor asks questions, offers suggestions, invents stage business, and creates characterization in harmony with the directorial pattern and the acting ensemble. When there is a serious disagreement between actor and director (a not uncommon occurrence), the disciplined actor seeks to work it out through discussion and compromise and will finally yield if the director cannot be persuaded otherwise. Persistent, willful disobedience has no place in the serious theatre and is not tolerated by it.

The Actor's Approach: Two Traditional Methods

How does an actor approach a role? How does he or she prepare to simulate a character? to embody a character? to create stage magic in a performance? These questions have been answered in many ways, and they are still shrouded in subjectivity and controversy.

Historically, the answers have generally gravitated toward one or the other of two basic methods, the one often called "external" or "technical," and the other often called "internal" or "truthful." These terms are inexact and even somewhat misleading; nevertheless, their historical importance and wide dissemination demand that we pay them some attention at the outset of this discussion.

The external–internal dichotomy refers back to the basic paradox of the theatre itself and to the fact that the actor both simulates and embodies his role. The external methods of approaching a role have concentrated on the actor's acquisition of technique, on development of virtuoso abilities, and on facility at simulating emotions and behaviors without regard to personal feelings. Diderot, of course, who first articulated the paradox, was an extremist in this position, contending that the best acting was done with cool dispassion and that "the great actor watches appearances . . . he has rehearsed to himself every particle of his despair. He knows exactly when he must . . . shed tears; and you will see him weep at the word, at the syllable, he has chosen, not a second sooner or later. . . . At the very moment when he touches your heart he is listening to his own voice." Believers in such an external approach treat the actor's performance as an analogue of reality rather than a direct embodiment of it, a calculated *presentation* of a character's life rather than its living representation on stage.

Contrarily, internal methods have focused on the actor's personal assumption of his character, his "use of himself" in the portrayal of his role and his actual "experiencing" of the events that he goes through as he embodies his role. These methods tend to expand the psychological dimensions of a performance and to aid the actor in assimilating the physiological reality of his character—down to the heartbeats and flushes and hormonal activities the character would undergo if the dramatized situation were real. Internal methods profess to reach the actor's rationally uncontrollable states and to awaken in him feelings and reflexes that are beyond sheer technical manipulation. Konstantin Stanislavski, the founder of the Moscow Art Theatre (1898) and one of the all-time great teachers of acting, is most closely associated with internalized acting; his "System," developed over the last three decades of his life, was based on the maxim "You must live the life of your character on stage." In order to achieve this end, he developed research into the subconscious, vigorously studied the intricacies of the lives of characters he was to play, and demanded that his actors be "in character" not only during intermissions and while waiting for cues in the wings, but for the entire day of the performance. It is the actor's "sense of truth which supervises all of his inner and physical activity," said Stanislavski. "It is only when his sense of truth is developed that he will . . . express the state of the person he is portraying and . . . not merely serve the purposes of external beauty, as all sorts of conventional gestures and poses do."

The follower of the internal approach is likely to judge the external performance to be "hollow," "shallow," "merely technical," "empty," "unfeeling," or "cold." "I didn't believe it" is the frequent complaint of the Stanislavski adherent. The externalist's criticisms, by contrast, are usually couched in terms such as "unclear," "muddy," "self-indulgent," "overemotional," "melodramatic," "sentimental," "unfocused," and "confused." Partisans for one or the other position are often more distinguishable by their criticisms of other performances than by significant accomplishments of their own.

Integrated Methods

The two traditional methods have had an extraordinary impact on the theatre of the present century. European acting has been responsive to many of the presentational techniques suggested by Diderot, whereas American acting has been particularly influenced by the teaching of Stanislavski—and by the acting of several of Stanislavksi's followers who studied at the late Lee Strasberg's celebrated Actors Studio in the 1950s and 1960s. Strasberg's variation of the Stanislavski System (actually it was a variation of an early version—subsequently discarded—of Stanislavski's system) soon became widely known in the United States simply as "the Method," or as "Method acting." Though to a lesser extent today than in past years, Strasberg's Method continues to attract adherents. Focusing directly on the problem of how the actor can "make his real feelings expressive on the stage," Strasberg, unlike Stanislavski, privileged the actor over the dramatic character and generated an acting style that can be

THE ACTORS STUDIO

The most influential school of acting in the United States has been New York's Actors Studio, which was founded by director Elia Kazan and others in 1947 and achieved prominence following the appointment of Lee Strasberg (1901–1982) as artistic director in 1951. Strasberg, an Austrian by birth and a New Yorker by upbringing, proved a magnetic teacher and acting theorist, and his classes revolutionized American acting, producing such notable performers as Marlon Brando, James Dean, Julie Harris, Paul Newman, Geraldine Page, Shelley Winters, Al Pacino, Ellen Burstyn, and Marilyn Monroe. The Studio is now headed by director Frank Cosaro.

The Studio is not actually a school, but rather an association of professional actors who gather at weekly sessions to work on acting problems. The methodology of the Studio derives in part from Stanislavski and in part from the working methods of the Group Theatre—a pre–World War II acting ensemble that included Kazan, Strasberg, and playwright Clifford Odets. But Strasberg himself proved the key inspiration of Studio teaching and of the American love affair with "method acting" attributed to the Studio work.

Strasberg's work is not reducible to simple formulas; for the Studio is a working laboratory, and the Studio work is personal rather than theoretical, direct rather than general. Much of the mythology that has arisen about the Studio—that actors are encouraged to mumble their lines and scratch their jaws in the service of naturalness—is quite fallacious. Strasberg was a fierce exponent of firm performance discipline and well-studied acting technique; insofar as the Studio developed a reputation for producing actors that mumbled and fidgeted, this seems to have been only a response to the personal idiosyncracies of Marlon Brando, the Studio's first celebrated "graduate."

Strasberg demanded great depths of character relationships from his actors, and he went to almost any length to get them. Explanation was only one of his tools, but it is the only one that can be made available to readers. The following quotes are from Strasberg himself:*

The human being who acts is the human being who lives. That is a terrifying circumstance. Essentially the actor acts a fiction, a dream; in life the stimuli to which we respond are always real. The actor must constantly respond to stimuli that are imaginary. And yet this must happen not only just as it happens in life, but actually more fully and more expressively. Although the actor can do things in life quite easily, when he has to do the same thing on the stage under fictitious conditions he has difficulty because he is not equipped as a human being merely to play-act at imitating life. He must somehow believe. He must somehow be able to convince himself of the rightness of what he is doing in order to do things fully on the stage.

When the actor explores fully the reality of any given object, he comes up with greater dramatic possibilities. These are so inherent in reality that we have a common phrase to describe them. We say, "Only in life could such things happen." We mean that those things are so genuinely dramatic that they could never be just made up. . . .

The true meaning of "natural" or "nature" refers to a thing so fully lived and so fully experienced that only rarely does an actor permit himself that kind of experience on the stage. Only great actors do it on the stage, whereas in life every human being to some extent does it. On the stage it takes the peculiar mentality of the actor to give himself to imaginary things with the same kind of fullness that we ordinarily evince only in giving ourselves to real things. The actor has to evoke that reality on the stage in order to live fully in it and with it.

---

*Quotations from Robert Hethmon, *Strasberg at the Actors Studio* (New York: Viking Press, 1965), pp. 78, 197–98.

highly idiosyncratic to the individual performer, who may be thereby encouraged to bring an entire repertoire of personal behavior into performance. Celebrated midcentury actors like Marlon Brando, James Dean, Paul Newman, and Julie Harris were Strasberg students, as were movie celebrities like Marilyn Monroe; they were perhaps drawn in to the Method by the opportunity to transform their personal idiosyncrasies into recognized art (see box at left).

The division of acting into easily defined, easily opposed "schools" has provided convenient grounds for an overly simplified debate in theatre greenrooms and acting classrooms around the world; all too often, quarrels between Method and technical acting theories obscure rather than clarify the profound — and complicated — art of the actor. Much of the division can now be ruled obsolete: much of what passes for Strasberg-inspired Method acting is little more than intentional shuffling, stumbling, and slurring calculated to convince an audience that the actor is "real." Much of what is called technical acting involves no technique at all beyond the ability to mouth schoolboy rhetoric and look handsome.

The contemporary theatre has come to realize that acting involves *both* simulation and embodiment, *both* impersonation and virtuosity, and that, therefore, *both* external and internal processes are involved; the debate between them is irrelevant. Acting approaches of the present day thus tend to integrate the best of the traditional methods and to combine these with new approaches suggested by recent discoveries in psychology and communications, stressing all the while a contemporary awareness of human identity and of the function of the actor in creating and theatricalizing that identity.

The integrated methods of approach favored by most teachers of acting today encourage the student to study the *situational intentions* of the character, the *variety of tactics* the character can employ in the fulfillment of those intentions, and the specific *mode of per-*

EMOTION IN ACTING

If emotion is a state, the actor should never take cognizance of it. In fact we can never take cognizance of an emotion when we are in its grip, but only when it has passed. Otherwise the emotion disappears. The actor lives uniquely in the present; he is continually jumping from one present to the next. In the course of these successive presents he executes a series of actions which deposit upon him a sort of sweat which is nothing else but the state of emotion. This sweat is to his acting what juice is to fruit. But once he starts perceiving and taking cognizance of his state of emotion, the sweat evaporates forthwith, the emotion disappears and the acting dries up. . . . We cannot think "I am moved" without at once ceasing to be so. [Therefore] . . . no one in a theatre should allude to the fragile phenomenon, emotion. Everyone, both players and audience alike, though under its influence, must concern themselves with actions.

Jean-Louis Barrault

---

formance demanded by the playwright and/or the director.

By "situational intentions" we mean the goals or desires the characters hope to achieve: the victories they have set ahead for themselves. Romeo's intention, for example, is first to win the love of Juliet, then to marry her — and then to join her in Heaven. Hecuba's intention is to shame the Athenians; Monsieur Jourdain's intention is to awe his family and friends. An actor concentrating as fully as possible on such intentions will focus energy, drive out stage fright, and set up the foundation for the fullest use of his or her instrument.

By "tactics" we refer to those actions by which the character moves through the play, as propelled by personal intentions. Romeo woos Juliet through his expressive use of lan-

Playing "ordinary people" in realistic plays is often the biggest challenge for an actor, since the audience quickly understands the characters — and consequently makes great demands on the performers. Neil Simon's Broadway Bound *is a highly realistic, and even autobiographical, play. Jonathan Silverman is the young writer, shown here with Jason Alexander, who plays his older brother Stanley; Gene Saks directed. (Photo: Martha Swope and Associates.)*

guage, his kisses, and his ardent behavior. Hecuba shames the Athenians by taunting them for their weakness and by defeating their rhetoric with her own more noble recitations. Jourdain awes his family — or tries mightily to do so — by parading in what he considers to be fashionable garments. The point is not that the characters must succeed with their tactics or even that they must fulfill their intentions — for those matters are finally determined by the playwright, not the actor — but that the actor must be fully engaged in the pursuit of the character's intentions and quite imaginative in employing tactics to get what the character wants. An actor who is fully and powerfully engaged, who commands the language of the play and the action of the dramatized situation, can create a character who is magnificent even in defeat: he or she can thus transport the audience and deliver a fully theatrical performance.

By "mode of performance" we mean the intended relationship between the play's characters and its audience. For example, the actor must know whether the audience is expected to empathize with the characters, to analyze them, to be socially instructed by them, or merely to be entertained by them. The contemporary theatre has utilized many different performance modes, some entirely realistic, others radically antirealist in tone and structure. We have seen how the theatre of Bertolt Brecht, for example, theoretically eschews "theatre magic" altogether and demands that the actors simulate their characters without fully embodying them. Other performance modes that have adopted and created distinctive theatrical conventions include improvisational theatre, street theatre, music theatre, and the "holy theatre" of Jerzy Grotowski. All of these impose, for the actor, performance requirements quite beyond the impersonation of character through intentions and tactics.

It is at the junction of tactics, intentions, and performance modes that simulation, embodiment, and virtuosity come together. For they all stand upon the same foundation: the actor's assumption of the character's intentions and the actor's committed pursuit of the character's goals. Forceful tactics derived from that pursuit, such as power and precision in speaking, articulate wit, authoritative bearing, and the implicit threat of pent-up passions, give an acting performance its strength; seductive tactics derived from the same pursuit, such as poetic sensitivity, disarming agreeability, sexual enticement, and evocative nuance, create the magnetism of stage performance.

The aspects of acting, separate in this analysis, come together again in both the actor's mind and in that of the audience. Even Brecht found, despite his theories, that performances under his direction created the very magic he decried and occasioned incontrovertible examples of character embodiment. Great stylized performances are both "felt" by the actors and "believed" by audiences; technical virtuosity, the actor's ability to shift easily and uninhibitedly among a great variety of tactics and to commit fully to a compelling set of character intentions, underlies great acting in any style and any performance motif.

Finally, every actor finds a personal method of approaching a role. Moreover, every actor learns eventually that the process is an ever-changing one: every role is different, every role makes different demands on the actor's

> ## "EVERYBODY UNDERSTANDS FRUSTRATION"
>
> One time I had this scene where I was to walk into this actress' dressing room and say something like "I love you; will you marry me?" We managed to make it better by having the girl go into her bathroom and close the door and I had to say those lines to a closed door. I learned to work with counterpoint. To make the material more interesting I would find ways to create obstacles for the character—frustrate him in what he wants to accomplish. That makes the character more sympathetic, because everybody understands frustration.
>
> Jack Lemmon

instrument, and every role strikes different chords within the actor's own psychological experience and understanding. An accomplished actor's method will change with each role, with each director, and to a certain extent with each rehearsal and each performance. The more flexible the actor's approach, the more versatile he can be and the more capable he is of meeting the multiple demands of his art. The more encompassing his method, the more unblinking his self-analysis and the more sophisticated his technique, the more he will be able to apply himself rigorously and creatively, which will lead him further and further into the depth and breadth of his art.

THE ACTOR'S ROUTINE

In essence, the actor's professional routine consists of three stages: auditioning, rehearsal, and performing. The first is the way the actor gets a role, the second is the way the actor learns it, and the last is the way the actor produces it, either night after night on a stage or one time for film or taping. Each of these stages merits independent consideration, for each imposes certain special demands on the actor's instrument and on his approach.

Auditioning

For all but the most established professionals, auditioning is the primary process by which acting roles are awarded. A young actor may audition literally hundreds of times a year. In the film world, celebrated performers may be required to audition only if their careers are perceived to be declining: two of the more famous (and successful) auditions in American film history were undertaken by Frank Sinatra for *From Here to Eternity* and by Marlon Brando for *The Godfather*. Stage actors are customarily asked to audition no matter how experienced or famous they are.

In an audition the actor has an opportunity to demonstrate to the director (or producer, or casting director) how well he or she can fulfill the role sought; in order to show this, the actor presents either a prepared reading (which may be taken from any play) or a "cold reading" from the script whose production is planned.

Every actor who is seriously planning for a career in the theatre will prepare several audition pieces to have at the ready in case an audition opportunity presents itself. For the most part these pieces will be one- or two-minute monologues from plays, although sometimes short narrative cuttings from novels, stories, and poems are used. Each audition piece must be carefully edited for timing and content (some alteration of the text, so as to make a continuous speech out of two or three shorter speeches, is generally permissible); the piece is then memorized and simply staged. The staging requirements should be flexible to permit adjustments to the size of the audition place (which might be a stage but could just as well be an agent's office) and should

not rely on costume or particular pieces of furniture. Most actors prepare a variety of these pieces, for although auditions generally specify two contrasting selections (one verse and one prose, or one serious and one comic, or one classical and one modern), an extra piece that fits a particular casting situation can often come in handy. An actor's audition pieces are as essential as calling cards in the professional theatre world and in many academies as well; they should be carefully developed, coached, and rehearsed, and they should be performed with assurance and poise.

The qualities a director looks for at an audition vary from one situation to another, but generally they include the actor's ease at handling the role; naturalness of delivery; physical, vocal, and emotional suitability for the part; and spontaneity, power, and charm. Most directors also look for an actor who is well trained and disciplined and capable of mastering the technical demands of the part, who will complement the company ensemble, and who can convey that intangible presence that makes for "theatre magic." In short, the audition can show the director that the actor not only knows his or her craft, but also will lend the production a special excitement.

Rehearsing

Plays are ordinarily rehearsed in a matter of weeks: a normal period of rehearsal ranges from ten weeks for complex or experimental productions to just one week for many summer stock operations. Much longer rehearsal periods, however, are not unheard of; indeed, the productions of Stanislavski and Bertolt Brecht were frequently rehearsed for a year or more. Three to five weeks is the customary rehearsal period for American professional productions—but it should be noted that these are forty-hour weeks, and they are usually followed by several days (or weeks) of previews and/or "out-of-town" tryouts, with additional rehearsals between performances.

HOW TO AUDITION

Doubtless many readers of this book will wish to audition for a play at some time in their lives. It is a wonderful experience, provided one is prepared to deal with the chance of rejection; for it energizes the mind and body in a one-to-one relationship that has no exact equal anywhere else.

There can be no consensus as to what sort of audition will be successful in any given circumstance, since directors vary widely in what they are looking for—and what they are *not* looking for—and a certain amount of interpersonal chemistry inevitably influences the final decisions. However, these general points about auditioning might prove useful to the beginner.

Audition pieces should always be selected from material suitable to the actor. For example, an inexperienced young person should not prepare a speech of King Lear's for audition purposes, for this role would almost surely be quite beyond his grasp; far better that he prepare a piece reasonably in concert with his own age and experience.

Similarly, audition pieces should be suited to the role sought or the play auditioned for. It would be foolish even for a veteran performer to prepare material from *King Lear* if the play being cast were a light comedy; only the most creative casting director could get any idea from the Lear audition of how the actor would come across if given a role in the play under consideration.

Auditions should evoke the actor's most theatrically interesting qualities. They should do something to "grab" the attention of the director; otherwise they fail, no matter how competently performed. An audition, after all, is not a classroom assignment: it is an appeal to the director that should say—should actually *scream*—"Look no farther, you've found what you're looking for!" All auditions, whether of the prepared or the cold-reading variety, should be designed to bring out the actor's ability to concentrate on situational objectives and to employ engaging tactics, thus giving evidence of the actor's range within the required context; only then can the director get a valid idea of the actor's potential contribution to the excitement of his planned theatrical experience.

Auditions should be given with confidence and without extensive preamble, apology, or explanation. Excessive nervousness or slavish deference to the director, though they be occasioned by nothing more than shyness, can freeze the actor and ruin an audition; conversely, the bluster that sometimes is attempted to cover shyness is likely to read as an attitude of superiority or defiance, which is rarely encouraged. Continual auditioning is the best single means of developing calm and powerful auditioning; every actor with professional ambitions should audition as often as possible and under as many sorts of circumstances as present themselves.

Auditions should be short. In some professional situations the actor has no control whatever over the amount of time allotted for auditions, and the audition is routinely cut off after just ten or fifteen seconds. While most directors dislike cutting auditions off in mid-course, they do learn most of what they want to know in a few moments and allow the audition to continue only as a matter of courtesy. Thus the first few moments of an audition count enormously, and the best auditioners learn to get themselves across in a very short time.

Auditions can be practiced; prepared auditions can be coached and rehearsed successfully, and cold-reading techniques can be developed. But nothing demonstrates a fine actor so much, in an audition, as the confidence, control, and authority that come with training and experience. No actor should concentrate exclusively on developing an "audition method," for the audition can afford only a glimpse of the performer's total capabilities. The best preparation an actor can make for auditions is to look to his or her whole development as an actor.

During the rehearsal period the actor studies and learns the role. Some things investigated in this period are the character's biography; the subtext (the unspoken communications) of the play; the character's thoughts, fears, and fantasies; the character's objectives; and the world envisioned by the play and the playwright. The director almost certainly will lead discussions, offer opinions, and issue directives with respect to some or all of these matters; the director may also provide reading materials, pictures, and music to aid the actor in his research.

The actor must memorize lines, stage movements ("blocking"), and directed stage actions ("business") during the rehearsal period. He or she must also be prepared to rememorize these if they are changed, as they frequently are: in the rehearsal of new plays it is not unusual for entire acts to be rewritten between rehearsals and for large segments to be changed, added, or written out overnight.

Memorization usually presents no great problem for young actors, to whom it tends to come naturally (children in plays frequently memorize not only their own lines but every-

Comedy requires a deep commitment to the passions of the characters; although the action is amusing to the audience, it is dead serious to the characters. Here Jeff Goldblum, as Malvolio, presses his unwanted attentions on Michelle Pfeiffer, Lady Olivia, in Shakespeare's comedy Twelfth Night *at the New York Shakespeare Festival, 1989. This production played at the large, outdoor Delacorte Theatre in Central Park; both actors wear body microphones for electronic sound enhancement. (Photo: George Joseph.)*

one else's, without even meaning to); however, it seems to become more difficult as one gets older. But at whatever age, memorization of lines remains one of the easier problems the actor is called upon to solve, even though it is the one many naive audience members think would be the most difficult. Adequate memorization merely provides the basis from which the actor learns a part; the important memory goal of the actor is not simply to get the lines down, but to do it *fast* so that most of the rehearsal time can be devoted to concentrating on other things.

The rehearsal period is a time for experimentation and discovery. It is a time for the actor to get close to his character's beliefs and intentions, to steep himself in the internal aspects of characterization that lead to fully engaged physical, intellectual, and emotional performance. It is a time to search the play's text and the director's mind for clues as to how the character behaves and what results the character aims for in the play's situation. And it is a time to experiment, both alone and in rehearsal with other actors, with the possibilities of subtle interactions that these investigations develop.

Externally, rehearsal is a time for the actor to experiment with timing and delivery of both lines and business; to integrate the staged movements, given by the director, with the text, given by the playwright, and to meld these into a fluid series of actions that build and illuminate by the admixture of his own personally initiated behavior. It is a time to suggest movement and "business" possibilities to the director (presuming the director is the sort who accepts suggestions, as virtually all do nowadays) and to work out details of complicated sequences with the other actors. It is also a time to "get secure" in both lines and business by constant repetition — in fact, the French word for "rehearsal" is *répétition*. And it affords an opportunity to explore all the possibilities of the role — to look for ways to improve the actor's original plan for its realization and to test various possibilities with the director.

Thus the rehearsal of a play is an extremely creative time for an actor; it is by no means a routine or boring work assignment — and indeed for this reason some actors enjoy the rehearsal process even more than the performance phase of production. At its best, a rehearsal is both spontaneous and disciplined, a combination of repetition and change, of trying and "setting," of making patterns and breaking them and then making them anew. It is an exciting time, no less so because it invariably includes many moments of distress, frustration, and despair; it is a time, above all, when the actor learns a great deal about acting and, ideally, about human interaction on many levels.

Performing

Performing, finally, is what the theatre is "about," and it is before an audience in a live performance that the actor's mettle is put to the ultimate test.

Sometimes the results are quite startling. The actor who has been brilliant in rehearsal can crumble before an audience and completely lose the "edge" of his performance in the face of stage fright and apprehension. Or — and this is more likely — an actor who seemed fairly unexciting in rehearsal can suddenly take fire in performance and dazzle the audience with unexpected energy, subtlety, and depth: one celebrated example of this phenomenon was achieved by Lee J. Cobb in the original production of Arthur Miller's *Death of a Salesman,* in which Cobb had the title role. Roles rehearsed in all solemnity can suddenly turn comical in performance; conversely, roles developed for comic potential in rehearsal may be received soberly by an audience and lose their comedic aspect entirely.

Sudden and dramatic change, however, is not the norm as the performance phase replaces rehearsal: most actors cross over from final dress rehearsal to opening night with only the slightest shift; indeed, this is generally thought to be the goal of a disciplined

Solo performance is perhaps the actor's greatest challenge. For the Broadway production of Jane Wagner's The Search for Intelligent Life in the Universe, *actress Lily Tomlin played all the parts — and won the 1986 Tony Award for best actress of the year.*

in response to the first waves of laughter or applause, is similarly frowned upon in all but the most inartistic of theatres today.

Nevertheless, a fundamental shift does occur in the actor's awareness between rehearsal and performance, and this cannot and should not be denied; indeed, it is essential to the creation of theatre art. The shift is set up by an elementary feedback: the actor is inevitably aware, with at least a portion of his mind, of the audience's reactions to his own performance and that of the other players; there is always, in any acting performance, a subtle adjustment to the audience that sees it. The outward manifestations of this adjustment are usually all but imperceptible: the split-second hold for a laugh to die down, the slight special projection of a certain line to ensure that it reaches the back row, the quick turn of a head to make a characterization or plot transition extra clear.

In addition, the best actors consistently radiate a quality known to the theatre world as "presence." It is a rather difficult quality to describe, but it has the effect of making both the character whom the actor portrays and the "self" of the actor who represents that character especially vibrant and "in the present" for the audience; it is the quality of an actor who takes the stage and acknowledges, in some inexplicable yet indelible manner, that he or she is there *to be seen.* Performance is not a one-way statement given from the stage to the house; it is a two-way, participatory communication between the actors and the audience, in which the former employ text and movement, and the latter employ applause, laughter, silence, and attention.

Even when the audience is silent and invisible — and, owing to the brightness of stage lights, the audience is frequently invisible to the actor — the performer "feels" their presence. There is nothing extrasensory about this: the absence of sound is itself a signal; for when several hundred people sit without shuffling, coughing, or muttering, their silence betokens a level of attention for which the actor

and professional rehearsal schedule. "Holding back until opening night," an acting practice occasionally employed in the past century, is quite universally disavowed today, and opening-night recklessness is viewed as a sure sign of the amateur, who relies primarily on guts and adrenalin to get through the evening. Deliberate revisions of a role in performance, customarily strives. Laughter, gasps, sighs, and applause similarly feed back into the actor's consciousness — and unconsciousness — and spur (or sometimes, alas, distract) his efforts. The veteran actor can determine quickly how to ride the crest of audience laughter and how to hold the next line just long enough that it will pierce the lingering chuckles but not be overridden by them; he also knows how to vary his pace and/or redouble his energy when he senses restlessness or boredom on the other side of the curtain line. "Performance technique," or the art of "reading an audience," is more instinctual than learned. It is not dissimilar to the technique achieved by the effective classroom lecturer or TV talk show host or even by the accomplished conversationalist. The timing it requires is of such complexity that no actor could master it rationally; he or she can develop it only out of experience — both on stage and off.

Professional stage actors face a special problem unknown to their film counterparts and seldom experienced by amateurs in the theatre: the problem of maintaining a high level of spontaneity through many, many performances. Some professional play productions perform continuously for years, and actors may well find themselves in the position — fortunately for their finances, awkwardly for their art — of performing the same part eight times a week, fifty-two weeks a year, with no end in sight. Of course the routine can vary with vacations and cast substitutions; and in fact very few actors ever play a role continuously for more than a year or two, but the problem becomes intense even after only a few weeks. How, as they say in the trade, does the actor "keep it fresh"?

Each actor has his or her own way of addressing this problem. Some rely on their total immersion in the role and contend that by "living the life of the character" they can keep themselves equally alert from first performance to last. Others turn to technical experiments — reworking their delivery and trying constantly to find better ways of saying their lines, expressing their characters, and achieving their objectives. Still others concentrate on the relationships within the play and try with every performance to "find something new" in each relationship as it unfolds on stage. Some actors, it must be admitted, resort to childish measures, rewriting dialogue as they go or trying to break the concentration of the other actors; this sort of behavior is abhorrent, but it is indicative of the seriousness of the actor's problems of combating boredom in a long-running production and the lengths to which some will go to solve them.

The actor's performance does not end with the play, for it certainly extends into the paratheatrical moments of the curtain call — in which the actor-audience communion is direct and unmistakable — and it can even be said to extend to the dressing-room post mortem, in which the actor reflects upon what was done today and how it might be done better tomorrow. Sometimes the postmortem of a play is handled quite specifically by the director, who may give notes to the cast; more typically, in professional situations, the actor simply relies on self-criticism, often measured against comments from friends and fellow cast members, from the stage manager, and from reviews in the press. For there is no performer who leaves the stage in the spirit of a factory worker leaving the plant. If there has been a shift up from the rehearsal phase to the performance phase, there is now a shift down (or a letdown) that follows the curtain call — a reentry into a world where actions and reactions are likely to be a little more calm. There would be no stage fright if there were nothing to be frightened *about,* and the conquering of one's own anxiety — sometimes translated as conquering of the audience: "I really killed them tonight" — fills the actor at the final curtain with a sense of awe, elation . . . and emptiness. It is perhaps this feeling that draws the actor ever more deeply into the profession, for it is a feeling known to the rankest amateur in a high school pageant as well as to the most experienced professional in a Broadway or

West End run. It is the theatre's "high," and because it is a high that accompanies an inexpressible void, it leads to addiction

THE ACTOR IN LIFE

Acting is an art. It can also be a disease.

Actors are privileged people. They get to live the lives of some of the world's greatest and best-known characters: Romeo, Juliet, Phèdre, Cyrano, St. Joan, and Willy Loman. They get to fight for honor, hunger for salvation, battle for justice, die for love, kill for passion. They get to die many times before their deaths, to duel fabulous enemies, to love magnificent lovers, and to live through an infinite variety of human experiences that, though imaginary, are publicly engaged. They get to reenter the innocence of childhood without suffering its consequences and to participate in every sort of adult villainy without reckoning its responsibility. They get to fantasize freely and be seen doing so—and they get paid for it.

Millions of people want to be actors. It looks easy and, at least for some people, it *is* easy. It looks exciting, and there can be no questions that it *is* exciting, *very* exciting; in fact, amateurs act in theatres all over the world without any hope of getting paid merely to experience that excitement. Acting addicts, as a consequence, are common. People who will not wait ten minutes at a supermarket checkout stand will wait ten years to get a role in a Hollywood film or a Broadway play. The acting unions are the only unions in the world that have ever negotiated a *lower* wage for some of their members in order to allow them to perform at substandard salaries. To the true acting addict there is nothing else; acting becomes the sole preoccupation.

The addicted actor—the actor obsessed with acting for its own sake—is probably not a very good actor, for fine acting demands an open mind, a mind capable of taking in stimuli from all sorts of directions, not merely from the theatrical environment. An actor who knows nothing but acting has no range. First and foremost, actors must represent human beings, and to do that they must know something about humankind. Thus the proper study of acting is Life, abetted but not supplanted by the craft of the trade. Common sense, acute powers of observation and perception, tolerance and understanding for all human beings, and a sound general knowledge of one's own society and culture are prime requisites for the actor—as well as training, business acumen, and a realistic vision of one's own potential.

A lifetime professional career in acting is the goal of many but the accomplishment of very few. Statistically, the chances of one's developing a long-standing acting career are quite small; only those individuals possessed of great talent, skill, persistence, and personal fortitude stand any chance of succeeding—and even then it is only a chance. But the excitement of acting is not the exclusive preserve of those who attain lifetime professional careers; on the contrary, it may be argued that the happiest and most artistically fulfilled actors are those for whom performance is only an avocation. The excitement of acting, finally, is not dependent on monetary reward, a billing above the title, or the size of one's roles, but on the actor's engagement with drama and with dramatized situations—in short, on a personal synchronization with the theatre itself, of which acting is the very evanescent but still solid center.

He is an anomalous figure in the theatre.

In his home he is the master of the stage, the initiator of all theatrical art. Facing his writing paper, he is profoundly in control: actions cascade through his head, characters populate his imagination, great scenes parade across his vision, words and speeches pour from his pen. It is to be *his* play, *his* thoughts, *his* people, and *his* words that will resound through the theatres of the world, that will be praised in the press, immortalized in handsomely bound volumes, and examined diligently in the universities. It is he, the playwright, who will win the Pulitzer Prize and the Critics Circle Award and who perhaps will one day sit next to some contemporary Einstein or Schweitzer when the Nobel laureates are lionized at Stockholm.

In the theatre, however, he is the lonely figure who huddles uncomfortably over a legal pad, in a back row, scarcely noticed by the actors and directors who are rehearsing his play, certain in the back of his mind that the theatre is nothing more than an instrument created for the purpose of diluting his ideas and massacring his manuscript.

Has there ever been such an anomaly? For the playwright is both the most central and

CHAPTER 4

THE PLAYWRIGHT

George Wolfe is author and director of Jelly's Last Jam, *a Broadway sensation in 1992. The musical tells the story of a famed musician, Jelly Roll Morton, performed by Gregory Hines (right), shown here being counseled by "The Chimney Man," a ghostly philosopher, played by Keith David. (Photo: Martha Swope and Associates.)*

the most peripheral figure in the theatrical event.

He is central in the most obvious ways. He provides the point of origin for virtually every play production—the script, which is the rallying point around which the director or producer gathers the troops.

And yet that point of origin is also a point of departure. The days when a Shakespeare or a Molière would gather actors around, read his text to them, and then coach them in its proper execution are long gone, replaced by a more specialized theatrical hierarchy in which the director is interposed as the playwright's representative to the theatrical enterprise and its constituent members. More and more, the playwright's function is to write the play and then disappear, for once the script has been typed, duplicated, and distributed, the playwright's physical participation is relegated mainly to serving as the director's sounding board and rewrite person. Indeed, the playwright's mere physical presence in the rehearsal hall can become an embarrassment, more tolerated than welcomed and sometimes not even tolerated.

Fundamentally, the playwright today is considered an independent artist, whose work, like that of the novelist or poet, is executed primarily, if not exclusively, in isolation. There are exceptions, of course: some playwrights work out of the improvisations of actors, and others participate quite fully in rehearsals, even to the point of serving as the initial director of their plays (as Edward Albee, Sam Shepard, and George C. Wolfe often do) or, more extraordinarily, by acting in them (as Tennessee Williams and Michael Christofer have done).

But the exceptions do not, in this case, disprove the rule; since the age of romanticism, the image of the playwright has turned increasingly from that of theatre coworker and mentor to that of isolated observer and social critic. In the long run, this change should occasion no lamentation; for if theatre production now demands collaboration and compromise, the art of the theatre still requires individuality, clarity of vision, sharpness of approach, original sensitivity, and a devotion to personal truth if it is to challenge the artists who are called upon to fulfill it and the audiences who will pay money to experience it. It is often said that Shakespeare and Molière wrote great plays because they could tailor their parts to the talents of actors whom they knew well. It seems far more likely that they wrote great plays in spite of this, for at the hands of lesser writers, that sort of enterprise produces sheer hack work that simply combines the limitations of the actors with those of the author. Whether writing from inside an acting company or in submission to one, the playwright strives to give life to a unique vision, to create material that transcends what has gone before, both in writing and in performance.

Therefore the *independence* of the playwright is perhaps his most important charac-teristic. Playwrights must seek from life, from their own lives—and not from the theatrical establishment—the material that will translate into exciting and meaningful and entertaining theatre; and their views must be intensely personal, grounded in their own perceptions and philosophy, in order to ring true. We look to the theatre for a measure of leadership, for personal enlightenment derived from another's experience, for fresh perspectives, new visions. In other words, simple mastery of certain conventional techniques will not suffice to enable the playwright to expand our lives.

WE ARE ALL PLAYWRIGHTS

For playwriting is not just something we learn, it's something we already do. All of us. Every day—or night.

Every night, dreams come to us in our sleep. Or, rather, they *seem* to come to us: in fact, we create them. For each of us has our own playwright-in-residence, and designer-in-residence, bringing to our semiconscious minds, often in equal measure, fantasies and realities, imaginary people and real ones, idealized memories and gruesome terrors, mirages and nightmares, delusions of grandeur and depictions of our own demise. The situations and characters of our dreams are our own creations: drawn from our careful observations, colored by our unconscious phobias and fancies, stylized into associations of words, scenes, and "stagings" that ring with deep resonance of our innermost plans, fears, and secrets. We all know what it is to create a play out of our imaginations: we do it every night.

Therefore, there is little conformity among playwrights, nor are there easily identified "schools" of associated writers; nor have "rules" of playwriting been laid down with any demonstrable sustained success. Playwrights may come from anywhere.

THE PLAYWRIGHT'S CAREER

How does a person become a playwright? Writing plays, naturally, is the first (and most important) step. But getting that original play produced is almost as challenging.

There are literally hundreds of "break in" opportunities for playwrights to develop their scripts in open rehearsals or in developmental workshop productions or staged "readings." And sometimes a playwright can realize (or can produce himself or herself), a fully staged production.

Many of these developmental opportunities are available through universities. David Hwang's *FOB* was first presented at his college dormitory at Stanford; Wendy Wasserstein's *Uncommon Women and Others* was first presented at the Yale Drama School.

Virtually all regional professional theatres present new plays from time to time, and many—if not most of them—actively solicit new works, usually presenting them first in script-in-hand readings or special workshops, where the work is presented and critiqued by other writers and company artists. Many prize-winning plays have originated, for example, at the Yale Repertory Theatre Winterfest of New Plays, or the Humana New Play Festival at the Actors Theatre of Louisville. Indeed, most important American plays of the 1980s and beyond have seen their first presentation in readings or workshops at theatres like these, although applicants must realize that the competition for workshop slots at these premier theatres is, naturally, quite fierce. An annual publication, *Dramatists Sourcebook* (published by Theatre Communications Group in New York) lists all theatres that solicit new work and identifies any special areas of interest (such as Hispanic theatre) that these theatres might have.

There are also certain "developmental" theatre companies totally devoted to finding, and developing, new scripts. The National Playwrights Conference (at the Eugene O'Neill Center in Waterford, Connecticut, with year-round offices in New York) receives hundreds of applications each year—and selects nine to twelve plays to present, in staged readings, each summer. August Wilson first came to prominence through his "discovery" at the Playwrights Conference.

Finally, there are dramatic contests, fellowship and grant opportunities, commercial reading and critique services, and literary/dramatic agents that aspiring playwrights may consider as they try to build a career in this field; the *Dramatists Sourcebook* is a useful guide to all of these areas. It should be borne in mind, however, that playwriting is an extraordinarily competitive field and that the quality of the work—not the number of contacts—is far and away the critical factor.

LITERARY AND NONLITERARY ASPECTS OF PLAYWRITING

Since drama is often thought of as a form of literature (and is taught in departments of literature) and since many dramatic authors begin (or double) as poets or novelists, it may seem convenient to think of playwriting as primarily a literary activity. It is not. Etymology helps here: *playwright* is not *playwrite,* and writing for the theatre entails considerations not common to other literary forms. Although by homonymic coincidence the words *write* and *wright* sound alike, a "playwright" is a person who *makes* plays, just as a wheelwright is a person who makes wheels. This distinction is particularly important, because some plays, or portions of plays, are never written at all. Improvisational plays, certain rituals, whole scenes of comic business, subtextual behaviors, and many documentary dramas are created largely or entirely in performance, or are learned simply through oral improvisation and repetition. Some are created with a tape recorder and multiple imaginations and may or may not be committed to writing after the performance is concluded. And others, although dramatic in structure, are entirely nonverbal; that is, they include no dialogue, no words, and very little that is actually written other than an outline of mimetic effects.

So drama is a branch of literature, but it is a very special and distinctive branch. It is not merely an arrangement of words on a page; it is a conceptualization of the interactions of myriad elements in the theatrical medium: movement, speech, scenery, costume, staging, music, spectacle, and silence. It is a literature whose impact depends on a collective endeavor and whose appreciation must be, in large part, spontaneous and immediate; there can be no thought in the drama of relying purely on effects that are perceivable through solitary reading.

A play attains its finished form only in performance upon the stage: the written script is not the final play but the *blueprint* for the play, the written foundation for the production that is the play's complete realization. Some of a play's most effective writing may look very clumsy as it appears in print, as for example:

"Oh! Oh! Oh!"

(Shakespeare's *Othello*)

"Howl, howl, howl, howl!"

(Shakespeare's *King Lear*)

"No, no, the drink, the drink. O my dear Hamlet,
The drink, the drink! I am poisoned."

(Shakespeare's *Hamlet*)

These apparently unsophisticated lines of dialogue in fact provide great dramatic climaxes in an impassioned performance; they are *pretexts for great acting*, the creation of which is far more crucial than literary eloquence to the art of playwriting.

Of course some formal literary values are as important to the theatre as they are to other branches of literature: allusional complexity, descriptive precision, poetic imagery, metaphoric implication, and a careful crafting of verbal rhythms, cadences, and textures all contribute powerfully to dramatic effect. But they are effective only insofar as they are fully integrated with the whole of the theatrical medium, as they stimulate action and behavior through stage space and stage time in a way that commands audience attention and involvement. Mere literary brilliance is insufficient as theatre, as a great many successful novelists and poets have learned to their chagrin when they attempted to write plays.

PLAYWRITING AS EVENT WRITING

The core of every play is action. In contrast to other literary forms, the inner structure of a play is never a series of abstract observations or a collage of descriptions and moralizings; it is an ordering of observable, dramatizable *events*. These events are the basic building blocks of the play, regardless of its style or genre or theme.

Fundamentally, the playwright works with but two tools, both representing the externals of human behavior: dialogue and physical action. The inner story and theme of a play — the psychology of the characters, the viewpoint of the author, the impact of the social environment — must be inferred, by the audience, from outward appearances, from the play's events as the audience sees them. Whatever the playwright's intended message and whatever the playwright's perspective on the function and process of playwriting itself, the play cannot be put together until the playwright has conceived of an event — and then a series of related events — designed to be enacted on a stage. It is this series of related events that constitutes the play's scenario or, more formally, its plot.

The events of drama are, by their nature, compelling. Some are bold and unusual, such as the scene in which Prometheus is chained to his rock. Some are subdued, as the vision of the Trojan women leaving their devastated

The best way for a writer to create credible characters is to know those characters well. Young writers, therefore, are often urged to write about people they know, and the first plays of many dramatists are about their own families. Tennessee Williams's The Glass Menagerie *is such a play, written about Williams's life as a young shipping clerk. Shown here in the 1991 McCarter Theatre production directed by Emily Mann, with Shirley Knight as Amanda and Dylan McDermott as her son Tom. (Tennessee Williams's given name was Tom, and Williams has long admitted that his own mother served as a model for the role of Amanda.) (Photo: T. Charles Erickson.)*

city at that play's end. Some are seemingly quite ordinary, as in the domestic sequences depicted in most modern realist plays. But they are always aimed at creating a memorable impression. To begin playwriting, one must first conceptualize events and envision them enacted in such a way as to hold the attention of an audience.

The events of a play can be connected to each other in a strict chronological, cause-effect continuity. This has been a goal of the realistic theatre, in which dramatic events are arranged to convey a lifelike progression of experiences in time. Such plays are said to be *continuous* in structure and *linear* in chronology, and they can be analyzed like sociological events, with the audience simply watching them unfold as it might watch a family quarrel in progress in an adjoining apartment.

Continuous linearity is by no means considered a requirement for play construction (although it was in the days of the neoclassic "Rules"). Many plays are discontinuous and/ or nonlinear. The surviving plays of ancient

Greece are highly discontinuous, with odes alternating with episodes in the tragedies and a whole host of nonlinear theatrical inventions popping in and out during the comedies. Shakespeare's plays are structured in a highly complex arrangement of time shifts, place shifts, style shifts, songs and subplots ingeniously integrated around a basic theme or investigation of character. And many contemporary plays break with chronological linearity altogether, flashing instantly backward and forward through time to incorporate character memories, character fantasies, direct expressions of the playwright's social manifesto, historical exposition, comic relief, or any other ingredient the playwright can successfully work in.

Linear, point-to-point storytelling still has not disappeared from the theatre — indeed, it remains the basic architecture of most popular and serious plays — but modern (and postmodern) audiences have proven increasingly receptive to less conventional structures: the exuberance of the music hall, for instance, inspired the structuring of Joan Littlewood's *Oh, What a Lovely War!,* the minstrel show served as a structure for George C. Wolfe's *The Colored Museum,* and the didacticism of the lecture hall underlay much of the theatre of Bertolt Brecht. Nonlinear, discontinuous, and even stream-of-consciousness structures can provide powerful and sustained dramatic impact in the theatre, provided they are based in the dramatization of events that the audience can put together in some sort of meaningful and satisfying fashion.

THE QUALITIES OF A FINE PLAY

As with any art form, the qualities that make up a good play can be discussed individually, but it is only in their combination, only in their interaction — only in ways that cannot be dissected or measured — that these qualities have meaning.

Credibility and Intrigue

To say that a play must be credible is not at all to say that it has to be lifelike, for fantasy, ritual, and absurdity have all proven to be enduringly popular theatrical modes. The demand of credibility is an audience-imposed demand, and it has to do with the play's internal consistency: the actions must flow logically from the characters, the situation, and the theatrical context that the playwright provides. In other words, we might say that credibility is the audience's demand that what happens in Act II makes sense in terms of what happened in Act I.

Credibility demands, for example, that the characters in a play appear to act out of their own individual interests, instincts, and intentions rather than serving as mere pawns for the development of theatrical plot or effect, as empty disseminators of propaganda. Credibility means that characters must maintain consistency within themselves: that their thoughts, feelings, hopes, fears, and plans must appear to flow from human needs rather than purely theatrical ones. Credibility also demands that human characters appear to act and think like human beings (even in humanly impossible situations) and not purely as thematic automatons. Credibility, in short, is the essence of a contract between author and audience, whereby the audience agrees to view the characters as "people" so long as the author abides by the agreement not to shatter that belief in order to accomplish other purposes.

Thus James Barrie's famous play *Peter Pan,* while undeniably fantastical, creates a cast of characters wholly appropriate to their highly imaginary situation and internally consistent in their actions within the context of their developing experience. All their aspirations (including those of the dog!) are human ones, and their urgencies are so believable that when Tinker Bell steps out of the play's context to ask the audience to demonstrate its belief in fairies, the audience is willing to applaud its approval. At that moment, the world of the

What's in the box? A standard thriller technique, here used in Paul Giovanni's The Crucifer of Blood, *is to intrigue the audience with mysterious locked boxes. This one, opened by a soldier's sword in India, will provoke an investigation from Sherlock Holmes on London's Baker Street. From American Conservatory Theatre. (Photo: William Ganslen.)*

play becomes more credible, more "real," than that of the audience. So much for the power—and consequently the necessity—of dramatic credibility.

Intrigue is that quality of a play which makes us curious (sometimes fervently so) to see "what happens next." Sheer plot intrigue—which is sometimes called "suspense" in that it leaves us suspended (that is, "hanging")—is one of the most powerful of dramatic approaches. Whole plays can be based on little more than artfully contrived plotting designed to keep the audience in a continual state of anticipation and wonder. Plot, however, is only one of the elements of a play that can support intrigue. Most plays that aspire to deeper insights than whodunits or farces develop intrigue in character as well, and even in theme. Most of the great plays, in fact, demand that we ask not so much "What will happen?" as "What does this mean?" Most great plays, in other words, make us care

about the characters and invite us to probe the mysteries of the human condition.

Writers of tragedy tend to dispense with plot intrigue altogether. The Greek tragedies were retellings of well-known legends whose conclusions were known to the audience before they even entered the theatre. Shakespeare also used earlier works as the bases for his tragedies; on occasion—in *Romeo and Juliet,* for instance—he even reminded his audience of the play's ending in its first words. Peter Shaffer's *Equus* is a modern tragedy whose most significant incident is described early in the play in order that it may be analyzed (by characters and audience) for the balance of the play, which culminates in an enactment of the same incident. Intrigue of character depends on the author's ability first to present characters who are so fascinating that we want to understand them better—and then to devise situations and scenes that deepen our fascination with each successive revelation.

Surprise is an essential ingredient of intrigue: a play that is truly intriguing is one that leads us to expect surprises and then appropriately rewards our expectations. The plays of Harold Pinter, which are filled with abrupt, almost inexplicable transitions, intense pauses and glances, and elliptical dialogue that seems to contain innuendoes that we don't fully comprehend, create an almost palpable sense of foreboding and spookiness that plunges the audience deeper and deeper into Pinteresque moods and reveries. The plays of Tom Stoppard, by contrast, race glibly through brilliant rhetorical flights of language that always manage to stay one step ahead of the audience's capability to follow, keeping the audience breathless while forcing them to remain intellectually alert.

Sometimes a playwright's theme can provide sufficient intrigue in itself to engage an audience's deepest attention. "What is the playwright getting at?" we wonder, and this question can lead us, for a while at least, to follow closely a dialogue that would hold no interest for us if overheard in a real-life situation. The mere fact that the author has seen fit to incorporate such dialogue in a play — and moreover that many people have labored to get that play to the point of production — is sufficient to confer a modicum of intrigue. But, of course, the audience must soon receive some sort of intellectual or emotional or "entertainment" reward for its attention.

Intrigue draws us into the world of a play; credibility keeps us there. In the best plays the two are sustained throughout the course of the action in a fine tension of opposites: intrigue demanding surprise, credibility demanding consistency. Combined, they generate a kind of "believable wonder," which is the fundamental state of drama. All the credibility in the world will not suffice by itself to make a play interesting, and all the intrigue that craft can contrive will fail to make an incredible play palatable. The integration of the two must be explored by the playwright in order to establish that shared ground which satisfies both human inertia and human potential, which transcends our expectations but not our credulity.

Speakability, Stageability, and Flow

The dialogue of drama is written upon the page, but it must be spoken by an actor and staged by a director. Thus the goal of the dramatist is to fabricate dialogue that is both actable and stageable and that flows in a progression leading to theatrical impact.

One of the most common faults in the work of the beginning playwright — sometimes even when that playwright is an established novelist or poet — is that the lines lack "speakability." This is not to say that play dialogue must resemble ordinary speech. No one imagines people in life speaking like characters out of the works of Aeschylus, Shakespeare,

Surprise! Steven Berkoff's dark comedy Kvetch *is filled with sudden discoveries. It was written in part out of experiences from his childhood. Odyssey Theatre Ensemble, 1986.*

PINTER AND STOPPARD

Harold Pinter and Tom Stoppard, contemporary British playwrights, exemplify sharply contrasting dramatic styles. The following samples are reasonably typical of their respective works.

From Pinter's *Silence* (1969):

BATES: (*moves to* ELLEN) Will we meet tonight?
ELLEN: I don't know. (*Pause*)
BATES: Come with me tonight.
ELLEN: Where?
BATES: Anywhere. For a walk. (*Pause*)
ELLEN: I don't want to walk.
BATES: Why not? (*Pause*)
ELLEN: I want to go somewhere else. (*Pause*)
BATES: Where?
ELLEN: I don't know. (*Pause*)
BATES: What's wrong with a walk?
ELLEN: I don't want to walk. (*Pause*)
BATES: What do you want to do?
ELLEN: I don't know. (*Pause*)
BATES: Do you want to go somewhere else?
ELLEN: Yes.
BATES: Where?
ELLEN: I don't know. (*Pause*)

From Stoppard's *Dirty Linen* (1976):

COCKLEBURY-SMYTHE: May I be the first to welcome you to Room 3B. You will find the working conditions primitive, the hours antisocial, the amenities non-existent and the catering beneath contempt. On top of that the people are for the most part very boring, with interests either so generalized as to mimic wholesale ignorance or so particular as to be lunatic obsessions. Their level of conversation would pass without comment in the lavatory of a mixed comprehensive and the lavatories, by the way, are few and far between.

Mirrored surfaces on floor and backdrop amplify the empty communication between Bates and Ellen in the Royal Shakespeare Company's 1969 production of Harold Pinter's Silence, *directed by Peter Hall. (Photo: Zoë Dominic.)*

Shaw, or Giraudoux, or even like contemporary characters fashioned by Harold Pinter or Edward Albee; a brilliantly styled language has been a feature of most of the great plays in theatre history, and naturalness or superrealism is not, by itself, a dramatic virtue—nor is its absence a dramatic fault.

Rather, speakability means that a line of dialogue should be so written that it achieves its maximum impact when *spoken*. In order to accomplish this, the playwright must be closely attuned to the "audial shape" of dialogue; the rhythm of sound that creates emphasis, meaning, focus, and power. Verbal lullabies and climaxes, fast punch lines, sonorous lamentations, sparkling epigrams and devastating expletives, significant pauses and electrifying whispers—these are some of the devices of dialogue that impart audial shape to great plays written by master dramatists.

Speakability also requires that the spoken line seem to emanate from the character who utters it and that it contain, in its syntax, vocabulary, and mode of expression, the marks of that character's milieu and his personality. The spoken line is not merely an expression of the author's perspective; it is the basis from which the actor develops characterization and the acting ensemble creates a play's style. Thus the mastery of dramatic dialogue writing demands more than mere semantic skills; it requires a constant awareness of the purposes and tactics underlying human communication, as well as of the multiple psychological and aesthetic properties of language.

Stageability, of course, requires that dialogue be written so it can be spoken effectively upon a stage, but it also requires something more: dialogue must be conceived as an integral element of a particular staged situation, in which setting, physical action, and spoken dialogue are inextricably combined. *Romeo and Juliet* affords a splendid illustration of the successful integration of lyrical dramatic dialogue and physical stage behavior (together with a multitude of stage properties) into a dramatic unity that simply cannot be expressed outside the theatrical context itself. A stageable script is one in which staging and stage business—as well as design and the acting demands—are neither adornments for the dialogue nor sugarcoating for the writer's opinions, but are intrinsic to the very nature of the play.

Both speakability and stageability are contingent upon human limitations: those of the actors and directors as well as those of the audience. Speakability must take into account that the actor must breathe from time to time, for example, and that the audience can take in only so many metaphors in a single spoken sentence. Stageability must reckon with the forces of gravity and inertia, which both the poet and the novelist may conveniently ignore. The playwright need not simply succumb to the common denominator—all the great playwrights strive to extend the capacities of actors and audience alike—but still must not forget that the theatre is fundamentally a human event that cannot transcend human capabilities.

A speakable and stageable script flows rather than stumbles; this is true for nonlinear plays as well as for more straightforwardly structured ones. Flow consists above all in the creation of a continual stream of *information,* and a play that flows is one that is continually saying something, doing something, and meaning something to the audience. To serve this end, the playwright should address such technical problems as scene shifting, entrances and exits, and act breaks (intermissions) as early as possible in the scriptwriting process. Furthermore, in drafting scenes, the writer should be aware that needless waits, arid expositions (no matter how "necessary" to the plot), inane ramblings on the part of the characters, and incomprehensible plot developments can sink the sturdiest script in a sea of audience apathy.

The combined demands of speakability, stageability, and dramatic flow apply in some measure to the crafting of any play; hence every professional playwright necessarily develops certain skills to meet these demands. In

Stageability is a matter of the highest importance in farce. The dialogue for this clumsily urgent seduction scene from Feydeau's Hotel Paradiso *is of relatively little importance. Staged by director Tom Moore at American Conservatory Theatre with actors Elizabeth Huddle and Raye Birk. (Photo: William Ganslen, ACT.)*

many theatrical eras in the past, playwriting was considered so technically demanding that craft appeared to be all that was involved, and playwrights spent long in-house apprenticeships as "company men" learning their skills through continual exposure to theatrical rehearsal and performance. Even today, many playwrights come to their craft after decades of experience as actors, stage managers, or directors. But craft—which is largely an understanding of what has worked before—is not the sole determinant of the good play, and a blind reliance on craft has never led to great

writing in any genre. With his *Waiting for Godot* in 1953, Samuel Beckett virtually rewrote the book on playwriting, teaching actors and directors new lessons about what is speakable and stageable and introducing audiences to a kind of dramatic flow that was radically different from anything they had ever seen before. Great playwriting, it would seem, always straddles the line between solid craft and brilliant innovation; it is always based in a theatre wisdom that both understands the conventional and seeks, consciously or unconsciously, to improve upon it.

Richness

Depth, subtlety, fineness, quality, wholeness, and inevitability — these are words often called into service on behalf of plays that we like. They are fundamentally subjective terms, easier to apply than to define or defend, for the fact is that when a play pleases us, when it "works," the feelings of pleasure and stimulation it affords are quite beyond the verbal level. Certainly *richness* is one of the qualities common to plays that leave us with this sense of satisfaction — richness of *detail,* and richness of *dimension*.

A play that is rich with detail is not necessarily one that is rife with detail; it is simply one whose every detail fortifies our insight into the world of the play. For going to a play is in part a matter of paying a visit to the playwright's world, and the more vividly created that world, the greater the play's final impact. The best plays of Anton Chekhov, for example, portray in loving and incisive detail the end-of-a-century, end-of-an-era world of provincial Russia before the Revolution: attending a well-mounted production of Chekhov's *The Three Sisters* is like stepping backward in time into an adventure no travel agent could possibly book. Similarly, to attend a play by Bernard Shaw is to venture into a dazzling Edwardian milieu brimming with bright rhetoric and to be caught up in a flurry of intellectual activity whose every speech gives occasion for thought or laughter — or both. And a play by Tennessee Williams is a journey into complex lives lived in steamy Southern towns, a journey into a firmer, deeper, broader set of impressions than could ever be provided by a guided tour. Each of these playwrights exhibits an extraordinary skill in the selection of meaningful detail.

Richness of detail — in movement, in language, in character outlook, in environmental features — lends a play authority, an aura of sureness. It surrounds the play's characters as a city surrounds a home and gives them a cultural context in which to exist. It lends a play specificity — the feeling that it deals with specific people engaged in specific tasks in a specific place. In short, richness of detail makes a play authentic. It also makes it informative and, therefore, memorable.

Richness is not an easy quality to develop in writing. It demands a certain richness in the resources and capabilities of the author: a gift for close observation, an uninhibited imagination, and an astute sense of what to leave out as well as what to include. A person who can recollect personal experiences in great detail, who can create convincing situations, peoples, locales, and conversations when called upon to do so, and who is closely attuned to nuance can perhaps work these talents into the writing of plays. Training programs for playwrights frequently assign exercises in observation and require the writing of imaginative or evocative description. These exercises can be useful, but only up to a point. For true richness tends to be a characteristic of the work of the mature writer, and all too often attempts to foster it in the young only result in counterfeit richness, a product of imitation rather than of observation and personal creativity.

Beyond question, *depth of characterization* is the single most important factor in determining a play's richness of dimension. It also presents perhaps the greatest single stumbling block for novice playwrights, who tend either to write all characters "in the same voice" (normally the author's own) or to divide them into two camps: the good ones and the bad ones. Although shallowness of characterization can sometimes be offset by strengths in other dramatic areas, a play that lacks sound character development can rarely achieve the profound embodiment of the human condition that represents theatre at its best.

Depth of characterization requires that every character possess, at least to a certain extent, an independence of intention, expression, and motivation; moreover, these characteristics

Even in a musical drama, characters can be drawn in depth. The milkman Tevya, in Jerry Bock's Fiddler on the Roof, *is a character of profound warmth, richness, and complexity. From the Komische Oper Berlin production directed by the late Walter Felsenstein, 1971. (Photo: Arwid Lagenpusch.)*

must appear sensible in the light of our general knowledge of psychology and human behavior. In plays as in life, all characters must act from motives that appear reasonable *to them* (if not to those watching them, or those affected by them). Moreover, the writer should bear in mind that every character is, *to himself,* an extremely important and worthwhile person, even though he may be haunted by self-doubts or may perceive himself to be despised by others. These observations apply in even the most nonrealistic of plays. The great villains of drama — Hermes in *Prometheus,* Menelaus in *The Trojan Women,* Satan in the York Cycle, and Iago in *Othello,* for example — all convey the impression that they believe in themselves and in the fundamental "rightness" of their cause; and even if we never completely understand their ultimate motivations (as we do not completely understand the motivations of historical villains like Hitler, Caligula, and John Wilkes Booth), we can sense at the bot-

tom of their behavior a certain validity of purpose, however twisted or perverse.

Depth of characterization requires that the characters convey the complexity of real human beings and do not simply represent thematic integers in the playwright's grand design. Even in a theatre in which the psychology of characterization takes second place to the promulgation of ideas, the "ideas" that are worth exploring theatrically are concerned with people and their behavior; and if the complexity of people and the purposes for their behavior are not conveyed in the writer's work, the ideas he or she wishes to get across can only appear trivial and ill-conceived.

The realistic theatre, particularly in the turn-of-the-century domestic plays of Chekhov, Strindberg, and Maxim Gorky, has provided many works in which the psychological dimensions of the characters dominate all other aspects of the theatrical experience. By the mid-twentieth century, this approach had become equally important in the American theatre, most notably in the searching, probing dramas of Tennessee Williams, Arthur Miller, Eugene O'Neill, and William Inge. The psychiatric process itself has stood at the core of the action in several plays, including Williams's *Suddenly Last Summer,* Miller's *After the Fall,* Shaffer's *Equus,* and the 1941 American musical *Lady in the Dark,* each of which portrays a principal character undergoing analysis or psychotherapy. The psychological sophistication of modern theatre audiences has afforded playwrights an expanded opportunity to explore and dramatize their characters in greater and greater depth and has helped to make the "case study" drama a major genre of the current theatre.

Gravity and Pertinence

Gravity and pertinence are terms used to describe the importance of a play's theme and its overall relevance to the concerns of the intended audience.

To say that a play has gravity is to say simply that its central theme is one of serious and lasting significance in humanity's spiritual, moral, or intellectual life. All the world's major dramas — whatever their genre — are concerned fundamentally with life problems about which human beings regularly seek lucidity and enlightenment. Even comedies and farces deal with universal issues — issues such as adultery, aging, marital discord, religious and financial intimidation, personal and romantic insecurity, social ambition — and no amount of surface slapstick or badinage should obscure the fact that these issues are serious daily preoccupations of the human species.

Obviously, then, gravity does not mean somberness, which indeed often only signifies an attempt to imitate profundity. Quite to the contrary, gravity is more usually attended by a considerable release of theatrical energy, owing precisely to the universality of its appeal: when an audience truly understands and deeply identifies with the experiences set forth by the playwright, even the darkest tragedy radiates power, animation, and light.

If a play has the quality of pertinence, it relates in some fashion to the current personal concerns of its audience. These concerns can be timeless, or they can be quite ephemeral.

Plays about current political situations or personalities usually rely heavily on pertinence to attract their audiences. Writers of such plays, of course, must be aware that their work may be quickly outdated; for that reason, most producers are loath to have anything to do with any but the most promising topical plays. Indeed, many highly topical plays that do find their way into production require extensive adaptation and "updating" before they can be successfully revived.

More timeless concerns — such as the conflicts between passion and practicality (as in *Romeo and Juliet*) or between salvation and material well-being (as in *Waiting for Godot*) — lead to a kind of theatre that achieves pertinence without being merely topical or trendy and that engages the attention of the audience without regard to the current or local scene.

If we think of the mind of the author as a wheel turning in space, and the mind of the audience as another wheel similarly turning, pertinence would be the axle that connects them and makes them turn in some sort of synchronization. If that axle is missing, if a

Larry Gelbart's Mastergate *is a satire about American politics, specifically the Iran-Contra investigations of the late 1980s; the characters, including "Major Manley Battle" (pictured), are satiric representations of contemporary public figures. Satire's appeal is generally limited to the period of time its subject matter is relevant ("Satire is what closes Saturday night" said playwright George S. Kaufman); some, however, stand the test of time. From the American Repertory Theatre production directed by Michael Engler; Daniel Von Bargen is the actor. (Photo: Richard Feldman.)*

play does not stimulate the audience to consider, in its own frame of reference, the issues raised by the playwright, then the theatre has failed: it has committed the unforgivable sin of boring the audience.

Compression, Economy, and Intensity

Compression, economy, and intensity make up another set of related aspects of the finest plays.

Compression refers to the playwright's skill at condensing a story (which may span many days, even years, of chronological time) into a theatrical time frame; *economy* relates to her skill at eliminating or consolidating characters, events, locales, and words in the service of compression. We have seen how Shakespeare combined these skills in creating the "two-hour traffic of the stage" which is *Romeo and Juliet.* Unlike other literary or visual art forms that can be examined in private and at the leisure of the observer, a play must be structured to unfold in a public setting and at a predetermined pace. If the playwright can manage to meet these needs and at the same time to make every scene, every incident, every character, every word deliver an impact, he or she has satisfied the dramatic demand for *intensity.*

Many beginning playwrights attempt to convert a story to a play in the most obvious way: by writing a separate scene for every event described in the story (and sometimes including a different setting and supporting cast for each scene). Economy and compression, however, require that most stories be restructured in order to be dramatically viable. If the play is to be basically realistic, the playwright has traditionally reworked the story so as to have all the events occur in one location, or perhaps in two locations with an act break between to allow for scenery changes. Events that are integral to the story but cannot be shown within the devised settings can simply be reported (as in Bernard Shaw's *Misalliance,*

for example, in which an airplane crash occurs offstage, as the onstage characters gawk and exclaim). More common today is the use of theatricalist techniques which permit an integration of settings so that events occurring in various places can be presented on the same set without intermission. Similarly, economy and compression commonly dictate the deletion or combination of certain characters who appear in the story and the reduction of important expository passages to a line or two of dialogue.

The effects of economy and compression are both financial and aesthetic. Obviously, when scenery changes and a number of characters are held to a minimum, the costs of production are minimized as well. But beyond that, compression and economy in playwriting serve to stimulate intrigue and focus audience expectation: a tightly written play gives us the feeling that we are on the trail of something important and that our quarry is right around the next bend. In other words, economy and compression actually lead to intensity, and dramatic intensity is one of the theatre's most powerful attributes. Dramatic intensity can take many forms. It can be harsh, abrasive, explosive, eminently physical or overtly calm. It can be ruminative, it can be tender, it can be comic. But whenever it occurs and in whatever mood or context, it conveys to the audience an ineradicable feeling that this moment in theatre is unique and its revelations are profound. Intensity in the theatre does not come about by happy accident, obviously, but neither can it be straightforwardly injected at the whim of the playwright. It must evolve out of a careful development of issues, through the increasing urgency of character goals and intentions and the focused actions and interactions of the plot that draw characters and their conflicts ever closer to some sort of climactic confrontation. A play must spiral inward toward its core; that is, its compression must increase, its mood must intensify, as it circles toward its dénouement. Too many tangential diversions can deflect it

Athol Fugard's My Children! My Africa! *ends tragically; but before it does, South African township teacher Mr. M. (played here by Brock Peters) and his visiting pupil Isabel (Nancy Travis) share an exquisite moment of triumph, which makes the resulting tragedy all the more poignant and insupportable. La Jolla Playhouse production, 1990. (Photo: Micha Langer.)*

from this course and render it formless and apparently devoid of purpose.

Celebration

Finally, a fine play celebrates life; it does not merely depict or analyze or criticize it.

The first plays were presented at festivals that, though perhaps haunted by angry or capricious gods, were essentially joyful celebrations. Even the darkest of the ancient Greek tragedies sought to transcend the more negative aspects of existence and to exalt the human spirit, for the whole of Greek theatre was informed by the positive (and therapeutic) elements of the Dionysian festival: spring, fertility, the gaiety and solidarity of public communion.

The theatre can never successfully venture too far from this source. A purely didactic theatre has never *in fact* satisfied the public's expectations of theatre, and the merely grim depiction of ordinary life has proved equally inadequate to this art form. Although the word "theatrical" is often debased to suggest something like "glittery" or "showy," it should instead be used to connote an accord with the theatre's most fundamental aspirations: to go beyond known experience, to illuminate life, and to raise existence to the level of an art.

This "celebration" of which drama is capable can easily be perverted. Whole eras have been dedicated to a theatre that was deemed acceptable only insofar as it was "uplifting," and in those times many of the greatest tragedies were drastically revised so as to include happy endings and none but the most noble sentiments. Other dramas, in our own times, have been self-consciously written in "elevated" tones, in pale imitation of the more vigorous poetry of Shakespeare or Sophocles. These dramas do not celebrate life—they try to whitewash it and to build a dramatic style that is independent of reality; to most observers these works seem but affectations.

The truest and most exciting theatre, whether played out on the tragic stage or in the music hall, in the innyard or behind the proscenium, has always been based on those dramas that were written out of a passionate, personal vision of reality and a deep devotion to the aim of extracting and expressing life's magnificence. For the theatre is fundamentally an affirmation in all its aspects. Like the writing of plays, the acts of putting them on, performing in them, and attending them are also acts of affirmation: they attest to a desire to share and to communicate; they celebrate human existence and participation and communion. Purely bitter plays, no matter how justly based or how well grounded in experience, remain incomplete and unsatisfying as theatre, which simply is not an effective medium for the conveyance of unalloyed pessimism. Even the bleakest of modern plays radiates a persistent hopefulness—even joyousness—as represented archetypally by Samuel Beckett's two old men singing, punning, and pantomiming so engagingly in the forlorn shadow of their leafless tree as they wait for Godot.

THE PLAYWRIGHT'S PROCESS

How does one go about writing a play?

It is important that one know the elements of a play, as discussed in Chapter 2, and the characteristics of the best plays—credibility, intrigue, richness in detail and characterization, gravity, pertinence, compression, economy, intensity, and celebration—as discussed in the preceding sections. But that is not enough; one must still confront the practical task of writing.

The blank sheet of paper is the writer's nemesis. It is the accuser, the goad and critic that coldly commands action even as it threatens humiliation.

There is no consensus among writers as to where to begin. Some prefer to begin with a story line or a plot outline. Some begin with a real event and write the play to explain why that event occurred. Some begin with a real character or set of characters and develop a plot around them. Some begin with a setting and try to animate it with characters and actions. Some begin with a theatrical effect, or an idea for a new form of theatrical expression. Some write entirely from personal experience. Some adapt a story or a legend, others a biography of a famous person, others a play by an earlier playwright, and others simply expand upon a remembered dream.

"Theatre of fact" usually begins with a document, such as the transcript of a trial or a committee hearing. Other documentary forms might begin with a tape recorder and a situation contrived by the playwright. Some plays are created out of actors' improvisations or acting class exercises. Some are compilations of material written over the course of many years or collected from many sources.

The fact is, writers tend to begin with whatever works for *them* and accords with their immediate aims. Since playwrights usually work alone, at least in the initial stages, they can do as they please whenever they want: there is no norm. On the other hand, certain "steps" can be followed as introductory exercises to playwriting, and these may in fact lead to the creation of an entire play.

Dialogue

Transcription of dialogue from previous observation and experience—that is, the writing down of *remembered dialogue* from overheard conversations or from conversations in which

Jake's Women, by Neil Simon, is a semiautobiographical play that moves into fantasy: the play's protagonist, Jake, is continually confronted by the women in his present life, and those living only in his imagination (his late wife, his daughter as a child). In writing the play, Simon has necessarily imagined dialogue as it might take place between living and now-deceased "real" people. From the Old Globe Theatre premiere, 1990, with Peter Coyote as Jake, Candice Azzara as his sister, and Joyce Van Patten as his analyst. (The play was rewritten, and a new production was mounted for Broadway in 1992.) (Photo: William Gullette.)

the author has participated—is a fundamental playwriting exercise; probably most finished plays in fact contain such scenes. Because we remember conversations only selectively and subjectively, a certain amount of fictionalizing and shading inevitably creeps into these transcriptions; and often without even meaning to do so, authors also transform people in their memory into characters in their scenes.

Writing scenes of *imagined dialogue* is the logical next step in this exercise, for all the author need do now is to extend the situation beyond its remembered reality into the area of "what might have happened." The dialogue then constructed will be essentially original, yet in keeping with the personalized "characters" developed in the earlier transcription. The characters now react and respond as dramatic figures, interacting with each other freshly and under the control of the author. Many fine plays have resulted from the author's working out, in plot and dialogue, hypothetical relations between real people who never actually confronted each other in life; indeed, many plays are inspired by the author's notion of what *should* have happened among people who evaded the very confrontations that she wishes them to experience. In this way, the theatre has often been used as a form of psychotherapy, with the patient-playwright simply acting out—in imagination or with words on paper—certain obligatory scenes in her life that never in fact occurred.

Conflict

Writing scenes of *forced conflict* accelerates the exercise and becomes a third step toward the creation of a play. Scenes of separation, loss, crucial decision, rejection, or emotional breakthrough are climactic scenes in a play and usually help enormously to define its structure. If a writer can create a convincing scene of high conflict that gets inside *each* of the characters involved and not merely one of them, then there is a good chance of making that scene the core of an exciting play—especially if it incorporates some subtlety and is not dependent entirely on shouting and denunciation. What is more, such a scene will be highly actable in its own right and thus can serve as a valuable tool for demonstrating the writer's potential.

> ## "CONSIDER THE ACTOR"
>
> If this is the dramatist's day, he will be wise to consider the actor, not as a mere appendage to his work, but as its very life-giver. Let him realize that the more he can learn to ask of the actor the more he will gain for his play. But asking is giving. He must give opportunity.
>
> Harley Granville-Barker

Exercises that result in scripted scenes—even if the scenes are just a page or two in length—have the advantage of allowing the writer to test his work as it progresses. For a short scene is easily producible: all it requires is a group of agreeable actors and a modest investment of time, and the playwright can quickly assess the total impact. The costs and difficulties of testing a complete play, on the other hand, may well prove insurmountable for the inexperienced playwright. Moreover, the performance of a short original scene can sometimes develop such impact as to generate enthusiasm for the theatrical collaboration needed for a fuller theatrical experience. Most playwrights today see their words staged first in the form of acted original scenes, either in colleges and universities or in professional theatre laboratories or community playreading groups.

Structure

Developing a complete play demands more than stringing together a number of scenes, of course, and at some point in the scene-writing process the playwright inevitably con-

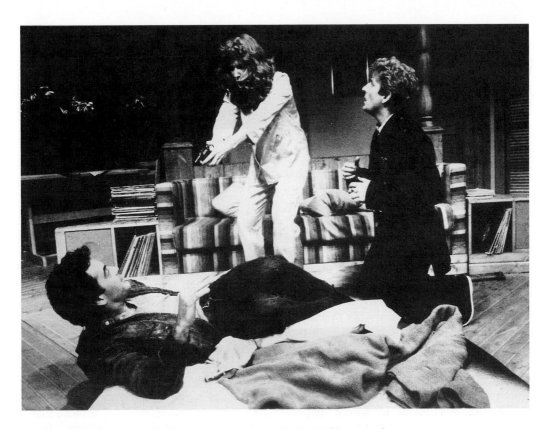

If a gun appears in the first act, it has to be fired by the third act. This tongue-in-cheek "rule" of theatre (said to be first uttered by Chekhov) implies a valid precept: exposition should lead to actions, which should lead to climax and resolution. This means a dramatic structure that can deliver an escalating momentum of excitement. The photograph is from Astronauts, *by Claudia Reilly, staged at the Humana Festival at the Actors Theatre of Louisville. On the ground is John Shepard; Peggity Price holds the gun on him. (Photo: David S. Talbott.)*

fronts the need for structure. Many playwrights develop outlines for their plays after writing a scene or two; some have an outline ready before any scenes are written or even thought of. Other playwrights never write down anything except dialogue and stage directions, yet find an overall structure asserting itself almost unconsciously as the writing progresses. But the beginner should bear in mind that intrigue, thematic development, compression, and even credibility depend upon a carefully built structure and that it is an axiom of theatre that most playwriting is in fact *rewriting*—rewriting aimed principally at organiz-ing and reorganizing the play's staged actions and events.

A strong dramatic structure compels interest and attention. It creates intrigue by establishing certain expectations—both in the characters and in the audience—and then by creating new and bigger expectations out of the fulfillment of the first ones. A good dramatic structure keeps us always wanting more until the final curtain call, and at the end it leaves us with a sense of the inevitability of the play's conclusion, a sense that what happened on stage was precisely as it had to be. A great structure makes us comfortable and receptive; we feel in good hands, expertly led through whatever terrain the play may take us. And we are willing, therefore, to abandon ourselves to a celebration of vital and ineffable matters.

THE PLAYWRIGHT'S REWARDS

There will always be a need for playwrights, for the theatre never abandons its clamor for new and better dramatic works. Hundreds of producers today are so anxious to discover new authors and new scripts that they will read (or instruct an associate to read) everything that comes their way; thus a truly fine play need not go unnoticed for long. What is more, playwrights are the only artists in the theatre who can bring their work to the first stage of completion without any outside professional help at all; they do not need to be auditioned, interviewed, hired, cast, or contracted to an agent in order to come up with the world's greatest dramatic manuscript. And the rewards that await the successful playwright are absolutely staggering: they are the most fully celebrated artists of the theatre, for not only do they receive remuneration com-

---

START AT THE BEGINNING

All those awards, all that stuff, I take them and I hang them on my wall. But then I turn around and my typewriter's sitting there, and it doesn't know from awards. I always tell people I'm a struggling playwright. I'm struggling to get the next play down on paper. You start at the beginning each time you sit down. Nothing you've written before has any bearing on what you're going to write now.

August Wilson

---

mensurate with their success but they also acquire enormous influence and prestige on the basis of their personal vision. The public may adore an actor and it may admire a director or designer, but it *listens* to the playwright, who in Western culture has always assumed the role of prophet. Playwriting at its best is more than a profession and it is more than a component of the theatrical machine. It is a creative act that enlarges human experience and enriches our awe and appreciation of life.

The actor and the playscript may be at the core of the theatrical experience, but they are by no means the sum of it. Indeed, in the view of many spectators and participants, the primacy of acting and playwriting is extremely debatable.

For acting and textual brilliance are not isolated components capable of full expression in and by themselves. In even the most primitive of dramas the theatrical experience always has a "look" and a "sound" and a "shape," a visual and aural impact, that can be achieved only through *design*. And the execution of that design always entails a measure of *technology*. In many ways and at many times, the theatre has had occasion to celebrate the artistic talent of its designers and the engineering capability of its technicians, for many of the world's great aesthetic and technological innovations have been made public primarily through theatrical exploitation.

Therefore, in examining a play it is hardly sufficient to inquire merely as to what it is "about." We must also ask, How does it look? How does it sound? How is it built? How does it run? These questions bring us face to face with a veritable army of "backstage" personnel: the artists and technicians who, to greater or lesser degree, create and make possible what Aristotle called the "spectacle" of

CHAPTER **5**

DESIGNERS AND TECHNICIANS

theatre, who are responsible for the overall appearance, orchestration, and management of the theatrical experience.

It is customary for purposes of discussion to divide design functions into a series of components — scenery, lighting, make-up, and so forth — and to a certain extent this categorization is appropriate; most productions involve separate "departments" of design, each with its own designers, assistants, and crews. Nonetheless, it must be borne in mind that all the design functions of a production are interrelated, that the appearance of scenery, for example, is heavily dependent on the light that falls upon it, and the look of a costume is greatly affected by the actress's make-up and hairstyle — to say nothing of her acting and her bearing. In listing the various contributing "arts" of theatrical design, therefore, we must recognize that in abstracting each of them for separate examination, we are attempting only to clarify certain traditional practices, and that no single design art can be fully realized in isolation.

Similarly, the ordering of these separate arts can only be one of convenience, for no fundamental hierarchy exists among them. It is for a certain convenience, therefore, that we shall first discuss the theatre's architecture, scenery, and lighting and then deal with costuming, make-up, and technical production.

ARCHITECTURE

The theatre architect is, as a rule, the most anonymous of all major theatre artists. Although responsible for the theatre building itself and therefore for the basic spatial relationship between actors and audience — the "sight lines" of dramatic representation — the architect is rarely known to the theatre audience, almost never cited in the theatre program, and frequently unknown even to the artists who labor in the building. The divorce between the art of theatre and the art of theatre building is astonishing in this otherwise most collaborative endeavor.

Fortunately, there are some exceptions to this rule — exceptions that illustrate quite well the advantages of a theatre architecture developed hand in glove with the artistry that will utilize it.

The Bayreuth (Germany) Festspielhaus, conceived by opera composer-author Richard Wagner in association with "stage master" Carl Brandt and architect Otto Brückwald, was specifically designed as a showcase for the Wagnerian masterworks. The theatre, completed in 1876, features a steeply inclined, fan-shaped auditorium with continental seating instead of boxes and aisles; this arrangement was calculated to maximize the impact of grand scenic illusions that were painted so as to present roughly the same perspective from every seat in the house. The Bayreuth stage also features elaborate machinery and a mammoth sunken orchestra pit to facilitate the grandiose spectacle of the Wagnerian operas. This theatre still stands as a masterpiece of proscenium-type architecture, and it still succeeds brilliantly in the purposes for which it was designed.

Alternatively, the "thrust" stage built at Stratford, Ontario, in 1957 to specifications developed by Sir Tyrone Guthrie, in collaboration with scene designer Tanya Moiseiwitsch and architect Robert Fairfield, returned to the more "open" staging area of the ancient Greeks and Elizabethans. This design provided director Guthrie with a versatile acting platform and architectural background for his fast-moving, fast-paced classical revivals. The Stratford Festival Theatre served as a model not only for the later Guthrie Theatre in Minneapolis (1963), but also for a whole generation of American regional theatres that followed (see photograph of Pamela Brown Auditorium, this chapter).

The Wagnerian and "Guthrian" stages, although quite unlike in concept, both exemplify the potential of the theatre building mutually conceived by the architect and the theatre artist. Such a collaboration can be crucial to the development of a theatre aesthetic, as well as to providing stages suitable for the

A modern thrust stage, with vomitoria. The Pamela Brown Auditorium, one of two stages at the Actors Theatre of Louisville. (Photo: David S. Talbott.)

performances created upon them. Today, in most professional theatre companies and in community or university theatres, those who direct there are frankly expected to play a leading role in the planning of any new theatre structure, not only in the conception phase but in the design and construction phases as well.

What is theatre architecture? Basically, it is the "hard stuff" of a theatre building—that which is more or less permanent, more or less impervious to alteration by designer and director from one show to the next. Essentially, the theatre architect designs a stage for performance, a system of machinery for handling scenery (loading and unloading, hanging, shifting, and storage), a seating system for the audience (including conveniences such as lobbies, rest rooms, bars, and aisles), and both open and closed spaces for the day-to-day operation of the theatre enterprise (a box office,

dressing rooms, storage areas, rehearsal halls, administrative offices, control booths, lighting positions, quick-change rooms, crossover spaces, loading platforms, stage doors, fire escapes, wiring and access spaces). Needless to say, the manner in which any of these basic responsibilities is carried out (or not carried out) can affect the quality and character, the look and sound and "feel" of every single production that takes place in the building.

Inasmuch as theatre architecture is hard stuff that may survive its conceivers and constructors by many years—or centuries—it must be designed with a view to versatility. The design of the ancient Greek theatre and that of the "thrust" stage of Elizabethan times provide versatility largely by dint of their structural simplicity, which requires only a modest performing area, giving way on three sides to upward-sloping rows of seats, and backed on the fourth side by a building feature that permits the entrance and exit of actors through doorways—and possibly through balconies and windows. By being scenically inexplicit, these stages are suitable for the production of an enormous range of plays with but the slightest temporary additions of furniture, drapery, and/or special set pieces. The proscenium stage, when outfitted with proper machinery—fly galleries to hoist scenery out of sight, turntables and/or rolling wagons to move scenic units on and off laterally, and elevators to raise and lower actors, platforms, and entire orchestra pits—affords great versatility in a different direction, by dint of its scenic flexibility.

But versatility is not the sole criterion of aesthetic quality in theatre design; indeed, one of the intriguing perplexities of modern stage architecture has been the relative lack of enthusiasm accorded by theatre artists and audiences alike to theatres designed to convert from proscenium to thrust format at the throw of a few switches. The Vivian Beaumont Theatre at Lincoln Center (New York City) is a case in point. The stage of that theatre, designed by noted set designer Jo Mielziner in the early 1960s, includes a convertible thrust that can easily be turned into proscenium-format seating at the request of any individual director. Desirable as this feature seemed at the time it was built, the Beaumont Theatre and others like it appear somehow to lack the "tone" or "personality" that distinguishes the great playhouses. By way of explaining this curious lack, one might suggest that ultimately it is neither versatility nor practicality that characterizes the finest theatre buildings, but rather an aura of momentousness and vitality, and that this requires a certain specificity of design. All the great theatres—those most loved by audiences and performers alike—convey individuality (even eccentricity) and solid authority; they convey the sense that this is a house that has seen many great moments and will yet see many more. An omniflexible or institutionally

mechanical theatre structure may inhibit this feeling and rob a theatre of identity.

The Evolution of Theatre Architecture

Despite its largely anonymous instigation, theatre architecture has long been one of the glories of the Western world. The Greek theatres, which evolved out of a pagan rite celebrated on a hillside, rank high among the magnificent relics of antiquity: the surviving theatre at Epidaurus is only one of many from the fourth century B.C. that still resound from time to time with revivals of the same great plays that thrilled audiences in the Hellenistic Age. The theatres of ancient Rome were so grandiose in conception and execution that only hyperbole, it appears, could convey their proper character. For example, can we believe Pliny's account of an 80,000-seat theatre built in three stories, one each of marble, glass, and gilt? Or of the two theatres built back to back that, filled with spectators, rotated on a pivot to join in a huge amphitheatre that was then flooded for sea battle scenes?

Later times have given us only a few names of architects, but many more fine theatres. Of Peter Street, the architect of Shakespeare's Globe and Henslowe's Fortune, history unfortunately tells us little beyond the notation that his theatres were provocative of the best in dramatic art. The Teatro Olimpico in Vicenza, Italy, was designed by the famed Andrea Palladio and is the oldest extant theatre of known design and known architect—it was built in 1584, and it not only survives intact but also continues to be used for opera and dramatic presentations. Other theatres surviving from earlier eras, such as the elegant eighteenth-century court theatre at Drottningholm, Sweden, and the opulent nineteenth-century romantic structure built for the Paris Opera, are cultural landmarks as well as theatrically significant sites of contemporary production.

Today we are in the midst of an explosion of theatrical construction that began just after the close of World War II. Since then, performing arts centers have sprung up in almost every fair-sized American and European city; each year in the United States alone, ground is broken for literally dozens of first-class theatres, on campuses, in suburban communities, and in major urban renewal projects in the heart of "central downtown."

What we are seeing today might well be the beginning of a golden age of theatrical architecture, an age marked by a growing public willingness to lend financial support as well as by a greatly increased understanding of the need for extensive collaboration between theatre artists and architects in order to reconcile the needs for theatrical "tone" and atmosphere with those of practical flexibility and operational ease.

Staging Formats

The two principal types of modern theatre building are the proscenium stage design and the thrust stage design. These two basic types account for more than 95 percent of the professional theatres in Europe and America today and for the bulk of amateur stages as well.

Four basic theatre spaces. The architect's first decisions are, Where is the stage? Where is the audience? The arena, proscenium, thrust, and neutral "black box" formats constitute the realm of possibilities. (Drawing: John von Szeliski.)

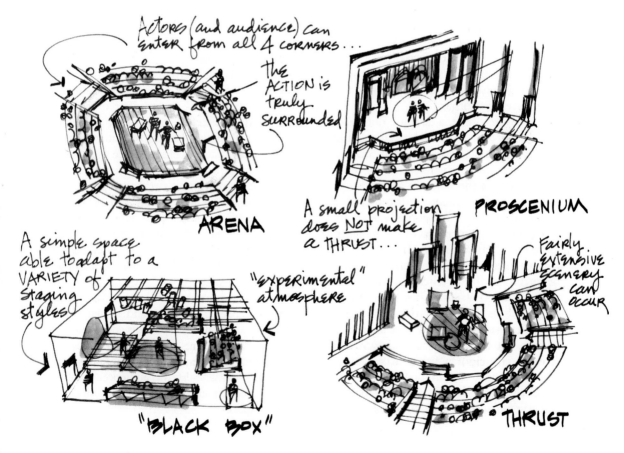

The *proscenium* theatre is essentially a rectangular room with the audience on one side facing the stage on the other, the two separated by an arch (the proscenium arch) through which the audience peers. This creates the well-known "picture frame" stage, with the arch serving as the frame for the action going on within. The proscenium format developed in Italy during the Renaissance as a mode of presenting elaborate court masques and other court entertainments; because it put the audience on but one side of the action, it allowed extensive "hidden" areas backstage for the scene shifting and trickery involved in creating the illusions and fantasies so admired at the time. The proscenium theatre achieved its fullest realization in the baroque era, and some of the surviving court theatres and opera houses of Europe testify eloquently to the splendor of that age. Modern proscenium theatres, following the Bayreuth model with its fan-shaped, unobstructed auditorium (instead of the horseshoe-shaped, boxed and galleried auditorium of earlier eras), have proven particularly serviceable for the use of realistic scenery and for the presentation of scenic spectaculars. Virtually all Broadway theatres feature the proscenium format.

The *thrust* format, a design pioneered only recently in North America by Tyrone Guthrie, was in fact the favored format in ancient Greece and Elizabethan England. Because it places much of the action in the midst of the audience, it is a more actor-centered than scenery-centered theatre configuration. In the thrust format the members of the audience are more aware of each other than they are in a darkened proscenium "fan," and their viewing perspectives differ radically, depending on their seating locations. When the acting platform or thrust has access from tunnels (*vomitoria*) that come up through the audience, the stage can be flooded by actors in a matter of seconds, creating a whirlwind of movement that is dazzling and immediate—the thrust stage's alternative to elaborate stage machinery and painted scenes. That is not at all to say that there can be no scenery on a thrust stage, but merely that major scenic pieces tend to be placed behind the action rather than surrounding it, leaving a major acting space, scenically quite neutral, projecting into the center of the audience.

A third theatrical configuration is the *arena format,* in which the audience surrounds the action on all sides; one American regional theatre, the Arena Stage in Washington, D.C., has presented an arena season regularly since 1950. Arena staging dispenses with all scenery except floor treatments, furniture, and out-of-the way hanging or standing pieces, and focuses audience attention sharply and simply on the actors. The long-standing success of the Washington Arena Stage testifies to the viability of this format; however, since no other major theatre has followed Washington's example (and indeed since the Arena Stage itself has built an adjacent proscenium theatre as a second space), it would appear that arena staging is destined to remain an interesting novelty rather than to initiate a staging revolution.

A final staging alternative is afforded by the so-called *black box* theatre, a formatless space that can be adjusted to any desired arrangement and is therefore particularly useful in experimental, environmental, or academic stagings. Usually painted black (hence the name), this type of theatre consists of a bare room fitted with omniflexible overhead lighting; in this room, stages and seating can be set up in any configuration—proscenium, thrust, arena, or two-sided "center stage"—or the action can occur at selected spots interspersed throughout the room: an "environmental" staging. The black box allows the director/creator to develop a near-infinite variety of actor-audience interactions and to make use of highly unusual scenic designs and/or mechanisms. "Happenings," participatory dramas, participatory rituals, and seminar plays—all of which demand active audience involvement—are frequently best presented in these sorts of spaces.

▲ *Scenery, costumes, and lighting set Shakespeare's* A Midsummer Night's Dream *in a colorful and sensual Caribbean landscape for this 1987 New York Shakespeare Festival production. Scenery by Andrew Jackness, costumes by Frank Krenz, lighting by Peter Kaczorowski. (Photo: George Joseph.)*

▼ *Patricia Goheen's inventively constructed and "found" costume elements for the "Pyramus and Thisbe" performers, juxtaposed against the formal wear of Theseus and Hippolyta, prove delightful in this 1988 Colorado Shakespeare Festival version of* A Midsummer Night's Dream. *Scenery and photograph by Douglas-Scott Goheen.*

▲ *An earthy* A Midsummer Night's Dream *was designed by Cliff Faulkner (scenery) and Shigeru Yaji (costumes) for South Coast Repertory Theatre in 1989. Here Oberon and Titania, the King and Queen of Fairies, frolic on the sandy ground. (Photo: Christopher Gross.)*

Shawn Judge as Cassandra, in "The Clytemnestra Plays," a combined production of Aeschylus' Agamemnon *and Sophocles'* Electra, *directed by Garland Wright at the Minneapolis Guthrie Theatre, 1991, with costume design by Susan Hilferty and lighting by Marcus Dilliard.*

Starlight Express is never static; the roller-skating musical features an "erector-set" design by John Napier that encircles the theatre audience and includes rising and descending ramps and straightaways for the whizzing-by performers. From the 1987 Broadway production. (Photo: Martha Swope and Associates.)

Other Architectural Considerations

Designing a theatre involves a great deal more than choosing a staging format.

It involves creating a seating space that is suited to the requirements of the expected audience; this may mean one thing in a sophisticated urban area, another in a rural outpost, yet another on a college campus. Different audiences have different comfort demands; they also differ in their emotional and intellectual responses to their surroundings. If the seats are too hard or too soft, for example, or if the ambience of the auditorium is intimidating, audiences may refuse to see the merits in any play.

Designing a theatre involves providing for effective communications systems, sight lines, and stage mechanisms for the sorts of productions the theatre will handle. This means there must be adequate wiring, soundproofing, and rigging, as well as a good use of backstage and onstage spaces, both open and enclosed — and often that means calling in a consultant who specializes in ascertaining the most practical design for the widest variety of uses.

The actual concrete wall of the Bouffes du Nord theatre in Paris provides most of the basic "scenery" for Peter Brook's 1986 Mahabharata —*and for all other works performed in this surprising theatre, which was in ruins when Brook rediscovered it in an old abandoned building. Instead of renovating the theatre, Brook decided to retain the collapsed and partially burned-out interior pretty much as he found it. (Photo: Gilles Abegg.)*

Theatre building also involves principles of acoustics, which can determine whether actors' voices will be heard, given a normal volume level, in all parts of the house, and whether singers' voices can be heard when the orchestra is playing. As a science, acoustics is maddeningly inexact so that the best results come only after much experience and testing.

Theatre architecture involves the art of lighting, for no lighting designer can possibly overcome the limitations imposed by poorly located, permanently installed lighting positions. One of the sadder aspects of many older theatres is the jungle gym of exposed pipes and lighting instruments awkwardly strapped to gilded cupids in a latter-day attempt to make up for antiquated lighting systems.

And finally, designing and building a theatre involves a love of theatre, an emotional and aesthetic understanding that a theatre is not merely a room, not merely a hall, and not merely an institutional building with certain features, but a permanent home for the portrayal of human concerns and a repository of twenty-five hundred years of glorious tradition. Such a place must be functional and flexible, to be sure, but it is also deserving of more: it deserves to have the distinctive identity that comes from the architect's ineffable sense of purpose and passion and theatrical imagination.

SCENERY

Scenery is likely to be the first thing we think of under the general category of theatrical design; if a production is said to be "designed by Jane Jones," we may simply assume that this means the scenery was designed by Jane Jones. Scenery is usually the first thing we see of a play, either at the rise of the curtain in a traditional proscenium production or as we enter the theatre where there is no curtain.

And yet scenery, as considered apart from architecture, is a relatively new phenomenon in the theatre. It was not needed for the dithyramb, and it probably played little part in Greek tragedy or comedy save to afford entry, exit, and sometimes expanded acting space for actors; such rotating prisms, rolling platforms, and painted panels as were used in the Greek theatre probably had no representational significance. In other words, none of these features was intended to disguise the fact that the play's action took place in a Greek theatre. The same is more or less true of the Roman theatre, the medieval theatre, and the outdoor Elizabethan theatre — apart from a few set pieces that were painted and otherwise detailed to resemble free-standing walls, trees, caves, thrones, tombs, porches, and the inevitable Hellmouth — for virtually all visual aspects of public outdoor staging prior to the seventeenth century were dictated by the architecture of the theatre structure itself.

It was the development of indoor stages, artificially illuminated, that fostered the first great phase of scene design: the period of painted, flat scenery. Working indoors out of the reach of the elements, designers of Renaissance spectacles and court masques were free

A grand rococo theatre becomes the stage setting for this 1987 production of Pirandello's metatheatrical comedy Tonight We Improvise *at the Thèâtre de la Ville, in Paris. The "theatre within a theatre" design is particularly Pirandellian. (Photo: Gilles Abegg.)*

Richard Seger's set for The Girl of the Golden West, *an early (1905) American drama by David Belasco, exemplifies the realism of Belasco's period. "Aged" wooden planks are used for flooring, walls, counter, furniture, and roof timbers; the set has the look, feel, and smell of its time. From an American Conservatory Theatre production. (Photo: William Gonsler.)*

greater than) the playwright's; and for almost two hundred years thereafter, flat scenery, painted in exquisite perspective, took on even greater sophistication under the brilliant artists of the theatre's baroque, rococo, and romantic epochs. The proscenium format, which was developed primarily to show off elegant settings, utterly dominated theatre architecture for all that time. It was not until the beginning of the present century that scenery went into its second major phase—the modern one—which can be said to continue in various fashions today.

Modern scenery is of two basic types: realistic and abstract. Often the two types are used in combination and often the line between them is difficult to draw, but in their separate ways both have contributed mightily to the important position of scenery in the theatrical experience today.

Realistic settings carry on the tradition of "illusionism" established in eighteenth-century painted perspective stagings; the familiar "box set" of modern realistic or naturalistic theatre is essentially a series of interconnected flats of framed canvas painted to resemble walls and ceilings, filled with real furniture and real properties taken from ordinary real-world environments. This type of set, a development of the early nineteenth century, is very much alive today and is indeed the major scenic format for contemporary domestic drama (particularly comedy) of New York's Broadway, London's West End, and most community and college theatres across America. No longer particularly voguish, the box set rarely wins design awards; but it admirably fulfills the staging requirements of a great many domestic comedies, thrillers, and serious linearly structured dramas, particularly those requiring interior settings. Advances in scenic construction and technology have made the box set an absolute marvel of lifelike appearance and detail.

Box sets and other forms of realistic painted scenery can be immensely useful in designating a play's locale. The cleverly painted wings

for the first time to erect painted canvases and temporary wooden structures without fear of having the colors run and the supports rot out or blow away. And with the advent of controllable indoor lighting, they could illuminate their settings and acting areas as they wished without calling attention to the permanent structures behind: they could, in short, create both realistic illusion and decorative spectacle without having to contend with bad weather, bird droppings, and extraneous architectural interference.

The result was a series of scene design revelations that brought the names of a new class of theatre artists—designers—to public consciousness, designers such as the Italians Aristotile da Sangallo (1481–1551), Sebastiano Serlio (1475–1554), and Giacomo Torelli (1604–1678), the Englishman Inigo Jones (1573–1652), and the Frenchman Jean Berain (c.1637–1711). By the beginning of the eighteenth century, the scene designer's art had attained a prominence equal to (or perhaps and drops of the era of flat, perspective-painted scenery portrayed with great precision the drawing rooms, conservatories, ballrooms, reception halls, parlors, libraries, servants' quarters, professional offices, and factory yards of many a dramatist's imagination or prescription. The box set served to heighten the verisimilitude by adding three-dimensional features: suitable doors to enter through, windows to peer through, bookcases to hide revolvers in, and grandfather clocks to hide characters in. The public fascination with realistic scenery reached its high-water mark in the ultrarealist "theatre of the fourth wall removed," in which the box set was used to such advantage that it helped to foster a uniquely architectural theory of theatre — that it should always represent life "with one wall removed."

The most talked-about scenic design today, however, tends to be more plastic than rigid, more kinetic than stable, more symbolic and evocative than realistic and explicit. In other words, abstract scenography is distinctly gaining ground.

The movement toward scenic abstraction began with the theoretical (and occasionally practical) works of designers Adolphe Appia (1862–1928) and Gordon Craig (1872–1966), both of whom urged the fluid use of space, form, and light as a fundamental principle of dramatic design. Aided by technological advances in lighting and motorized scene shifting, the movement toward a more plastic scenography has inspired a great many impressive abstract stylizations. Projections, shafts and walls of light, transparent scrims, outsized graphics and photoreproductions, sculptural configurations, metals both polished and coarse, mirrored and burlaped surfaces both hard and soft, "floating" walls and rising staircases, and wholly "found" or wholly "surreal" environments: all these have become major media for many contemporary scene designers.

These more plastic and more abstract settings can establish locales if need be, but they are perhaps more effective in establishing

Ming Cho Lee's great realistic setting for Patrick Meyer's adventure drama K-2 portrays a ledge in the Himalayan mountains. It even feels cold. (Photo: Martha Swope and Associates.)

THE HIDDEN ENERGY

A stage setting has no independent life of its own. Its emphasis is directed toward the performance. In the absence of the actor it does not exist. Strange as it may seem, this simple and fundamental principle of stage design still seems to be widely misunderstood. . . .

A scene on the stage is . . . like a mixture of chemical elements held in solution. The actor adds the one element that releases the hidden energy of the whole. Meanwhile, wanting the actor, the various elements which go into the setting remain suspended, as it were, in an indefinable tension. To create this suspense, this tension, is the essence of . . . stage designing.

The designer must strive to achieve . . . a kind of embodied impulse. When the curtain rises we feel a frenzy of excitement focused like a burning-glass upon the actors. Everything on the stage becomes a part of the life of the instant. The play becomes a voice out of a whirlwind.

Robert Edmund Jones

moods and styles. Of course, mood and style can be established to some extent by realistic scenery as well: by creating a theatrical space that is tall and airy, for example, or cramped and squat, by using or withholding color and clutter, the designer in any mode can define an environment in such a way that the action of the play takes on a highly special tone. But with the extension into nonrealistic abstraction, the designer can greatly elaborate upon tone and develop it into a highly specific sensory approach.

The dark walls and cobwebby interiors designed by Edward Gorey for the Broadway production of *Dracula* (1977), for example, were a significant factor in the play's communication of fascinating horror. The bare but shiny white walls and lacy black catwalks de-

signed by Sally Jacobs for the 1970 Peter Brook production of *A Midsummer Night's Dream* focused all attention on the poetry of the human relationships in that famous Shakespearean revival. The remarkable "found object"—a complete nineteenth-century iron foundry—that served as the surround for Eugene Lee's basic set in the original Harold Prince production of *Sweeney Todd* (1979) indelibly conveyed the underlying theme of industrial oppression. Designer Eiko Ishioka's soaring white ramp, arcing through a brilliant Chinese-red background, epitomized the racial conflict and the psychosexual theme of David Hwang's *M. Butterfly* in 1988. And

Sally Jacobs's bare white walls for this internationally celebrated 1970 production of A Midsummer Night's Dream, *directed by Peter Brook, were in stark contrast to the then-standard woody romanticism expected for this play. But the abstraction brilliantly served both the actors (who employed various circus techniques, such as the illustrated plate-twirling) and the text. (Photo: Holte Photographics.)*

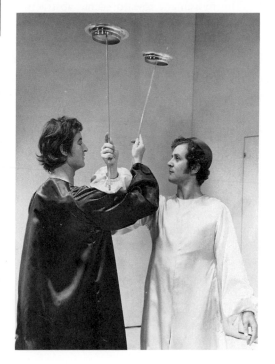

Eiko Ishioka's stunning set for David Henry Hwang's M. Butterfly *employs minimal details: soaring white ramp, black floor, glossy Chinese-red chairs, and a red surround, contrasting purity and passion in this 1987 Broadway play of East-West cultural (and male-female sexual) tensions. (Photo: Martha Swope and Associates.)*

Tony Walton's boldly colorful, brashly cartoonish street scenes for the 1992 Broadway revival of *Guys and Dolls* animated the play's New York City setting with a giddy, unworldly, and unthinking nostalgia, allowing current audiences to bask in Runyon's fantasy Manhattan—while just outside the door, on real New York City streets, contemporary urban agony and despair dominated the scene.

Specifically postmodern design elements, too, have made their appearance in the theatre of the 1980s and 1990s. Because the postmodern emphasizes disharmonies and associations, it travels in a somewhat different path from the departures of modernist innovators Craig and Appia; postmodern design can be recognized by the conscious disruption of "unifying" stylistic themes, replacing them with apparently random assemblages of different and unrelated styles, some "quoting" other historical periods or intellectual sources.

Postmodern design often reconfigures, or refers to, the theatre facility itself, with painted scenery made to look specifically scenic, particularly in contrast to seemingly arbitrary "found objects" strewn about the set, and with designed units meant to comment on—and to mock—their own "theatricality." Richard Hudson's setting and costumes for David Hirson's 1990 *La Bête*, a play set in 1654, ironically juxtaposes classical, neoclassical, baroque, and contemporary images with superbly ironic, and hilarious, effect.

The best scenic design today goes far beyond mere "backing" for the action of a play; it creates a basic visual and spatial architecture of performance, an architecture that when fully realized, becomes *intrinsic to the action.* Consider, for example, the multilevel, multiroomed setting designed by Jo Mielziner for the original production of Arthur Miller's American classic *Death of a Salesman.* This set,

Ocean waves create the Baltic seacoast in this 1991 Hamlet, *designed by Antony McDonald and staged by Ron Daniels at the American Repertory Theatre. The waves were handpainted on a giant canvas backdrop. (Photo: Richard Feldman.)*

which provided a cutaway view of both floors of the salesman's house, permitting the simultaneous staging of activity in the kitchen and in the upstairs bedrooms, caused playwright Miller (and director Elia Kazan) to restructure the play so that events originally planned to evolve sequentially could be performed simultaneously, thereby tremendously increasing the intensity and impact of the action. The simple but brilliant setting devised by Andrew Jackness for the stage production of Arthur Kopit's *Wings*—a series of twirling eight-foot squares of mirror and black scrim—created a striking image of mental recesses and led to a series of actions in which characters moved forward and back through whirling and indefinite perceptibility, a splendidly appropriate use of scenery for this play, which deals with a stroke and its accompanying perceptual distortions. And the many brilliant

designs of Joseph Svoboda, who is certainly Europe's most celebrated "scenographer" (his own term) in the second half of this century, are nothing short of dramatic architecture in action. Svoboda has made highly imaginative use of a whole array of contemporary technologies, including laser beams, computerized slide and film projections, pneumatic mirrors, low-voltage lighting instruments, aerosol sprays, and innovative stage machinery, to create a body of scenic design unrivaled for theatrical impact and expressive dramaturgy. Speaking of "dramatic space" as "psychoplastic," Svoboda has said: "The goal of a designer can no longer be a description of a copy of actuality, but the creation of its multidimensional model." And for Svoboda—as for most contemporary designers—that multidimensional model is a dynamic one, flowing through time as well as space, and responding to the inner

Jo Mielziner's celebrated two-story cutaway set for Arthur Miller's Death of a Salesman, *1949. Mielziner's own rendering of the set shows Willy coming into the ground floor dining area while his two sons sit up in their bedroom upstairs. Willy's wife is barely visible sleeping in her bed at left.*

biological and psychological rhythms of the actors and the dramatic actions.

Thus the functions of scenery design are both practical and abstract, both concrete and imaginative. Although it is a latecomer to theatre history, scenery has occasionally overwhelmed the drama itself: in the 1730s, in the "mute spectacles" of Jean-Nicholas Servandoni, whole performances were arranged with nothing but scene designs, lighting, music, and posed actors; Svoboda's *Diapolyekran* and *Lanterna Magika* have accomplished the same in more recent years (the 1960s and 1970s). Scenery's place in the theatre is not inevitable—the theatre has managed in the past without it and still does so from time to time—but its future looks very secure. It has

the capacity, when well used, to develop enormous visual, emotional, aesthetic, and dramatic impact, lending the theatre a conjunction with artistic technology that it can in no other way acquire.

The Scene Designer's Media

The traditional media of scenery design—wood, canvas, and paint—have in recent times been extended to include steel, plastics, and projected images. Designing and building scenic components from each of these sources is the first area of training for every scenic designer.

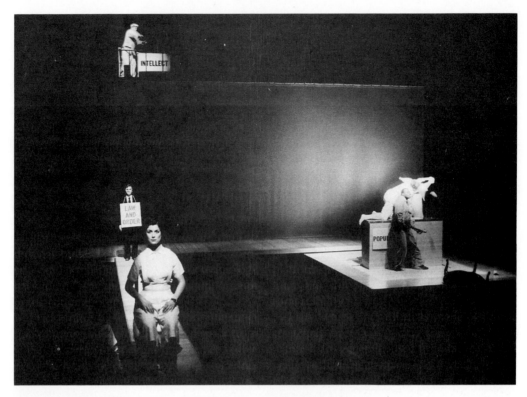

Seemingly disconnected elements are compiled in an overall theatrical effect, in Robert Wilson and Tomm Kamm's setting for Wilson's the CIVIL warS, which Wilson also directed at the American Repertory Theatre. (Photo: Richard Feldman.)

Platforms, flats, and draperies are the traditional building blocks of fixed stage scenery — and no changes in aesthetics or technology have in any way diminished their importance in the contemporary theatre.

Platforming serves the all-important function of giving the actor an elevated space from which to perform, making him or her visible over the heads of other actors and stage furniture; a stage setting that utilizes several artfully arranged platforming levels (of increasing height toward the back of the stage), together with appropriate connecting staircases and ramps or "raked" platform units, can permit dozens of actors to be seen simultaneously. Platforms can be created in virtually any size

and shape; what is more, with the growing use of steel in stage platform construction, platform support can be fairly open, allowing huge but still "lacy" settings of great structural stability.

Flats, which are ordinarily made of canvas stretched over a wooden frame and then painted, are generally used to indicate vertical walls (realistic or abstract) and to define space. Flats can be pierced with windows, doors, and open archways; they can be adorned with moldings, paintings, hangings, bookcases, or fireplaces; they can be turned horizontally to serve as ceilings; they can be "tracked" onto the stage in grooves, as they were in the eighteenth century, or "flown" down from the overhead flies, as they often are in repertory theatres that store many settings at one time. The flat is an immensely versatile workhorse that has almost become a symbol of the theatre itself.

Drapery is the great neutral stuff of stage settings; it is often used to bridge the gap between the setting itself and the permanent features of the theatre building, and occasionally it is used in somewhat more realistic fashion as well. The stage curtain of a proscenium theatre is one form of hanging drapery—when the curtain rises or parts or is pulled diagonally upward (the "opera drape") at the beginning of a play, it signals the drama's first engagement of the audience. Another form of hanging drapery is used conventionally to mask (hide) the stage lighting above the set (this is called a "drapery border"), and yet another is used to mask the machinery and personnel behind the flats (the "drapery legs" or "wings"). Black drapery at the rear of the stage can provide a neutral backdrop to the action of a play, and frequently a whole set of drapery, usually black, is used as the entire setting for readings, chamber productions, and "reader's theatre" productions. Sometimes this sort of scenery is deemed suitable even for full-scale theatricalizations, and a theatre possessing such a "set of blacks" is able to present

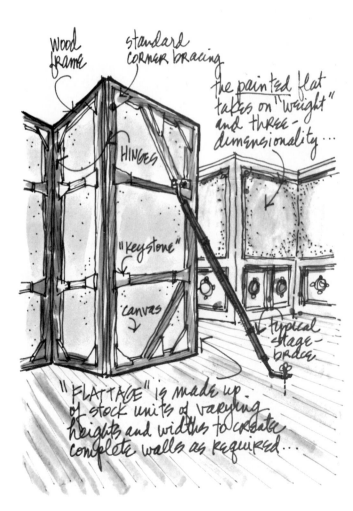

wood frame

standard corner bracing

the painted flat takes on "weight" and three-dimensionality...

HINGES

"keystone"

canvas

typical stage-brace

"FLATTAGE" is made up of stock units of varying heights and widths to create complete walls as required...

The "flat" is an inexpensive way to create the illusion of an interior or exterior wall. Light, easy to move and to store, flats can be repainted almost indefinitely to create a variety of settings. (Drawing: John von Szeliski.)

many plays with a minimal expenditure of scenery time or budget. A final drapery found in most well-equipped theatres is the *cyclorama,* a hanging fabric stretched taut between upper and lower pipes and curved to surround the rear and sides of the stage. Colored white, gray, or gray-blue, the "cyc" can be lighted with stronger colors to represent a variety of "skyscapes" with great effectiveness; it can also be used for abstract backgrounds and projections.

In addition to the three primary components of stage settings, many productions make use of the special one-of-a-kind "set piece," which frequently becomes the focal point for an overall setting design or even for the action of a whole play. The tree in *Waiting for Godot,* for example, is the primary scenic feature of that play's setting, symbolizing both life and death. The moment when Vladimir and Estragon "do the tree" — a calisthenic exercise in which each man stands on one leg and tries to assume the shape of the tree — is a profound moment of theatre in which set piece and actors coalesce in a single image, referred to in the text of the play, of the triple crucifixion on Calvary where two thieves died alongside Christ. Similarly, the massive supply wagon hauled by Mother Courage in Bertolt Brecht's epic play of that name gives rise to a

Sheets of plastic, corrugated plastic grating, and open steel scaffolding are some of the contemporary scene designer's media in this production of Julius Caesar *in Atlanta. (Photo: Charles M. Rafshoon.)*

Robert Wilson, who designs or codesigns (as here, with Jennifer Tipton) the lighting for his productions, paints the stage with lights from various sources, including lasers, and coming from unusual positions, including beneath the stage. Shown here: light as scenery in his 1986 Alcestis *at the American Repertory Theatre. (Photo: Richard Feldman.)*

powerful visual impression of struggle and travail that may last long after the words of the characters are forgotten. And what would *Prometheus Bound* be without its striking set piece, Prometheus' rock and chains? No matter how stylized this element may have been in its original realization, it must have radiated to the Athenian audience a visual poetry every bit as eloquent as the verbal poetry with which Aeschylus supported it. Individual set pieces indeed tax the imagination of author, director, designer and scene technician alike, and the masterpieces of scenic invention can long outlive their makers in the memory of the audience.

A host of modern materials and technological inventions add to the primary compo-nents and set pieces from which scenery is created.

Light as scenery, apart from the stage lighting discussed later, can create walls, images, even (with laser holography) three-dimensional visualizations. Banks of sharply focused light sent through dense atmospheres, enhanced by smoke or dust or fog, can create trenches of light that have the appearance of massive solidity and yet can be made to disappear at the flick of a switch. Carefully controlled slide projections can provide images either realistic or abstract, fixed or fluid, precise or indefinite.

Scrim, which is a loosely woven fabric that looks opaque when lit from one side and transparent when lit from the other, has been a staple of theatre "magic" for many years.

Stage machinery — turntables, elevators, hoists, rolling carts and wagons, and the like — can be used to create a veritable dance of scenic elements to accompany and support dramatic action. The ancient Greeks apparently understood the importance of mechanical devices quite well, as did Shakespeare with his winched thrones and disappearing witches. Tricks and sleight of hand (called, in the medieval theatre, "trucs" and "feynts") have always imparted a certain sparkle of mystery to the theatre and hence will always play a part in the designer's art.

Sound also must be taken into consideration by the designer, who must plan for the footfalls of the actor as well as for the visual elements behind, around, and underneath him. The floor of a stage designed for the production of Japanese Noh drama, for example, has a characteristic look and produces a character-

istic sound; it is meant to be stamped upon, and it must sound just so. Joseph Svoboda has designed a stage floor for *Faust* that can be either resonant or silent depending on the arrangement of certain mechanisms concealed underneath; when Faust walks upstage his steps reverberate; when he turns and walks downstage his steps are silent — and we know Mephistopheles has taken his body.

Properties and furniture, which are often handled by a separate artist working under the guidance of the scene designer, are crucial not only in establishing realism but also in enhancing mood and style. Although furniture is most often used in the theatre just as it is in life — to sit upon, lie upon, and so forth — it also has a crucial stylistic importance; often stage furniture is designed and built in highly imaginative ways to convey a special visual impact when coordinated with the setting. Properties such as ash trays, tele-

Oceanus "flies" to visit Prometheus on his rock, via a strong cable in the Paris production. Flying machinery has existed in the theatre since ancient Greek times. (Photo: Marc Enguerand.)

Properties figure prominently in production design, as in this photograph from the Actors Theatre of Louisville production of Odon von Horvath's Tales from the Vienna Woods, *produced as part of the company's 1991 Classics in Context Festival that focused on the theatre of Weimar Germany. (Photo: Richard C. Trigg.)*

phones, letters, and tableware are often functional in realistic plays, but they can also have aesthetic importance and are therefore quite carefully selected—or else specially designed. Frequently, furniture pieces or properties have considerable symbolic significance, as in the case of the thrones in Shakespeare's *Richard III,* for example, or the glass figurines in Williams's *Glass Menagerie.*

The Scene Designer at Work

The scene designer's work inevitably begins with a reading and rereading of the play, discussions with the director, and a consideration of the type of theatre in which the play is to be produced. This step is usually followed with a series of visualizations—either sketches, drawings, collected illustrations (for example, clippings from magazines, notations from historical sources, color ideas, spatial concepts), or three-dimensional models. Whatever the scenic inspiration, it must ultimately be rendered in a fashion suitable to serve as a guide for construction—which ordinarily means, minimally, a full set of working drawings explaining in precise technical detail the construction practices to be used. All along the way, of course, the designer must reckon with budgetary restraints and the skills of the construction staff available to execute and install the finished design. Part architect, part engineer, part painter, part decorator, part builder, part interpretive genius, part accountant, the scene designer today is one of the theatre's premier artists/craftspeople.

LIGHTING

The very word *theatre,* meaning "seeing place," implies the crucial function of light. Light is the basic condition for theatrical appearance; without light, nothing is to be seen.

The use of light for dramatic effect, as distinct from pure illumination, can be traced back to the earliest surviving plays: *Agamemnon,* by Aeschylus, was staged so that the watchman's spotting of the signal fire heralding Agamemnon's return to Argos coincided with the actual sunrise over the Athenian *skene* (stagehouse); it is also probable that the burning of Troy at the conclusion of Euripides' *The Trojan Women* was staged to coincide with the hour when sunset reddened the Attic sky. Modern plays commonly use light in metaphoric and symbolic ways: the blinking neon light that regularly reddens Blanche's quarters in Tennessee Williams's *A Streetcar Named Desire* affords one example; another is the searching followspot demanded by Samuel Beckett to train upon the hapless, trapped characters in his play entitled *Play.*

It is customary to think of theatre lighting as a relatively recent technology, dating from the invention of electricity. Nothing could be more misleading; lighting has always been a major theatrical consideration. The Greeks paid a great deal of attention to the proper orientation of their theatres to take best advantage of the sun's rays. The medieval outdoor theatre, although as dependent on sunlight as was the Greek theatre, made use of several devices to redirect sunlight, including the haloes made of reflective metal that were used to surround Jesus and his disciples with a focused and intensified illumination; in one production a brightly polished metal basin was held over Jesus' head to concentrate the sun's rays—and surviving instructions tell the medieval stagehands to substitute torches for the bowl in case of cloudy skies!

It was in indoor stagings, however, that lighting technology attained its first significant sophistication—and this as early as the Middle Ages. In a 1439 production of the *Annunciation* in Florence, one thousand oil lamps were used for illumination, plus a host of candles that were lighted by a "ray of fire" that shot through the cathedral. One can imagine the spectacle. Leonardo da Vinci designed a 1490 production of *Paradise* with twinkling stars and backlit zodiac signs on colored glass; by the sixteenth century the great festival lighting of indoor theatres, located in manor houses and public halls, would serve as a symbol of the intellectual and artistic achievements of the Renaissance itself, a mark of the luxury, technical wizardry, and ostentatious, exuberant humanism of the times. People went to the theatres in those times simply to revel in light and escape the outside gloom—in rather the same way that Americans, earlier in this century, populated air-conditioned movie theatres largely to escape the heat of summer days. The indoor stages of the Renaissance have perhaps never been equaled in terms of sheer opulence of illumination—and the entire effect was created simply from tallow, wax, and fireworks. Raphael "painted" the name of his patron, Pope Leo X, with thirteen lighted chandeliers in a 1519 dramatic production; Sebastiano Serlio, whose development of flat painted scenery was mentioned earlier, included sparkling panes of colored glass, illuminated from behind, to make a veritable jewel box of that scenery (an effect which, unfortunately, is not captured in the woodcuts that have come down to us as illustrations of this work). As the Renaissance spirit give way to the lavish Royal theatre of the age of Louis XIV, the "Sun King," artificial illumination calculated to match Louis's presumed incendiary brilliance developed apace: one 1664 presentation at Versailles featured 20,000 colored lanterns, hundreds of transparent veils and bowls of colored water, and a massive display of fireworks.

It was the invention of the gaslight in the nineteenth century and the development of electricity shortly thereafter—first in carbon arc and "limelight" electrical lighting and then in incandescence—that brought stage lighting into its modern phase and made it less strictly showy and more pertinent to individual works and dramatic action. Ease and flexibility of control is the cardinal virtue of both gas and electricity. A single operator at a "gas table" could, by throwing a valve, raise or dim the intensity of any individual light or of a preselected "gang" of lights—just as we can raise or lower the fire on a gas range by turning a knob. And, of course, with electricity—which was introduced in American theatres in 1879 and in European theatres the following year—the great fire hazard of live flame, a danger that had plagued the theatre for centuries and claimed three buildings a year on average (including Shakespeare's Globe), was at last over. The fire crews, which had been a permanent, twenty-four-hour staff in the employ of every major theatre in the early nineteenth century, were dismissed; and the deterioration of scenery and costumes from heat, smoke, and carbon pollution of flame lighting similarly came to a halt. Incandescent lighting also had the great advantage of being fully self-starting—it did not need to be relit or kept alive by "pilots"—and it could easily be switched off, dimmed up and down, and reganged or reconnected simply by fastening and unfastening flexible wires. Within a few years of its introduction, electricity became the primary medium of stage lighting in the Western world, and great dynamo generators—for electricity was used in the theatre long before it was commercially available from municipal power supplies—were installed as essential equipment in the basements of theatres from Vienna to San Francisco.

Electricity provides the enormous flexibility of lighting that we know and use today. The incandescent filament is a reasonably small, reasonably cool point of light that can

LIMITS OF ELECTRICITY

For all the efficiency, economy, safety, and extraordinary flexibility of electric lighting, it is by no means regarded universally as an unmixed blessing for the theatre. Gone is the "living flame" that for eight hundred years had illuminated indoor theatrical performance, and gone with it the warm, mellow, flickering glow cast by gaslight and, more particularly, by candlelight. Undeniably, the very strengths of electrical lighting—its uniform beam, its whiteness, its precision—have also contributed a certain sterility, coldness, and harshness, and for this reason its nearly exclusive use in the theatre today is seen by some as a definite step in the wrong direction. As candlelight and gaslight have returned in recent years to many restaurants, homes, and even street corners—almost always in successful conjunction with incandescent or even fluorescent lighting—so a few designers now are attempting to reintegrate the "living flame" into stage lighting. The great electrical revolution of the past hundred years need not forever define the future of stage illumination.

be focused, reflected, aimed, shaped, and colored by a great variety of devices invented and adapted for those purposes; and electric light can be trained in innumerable ways upon actors, scenery, audience, or combinations of these to create realistic and/or atmospheric effects, through dimensionality, focus, animation, distortion, diffusion, and overwhelming radiance. Today, thanks to the added sophistication of computer technology and microelectronics, it is not uncommon to see theatres with nearly a thousand lighting instruments all under the complete control of a single technician seated in a comfortable booth above the audience.

Natasha Katz's intense downlighting keeps our attention on Edmund (Jonathan Fried), his sword drawn before his duel with Edgar (deep background). For the 1991 Adrian Hall production of King Lear *at the American Repertory Theatre. (Photo: Richard Feldman.)*

Modern Lighting Design

Today, the lighting for any given production is likely to have been conceived and directly supervised by a professional lighting designer, a species of theatre artist who has appeared as a principal member of the production team only in the past two or three decades.

By skillfully working with lighting instruments, hanging positions, angles, colors, shadows, and moment-to-moment adjustment of intensity and directionality, the lighting designer can illuminate a dramatic production in a great variety of subtle and complex ways. The way in which the lighting designer uses the medium to blend the more rigid design elements (architecture and scenery) with the evolving patterns of the movements of the actors, and the meanings of the play, can be a crucial factor in a production's artistic and theatrical success.

Visibility and *focus* are the primary considerations of lighting design: visibility assures that the audience sees what it wants to see, and focus assures that they see what they are *supposed* to see without undue distraction. Visibility, then, is the passive accomplishment of lighting design and focus is its active accomplishment. The spotlight used in contemporary theatre, a development of the twentieth century, has fostered something akin to a revolution in staging, which now routinely features a darkened auditorium (a rarity prior to this century) and a deliberate effort to illuminate certain characters (or props or set pieces) more than others — in other words, to direct the audience's attention toward those visual elements that are dramatically the most significant.

Realism and *atmosphere* also are frequent goals of the lighting designer, and both can be achieved largely through the color and direction of lighting. Realistic lighting can be created to appear as if emanating from familiar sources: from the sun, for example, or from "practical" (real) lamps on the stage, or from moonlight, fire, street lights, neon signs, or the headlights of moving automobiles. Atmospheric lighting, which may or may not suggest a familiar source, can be used to evoke a mood appropriate to a play's action: sparkly, for example, or gloomy, oppressive, nightmarish, austere, verdant, smoky, funereal, or regal.

Sharp, bold lighting designs are frequently employed to create highly theatrical effects — for glittery entertainments in the Broadway musical tradition, for example, or for harsher experimental stagings like those often associated with the plays and theories of Bertolt Brecht. Brecht's concept of a "didactic" theatre suggested the lighting be bright, cold (uncolored), and specifically "unmagical"; Brecht suggested, in fact, that the lighting instruments themselves be made part of the setting, placed in full view of the audience, and this "theatricalist" use of the lighting instruments themselves is now in widespread use even in nondidactic plays. The splashy musical, more romantically, often makes use of footlights, banks of colored border lights, onstage "tracer" lights that flash on and off in sequence, followspots, and high-voltage incandescence that makes a finale seem to burn up the stage; in fact, this traditional exploitation of light has done as much to give Broadway the name "Great White Way" as have the famous billboards and marquees that line the street.

Stylized lighting effects are often used to express radical changes of mood or event; indeed, the use of lighting alone to signal a complete change of scene is an increasingly common theatrical expedient. Merely by switching from full front to full overhead lighting, for example, a technician can throw a character into silhouette and make his figure appear suddenly ominous, grotesque, or isolated. The illumination of an actor with odd lighting colors, such as green, or from odd lighting positions, such as from below, can create mysterious, unsettling effects. The use of followspots can metaphorically put a character "on the spot" and convey a specific sense of unspeakable terror. Highly expressive lighting and projections, when applied to a production utilizing only a cyclorama, a set piece, sculp-

Tom Ruzika's downlighting silhouettes concentration camp victims against the highlighted prison fencing, in the South Coast Repertory Theatre production of Cecil P. Taylor's Good, *directed by David Emmes. (Photo: Christopher Gross.)*

ture, or stage mechanism and neutrally clad actors, can create an infinite variety of convincing theatrical environments for all but the most resolutely realistic of plays; it is here, in the area of stylization and expressive theatricality, that the modern lighting designer has made the most significant mark.

Robert Wilson uses lighting in both subtle and flamboyant fashions. The lighting for his 1992 production of Einstein at the Beach *has the effect of seeming to magically propel a character beyond an imprisoning "jail" of steel bars. (Photo: Martha Swope Associates/William Gibson.)*

The Lighting Designer at Work

The lighting designer ordinarily conceives a lighting design out of a synthesis of many discrete elements: the play, the director's approach or concept, the characteristics of the theatre building (lighting positions, control facilities, and wiring system), the basic scenery design, the costumes and movements of the actors, and the available lighting instruments. Occasionally the availability of an experienced lighting crew must also be a consideration.

Because not all of these variables can be known from the outset — the stage movement, for example, may change from one day to the next right up to the final dress rehearsal — the lighting designer must possess a certain skill at making adjustments and must have the opportunity to exercise a certain amount of control, or at least to voice concerns with regard to areas affecting lighting problems.

Ordinarily, the two major preparations required of the lighting designer are the light plot and the cue sheet. A light plot is a plan or series of plans showing the placement of each lighting instrument; its type, wattage, and size; its wiring and connection to an appropriate dimmer; its color; and any special instructions as to its use. A cue sheet is a list of the occasions, referred to by number and keyed to the script of the play (or, in final form, the more fully annotated stage manager's script), when lights change, either in intensity or in their use. These two documents — light plot and cue sheet — are developed in consultation with the director, who may take a major or minor role in the consultation depending on his or her interest and expertise. Inasmuch as some productions use literally hundreds of lighting instruments and require literally thousands of individual cues, the complexity of these documents can be extraordinary; weeks and months may go into their preparation.

The lighting designer works with a number of different sorts of lighting instruments and must know the properties of each instrument well enough to anticipate fully how it will perform when hung and focused on the stage. Few theatres have the time or space flexibility to permit much on-site experimentation in lighting design; thus most of the development of light plot and cue sheet must take place in the imagination and, where possible, in workshop or free experimentation apart from the working facility. This requirement places a premium on the designer's ability to predict instrument performance from various distances and angles and with various color elements installed; it also demands a sharp awareness of how various lights will reflect off different surfaces.

Ordinarily the lighting designer develops the plot and cue sheet gradually, over the course of regular discussions with the director and after attending some rehearsals, studying a model of the setting and perhaps some of the completed set pieces, and looking at the actual fabrics purchased for costuming. At a certain point, with the plot complete, the lights are mounted (hung) in appropriate positions, attached to the theatre's wiring system (or wired separately), "patched" to proper dimmers, focused (aimed) in the desired directions, and colored by the attachment of frames containing "gelatins" (actually thin, transparent sheets of colored plastic). Ideally, the stage setting is finished and in position when all this occurs, but this ideal is rarely fully achieved, particularly on Broadway, where theatres are rented only a short time before the opening performance.

Once the instruments are in place and functioning, the lighting designer begins setting the intensities of each instrument for each cue, a painstaking process involving the recording of thousands of individual numerical decisions on a series of cue sheets for the precise instruction of technicians who must effect the cues. Computer technology has vastly simplified this process for those theatres able to afford "computer boards"; with or without computers, however, much time and care inevitably go into this process, which is vital to the development and execution of a fully satisfying lighting design.

Finally, the lighting designer presides over the working and timing of the cues, making certain that in actual operation the lights shift as subtly or as boldly, as grandly or as imperceptibly, as is appropriate for the play's action and for the design aesthetic.

It is out of thousands of details, most of which are pulled together in a single final week, that great lighting design springs. Gradations of light, difficult to measure in isolation, can have vastly differing impacts in the moment-to-moment focus and feel of a play. Since light is a medium rather than an object, the audience is rarely if ever directly aware of it — they are aware only of its illuminated target. Therefore the lighting designer's work is poorly understood by the theatregoing public at large. But everyone who works professionally in the theatre, from the set and costume designer to the director to the actor, knows what a crucial role lighting plays in the success of the theatre venture. As the "Old Actor" says as he departs the stage in off-Broadway's longest running hit, *The Fantasticks:* "Remember me — in light!" The light that illuminates the theatre also glorifies it; it is a symbol of revelation — of knowledge and humanity — upon which the theatrical impulse finally rests.

G. W. Mercier's fanciful costume is part of the delight in John Milligan's performance as Launce, in the 1991 Alabama Shakespeare Festival production of The Two Gentlemen of Verona, *directed by Festival artistic director Kent Thompson.*

COSTUME

Costume has always been a major element in the theatrical experience, a vehicle for the "dressing up" that actors and audiences alike have at all times felt to be necessary for the fullest degree of theatrical satisfaction. Costume serves both ceremonial and illustrative functions.

The Functions of Costume

The first theatrical costumes were essentially ceremonial vestments. The *himation* of the early Aeschylean actor was derived from the garment worn by the priest-chanter of the dithyramb; the comic and satyr costumes, with their use of phalluses and goatskins, were likewise derived from more primitive god-centered rites. The priests who first enacted the *Quem Queritis* trope in medieval Europe simply wore their sacred albs, hooded to indicate an outdoor scene but otherwise unaltered; the actors of the classic Japanese Noh drama even today wear costumes that relate more to spiritual sources than to secular life.

These ancient and original uses of costuming served primarily to separate the actor from the audience, to "elevate" the actor to a quasi-divine status. The thick-soled footwear (*kothurnoi*) worn by Greek actors in the fourth century B.C. were calculated to enhance this ceremonial effect by greatly increasing the height of the wearers, thereby "dressing them up" both figuratively and literally.

The shift of stress in costuming from a "dressing up" of the actor to a defining of the character came about gradually in the theatre's history. In the Elizabethan theatre the costumes often had an almost regal ceremonial quality because the acting companies frequently solicited the cast-off raiment of the nobility; English theatre of this time was known throughout Europe for the splendor of its costuming, but apparently little effort was made to suit costume to characterization. Moreover, it was not unusual in Shakespeare's time for some actors to wear contemporary garb on stage while others wore costumes expressive of the period of the play. In Renaissance Italy, costuming developed a high degree of stylization in the *commedia dell'arte,* where each of the recurring characters wore a distinctive and arresting costume that brightly and instantly signified a particular age, intelligence, and disposition. The same characters and the same costumes can be seen today in contemporary *commedia* productions, and they are still as eloquent and entertaining as they were four hundred years ago.

Modern costuming took on much of its present character in the eighteenth and nineteenth centuries, when certain realistic considerations took control of the Western theatre. These centuries witnessed a great deal of radical social change that led to, among other things, the widespread acceptance of science and its methods and a great fascination with detail and accuracy. These trends coalesced in the European (and eventually the American) theatre with a series of productions in which historical accuracy served as the guiding principle. For the first time, a massive effort was made to ensure that the design of every costume in a play (and every prop and every set piece as well) accorded with an authentic "period" source. Thus a production of *Julius Caesar* would be intensively researched to re-create the clothing worn in Rome in the first century A.D., a *Hamlet* would be designed to mirror the records of medieval Denmark, and a *Romeo and Juliet* would seek to re-create, in detail, the world of Renaissance Verona.

The movement toward historical accuracy and the devotion with which it was pursued led ultimately to a widespread change in the philosophy of costume design that persists to this day. For although historical accuracy itself is no longer the ultimate goal of costume design, stylistic consistency and overall design control have proven to be lasting principles. Costuming today stresses, in addition to an imaginative aesthetic creativity, a coordinated dramatic suitability as well; thus the influence of realism, with its attendant emphasis on historical accuracy, has fostered coherent and principled design in place of the near anarchy that once obtained.

This does not mean that costuming has lost touch with its ancient origins. On the one hand, we can still capture in the combination of bright stage lights and grotesque or exotic costumes the ceremonial magic conjured by ancient priests and modern-day shamans alike. What is more, our potential for capturing that magic is probably *enhanced* by costume consistency and control.

On the other hand, however, costuming has gained a great deal by its commitment to character definition and dramatic suitability. Costuming can provide the audience's first clues to a character's profession, wealth, class status, tastes, and self-image. More subtly, costume can symbolize human vices and virtues: sloth, vanity, benevolence, pride, generosity, for example. Some costumes are intrinsic to the characters who wear them—as Hamlet's "inky cloak" or Harlequin's parti-colored tights. By judicious use of color, shape, and fabric, costume designers can imbue every character

Costuming can signal a drastically reconceived production, as in the celebrated
Kabuki Medea, *which was conceived, directed, and designed by Shozo Sato at the*
Wisdom Bridge Theatre in Chicago in 1983. The production has subsequently
toured the United States, and Sato has embarked on a series of such "Kabuki-ized"
ventures. (Photo: Jennifer Girard.)

in a play with individuality. The collective costuming of a play, in addition to setting a
historical period and creating an overall theatrical style, can also convey social and personal meanings supportive of the text's intent;
consider, for example, Tennessee Williams's direction in *A Streetcar Named Desire* that the
poker players are to wear shirts of "bright
primary colors," to contrast them with
Blanche du Bois's dead husband, one "Allen
Grey."

The specific challenge of the costume designer, then, is to impart patterns of meaning
and an aggregate theatrical excitement to what
must finally be *wearable clothing for the characters*. For costume, of course, is clothing; it
must be functional as well as meaningful and
aesthetic. The actor does not model his costume; he wears it, walks in it, sits in it, duels
in it, dances in it, tumbles downstairs in it.
The costume designer thus cannot be content
merely to draw pictures on paper but must
also design workable, danceable, actable clothing for which cutting, stitching, fitting, and
quick-changing are as important considerations
as color coordination and historical context.

The costume as clothing gives rise to both
ensemble and individual impressions. As one
of an ensemble, the costume an actor wears
contributes not only to a play's overall symbolic effects, but also to its particularized milieu, to a specific "world" in which people are
seen to dress in special and perhaps unique
ways. This world may portray a period out of
the past, accurately rendered, or it may be
modern, or it may be a world fashioned out
of the purest fantasy; whatever the case, how-

ever, there is always a demand for a certain
costume coherence, even in the most inventive
and idiosyncratic productions. The very word
"costume," we might note, has the same root
meaning as "custom" and "customary"; and
the costumes of a particular world, theatrically
created, must be seen to represent the "customary costume" (or, in the same vein, the
"habitual habit") of the "inhabitants" of that
world. Costume, in other words, sets style; it
is the garb of choice for the general run of
people in the play.

And this leads us to an examination of the
importance of costume for the definition of
individual characters within the ensemble. A
character's adherence or nonadherence to the

IMPORTANCE OF SMALL DETAILS

The task of subtly distorting uniformity,
without destroying the desired illusion, is
a difficult one. Anton Chekhov's play *The
Three Sisters* presents a case in point. The
characters of the male players are clearly
defined in Chekhov's writing, but because
the men are all wearing military uniforms
they are theoretically similar in appearance. One of the few ways in which the
designer can help to differentiate between
characters is by the alteration of proportion; alterations such as these, which do
not show enough from the 'front' to make
the uniforms seem strange to the audience,
can be extremely effective, as well as helpful to the actor. In a London production
of *The Three Sisters*, Sir Michael Redgrave
wore a coat with a collar that was too low;
Sir John Gielgud one that was too high.
No one in the audience was unaware of
the characters' individuality, the talents of
these actors being what they are, but the
small details added to the scope of their
performances.

Motley

Costumes play major role in Luis Valdez's play and production of Zoot Suit, *in which the dress of 1940s Latinos living in the Los Angeles area becomes a metaphor for cultural pride and social advancement. Roberta Delgado Esparza, Daniel Valdez, Edward James Olmos, and Evelina Fernandez are featured in this Mark Taper Forum production. (Photo: Courtesy of the Mark Taper Forum.)*

"going dress" of the other characters in a play will always be loaded with significance. For costume is a character's way of expressing individuality and self-image: *it is the clothing he or she chooses to wear* within the context of the dress favored by his or her peers. When Hamlet wears his "inky cloak" to the royal court, for example, it signifies his refusal to adapt to his surroundings and the expectations of his superiors. It is both a mark of his character and a significant action in the play; it says a great deal about how he perceives himself and how he wants the world to see him. When Monsieur Jourdain in Molière's *The Bourgeois Gentleman* dons his fancy suit with the upside-down flowers and, later, his Turkish gown and grotesque turban, he is proclaiming (foolishly) to his peers that he is a person of elegance and refinement. And Estragon's unlaced shoes in *Waiting for Godot* represent — pathetically to be sure — his great wish to be unfettered, not "tied to Godot" but simply free, fed, and happy. Further, the battered bowler hats and smelly shoes that figure into that play, as well as the empty pockets in Vladimir's tattered overcoat, symbolize the fruitlessness of Gogo's and Didi's quest for salvation and at the same time suggest their reluctance to part with the familiar, the known quantity.

In Luis Valdez's *Zoot Suit,* the contemporary drama about Mexican-Americans in Los Angeles during World War II, the costume of the title acquires major significance, representing both the world of the play's central characters and the struggle of individual characters to stand apart from that world. Eugene Brieux's *The Red Robe* and Paul Claudel's *Satin Slipper* illustrate similar uses of costume elements as metaphor in modern (postromantic) drama.

The Costume Designer at Work

The costume designer works primarily with fabric—which comes in a variety of materials and weaves and can be cut, shaped, stitched, colored, and draped in innumerable ways. Aside from fabric, jewels, armor, feathers, fur, hair (real or simulated), and metallic ornamentation commonly figure into costume design.

The costume designer both selects and builds costume elements, usually in combination. The costumes for some plays are assembled entirely out of items ready at hand. For contemporary plays with modern settings, the costumes are often selected from the actors' own wardrobes or from department store racks. Sometimes a costume designer will acquire clothing from thrift shops and used clothing stores, particularly for plays set in the recent past; indeed, this is not unusual practice even for high-budget professional productions. In one celebrated instance, Louis Jouvet appealed to the citizens of Paris to donate costumes for the posthumous premiere of Jean Giraudoux's *The Madwoman of Chaillot,* and the clothing that poured into the Athénée theatre for that brilliant 1945 Parisian production signaled to the world that France had survived the scourge of Nazi occupation with its devotion to the theatre intact.

Even in a "fully designed, fully built" production, some costume elements are usually purchased, rented, or taken from costume storage; shoes, for example, are not ordinarily built from scratch for theatrical productions. Nonetheless, it is those productions that are designed and built for a given set of performances that test the full measure of the costume designer's imagination and ability. In these productions, subject only to the ultimate inspiration and control of the director, the costume designer can create a top-to-toe originality.

The comprehensive design for such a production begins with a series of sketches and material estimates—these usually proceed hand in hand—based on a thorough knowledge of the play, a clear agreement with the director on interpretation and style, research into necessary historical sources, and a firm understanding of the production monies and costume technologies available to the production organization. Generally, a separate costume sketch is made for each character, although choruses and "extras" are sometimes grouped in, or represented by, a single sketch; then, after such conferences with the director as needed to gain full support and approval, the sketches are developed into full-color renderings. When these are approved and the material estimates are "costed out" and budgeted, fabrics are purchased and appropriate sample swatches are attached to the corner of each rendering. Construction details are frequently included on the rendering itself, so that a single document conveys both the general look and specific construction of each costume.

The purchase of fabric is of course a crucial stage in costuming, for fabric is the basic medium of the costumer's art. Texture, weight, suppleness, and response to draping, dying, folding, crushing, twirling, and twisting are all considerations applied to the purchase of costume fabric. Velvet (and its synthetic substitute, velveteen), raw silk, woolens, and satin are the costumer's luxury fabrics; cottons, felt, burlap, and even painted canvas are less expensive and often quite appropriate for theatrical use. Coloring, "aging" (making a new fabric

Costume design does not always entail fresh construction; brilliant designs can often be a dramatic combination of existing garments and fabrics employed in unique ways. In Sam Shepard's A Lie of the Mind, *directed by the author, military decorations on an air corps flight jacket and an American flag ironically used as a scarf, create a provocative and indelible design element in a play that probes deeply into our national culture and mythos. Costume design by Rita Ryack. (Photo: Martha Swope and Associates.)*

appear old and used), and detailing are often achieved with dyes, appliques, and embroidery, and sometimes with paint, tie-dyes, and other special treatments (for example, the costume designers Motley—three women working under a single professional name—simulate leather by rubbing thick felt with moist yellow soap and spraying it down with brown paints).

Frequently, of course, printed or embossed fabrics with designs woven in are purchased for women's costumes or for male period attire.

The cutting, fitting, and stitching of original costumes are equally important stages in costume design. Most designers insist on at least some control over these procedures, for the cutting of a fabric determines the manner in which it drapes and moves, and the fitting of a costume determines its shape and silhouette. Needless to say, a "cutter" is a full-time professional in the theatre, and the designer must work in close collaboration with the cutter to achieve the intended result. Fitting and stitching (as well as refitting, restitching, and often re-refitting and re-restitching) are part of the obligatory and time-consuming backstage process by which the costume becomes a wearable garment for the actor and the actor "grows into" the theatrically costumed characterization.

Finally, the accessories of costume can greatly affect the impact of the basic design; occasionally they may even stand out in such a way as to "make" the costume or to obliterate it. Hairstyles and headdresses, since they frame the actor's face, will convey a visual message every time the actor speaks a line; they are obviously of paramount importance. Jewelry, sashes, purses, muffs, and other adornments and badges of various sorts have considerable dramatic impact insofar as they "read" from the audience—that is, insofar as the audience can see them clearly and take notice of what they may signify about the character. The lowly shoe, if unwisely chosen, can utterly destroy the artistry of a production, either by being simply unsuitable for the character or style of the play, or by being so badly fitted (or so unwieldy) that the actor stumbles awkwardly about the stage.

Good costuming for a play, whether arrived at through design and fabrication or through careful selection from the Army surplus store, creates a sense of character, period,

Costumes and accessories—masks, headdresses, parasols, purses, fire batons—make for a consummate costumography in this avant-garde production of The Bourgeois Gentleman *at the Théâtre de l'Est in Paris. (Photo: Marc Enguerand.)*

Witty irreverence and low-tech fantasy proved triumphant in the 1991 off-Broadway musical, Return to the Forbidden Planet, *which was billed as "Shakespeare's forgotten rock-and-roll masterpiece." This is the futuristic costume for a robotic Ariel (from Shakespeare's* Tempest*). (Photo: Martha Swope and Associates/Carol Rosegg.)*

style, and theatricality out of wearable garments. In harmony with scenery, make-up, and lighting, and with the play's interpretation and performance, costuming can have its maximum impact in a subtle way—by underlining the play's meaning and the characters' personalities—or it can frankly scream for attention and sometimes even become the "star of the show." Not a few musicals have succeeded primarily because the audience "came

out whistling the costumes," as a Shubert Alley phrase reminds us.

Certain theorists contend that costuming must at all times relegate itself to a subordinate role, and perhaps for most Western plays of the latter part of this century that has been a valid principle. But who is to say that the grand dancers of the Kabuki theatre, or the patchworked Arlecchino of the *commedia dell' arte,* or the stunningly garbed black-and-white mannequins of Cecil Beaton's creation in *My Fair Lady* represent any less a theatrical realization than their more modestly attired counterparts in other forms of theatre? Costume has always exerted a certain magical force in the theatre, lending a special magnitude to the actor's and the playwright's art. There are occasions when it seems altogether fitting and proper that this contribution should be celebrated in its own right.

SOUND DESIGN

The *sound designer* occupies a position of rapidly increasing importance in the theatre today. The sound designer's rise in prominence has been prompted by swiftly developing audio-technologies that now include computerized sampling devices, compact discs, miniaturized microphones and transmitters, and advances in electronic mixing and multiphonic sound. The influence of cinema is probably also a factor: modern audiences have become accustomed (and receptive) to near-continuous musical and sound underscoring for films and likewise for dramatic scenes in the theatre. These changes have made the sound technician's function vastly more demanding than that of the stagehand who just a few decades ago was expected to do little more than rattle a tin sheet to indicate thunder or play a scratchy record during scene changes.

As we have seen, the origins of theatre and music are intertwined (Aristotle included music as one of the six components of tragedy), and until about two hundred years ago no one even considered staging a play without music. Today the established popularity of the musical theatre, whether in the splashy Broadway format or the more socially expressive Brechtian one, exerts a continuing demand for both live and recorded sound that goes well beyond the simpler effects once required. Some sound "scores" for serious plays, such as the hoofbeats in *Equus,* the voices in *Wings,* and the offstage military band music at the end of *The Three Sisters,* are intrinsic to the text and indeed convey — often by contrast — the whole point of the actions they accompany. Finally, the amplification of live stage sound is becoming a major practice (much derided by many) in an attempt to give theatre the audible "boom-boom" punch of films, rock concerts, and certain religious revivals.

MAKE-UP

Make-up, which is essentially the design of the actor's face, occupies a curiously paradoxical position in the theatre.

In much modern production, make-up seems sorely neglected. It tends to be the last design technology to be considered; indeed, it is often applied (literally) for the first time at the final dress rehearsal — and sometimes not until just before the opening performance. Many directors spend little time planning for it, and rarely is an independent artist engaged to guide the make-up design of a contemporary play. Indeed, make-up is the only major design element whose planning and execution are often left entirely to the actor's decision.

And yet, ironically, make-up is one of the archetypal arts of the theatre, absolutely fundamental to the origins of drama. The earliest chanters of the dithyramb, like the spiritual leaders of primitive tribes today, invariably made themselves up in preparation for the performance of their holy rites: their make-up in later centuries inspired the Greek tragic and comic masks that are today the universal symbols of theatre itself.

Make-up and hair (the latter including facial hair) are key to the character's appearance. Beryl Reid and Bob Peck here play Lady Wishfort and Sir Wilfull Witwoud in Congreve's The Way of the World; costumes, make-up, and hairstyling help bring them back through the centuries. (Photo: Donald Cooper.)

The reason for this paradox resides in the changing emphasis of theatre aims. Make-up, like costuming, serves both ceremonial and illustrative functions. The illustrative function of make-up is unquestionably the most obvious one today — so much so that we tend to forget its other use altogether.

Illustrative make-up is the means by which the actor changes his appearance to resemble that of his character — or at least the appearance of his character as author, director, and

THE MAKE-UP KIT

Basic make-up consists of a foundation, color shadings, and various special applications.

The foundation is a basic color that is applied generally to the face and neck, and sometimes to other parts of the body as well. Greasepaint, the traditional foundation material, is a highly opaque and relatively inexpensive skin paint that can be purchased in tube or stick form in a variety of colors. Cake make-up, or "pancake" as it is commonly known, is also used for foundations; it is less messy than greasepaint, but also somewhat less flexible. Cake make-up comes in small plastic cases and is applied with a damp sponge. Most theatrical foundation colors are richer and deeper than the actor's normal skin color, so as to counteract the white and blue tones of stage lights. Foundations, whether of greasepaint or cake, should be applied thinly and evenly.

Color shading defines the facial structure and exaggerates its dimensions so as to give the face a sculptured appearance from a distance; ordinarily, the least imposing characteristics of the face are put in shadow and the prominent features are highlighted. Shading colors—which are universally called "liners" for some obscure reason—come in both grease and cake form, and are usually chosen to harmonize with the foundation color, as well as with the color of the actor's costume and the color of the lighting. Shadows are made with darker colors and highlights with light ones; both are applied with small brushes and blended into the foundation. Rouge, a special color application used to redden lips and cheeks, is usually applied along with the shading colors. When greasepaints are used, the make-up must be dusted with make-up powder to "set" it and prevent running.

A make-up pencil is regularly used to darken eyebrows and also to accentuate eyes and facial wrinkles.

Special applications may include false eyelashes or heavy mascara, facial hair (beards and moustaches, ordinarily made from crepe wool), nose putty and various other prosthetic materials, and various treatments for aging, wrinkling, scarring, and otherwise disfiguring the skin. A well-equipped make-up kit will include glue (spirit gum and liquid latex), solvents, synthetic hair, wax (to mask eyebrows), and hair whiteners in addition to the standard foundation and shading colors, so that the actor will be prepared to create a variety of make-ups without making additional trips to the make-up retailer.

actor imagine it. Make-up of this sort is particularly useful in helping to make a young actor look older or an old one look younger, and in making an actor of any age resemble a known historical figure or a fictitious character whose appearance is already set in the public imagination. Make-up gives Cyrano his great nose and Bardolf his red one; it turns the Caucasian Laurence Olivier into the Moorish Othello, and it makes Miss Sandy Duncan into Master Peter Pan. Make-up transformed the young Hal Holbrook into the old Mark Twain, and it permitted Cicely Tyson to portray a character's aging over an eighty-year period. Scars, deformities, bruises, beards, sunburn, frostbite, and scores of other facial embellishments, textures, and shadings can be mastered by the make-up artist's brush and can contribute significantly to realistic stagecraft when needed or desired.

A subtler use of make-up, but still within the realistic mode, is aimed at the evocation of psychological traits through physiognomic clues. For example, the modern make-up artist may try to suggest character by exaggerating or distorting the actor's natural eye placement, the size and shape of his mouth, the angularity of his nose, or the tilt of his eyebrows.

There can be no question that we do form impressions of a character's inner state on the basis of his observable physical characteristics—as Caesar notices and interprets Cassius's "lean and hungry look" so do we—and the skilled make-up artist can go far in enhancing the psychological texture of a play by the imaginative use of facial shapings and shadings.

Still another use of make-up, also within the realistic and practical spectrum, seeks merely to simplify and embolden the actor's features in order to make them distinct and expressive to every member of the audience. In theatre jargon this is known as creating a face that "reads" to the house—in other words, a face that conveys its fullest expression (that "can be read like a book") over a great distance. Make-ups that read in this way do so primarily by exaggerating highlights and shadows and by sharply defining specific features such as wrinkles, eyelashes, eyebrows, and jaw lines. Such simplified, emboldened, and subtly exaggerated make-up goes hand in hand with stage lighting and, in conjunction with it, creates an impression of realism far greater than any that could be achieved by make-up or lighting alone; in fact, a certain minimum level of make-up is thought by most actors and directors to be a necessity if only to prevent the actor from looking "washed out" in the glare of the stage lights.

Cyrano's famous nose is made of putty in this American Conservatory Theatre production. The Cyrano is Ray Reinhardt. (Photo: William Ganslen, ACT.)

Yet none of these realistic or practical uses of make-up truly touches upon its original theatrical use, which was aimed at announcing the actor as a performer and at establishing a milieu for acting that was neither realistic nor practical, but rather supernatural, mysterious, and calculatedly theatrical. For it was the white-lead make-up of Thespis and his fellows that endowed them with the same aspect of spiritual transcendence that warpaint provides for the celebrant in tribal rituals today: by making himself "up," the actor was preparing to ascend to a higher world; he was self-consciously assuming something of the power and divinity of the gods, and he was moreover offering to guide the audience on a divine adventure.

Today one still sees some obvious examples of such traditional make-up and "making up," particularly in the European and Asian theatres. The make-ups of the circus and the classic mime, two formats that developed in Europe out of the masked *commedia dell'arte* of centuries past, both use bold primary colors: white, black, and sometimes red for the mimist; these plus several more for the circus clown. Avant-garde and expressionist playwrights also frequently utilize similar sorts of abstracted make-ups, as did Jean Genet in *The Blacks,* which features black actors in clownish white-face, and Peter Handke, whose *Kaspar* featured similarly stylized facial painting. And the Japanese theatre, representative of much Asian practice, has always relied on the extreme colors and manelike wigs of the classical Noh and Kabuki now evolved into the violently expressive make-ups of the contemporary Tokyo avant-garde. The American theatre, which so far has witnessed only a small sampling of stylized make-ups, is perhaps due for an awakening to this fascinating approach to theatrical design.

But the realistic and symbolic functions of make-up are probably always combined to some extent in the theatre, for even the most stylized make-up is ultimately based on the human form, and even the most realistic make-up conveys an obvious theatricality. The theatre, after all, is never very far from human concerns, nor is it ever so immersed in the ordinary that it is completely mistaken for such. It might not be overly sentimental to suggest that when the American actor sits at a make-up table opening little bottles and tubes, moistening Chinese brushes and sharpening eyebrow pencils, more is going on than simple practical face-making: atavistic forces are at work, linking the actor not merely to the imagined physiognomy of his or her character or to the demands of facial projection in a large arena, but also, and more fundamentally, to the primitive celebrants who in ages past painted their faces to assure the world that they were leaving their temporal bodies and boldly venturing into the exalted domain of gods.

TECHNICAL PRODUCTION

We shall end this chapter with a discussion of theatre technicians.

They are the true proletariat of the theatre: the worker-artists whose functions, although various, all revolve around getting the production organized, built, installed, lit, and ready to open and then seeing that it runs. They far outnumber all the others — the actors, designers, writers, and directors — put together.

Because of their numbers, theatrical technicians are ordinarily marshaled into a hierarchical structure, with stage and house managers, technical directors, and production managers at the top, and carpenters, electricians, cutters, stitchers, wigmakers, publicists, make-up artists, stagehands, light and sound operators, prompters, and various running crews at the bottom. Top to bottom, however, they all play crucial roles in each theatrical presentation — and the "stage fright" of the actor playing Hamlet is not neccessarily any greater than that of the stagehand who must pull the curtain.

The great bulk of technical work in the

*We all dream, but theatre designers have the opportunity to re-create their
dreams — and the dreams of playwrights and directors — as artistic realizations. In
this 1989 American Repertory Theatre production of* Life is a Dream, *written by
Spanish Renaissance author Calderón de la Barca, designers Loy Arcenas (scenery),
Catherine Zuber (costumes), and Richard Riddell (lighting) create the highly surrealistic dreamworld. Anne Bogart directed. (Photo: Richard Feldman.)*

theatre is executed in accord with traditional
practices developed over centuries of theatrical
organizations and management; still, every
production poses a host of problems and situations in each technical area that are new to
the people asked to deal with them and, sometimes, new to the theatre itself. It is in the
junction of sound knowledge of craft with
creative imagination in the face of unantici-
pated problems that technological innovation
takes place; and the technical artists of the

theatre have always manifested an impressive
ingenuity at meeting unprecedented challenges
in creative ways.

Most theatrical crafts in the production
areas are learned through apprenticeship after
little or no preliminary instruction. Each of
the shops of the theatre — the scene shop, the
costume shop, the prop shop, and the make-
up room — is a laboratory of instruction as
well as a working unit of the theatre; most of
what is learned is acquired on site and in

action. Artistic components are never absent in the technical workings of the theatre: the painting of a set, the hanging of a lighting instrument, the timing of a scene shift, the sewing of a costume, and the calling of a sound cue are services that contribute mightily to the overall artistry of the enterprise. The technical crafts, therefore, are both learned and practiced in an aesthetic context, as a central activity of the theatrical venture. And although written and unwritten "textbooks" of stage practice can illustrate the traditional means of building a flat, cutting a pattern, organizing a rehearsal, and painting a prop, it is artistic sensitivity that ultimately determines the technical quality of a production, and it is artistic imagination that brings about the technical and technological advances.

Many separate production crafts go into building, promoting, managing, and running a show, and a separate textbook would be required to describe them all. Two of them, however, deserve special mention owing to the importance of their contribution to the growing art of stage production.

The *stage manager,* now often called the *production stage manager,* has the highly responsible position of overseeing all elements of production, coordinating all the director's work with that of the actors and the technical and design departments. At the beginning of rehearsals he or she is involved primarily in organizational work: scheduling calls and appointments, recording the blocking of actors, anticipating technical problems of quick costume changes, set shifts, and the like, and organizing the basic "calling" of the show — that is, the system by which lighting, sound, and scene shift cues are initiated. During performance, the stage manager actually runs the show, having final authority over the entire onstage and backstage operation; moreover, it

is the stage manager who ordinarily conducts understudy and replacement rehearsals in a professional run and who assumes the functions of the director when the director is absent or no longer employed by the production.

The *technical director,* who is also sometimes called the *production manager* (sometimes both titles exist in the same production) is generally in charge of the building and operation of scenery and stage machinery and may also have charge of the lighting crews and of all technical scheduling. The technical director must oversee the moving of scenery into and out of the theatre, assure all technical departments adequate "stage time" to do their jobs, establish policies and directives for scene shifting, special effects, and "strike" (the final removal of scenery from the theatre after a run), and, most importantly, make certain that everything is ready on time — no small order considering the massive technical complexities of theatre today.

The influence of Bertolt Brecht, as we have seen, has brought lighting instruments into plain view even for many "non-Brechtian" productions. It has also tended to pull the backstage technician into public awareness in recent years. A popular fascination with technology, together with a diminishing interest in stage "magic" or naturalistic illusion, has led to a scenography that deliberately incorporates the activities of scene technology as a visible aesthetic component of the theatre. Given this trend and the theatre's increasing use of newer and newer technical innovations — lasers and holograms, air cushions, videotape, and computerized slide projections, to name but a few — it would appear that the theatre technician is on the verge of being widely recognized as a full-fledged theatre artist and creator as well as a craftsperson and mechanic who executes the creations of others.

The room is already filled with people when she enters, a bit fussily, with a bundle of books and papers under her arm. Expectation, tension, and even a hint of panic can be sensed behind the muffled greetings, loose laughter, and choked conversation that greet her arrival.

She sits, and an assistant arranges chairs. Gradually, starting at the other end of that piece of furniture which suddenly has become "her" table, the others seat themselves. An edgy silence descends. Where are they going? What experiences lie ahead? What risks, what challenges, are to be demanded? What feelings, in the coming weeks and months, are going to be stirred to poignant reality?

Only she knows—or if she doesn't, no one does. It is in this silence, tender with hope and fear, that the director breaks ground for the production. It is here that plan begins to become work and idea begins to become art. It is the peak moment of directing and of the director.

This is an idealized picture, to be sure. There are many directors who deliberately avoid invoking an impression of "mystique" and whose primary efforts are directed toward dispelling awe, dread, or any form of personal tension among their associates. Nonetheless, the picture holds a measure of truth for every

CHAPTER **6**

THE DIRECTOR

The Irish-born, Harrow-educated playwright Richard Brinsley Sheridan wrote a century after the Restoration, but his "comedies of manners" were equally witty and delightful. His 1777 masterpiece, The School for Scandal, *is shown here in Paul Marcus's audacious 1988 production, mixing traditional design elements with contemporary props at the South Coast Repertory Theatre. Scenery by Cliff Faulkner, costumes by Shigeru Yaji. (Photo: Christopher Gross.)*

theatrical production, for the art of directing is an exercise in leadership, imagination, and control; in the director's hands, finally, rest the aspirations, neuroses, skills, and ideas of the entire theatrical company.

Directing is an art whose product is the most ambiguous, perhaps the most mysterious, in the theatre. The direction of a play is not visible like scenery or costumes; and unlike the actor's voice or the sound designer's score, it cannot be directly heard or sensed. And yet direction underlies everything we see and hear in the theatre. Utterly absorbed by the final theatrical experience, direction animates and defines that experience. A whole class of theatrical artists in our time has reached international eminence in this particular art. But what, exactly, is it?

At the *technical* level, the director is the person who organizes the production. This involves scheduling the work process and supervising the acting, designing, staging, and technical operation of the play. This is the easiest part of the directorial function.

At the more fundamental *artistic* level, the director inspires a creation of theatre with each production. He or she conceptualizes the play, gives it vision and purpose—both social and aesthetic—and inspires the company of artists to join together in collaboration.

It is in the conjunction of these levels, the technical and the artistic, that each director defines the directorial function anew. And it is with one foot in each that the director creates—through an adroit synthesis of text, materials, and available talent—a unique and vivid theatrical experience.

THE ARRIVAL
OF THE DIRECTOR:
A HISTORICAL OVERVIEW

Directing has been going on ever since theatre began, but there has not always been a director—that is, there has not always been an individual specifically charged solely with directorial functions and responsibilities. The evolution of the director as an independent theatre artist, less than a century ago, has had as much to do with the development of modern theatre as has any dramatic innovation. The gradual process of this evolution can be roughly divided into three phases.

Phase One: The Teacher-Directors

In the earliest days of the theatre and for some time thereafter, directing was considered a form of teaching. The Greeks called the director the *didaskalos,* which means "teacher," and in medieval times the director's designation, in all the various European languages, was "master." The underlying assumption of teaching, of course, is that a given subject is already known and understood; the teacher's task is simply to transmit what is known to persons yet unversed. The earliest directors, therefore, were simply asked to pass along the accumulated wisdom and techniques of "correct" performance within a "given" convention. Quite often the playwrights themselves served as directors, for who would be better qualified to "teach" a play than the person who wrote it? In one famous dramatic scene, Molière delightfully depicts himself directing one of his own plays; this is surely an effective model of the author-teacher-director for the seventeenth century and indeed for much of the theatre's history.

The teacher-director reached a pinnacle of influence, albeit anonymously, during the late Enlightenment and Victorian eras—during the eighteenth and nineteenth centuries—partly in response to the remarkable fascination of those times with science, scientific method, and humanistic research: the same dedication to rationalism that fostered a profusion of libraries, museums, and historic preservations also emphasized accuracy, consistency, and precision in the arts. The temper of the times led to major directorial changes in the theatre. For on the one hand, audiences were demanding revivals of classic plays—whose authors were no longer around to direct them—and on the other hand they were demanding that these revivals be historically edifying, that they have a museum-like authenticity. All this required research, organization, and comprehensive coordination; in other words, it demanded an independent director.

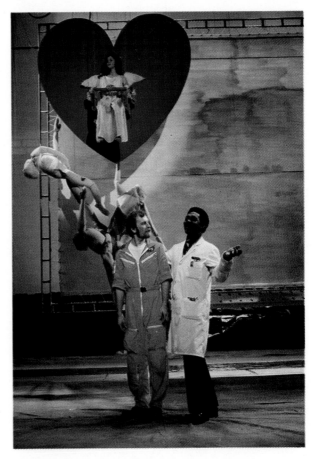

One of America's most exciting young stage directors in recent years has been Peter Sellars, who is also active as an opera director and as the artistic director for the Los Angeles International Theatre Festival. Illustrated is Sellars's typically unconventional staging of the Handel Opera, Orlando, *at the American Repertory Theatre in 1980–81.*

Most of the directors of this time—virtually all of them until the latter part of the nineteenth century—received no more recognition for their efforts than the museum director who created historical dioramas. Sometimes the directing was attributed to a famous acting star, such as the Englishman Charles Kean or the American Edwin Booth, when in fact the work was done by a lesser functionary; in Booth's case, for example, one D. W. Waller was the true director, but his name was all but buried in the program and never appeared in the reviews or publicity. Nevertheless, these teacher-directors who labored largely in the shadows began the art of directing as we know it today. They organized their productions around specific concepts, independently arrived at, and they dedicated themselves to creating unified and coherent theatrical works by "directing" an ensemble of actors, designers, and technicians toward established ends.

Phase Two: The Realistic Directors

The second stage in the development of modern-day directing began toward the end of the nineteenth century and brought to the fore a group of directors who restudied the conventions of theatrical presentation and strove in various ways to make them more lifelike.

George II, Duke of Saxe-Meiningen, was the first of this breed and is generally regarded as the first modern director. The duke, who headed a provincial troupe of actors in his rural duchy, presented a series of premieres and classical revivals throughout Europe in the late 1870s and 1880s that were dazzling in their harmonized acting, staging, and scenery. Although still historically "correct," the duke's productions featured an ensemble of performances rather than a hierarchy of "star, support, and supernumerary." All of his performers were vigorously rehearsed toward the development of individual, realistically conceived roles—which were then played out in highly organic, even volatile patterns of dramatic action. The stodgy line-up of spear carriers that had traditionally looked on while the star recited center stage was conspicuously absent from the Meiningen productions; so was the "super" who was customarily hired on the afternoon of performance, squeezed into a costume, and set upon the stage like so much living scenery. The totality of the Meiningen theatre aesthetic, embracing acting, interpretation, and design, was acclaimed throughout Europe: when the Meiningen troupe ceased

touring in 1890, the position of a director who would organize and rehearse an entire company toward a complexly and comprehensively fashioned theatrical presentation was firmly established.

In 1887 André Antoine began a movement of greater realism in Paris with his Théâtre Libre, and Konstantin Stanislavski initiated his even more celebrated Moscow Art Theatre in 1898; both of these directors, amateurs like the Duke of Saxe-Meiningen at the start of their careers, went on to develop wholly innovative techniques in acting and actor-coaching based on the staging concepts of the duke; both also theorized and worked pragmatically at the organizing of theatre companies, the development of a dramatic repertory, the re-education of theatregoing audiences, and the re-creation of an overall aesthetic of the theatre. Although both Antoine and Stanislavski were known primarily as naturalists—somewhat to their disadvantage, perhaps, for they had many other interests as well—they were above all idealists who sought to make the theatre a powerful social and artistic instrument for the expression of truth. Their ideals and their commitment virtually forced them to expand the directorial function into an all-encompassing and inspirational art.

The importance of these directors—and of certain other pioneers of the same spirit, including Harley Granville-Barker in England, David Belasco in America, and Otto Brahm in Germany—was not merely that they fostered the developing realist and naturalist drama, but also that they opened up the theatre to the almost infinite possibilities of psychological interpretation. Once the psychology of the human individual becomes crucial to the analysis and acting of plays, directors become more than teachers: they become part analyst, part therapist, and even part mystic; their *creative* function in play production has increased substantially. The rise of realism in the theatre of the late nineteenth and early twentieth centuries, and the rise of directors capable of bringing out realistic nuances and patterning them into highly theatrical productions, brought about an irreversible theatrical renovation that in turn irrevocably established the importance of the director.

Phase Three: The Stylizing Directors

Right on the heels of the realist phase of direction came a third phase—one that brought the director to the present position of power and recognition. This phase arrived with the directors who joined forces with nonrealist playwrights to create the modern antirealistic theatre. Their forces are still growing. They are the ones who demand of directing that it aim primarily at the creation of originality, theatricality, and style. The stylizing directors are unrestrained by rigid formulas with respect to verisimilitude or realistic behavior; their goal is to create sheer theatrical brilliance, beauty, and excitement, and to lead their collaborators in explorations of pure theatre and pure theatrical imagination.

Paul Fort, one of the first of these third-stage directors, launched his Théâtre d'Art in Paris in 1890 as a direct assault upon the realist principles espoused by Antoine. Similarly, Vsevolod Meyerhold, a one-time disciple of Stanislavski, began his theatre of "biomechanical constructivism" in Moscow to combat the master's realism. The movement toward stylized directing occasioned by these innovators and others like them introduced a lyricism and symbolism, an expressive and abstract use of design, an explosive theatricality, and certain intentionally contrived methods of acting that continue to the present day to have a profound effect on the theatre and its drama.

Perhaps the most influential proponent of this third-phase position of the director, however, was not himself a director at all, but an eminent designer and theorist: Gordon Craig. In a seminal essay entitled "The Art of the Theatre" (1905), Craig compared the director of a play to the captain of a ship: an absolutely indispensable leader whose rule, maintained by strict discipline, extends over every last facet of the enterprise. "Until discipline is understood in a theatre to be willing and reliant obedience to the manager [director] or captain," wrote Craig, "no supreme achievement can be accomplished." Craig's essay was aimed at a full-scale "Renaissance of the Art of the Theatre," in which a "systematic prograssion" of reform would overtake all the theatre arts—"acting, scenery, costuming, lighting, carpentering, singing, dancing, etc."—under the complete control and organizing genius of this newcomer to the ranks of theatrical artistry, the independent director.

The Contemporary Director

Craig's renaissance has surely arrived: this indeed is the "Age of the Director," an age in which the directorial function is fully established as the art of synthesizing script, design, and performance into a unique and splendid theatrical event that creates its own harmony and its own ineffable yet memorable distinction. If, as J. L. Styan says, "the theatre persists in communicating by a simultaneity of sensory impressions," it is above all the director who is charged with inspiring these impressions and ensuring this simultaneity.

Today, in a world of mass travel and mass communications, the exotic quickly becomes familiar and the familiar just as quickly becomes trite. Nothing is binding; the directorial function has shifted from teaching what is "proper" to creating what is stimulating and wondrous. At the beginning of a production the director faces a blank canvas but has at hand a generous palette. At his or her disposal are not only the underlying conventions of the time, but also all those of the past, which may be revived in an instant for novel effects and stunning juxtapositions. Our conglomerate theatre of today allows Shakespeare in modern dress, Greek tragedy à la Kabuki spectacle, theatre of the absurd as vaudevillian buffoonery, and romantic melodrama as campy satire.

Thus at the conception of a theatrical idea today—in the first moments of imagining a specific production—no question can be answered automatically, no style is obligatory, no interpretation is definitive. Jean-Paul Sartre has said about the whole of modern life that "man is condemned to be free"; in the theatre the director's freedom in the face of almost limitless possibilities leads to a certain existential anxiety that is both chilling and thrilling in its challenge.

DIRECTORIAL FUNCTIONS

Directing is not simply a craft; it is "directing" in the dictionary as well as in the theatrical sense: it is to lead, to supervise, to instruct, to give shape. In other words, it is to do what is necessary to make things "work." The director has final responsibility for *everything* that happens in a production, and so the "function" of a director must be, at least in part, subject to day-to-day demands and continuous improvisation.

Producer and Director

Part of what the director does in any given production will be determined by the possible existence of a *producer*. The producer is the person (or the institution) responsible for the financial support of the production: the producer may be a resident theatre, or a university theatre, or, as in Broadway or off-Broadway productions, an independent individual or partnership of individuals. In the regional theatre, the theatre's artistic director normally serves as the producer of each production in the theatre's season as well as the director of one or more plays; associate and/or freelance directors may be hired to direct other individual productions.

Where there is an active producer, separate from the director, it is the producer who is generally responsible for hiring the director, for establishing the production budget, and for determining the theatre facility and the production dates. The producer also normally plays an important role (if not *the* dominant role) in selecting the play, engaging the artistic staff (designers, technicians), and possibly even casting the actors.

As a result, functions listed below as "directorial" may in fact may be divided between the director and the producer. They remain "directorial" functions, however, inasmuch as they "direct" the artistic product that will finally appear on the stage.

Directorial Vision

Principally, the directorial function is one of *envisioning* the main lines of the production and providing artistic *leadership* necessary to realize that vision.

Envisioning, however, does not mean plotting out every detail in advance, nor does leadership mean dictatorship or tyranny. Directing means, quite literally, "giving direction," which implies choosing a point of focus and guiding everyone to face the same way. The talents of the play director are, in this regard, not unlike those of the bank director or the director of a research team: to provide goals, establish procedures, facilitate communication, drive the schedule, monitor the progress, encourage the timid, rein in the errant, heighten the stakes, refine the objectives, build the morale, and inspire absolute excellence from all and sundry. No two individuals will fulfill each of these functions in the same way, nor to the same degree. Directing clearly involves a confident and natural way of working with other people, as well as learned directorial technique. Artistic sensitivity, interpersonal skills, and an eagerness to accept responsibility (and exercise authority) should always be expected of the professional play director.

For purposes of discussion, individual directorial functions can be viewed as so many separate steps in the process of play production. The process, in fact, takes place over a period of weeks and sometimes years and is at no time as orderly as a schematic listing might suggest. Nonetheless, such a listing can help us to see the basic architecture of the directorial process and the progression of decisions and actions that bear upon the final production.

The steps divide easily into phases: a preparatory phase, which involves play selection, concept, staff selection, designing, and casting, and an implementing phase, which involves staging, coaching, pacing, coordinating, and presenting. All of these steps are continuous rather than segmented—a director is conceptualizing the production right up to the last minute and is pacing it at the instant the play is chosen—but they are generally centered in a time frame of relatively set order and organization.

Preparatory Phase

The preparatory phase of a production may take days or months or years; it is the director's dream world, wherein ideas germinate and begin to flower. Most directors are "in preparation" for several productions at once: even as one production is in rehearsal, others are taking shape in the mind. At various times these preparatory phases move from fancy to plain and from the world of dreams to the conference room, the rehearsal hall, and the scene shop.

Play Selection   The selection of a script is unquestionably the most critical single act of any director. The play is the essential theatrical product, so to speak: it is the basic element to which the audience responds—or thinks it responds—and it is universally perceived as the core of the theatrical experience. For this reason, play selection is the one directorial decision over which the producer—the provider of a pro-

duction's financial support—invariably reserves the right of review.

Three basic considerations go into play selection: the director's interest, the interest of the intended audience, and the capability of the director and producer to acquire, conceptualize, and produce the play.

Obviously, the director's interest is important because no director, save by chance, can create theatrical excitement from a script he or she finds dull and uninteresting. But at the same time it is part of the director's job to seek the excitement latent in a script and to imagine its various theatrical possibilities. Often a director who can envision the improvements to be gained by script revision, adaptation, or reinterpretation can discover plays that otherwise would be ignored; indeed, one of the marks of a great director is the ability to make us recognize the brilliance or beauty of a script we have unwittingly passed over.

The audience's interest is of even greater importance. It is the audience, after all, that makes the theatre possible; and the ability to assess an audience's needs and wants is absolutely fundamental to directing, both for pragmatic reasons (to ensure that an audience turns out to see the play) and for artistic reasons (to ensure that the play is satisfying and pertinent to those who come to see it). For a director directs not only the actors and designers but the audience as well and gives direction to their feelings and perceptions by the intellectual focus provided within the production. A director who discounts or ignores the interests—and the intelligence—of the audience stands little chance of creating any genuine theatrical impact.

Play selection that considers audience interest does not necessarily mean a reliance on the "tried and true"; quite the contrary, it means providing the audience with theatrical work that is fresh, fascinating, vigorous, and exciting. For some audiences, these ingredients can be provided by musicals, thrillers, and domestic comedies, for others by works of the European avant-garde, for others by plays of social protest and reform, for still others by new plays hot from the typewriters of yet unknown authors. There is an audience for every sort of good play, and it is the director's job to find that audience and attract it to the theatre. The audience demand is to be challenged as well as to be confirmed—and, in the long run, directors who lead their audiences are far more likely to gain artistic recognition than are those who either follow the audience or ignore them completely.

The capability of the director to produce the play adequately with available resources is the final requisite for sound play selection. Can the production rights to the play be acquired? Can a cast be brought together? a production staff? a theatre? Is there enough money? Interest alone—the director's and the audience's—will not buy the scripts, rent the theatre, pay for the electricity, or perform the roles. Considerations of quality must be factored in: are the available actors experienced enough to master the play's style? Is the costume budget adequate for the size of the cast and the period of the play? And finally, does the director understand this play well enough to bring out its ideas? A realistic consideration of one's own capabilities, together with an ability to assess the potential of one's expected collaborators, must be a significant factor in the critical decisions of play selection.

Concept More has been written in modern times about the director's role in conceptualizing a play than about any other directorial tasks; entire books have been devoted to the "directorial image," or the creation of the central concept that focuses and informs an entire production.

It is particularly with regard to those concepts that give unexpected and fresh insights into character, story, or style that the modern director has seized the imagination of the public. Like it or not (and there are many who do not), audiences and critics today are much more likely to admire (and remember) "high-concept" productions like Peter Brook's or A. J. Antoon's productions of *A Midsummer Night's Dream* (each illustrated in the chapter, Designers and Technicians) than they are "traditional" stagings of this sixteenth-century play.[1] Although the director runs a considerable risk with this kind of undertaking—for indeed Wild West Romeos, homosexual Hamlets, and Watergate Macbeths have more often been laughable than laudable—a brilliantly appropriate concept can completely captivate an audience by focusing a play production with such pertinence and meaning that it transcends time, place, and stylistic artifice to create profound, moving, and illuminating theatricalization.

The formation of a directorial concept takes place at both the conscious and the unconscious level; it takes place, in fact, whether the director wants it to or not. There is no avoiding it: it begins when the director first hears of a certain play, and it grows and develops as she reads the play, considers producing it, imagines its effects on an audience, and mentally experiments with possible modes of staging. The directorial concept is a product not only of the director's personal intelligence and vision, but also of the director's personal experiences that relate to the matters portrayed by the play as well as personal likes and lusts, appreciations and philosophical leanings, and desires concerning audience reaction to the final directorial product. The thought

---

[1]Indeed, what *is* a "traditional" staging of Shakespeare? We don't really know how the play was staged in Shakespeare's own time; what people call traditional staging is generally nineteenth-century staging, which is far removed from whatever Shakespeare intended. In truth, *all* stagings of Shakespeare and of other authors of his era are speculative and creative, governed by imaginative concepts as much as by historical research.

This "high-concept" production of Shakespeare's Twelfth Night *was directed, with jaundiced neoclassicism, by Andrei Serban in 1989, with scenery by Derek McLane and costumes by Catherine Zuber.*

processes by which the concept develops are both deductive and inductive, and they are set in motion with the first impressions the director receives from a play.

Concepts can be expressed in many ways. Often they are social statements ("this is a play about tyranny") or philosophical ones ("this is a play about self-knowledge"). Often they involve specific interpretations ("this is a play about a man who cannot make up his mind"), and often they invoke a particular genre of theatricality ("this is a revenge melodrama"). Frequently a director will state the concept psychodramatically ("this is a primitive ritual of puberty"), and frequently the concept is predominantly historical ("a play about fratricide in the Middle Ages") or imagistic ("a play about swords, sables, and skulls") or metatheatrical ("a play about playing"). Often

the conception of a play includes a basic tone ("sad," "heroic," "royal"), often a basic texture ("rich," "cerebral," "stark"). Diverse as these examples may seem, they all fall within the range of possibility in conceptualizing a single play: indeed, any one of them could be applied to Shakespeare's *Hamlet*, and probably at one time or another every one of them has been, as have hundreds of others besides.

The concept is the director's creation, and to a certain extent it remains primarily his or her own concern. It constitutes a personal organizing focus, the means of keeping the production aimed in a *specific* direction and impervious to deflection by tempting possibilities that might come to mind over the course of a production period. Therefore the concept, expressed succinctly but comprehensive in its implications, becomes the director's without the benefit of much conceptualization or with concepts flying in and out of the production process like so many blackbirds, but in today's multimedia, future-shocked world, theatrical excellence increasingly requires that the director have a strong and persistent conceptual vision.

Designer Selection   Although normally falling to the producer, the selection of production designers constitutes a vital step in the directorial process simply because both the playwright's script and the director's concept must ultimately be translated into concrete visual effects by a group of human beings of individual temperament, sensibility, and vision. The concept is the director's own creation, but its refinement and realization finally rest in the hands of collaborators, whose personal artistry and inclinations will inevitably play an enormous role in the shape and impact of the final product. Hence the selection of these individuals is by no means a mechanical or arbitrary task; it is a central directorial concern of great artistic consequence.

Director-designer teams are common in the theatre; some run for years, encompassing dozens of productions. Resident companies, whether national, regional, or community, often keep a core staff of directors and designers on the payroll year after year to facilitate continuing team relationships; most university theatre groups establish similar long-standing collaborations among faculty artists. Even the more fractious Broadway stage has its collaborations that span years and decades, although these teams work on a show-to-show basis rather than under continuing contract; Broadway directors frequently demand to work with certain designers whose work has proven sympathetic to their own in the past.

Ordinarily directors make every effort to find designers with whom they feel not only a personal compatibility but also a mutual respect and a synchrony of artistic and intellec-

starting point in choosing designers and actors, in initiating design discussions, and in setting the direction of the first rehearsals. Directing, of course, means giving *direction,* and the concept is the first and most decisive step in getting a particular production under way.

A great directorial concept has many qualities. It is specific, it is appropriate, it is evocative, it is visual, it is theatrical, it is concrete, it is original, and it is also a bit mysterious, a bit amusing. It *leads* the actors and the designers; and if it is truly inspired, it leads the director as well. Doubtless some play productions manage to attain a measure of success

The multi-hued sky in Robert Wilson's 1988 production of The Forest *silhouettes human, animal, and mythical creatures in an eerie arboreal setting. (Photo: Martha Swope Associates/Rebecca Lesher.)*

tual vision. Like all true collaborations, the most effective director-designer relationships result not in simple point-by-point agreement or master-slave autocracy, but in a give-and-take of ideas, plans, feelings, and hypotheses: a sense of sharing and complementary support.

Apart from these general considerations in designer selection, the director must look more specifically for the designers most appropriate for the play at hand: those whose abilities are best suited to the demands of the script and the director's conception of the production. Sometimes these specific considerations lead in a direction different from that generally indicated—away from the designer with whom the director feels most comfortable and toward the one who promises to be more helpful in narrowing and clarifying the director's concept. A designer's interest in a certain kind of scenic technology, for example, or in historical aestheticism or light cuing, can often help in many ways to sharpen the conceptual focus and provide insights through the design that will serve to inspire the production itself.

Designer selection, then, is a subtle and complicated process. The director chooses *people,* not colors or fabrics or instruments, and must select those people based on an estimate of their ultimate potential in the working conditions provided for them. Naturally the director will be interested in knowing something about the designer's previous work—and most designers can show prospective directors a résumé of experience and a portfolio of completed designs—but the director will also be interested in sounding out the designer's thinking and artistic sensibility. Like all decisions made in the developmental phase of production, the choice of designers will affect the entire production process; it is a choice that is difficult to retract, and the moment it is made it automatically closes certain directorial options and opens others that could prove either brilliant or catastrophic.

Designing The design phase of production marks the first step toward transforming vision into actuality: at this stage people turn ideas into concrete visual realizations.

The director's work in designing a production is generally suggestive and corrective; how well he or she succeeds in this delicate task is highly dependent on the personalities and predilections of the individuals involved. In theory, the director's and designer's goals in this phase are identical: actable space, wearable costumes, and an evocative, memorable, and meaningful appearance of the whole. In practice, each of the principals will have an independent perspective on what is actable, what is memorable, and what is evocative; moreover, each may have a different sense of the importance of sometimes contradictory values. A costume designer, for example, may place a higher value on the appearance of a garment than will the director, who may be more concerned with the actor's ability to move in it. A lighting designer may be greatly interested in the aesthetics of murkiness whereas a director may be more anxious that an actor's face be clearly seen at a particular moment. These are the sorts of artistic perspectives that must be reconciled in the design phase, which is essentially a collaboration in which the decisions are acknowledged to be subjective rather than "right" or "wrong"; it is a phase that demands qualities of leadership and artistic inspiration that are as sensitive as any the director may ever be called upon to exercise.

The design phase normally takes place in a series of personal conferences between director and designers, sometimes on a one-to-one basis and sometimes in group meetings. These are give-and-take affairs, for the most part, with the director doing most of the giving at the beginning and the designers taking over shortly thereafter. Often the first step is a collective meeting—the "first design conference"—at which the director discusses his or her concept in detail and suggests some possibilities for its visual realization: colors, images, spaces, textures, and technological implementations. Occasionally the director deliberately usurps a large measure of the designer's role, suggesting (or mandating) specific ground plans, sets, fabrics, and light colors and intensities, and proffering sketches of the finished work. Obviously, however, directors who so invade the designer's creative function risk losing precisely what they are trying to cultivate: the designer's talent and imagination. For this reason most professional directors seek primarily to stimulate, not stultify, the minds and abilities of the designers with whom they have chosen to work.

In the ensuing conferences, which are often conducted one on one and sometimes on an ad hoc basis, designers normally present their own conceptions and eventually provide the director with a progressive series of concrete visualizations: sketches (roughs), drawings, renderings, models, ground plans, working drawings, fabrics, technical details and devices. During these conferences the design evolves through a collaborative sharing, in which the director's involvement may range from minimal to maximal depending on how well the initial concept and the developing design seem to be cohering. Periodically—whenever the overall design effort reaches a stage requiring coordinated planning—full design conferences are called to review and compare current plans for scenery, costume, lighting, and property areas; these conferences afford opportunities for the designers to collaborate with each other instead of simply with the director.

The director's function at this stage of design is to approve or reject, as well as to suggest. As the person who sits at the top of the artistic hierarchy, the director has the last word on design matters, but that does not mean he or she can simply command the show into being: theatre design, like any creative process, cannot be summoned forth like an obedient servant. Moreover, wholesale rejection of a designer's work after the initial stages inevitably involves serious time loss and budgetary waste—not to mention the probability of some important staff resignations. For these reasons, the directorial effort must be committed from the outset to sound collaborative principles. Once under way, the director-designer collaboration must take the form of shared responsibility in a developing enterprise, not confrontation between warring artists attempting to seize the reins of aesthetic control.

Casting The cliché—"Casting is 90 percent of directing"—undeniably contains more than a germ of truth.

The people in a play—the actors—not only attract more audience attention than any other aspect of the play, but they also represent what the audience *cares* about and will remember the next day. They garner about 90 percent of all the interest an audience expends on a play, and if they squander that interest they can utterly destroy the effectiveness of any theatrical presentation.

When you look at theatre as a medium, you see many individual elements that are standardized and predictable: flats are made according to formula, lighting instruments are factory-calibrated to conform to precise specifications, color media are mathematically measured and numbered, and one theatre's black velours are virtually identical to those of another. The one absolutely unique ingredient of the theatre—as the audience sees it—is the actor. Actors are people, and as people they are exquisitely individual; moreover the audience, being human itself, is particularly attuned to the actor's human and idiosyncratic uniqueness. We would never mistake the Martin Dysart (in *Equus*)

Shakespeare called for Toby and his friends to hide behind a "box tree," but David Chambers set his intriguing South Coast Repertory Theatre production of Twelfth Night *in a kaleidoscopic Caribbean setting, and Toby and Andrew found themselves hilariously ensconced in tropical vegetation. (Photo: Christopher Gross.)*

of Richard Burton with the Dysart of Anthony Hopkins, or of Anthony Perkins, or of Alec McCowan. The actor's personality, physical and vocal characteristics, technical abilities, and sheer talent and "presence" weigh mightily in the final realization of every individual performance and in every ensemble of performances. A miscast or untalented or untrained actor can mar the effectiveness of any production even in a minor role; in a major role a poor performance simply ruins the play. Casting may not, in the end, account for 90 percent of the director's contribution, but there can be no doubt that bad casting renders all other efforts immaterial.

Most casting takes place in auditions, where the actor can be seen and heard by the director and associates either in a "cold" reading of material from the play to be produced or in a prepared presentation of previously developed material not necessarily related to the production at hand. Although "star" performers are often cast apart from auditions owing to their known ability to attract audiences to any production, most veteran professional actors regularly submit to auditioning; and the director's ability to detect an incipiently brilliant performance in the contrived audition format is a critical factor in effective casting.

The director looks for many things in an audition. Depending on the specific demands of the play and the rehearsal situation, the director may pay special attention to any or all of the following characteristics: the actor's training and experience, physical characteristics and vocal technique, suitability for the style of the play, perceived ability to impersonate a specific character in the play, personality traits that seem fitted to the material at hand, ability to understand the play and its milieu, personal liveliness and apparent stage "presence," past record of achievement, general deportment and attitude, apparent cooperativeness and "directability" in the context of an ensemble of actors in a collaborative enterprise, and overall attractiveness as a person with whom one must work closely over the next four to ten weeks. And the director might well be looking for a great many other things besides.

What is ultimately astonishing about the casting process is that most of the decisions based on these complex criteria are made not in agonizing conferences but in two- to four-minute "cold" auditions among perfect strangers! Indeed, this practice is often looked upon as a regrettable theatrical fact, but its very persistence indicates that a great many valid casting judgments can be made in a very short time—provided that time is used with wisdom and sensitivity.

Of course most of the decisions that are made that quickly—in the two- to four-minute initial audition—are "no" decisions; that is, those actors who are immediately perceived as wrong for the play, wrong for the part, or lacking in the desired level of proficiency, are winnowed out. Others may be winnowed out on the very subjective ground of apparent attitude—a dangerous ground because the director might mistake shyness for hostility or "audition jitters" for an exaggerated reserve.

Actors who survive the first audition are then "read" again, sometimes several times, and at this stage the director is involved more and more in the audition process, often coaching the actors to determine how rapidly they can acquire the qualities needed. Such "callbacks" can go on for days and even weeks in the professional theatre, limited only by the union requirement that actors receive pay for the fifth and ensuing calls; the frequency with which such payments are made amply attests to the care that attends final casting decisions in the professional theatre.

There is good casting and bad casting, of course, and there is also inspired casting. Many of the greatest performances in theatre history have been achieved by actors who at first glance might appear oddly suited to their roles: by Bert Lahr as Estragon in *Waiting for Godot,* for example, or by Laurence Olivier as the title character in John Osborne's *The Entertainer.* Franco Zeffirelli's casting of two inexperienced teenagers in his Royal Shakespeare Company production of *Romeo and Juliet,* much derided at the time, proved to be the spark of genius that made that celebrated production, and the film later adapted from it, two of the most memorable interpretations of the Shakespearean canon. And surely one of the finest King Lears in the American theatre was the late Michael O'Sullivan, who at the time he was cast in the role was still in his twenties and an unknown actor with the San Francisco Actor's Workshop. The ability to perceive an actor's unique and unexpected relationship to a specific role—and to chance that casting in place of a "safer" and more traditional choice—has always been the mark of the most daring and most successful film and play directors.

Implementation Phase

With the play selected and conceptualized, with the designers chosen and the designs under way, and with the actors auditioned and cast, the production moves from its perparatory phase to its implementation. It is here that the meeting described at the beginning of this chapter occurs; it is here in the silence between the completion of a plan and its execution that the blood begins to flow in a *corpus dramaticus* that heretofore lived only in the form of conversation and ink on paper.

The time structure of a production is a variable affair, but its direction is inevitably toward greater and greater tautness; that is, time becomes more and more precious as the play draws nearer and nearer to its opening performance. At the juncture between a production's developmental phase and its implementation, a major jump to a tighter time schedule takes place; what could conceivably be leisurely at the conceptual stage now becomes accelerated and intense. Now, because more and more must be done in less and less time, pressure becomes inevitable. Now the director's ability to maintain both leadership and creative inspiration under pressure—always an important element of professional skill—becomes absolutely crucial.

From the time of that first company meeting, the director controls the focus and consciousness of the entire cast and staff. As head of an ambitious and emotionally consuming enterprise, the director will be the repository of the company's collective artistic hopes—the focal point for the company's collective

Warner Shook's casting for The Kentucky Cycle *had to serve the nine different plays of the cycle; each actor had to play several roles, of varying ages, over many generations. Typecasting is useless in this situation: Katherine Hiler and Scott MacDonald play a young couple in this photo; later they play their aged descendants. (Photo: Jay Thompson.)*

frustration, its anxiety, and, on occasion, its despair. The company's shield against the intrusions of an outside world, the director is also the spokesperson for the enterprise to which the company has collectively dedicated itself. Directorial power or influence will not be substantially altered by any attempt the director may make to cultivate or repudiate it—it simply comes with the job, and with the need for every theatrical company to have a head, a focus, a direction. The manner in which the director uses that power, and the sensitivity with which he or she now brings the production into being, determines the nature of each director's individual brand of artistry.

Staging Staging—which essentially involves positioning actors on the set and moving them about in a theatrically effective manner — is certainly the most obvious of directorial functions. It is the one thing directors are always expected to do and to do well, and it is the one they are most often *seen* doing; it is no wonder that traditional textbooks on directing tend to be largely devoted to this function.

The medium of staging is the actor in space and time — with the space defined by the acting area and the settings, and the time defined by the duration of the theatrical event and the dynamics of its dramatic structure. The goals of staging are multiple and complementary: to create focus for the play's themes, to lend credibility to the play's characters, to generate interest in the play's action, to impart an aesthetic wholeness to the play's appearance, to provoke suspenseful involvement in the play's events, and, in general, to stimulate a fulfilling theatricality for the entire production.

The basic architecture of staging is called "blocking," which refers to the timing and placement of a character's entrances, exits, rises, crosses, embraces, and other major movements of all sorts. The "blocking pattern" that results from the interaction of characters in motion provides the framework of an overall staging; it is also the physical foundation of the actors' performance — and many actors have difficulty memorizing their lines until they know the blocking that will be associated with them.

The director may block a play either by preplanning the movements ("preblocking") on paper or by allowing the actors to improvise movement on a rehearsal set and then "fixing" the blocking sometime before the first performance. Often a combination of these methods is employed, with the director favoring one method or the other depending on the specific demands of the play, the rehearsal schedule, rapport with the acting company, or the director's own stage of preparation: complex or stylized plays and settings and short rehearsal periods usually dictate a great deal of preblocking; simple domestic plays and ex-

perienced acting ensembles are often accorded more room for improvisation. Each method can produce highly commendable results in the right hands and at the right time; both can present serious problems if misapplied or ineptly handled.

For the most part, the blocking of a play is "hidden" in the play's action; it tends to be effective insofar as it is *not* noticed and insofar as it simply brings other values into play and focuses the audience's attention on significant aspects of the drama. By providing a physical enhancement of the dramatic action and lending variety to the play's visual presentation, a good blocking pattern can play a large role in creating theatrical life and excitement.

But beyond this, there are moments when inspired blocking choices can create astonishing theatrical effects — effects that are not "hidden" at all but are so surprising and shocking that they compel intense consideration of specific dramatic moments and their implications. Such a *coup de théâtre* was achieved, for example, by director Peter Brook in his celebrated 1962 production of *King Lear,* when Paul Scofield, as Lear, suddenly rose and, with one violent sweep of his arm, overturned the huge oaken dining table at which he had been seated and sent pewter mugs crashing to the floor as he raged at his daughter Goneril's treachery. This stunning action actually led to a reevaluation of the character of both Lear and Goneril and of the relationship between this tempestuous and sporadically vulgar father and his socially ambitious daughter.

Some plays require quite specialized blocking for certain scenes — for duels, for example, or dances. Such scenes demand more than nuts-and-bolts blocking and are frequently directed by specialists, such as dueling masters or choreographers, working in concert with the director. These specialized situations are not at all rare in the theatre — almost every play that was written before the last century includes a duel or a dance or both — and the ability to stage an effective fight scene or choreographic interlude (or at least to supervise the staging of one) is certainly a requisite for

Staging battle scenes requires precise choreography: the fight must look dangerous but actually be safe. Usually a specialist — a fight choreographer — is assigned. Acting intensity, the use of real (if blunted) spears, throbbing music, and stage smoke make the battle scene exciting, but strict directorial control is required. JoAnne Akalaitis is the director of this 1989 production of Cymbeline *at the New York Shakespeare Festival. (Photo: George Joseph.)*

any director who aspires to work beyond the strictly realistic theatre.

"Business" is a theatre term that refers to small-scale movement — that which a character performs within the larger pattern of entrances and crosses and exits. Mixing a cocktail, answering a telephone, adjusting a tie, shaking hands, fiddling with a pencil, winking an eye, and drumming on a tabletop are all "bits of business" that can lend a character credibility, depth, and fascination. Much of the stage business in a performance is originated by the actor — usually spontaneously in the course of rehearsal — although it may be stimulated by a directorial suggestion or command. The director ultimately must select from among the rehearsal inventions and determine what business will become a part of the finished performance; when this determination is made, bits of business become part of the blocking plan.

Staging, then, in the largest sense, includes both hidden and bold blocking effects, specialized movements and small idiosyncratic behaviors, all combined into a complex pattern that creates meaning, impact, and style. Skillful staging unites the design elements of a production with the acting, creating an omnidynamic spatial interaction between actors, costumes, scenery, and audience, infusing the stage with life. Getting a play "on its feet," as the theatrical jargon puts it, is usually the first step in making it breathe; and the best staging is that which gives the actors the chance to breathe the air of the playwright's world and to awaken to the true vitality of the playwright's characters.

Actor-Coaching The director is the actor's coach, and in practice the director is likely to spend the largest share of his or her time exercising this particular function. The coach-

Acting "business" creates mood and atmosphere as well as subtle characterization. Here Trish Hawkins and Judd Hirsch smoke cigarettes in a production of Lanford Wilson's Talley's Folley *at Mark Taper Forum Theatre of Los Angeles. The manner in which actor holds cigarette, inhales or puffs smoke, and flicks ashes gives clues to character's personality. (Photo: Courtesy of the Mark Taper Forum.)*

ing begins at the first meeting with the cast.

Initially, it is the director who conveys the direction the production is expected to take: the concept, the interpretation, the intended "look" and style of the theatrical product. It is also the director who determines the schedule and process of work that will lead up to that final product. The director is the rehearsal leader and decides what activities — discussions, improvisations, games, exercises, lectures, research, blocking, or polishing — will occupy each rehearsal period; the director leads such activities with an eye to their ultimate goal.

Further, like the manager of an athletic team, the director is responsible for stimulating the best efforts of the cast and for instilling in them a high regard for teamwork (which in the theatre is called "ensemble") as well as for individual craft excellence and artistry. And, because the

work of the theatre invevitably demands of the actor a good measure of emotional, psychological, even irrational investment, the director has an opportunity (if not an obligation) to provide an atmosphere in which actors can feel free to liberate their powers of sensitivity and creativity. Good directors lead their cast; great directors inspire them.

The ways in which directors go about coaching actors are altogether various and probably more dependent on personality than on planning. Some directors are largely passive; they either "block and run," in the jargon of commercial theatre, or function primarily as a sounding board for actors' decisions about intention, action, or business. Conversely, there are directors closer to the popular stereotype, mercurial directors whose approaches at times verge on the despotic: they cajole, bully, plead, storm, and rage at their actors, involve themselves in every detail of motive and characterization, and turn every rehearsal into a mixture of acting class, group therapy session, and religious experience. Both methods, as experience teaches, can produce theatrical wizardry, and both can fail utterly; probably the determining factors either way are the

---

ACCORDING TO TEMPERAMENT

It is most important that the individuality of the actor, whatever be the character he is to interpret, be preserved, for individuality is an essential qualification of a great artist. So, at the outset, I suggest little to my people, in order to make them suggest more. I appeal to their imagination, emotion, and intelligence, and draw from them all I can. When I can get no more from them I then give them all there is in me. I coax and cajole, or bulldoze and torment, according to the temperament with which I have to deal.

David Belasco

Director Edward Payson Call directs actor Bill McCutcheon as Androcles in Shaw's Androcles and the Lion, *at the Denver Theatre Center. (Photo: Nicholas De Sciose.)*

strength of the director's ideas and the extent to which the cast is willing to accept his or her directorial authority.

Too little direction, of course, can be as stultifying to an actor as too much; the passive director runs the risk of defeating an actor's performance by failing to confirm it; that is, by withholding constructive response. Similarly, the extremely active director may, in a whirlwind of passion, overwhelm the actor's own creativity and squelch his efforts to build a sensitive performance, thereby condemning the production to oppressive dullness. For these and other reasons, most directors today strive to find a middle ground, somewhere between task-mastery and suggestion, from which they can provide the actor with both a goal and a disciplined path toward it while yet maintaining an atmosphere of creative freedom. Directors need not be actors themselves, but they must understand the paradoxes and

ambiguities inherent in that art if they are to help the actor fashion a solid and powerful performance. The greatest acting braves the unknown and flirts continuously with danger (the danger of exposure, of failure, of transparency, of artifice); the director must give the actor a careful balance of freedom and guidance in order to foster the confidence that leads to that kind of acting. Directors who are insensitive to this requirement—no matter how colorful their stormings and coaxings or how rational their discussions of the playwright's vision—are virtually certain to forfeit the performance rewards that arise from the great actor-director collaborations.

Pacing Despite all the director's responsibilities, pace is perhaps the only aspect of a theatrical production for which general audiences and theatre critics alike are certain to hold the director accountable. Frequently, newspaper reviews of productions devote whole paragraphs of praise or blame to the actors and designers and evaluate the director's contribution solely in terms of the play's pace: "well-paced" and "well-directed" are almost interchangeable plaudits in the theatre critic's lexicon; and when a critic pronounces a play "slow" or "dragging," everyone understands he or she is firing a barrage at the director.

To the novice director (or critic), pace appears to be primarily a function of the rate at which lines are said; hence a great many beginning directors attempt to make their productions more lively simply by instructing everyone to speak and move at a lively clip: "More energy!" and "Make it happen faster!" are somewhat generalized expressions of a director's suspicion that the production somehow lacks the proper pace.

But pace is fundamentally determined by a complex and composite time structure that must be developed to accommodate many variables, such as credibility, suspense, mood, style, and the natural rhythms of life: heartbeat, respiration, the duration of a spontaneous sob and an unexpected laugh. How much time is properly consumed, for example, by a moment of panic? a pregnant pause? a flash of remembrance? an agonized glance? a quick retort? These are the ingredients of pace and are not subject to the generalized "hurry-up" of the director who has not first discovered the pattern of rhythms inherent in a play.

The pace of a play should be determined largely by the quantity and quality of the information it conveys to the audience, and the director must decide how much time the audience requires to assimilate that information. In a farce, of course, the audience needs almost no time to synthesize information—therefore, farce generally is propelled rapidly, with the audience virtually assaulted with information coming as fast as the actors can get it out. A psychological drama, on the other hand, may require of the audience a deeper understanding of its characters and issues; sympathy is engendered as we have an opportunity to compare the characters' lives with our own, to put ourselves in their situations, and to engage in introspection even as we observe the action on stage. Similarly, political drama commonly demands of us a critical inquiry into our own societies and our own lives as part of our understanding of what is happening on stage; this form, too, demands time to linger over certain perfectly poised questions — and the pace of a production must give us that time.

As a symphony is composed of several movements, so a well-paced theatrical production will inevitably have its adagio, andante, and allegro tempos. Faster tempos tend to excite, to bedazzle, and to sharpen audience attention; slower ones give the audience a chance to consider and to augment the play's actions and ideas with their own reflections. Often directors speak in terms of "setting up" an audience with a rapid pace and then delivering a "payoff" with a powerful, more deliberately paced dramatic catharsis. The sheer mechanics of theatrical pacing demand the greatest skill and concentration on the part of both actor and director, and for both the perfection of dramatic timing (and most notably comic timing) is a mark of great theatrical artistry.

Directors vary in their manner of pacing plays, of course. Some wait until final rehearsals and then, martinet-like, stamp our rhythms on the stage floor with a stick or clap their hands in the back of the house. Some work out intricate timing patterns in the very first rehearsals and explore them in great detail with the actors as to motivation, inner monologue, and interpersonal effect. Directorial intervention of some sort is almost always present in the achievement of an excellent dramatic pace; it rarely occurs spontaneously. Actors trained to the realist manner often tend to work through material slowly and to savor certain moments all out of proportion to the information they convey; actors trained in a more technical manner just as often are "off

to the races" with dialogue, leaving the audience somewhat at sea about the meaning or importance of the matters at hand. And when a variety of actors, trained in different schools, come together in production for the first time, they can create such an arrhythmic pace that the play becomes virtually unintelligible until the director steps in to guide and control the tempo.

Coordinating In the final rehearsals the director's responsibility becomes more and more one of coordination: of bringing together the concept and the designs, the acting and the staging, the pace and the performance. Now all the production elements that were developed separately must be judged, adjusted, polished, and perfected in their fuller context. Costumes must be seen under lights, staging must be seen against scenery, pacing must include the shifting of sets, acting must coalesce with sound amplification, and the original concept must be reexamined in light of its emerging realization. Is the theme coming across? Are the actions coming across? Can the voices be heard and understood? Do the costumes read? Is the play focused? Is the play interesting? Do we care about the characters? about the themes? about anything? Does the production seem to *work?*

Timing and wholeness are governing concepts in this final coordinating phase of production. In assessing the play's overall timing, the director must be prepared to judge the play's effectiveness against its duration and to modify or even eliminate those parts of the production that simply overextend the play's potential for communicating information, feelings, or ideas. Last-minute cutting is always a painful process — certainly much labor and creative spirit have gone into those parts that will be cut — but many a production has been vastly improved by judicious pruning at this time. And in the interest of providing wholeness — that quality which unifies a play and gives it the stamp of taste the aesthetic as-

Scenes of vigorous conflict and peaceful contemplation by firelight alternate in Peter Brook's mesmerizing production of The Mahabharata, *an all-day performance that re-created portions of India's great epic poem for international Western audiences. Keeping the pace varied is particularly essential for extended dramas such as this. (Photos: Michel Dieuzaide.)*

surance—the best and bravest directors are willing in these final moments to eliminate those elements that fail to cohere with the play's overall appearance and significance. Often these elements hold a special meaning for the director; they may even have figured into his or her earliest conception of the production. But now, in the cold light of disciplined analysis, they look painfully like directorial indulgence or extraneous showing off. The best directors are those who can be most rigorous with themselves at this stage, for they are the ones who are capable not only of generating ideas but also of refining and focusing artistic form.

In the final rehearsals—the "technical rehearsals" when scenery, lighting, and sound are added, and the "dress rehearsals" when the actors don costumes and make-up for the first time—the director arrives at a crossroads: although remaining fundamentally responsible for every final decision about the timing and balance of theatrical elements, he or she must now "give over" the production to the actors and technicians who will execute it. Beyond this junction the director will be consumed, as it were, by the production and will disappear within

it in a matter of days: it will reflect the director's personal conceptions and directorial skills without reflecting the director's own *persona*. After contributing to everything that appears upon the stage and initiating much of it, the director must accept the fact that he or she will not be recognized in any single moment, any single act, any single costume or lighting cue. In these final rehearsals the director's presence normally becomes more a force for organization than a source of inspiration—clipboard in hand, he or she delivers hundreds of last-minute "notes" to actors, technicians, and stage managers in an effort to give the production that extra finesse which distinguishes the outstanding from the mediocre.

And what an extraordinary exchange of power has taken place between the first meeting of the cast and director and these final days! Whereas earlier the entire production was in the director's head and the cast waited in awe and expectation, now the actors hold the play in their heads and everyone confronts the unknowns of the play's reception. The actors have a new master now: the audience. It is in these days that even the most experienced actors confront their fundamental nakedness in performance: they must face the audience, and they must do it without benefit of directorial protection, with nothing to shield them save their costumes, characters, and lines. At these times the actor comes to see the director as no longer leader but partner, no longer parent but friend. Actors may indeed experience a certain feeling of betrayal; the director, after all, has abandoned them to face the audience alone, just as Good Deeds accompanied Everyman only to the brink of the grave. But then acting, like death, is a trial that cannot be shared.

Presenting It is an axiom of the theatre that nobody is more useless on opening night than the director. If all has progressed without major catastrophe and the production has successfully been "given over" to those who will run it and perform in it, the director's task on opening night consists chiefly in seeing and evaluating the production and gauging the audience response. This night may, of course, prove to be nothing but a calm between storms, and in the professional theatre it may simply be the first of a series of opening nights, one calculated to serve as a guide to future rehearsals, rewritings, and rethinkings; still, at this time the major work has reached a stopping point and invariably the director must shift perspectives accordingly.

The director in this last phase sometimes takes on certain responsibilities of a somewhat paratheatrical nature, such as writing directorial "notes" for use in newspaper stories and interviews, overseeing the house management, the dress of the ushers, the lobby decorations, the concession stands, or the "dressing of the house" (the spacing of spectators in a less than full house). The director may also play an active role as audience member by greeting patrons, chatting with critics, or leading the laughter and applause — although it should be stated that all of these activities are more common in community theatres than in professional ones.

More central to the directorial function in this final stage is the director's continuing evaluation of every production element in an effort to improve the audience impact. This may lead to changes at any time during the run of a play. In the professional theatre, new productions commonly go through a tryout period of two weeks or more — up to a year in a few cases — when the play is rehearsed and re-rehearsed daily between performances and material is deleted, revised, restaged, and freshly created in response to audience reception. Some quite famous plays have succeeded only because of such "doctoring" during tryout periods, and it is not at all uncommon in the contemporary commercial theatre for a director to be replaced during this phase in order to accelerate revision.

Even after the final opening, however, and throughout the run of a play, most directors attend performances periodically and follow up their visits with notes to the actors — either to encourage them to maintain spontaneity or to discourage them from revising the original directorial plan. One perhaps apocryphal show business story has it that the American director George Abbott once posted a rehearsal call late in a play's run in order to "take out the improvements."

Just as the actor might feel alone and somewhat betrayed in those empty moments prior to opening performance, so might the director feel a twinge of apartness at the ovation that follows the first performance. For it is in that curtain call ovation that the audience takes over the director's critic-mentor function and the director is consigned to anonymity. The actors, heady with the applause, suddenly remember that it is they who provide the essential ingredient of theatre, while the director, cheering the ensemble from the back of the house, suddenly realizes he or she is now just one of the crowd, one witness among many to the realization of his or her own intangible and now remote plans and ideas. In the professional theatre, it is at precisely this moment that the director's contract expires—a fitting reminder of the "giving over" that occurs in the direction of all plays. Only those directors who can derive genuine satisfaction from creating out of the medium of others' performance will thrive and prosper in directorial pursuits; those who aspire to public acclaim and adulation will most likely face perpetual frustration as practitioners of this all-encompassing and yet all-consuming art.

THE TRAINING OF A DIRECTOR

Traditionally, directors have come to their craft from a great many areas, usually after achieving distinction in another theatrical discipline: for example, Elia Kazan was first an actor, Gower Champion was a choreographer, Harold Prince was a producer, Peter Hunt was a lighting designer, Franco Zeffirelli was a scene designer, Robert Brustein was a drama critic, Harold Pinter was a playwright, Mike Nichols was an improvisational comedian and Robert Wilson was an architectural student. Still, in addition to a specialty, most of these directors have brought to their art a comprehensive knowledge of the theatre in its various aspects. Having distinction in one field is important chiefly insofar as it gives directors a certain confidence and authority—and it gives others a confidence in their exercise of that authority. But it is comprehensive knowledge that enables directors to collaborate successfully with actors, designers, managers, playwrights, and technicians with facility and enthusiasm.

New directors entering the profession today are more likely than not to have been trained in a dramatic graduate program or conservatory—and often they have supplemented this training with an apprenticeship at a repertory theatre. One of the most remarkable recent developments in the American theatre has been the emergence of a cadre of expertly trained directors: men and women with a broad understanding of the theatre and a disciplined approach to directorial creativity.

Well-trained directors will possess, in addition to the craft mastery of staging, actor-coaching, pacing, and production coordinating, a strong literary imagination and an ability to conceptualize intellectually and visually. They will be sensitive to interpersonal relationships, which will play an important role in both the onstage and offstage activities under their control. They will have a sound working knowledge of the history of the theatre, the various styles and masterworks of dramatic literature, the potential of various theatre technologies, and the design possibilities inherent in the use of theatrical space. They will have at their command resources in music, art, literature, and history; they will be able to research plays and investigate production possibilities without starting at absolute zero; and they will be able to base ideas and conceptions on sound social, psychological, and aesthetic understandings.

All these rather advanced skills can be effectively taught in a first-rate drama program, and for that reason today's top-flight theatre directors, more than any other group of stage artists, are likely to have studied in one or another of the rigorous drama programs now in place across the country. The accomplished director is perhaps the one all-around "expert" of the theatre; this it not to deride the director's function as a creative and imaginative force, but to emphasize his or her responsibility over a broad and highly complex enterprise. Nothing is truly irrelevant to the training of a director, for virtually every field of knowledge can be brought to bear upon theatre production. The distinctiveness of any production of the contemporary theatre is in large measure a reflection of the unique but comprehensive training of its *director*, who is responsible not only for the overall initiative and corrective authority that infuse the production, but also for the personal vision that inspires its singular *direction*.

The theatre has existed in many great periods — the Golden Age of Athens, the Elizabethan Era, the Age of Louis XIV — but one of the great periods of theatrical history is still going on. This is the period we call the modern, in addition to an onrush of avant-garde movements we may call (for the time being) the postmodern. Together, these make up the theatre of our times, a theatre that will likely be heralded for *all* times.

Modern drama can be said to date back to about 1875, and its roots lie deep in the social and political upheavals that developed out of the eighteenth century Enlightenment and dominated European and American culture in the nineteenth century. It is wise to look briefly at the premodern era so as to more fully understand our own.

Revolution characterizes those times. Political revolution in the United States (1776) and France (1789) irrevocably changed the political structure of the Western world, and industrial-technological revolution cataclysmically overhauled the economic and social systems of most of the world. In the wake of these developments came an explosion of public communication and transportation, a tremendous expansion of literacy, democracy, and public and private wealth, and a universal demographic shift from country to town.

CHAPTER 7

THE THEATRE OF OUR TIMES

These forces combined to create in Europe and the United States mass urban populations hungering for social communion and stimulation: a fertile ground for the citified and civilized theatre of our times.

Simultaneously, an intellectual revolution—in philosophy, in science, in social understanding, and in religion—was altering human consciousness in ways far transcending the effects of revolutionary muskets and industrial consolidation. The intellectual certainty of Louis XIV, whose divine right to rule was unquestioned in the seventeenth and early eighteenth centuries, appeared ludicrous in an age governed by secular scientific investigation. The clear-sightedness of a playwright such as Molière seemed simplistic in an age of existentialism signaled by the soul-searching, self-doubting analyses of Søren Kierkegaard.

The intellectual revolution was an exceedingly complex phenomenon that occurred in many spheres of thought and was to gain momentum with each passing decade. It continues to this day.

The Copernican theory had already made clear that human beings do not stand at the

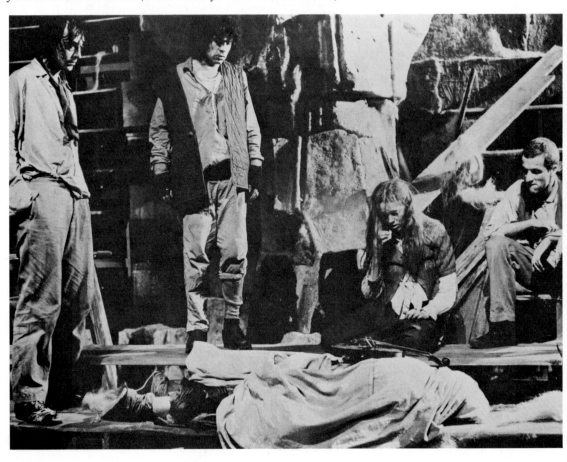

Elements of realism are everywhere apparent in this photograph of a modern production of Victor Hugo's romantic verse trilogy The Burgraves *(1843). Scenery, costume, make-up, and acting in this 1978 production—by the Théâtre de Gennevilliers in France—are realistically detailed, but the plot and language are from the romantic tradition. (Photo: Courtesy French Cultural Services.)*

geographic center of the universe, but rather that our world, indeed our universe, is swept up in a multiplicity of interstellar movements. Later scientists would press further than that, until eventually the revelations of Albert Einstein, Werner Heisenberg, and others would remove all our "hitching posts in space" and establish the human animal as little more than a transformation of kinetic energy, wobbling shiftily in a multigravitational atomic field marked by galaxies and black holes, neutrinos and quarks, matter and antimatter, all in a vast dance of inexplicable origin and doubtful destiny.

Nor was that "human animal" so vastly privileged over other species, it would seem. Darwin would argue that we *homo sapiens* are directly linked to other mammals — descended not from Adam and Eve, nor pre-Hellenic demigods, but from primal apes and prehistoric orangutans. Our morals and religions, anthropologist Ruth Benedict would argue, were not handed down to all humanity from a single source, but are instead a ranging complex of laws and traditions, wholly relative to the climes and cultures we inhabit. The work of Freud would disclose the existence of the Unconscious, a dark and lurking inner self aswarm with infantile urges, primordial fantasies, and suppressed fears and rages. The writings of Karl Marx would contend that all social behavior has its basis in economic greed, class struggle, and primal amorality. "Everlasting uncertainty and agitation" is the nature of human intercourse, according to Marx, and society comprises "two great hostile camps" continually engaged in civil war.

These and scores of other serious challenges to previous thinking were accompanied everywhere by public debate and dispute. By the turn of the present century, an investigative ferment had seized European and American civilization: data were being collected on every conceivable topic, and scientific questioning and testing replaced intuition and dogma as the accepted avenues to truth. Experimentation, exploration, documentation, and challenge became the marching orders of artist and intellectual alike.

The modern theatre has its roots in these political, social, and intellectual revolutions. Ever since its outset it has been a theatre of challenge, a theatre of experimentation. It has never been a theatre of rules or simple messages, nor has it been a theatre of demigods or of absolute heroes and villains. It has reflected, to a certain degree, the confusions of its times, but it has also struggled to clarify and to illuminate, to document and explore human destiny in a complex and uneasy universe.

THE PRECURSOR: ROMANTICISM

The first theatre to respond wholeheartedly to the challenge and experimentation of the Enlightenment was the theatre inspired by *romanticism,* an artistic movement that began in Europe in the late eighteenth century and reached its theatrical apogee in the nineteenth century with such works as Friedrich Schiller's *The Robbers* (1782), Johann Wolfgang von Goethe's *Faust* (Part 1, 1808), Victor Hugo's *Hernani* (1830), and the dramatization by Alexandre Dumas (Dumas *père*) of his novel *The Three Musketeers* (1844). Romanticism was a movement deliberately conceived in rebellion against the constraints of earlier conventions; romantic playwrights strove mightily — and self-consciously — to free dramaturgy from the strictures of neoclassic formulas by means of flamboyant verse, boisterous action, epic adventure, passionate feeling, and majestic style. With its emphasis on free-form, picaresque stories, exotic locales, outsized heroes and villains, and sprawling dramatic structure, romanticism gave rise to an imaginative and awesome theatricality that survives today primarily in the form of grand opera and "space odyssey" films.

Because of its emphasis on nonconformity and individuality and its refusal to accept rules for the theatre, romanticism is a true precursor of all modern dramatic movements and styles. Some of these, such as realism, can be seen as direct and even logical outgrowths of romanticism; others, such as the theatre of the absurd and the theatre of alienation, bear no obvious similarity to romanticism apart from their adventurousness and their conspicuous innovation. Some romantic strains, however, can be found in virtually all modern plays and play productions.

REALISM

Thus far, the movement that has had the most pervasive and long-lived effect on modern theatre is, beyond question, realism.

Realism has sought to create a drama without conventions or abstractions, in simple consonance with life itself. *Likeness to life* is realism's goal; and in pursuit of that goal it has renounced, among other things, idealized or prettified settings, versifications, contrived endings, and stylized costumes and performances.

Realism is a beguiling aesthetic philosophy, since the theatre has *always* taken "real life" as its fundamental subject; and so realism seems at first glance to be an appropriate style with which to approach the reality of existence. Instead of having actors represent characters, the realists would say, let us have the actors *be* those characters; instead of having dialogue stand for conversation, let us have dialogue that *is* conversation; instead of scenery and costumes that convey a sense of time and place and atmosphere, let us have scenery that is genuinely inhabitable and costumes that are real clothes.

It is perhaps unnecessary to point out that realism has its limits — that any dramatic piece must inevitably involve a certain shaping and stylization, no matter how lifelike its effect; the advocates of theatrical realism are well aware of this inevitability. Nevertheless, the ideology of realism was tested, during the last years of the nineteenth century and the first years of the present one, in every aspect of

theatre — acting, directing, design, and playwriting — and the results of those tests form a body of theatre that is both valid and meaningful and a style that remains enormously significant.

In essence, the realistic theatre is conceived to be a laboratory in which the nature of relationships, or the ills of society, or the symptoms of a dysfunctional family are "objectively" set down for the final judgment of an audience of impartial observers. Every aspect of realistic theatre should strictly adhere to the "scientific method" of the laboratory; nothing must ring false. The setting is to resemble the prescribed locale of the play as closely as possible; indeed, it is not unusual for much of the scenery to be acquired from a real-life environment and transported to the theatre (in one famous instance, American producer David Belasco went so far as to purchase a New York restaurant, dismantle it, and rebuild it within the confines of his Broadway stage). Costumes worn by characters in the realistic theatre follow the actual dress of "real" people of similar societal status; dialogue is prized as it re-creates the cadences and expressions of daily life.

Early on in the realist movement, the proscenium stage was modified to accommodate scenery constructed in box sets, with the walls given full dimension and with real bookcases, windows, fireplaces, swinging doors, and so forth built into the walls just as they are in a house interior. In the same vein, the acting of the realists was judged effective insofar as it was drawn from the behavior of life and insofar as the actors seemed to be genuinely speaking to each other instead of playing to the audience. A new aesthetic principle was spawned: "the theatre of the fourth wall," in which the life on stage was conceived to be the same as life in a real-world setting, except that, in the case of the stage, one wall — the proscenium opening — had been removed. Thus the "fourth wall" theatre was like a laboratory telescope and the stage like a microbiologist's slide: a living environment set up for judicious inspection by neutral observers.

And so realism presents its audience with an abundance of seemingly real-life "evidence" and permits each spectator to arrive at his or her own conclusions. There is some shaping of this evidence by author and performer alike, to be sure, but much of the excitement of the realistic theatre is occasioned by the genuine interpretive freedom it allows the audience and by the accessibility of its characters, whose behaviors are familiar enough to the average spectator that they may be easily assimilated and identified.

Moreover, in presenting its evidence from the surface of life, realism encourages us to delve into the mystery that lies beneath — for the exploration of life's mystery is the true, if unspoken, purpose of every realistic play. Realism's characters, like people in life, are defined by detail rather than by symbol or abstract idealization: like people we know, they are ultimately unpredictable, humanly complex rather than ideologically absolute.

The success of realism is well established; indeed, realism remains one of the dominant modes of drama to this day. At its most profound, when crafted and performed by consummately skilled artists, the realistic theatre can generate extremely powerful audience empathy by virtue of the insight and clarity it brings to real-world moments. In giving us characters, the realist playwright gives us *friends:* fellow travelers on the voyage of human discovery with whom we can compare thoughts and feelings. In the uncertainties and trepidations, the wistfulness, the halting eloquence and conversational syntax of these characters we recognize ourselves, and in that recognition we gain an understanding of our own struggles and a compassion for all human endeavors.

Pioneers of Realism

The realistic theatre had its beginnings in the four-year period that saw the premieres of *A Doll's House* (1879), *Ghosts* (1881), and *An Enemy of the People* (1882) by the Norwegian author Henrik Ibsen. Earlier in his career, Ibsen had been a stage director and dramatic poet, and his previous works for the theatre included the magnificent romantic/epic poem-play *Peer Gynt* (1867). With these three plays, which dealt, respectively, with the issues of woman's role in society, hereditary disease and mercy killing, and political hypocrisy, he turned to the realistic mode. Ordinary people populate Ibsen's realistic world, and the issues addressed in these dramas affect ordinary husband-wife, mother-son, and brother-brother relationships, played out in the interiors of ordinary homes. Controversial beyond measure in their own time, these plays retain their edge of pertinence even today and still have the power to inform, to move, and even to shock. The reason for their lasting impact lies in Ibsen's choice of issues and his skill at showing both sides through brilliantly captured psychological detail.

The realistic theatre spread rapidly throughout Europe as the controversy surrounding Ibsen's plays and themes stimulated other writers to follow suit. The result was a proliferation of "problem plays," as they were sometimes called, which focused genuine social concern through realistic dramatic portrayal. In Germany, Gerhart Hauptmann explored the plight of the middle and proletarian classes in several works, most notably in his masterpiece *The Weavers* (1892). In England, Irish-born George Bernard Shaw created a comedic realism through which he addressed such issues as slum landlordism (in *Widowers' Houses,* 1892), prostitution (in *Mrs. Warren's Profession,* 1902), and urban poverty (in *Major Barbara,* 1905). In France, under the encouragement of innovative director André Antoine, Eugène Brieux wrote a series of realistic problem plays that included *Damaged Goods* (1902), which deals with syphilis, and *Maternity* (1903), which deals with birth control. By the turn of the century realism was virtually the standard dramatic form in Europe.

Chekhov If the realistic theatre came to prominence with the plays of Henrik Ibsen, it attained its stylistic apogee in the major works of Anton Chekhov. Chekhov was a physician by training and a writer of fiction by vocation; toward the end of his career, in association with realist director Konstantin Stanislavski and the Moscow Art Theatre, he also achieved success as a playwright through a set of plays that portray the end of the czarist era in Russia with astonishing force and subtlety: *The Sea Gull* (1896), *Uncle Vanya* (1899), *The Three Sisters* (1901), and *The Cherry Orchard* (1904). The intricate craftsmanship of these plays has never been surpassed; even the minor characters seem to breathe the same air that we do.

Chekhov's technique is to create deeply complex relationships among his characters and to develop his plots and themes more or less between the lines. Every Chekhovian character is filled with secrets, none of which is ever fully revealed by the dialogue.

As an example of Chekhov's realist style, examine particularly the dialogue in the following scene between the army colonel Vershinin and Masha of *The Three Sisters;* the scene portrays Vershinin meeting Masha and her sisters Irina and Olga, whom Vershinin dimly remembers from past years in Moscow:

VERSHININ: I have the honor to introduce myself, my name is Vershinin. I am very, very glad to be in your house at last. How you have grown up! Aie-aie!

IRINA: Please sit down. We are delighted to see you.

VERSHININ: (*with animation*) How glad I am, how glad I am! But there are three of you sisters. I remember—three little girls. I don't remember your faces, but that your father, Colonel Prozorov, had three little girls I remember perfectly. How time passes! Hey-ho, how it passes! . . .

IRINA: From Moscow? You have come from Moscow?

VERSHININ: Yes. Your father was in command of a battery there, and I was an officer in the same brigade. (*To Masha*) Your face, now, I seem to remember.

MASHA: I don't remember you.

VERSHININ: So you are Olga, the eldest—and you are Masha—and you are Irina, the youngest—

OLGA: You come from Moscow?

VERSHININ: Yes. I studied in Moscow. . . . I used to visit you in Moscow.

Masha and Vershinin are destined to become lovers; their deepening, largely unspoken communion will provide one of the most haunting strains in the play. And how lifelike is the awkwardness of their first encounter! Vershinin's enthusiastic clichés ("how time passes") and interjections ("Aie-aie!") are the stuff of everyday discourse; the news that he comes from Moscow is repeated to the extent that it becomes amusing rather than informative, a revelation of character rather than of plot.

Masha's first exchange with Vershinin gives no direct indication of the future of their relationship; it is a crossed communication in which one character refuses to share in the other's memory. Is this a personal repudiation or is it a teasing provocation? The acting, not simply the text, must establish their developing rapport. The love between Vershinin and Masha will tax to the maximum the capabilities of the actors who play their parts to express deep feeling through subtle nuance, through the gestures, the glances, the tones of voice, and the shared understandings and sympathetic rhythms that distinguish lovers everywhere: it is a theme that strongly affects the mood of the play but is rarely explicit in the dialogue.

NATURALISM

Naturalism, a movement whose development paralleled that of realism but was in part independent of it, represents an even more extreme attempt to dramatize human reality without the appearance of dramaturgical shaping. The naturalists, who flourished primarily in France during the late nineteenth century (Emile Zola was their chief theoretician), based their aesthetics on nature and particularly on humanity's place in the natural (Darwinian) environment. To the naturalist, the human being was merely a biological phenomenon whose behavior was determined entirely by genetic and social circumstances. To portray a character as a hero, or even as a

Keith Baxter, as Vershinin, reaches for the hand of Maggie Smith, playing Masha, in the Stratford (Ontario) Festival production of The Three Sisters. *The contrast between the two actors' facial expressions reveals the cross-purposes of the play's character interactions. (Photo: Robert C. Ragsdale; courtesy of the Stratford Festival, Canada.)*

credible force for change in society, was anathema to the naturalist, who similarly eschewed dramatic conclusions or climaxes. Whereas realist plays at that time tended to deal with well-defined social issues — women's rights, inheritance laws, worker's pensions, and the like — naturalist plays offered nothing more than a "slice of life" in which the characters of the play were the play's entire subject; any topical issues that were brought in served merely to facilitate the interplay of personalities and highlight their situations, frustrations, and hopes.

The naturalists sought to eliminate every vestige of dramatic convention: "All the great successes of the stage are triumphs over convention," declared Zola. Their efforts in this direction are exemplified by August Strindberg's elimination of the time-passing intermission in *Miss Julie* (instead, a group of peasants, otherwise irrelevant to the plot, enter the kitchen setting between acts and dance to fill the time Miss Julie is spending in Jean's offstage bedroom), and by Arthur Schnitzler's elimination of conventional scene beginnings, endings, and climaxes in the interlocking series of cyclical love affairs that constitute the action of *La Ronde*.

Inasmuch as sheer verisimilitude, presented as "artlessly" as humanly possible, is the primary goal of the naturalist, the term *naturalism* is often applied to those realistic plays that seem most effectively lifelike. This is not a particularly felicitous use of the term, however, because it ignores the fundamental precept of naturalism — that the human being is a mere figure in the natural environment. Naturalism is not merely a matter of style; it is a philosophical concept concerning the nature of the human animal. And naturalist theatre represents a purposeful attempt to explore that concept, using extreme realism as its basic dramaturgy.

Eugene O'Neill, America's first great playwright, pioneered an earthy naturalistic style in his early plays, returning to that style in his autobiographical masterpiece *Long Day's Journey into Night* — a play so true to life that O'Neill forbade its production or publication until many years after his death. In our times, the dramas of Arthur Miller, Tennessee Williams, Robert Anderson, William Inge, and David Mamet are all strongly influenced by both realism and naturalism, which continue to have a commanding presence on the American stage. A more intense version of realism, called suprarealism, has emerged in recent decades.

Suprarealism: *Buried Child*

Buried Child, a play by American actor-author Sam Shepard, was originally produced at the Magic Theatre of San Francisco in 1978 and moved to New York's off-Broadway stage the following year. Shepard established himself as an American avant-garde playwright in the 1960s and 1970s with such works as *The Tooth of Crime, Operation Sidewinder, Angel City,* and *Curse of the Starving Class*. All of his plays have the characteristic of *suprarealism;* that is, they are ostensibly realistic but actually suffused with menacing obscurity and mythic symbolism, steadily seeking out patterns beneath everyday surfaces and meanings in the silences that punctuate ordinary conversation.

Buried Child is set in a decaying farmhouse in the American Middle West; the degenerate condition of the house is echoed by that of the family who inhabit it. The setting is realized in wholly realistic detail, down to the "pale, frayed carpet," the "upright lamp with a faded yellow shade," and the "large, old-fashioned brown TV" that is left on during much of the play. The dialogue, too, is of the everyday variety, but the incidents, the interactions, and the involvements of the play are just enough removed from the familiar to create an atmosphere of mystery, menace, and doom.

This scene, which comes near the beginning of the play, conveys something of the overriding spirit of *Buried Child*. In it, the

Tennessee Williams's The Glass Menagerie *is a memory play, drawing deeply on the author's own family and experiences. It was Williams's first major success (1945) and remains one of the most popular plays in the American theatre. Pictured here: Jim O'Connor, the "gentleman caller" (played by Jeff Weatherford) chats buoyantly with Amanda Wingfield (Shirley Knight), while Amanda's shy daughter Laura (Judy Kuhn) struggles with her inner terrors. At the McCarter Theatre, Princeton, New Jersey, 1991, directed by the McCarter's artistic director, Emily Mann. (Photo: T. Charles Erickson.)*

aged, irascible Dodge—who sits on a sofa watching the TV—calls in his middle-aged son, Tilden, over shouted objections of his offstage wife, Halie. Inexplicably, Tilden enters with an armload of freshly picked, unshucked corn:

DODGE: (*yelling off left*) Tilden!

HALIE'S VOICE: Dodge, what are you trying to do?

DODGE: (*yelling off left*) Tilden, get in here!

HALIE'S VOICE: Why do you enjoy stirring things up?

A confrontation in Buried Child, *centering on Bradley's artificial leg and a bouquet of flowers. From 1979 American Conservatory Theatre production, directed by Edward Hastings. (Photo: William Ganslen, ACT.)*

DODGE: I don't enjoy anything!

HALIE'S VOICE: That's a terrible thing to say.

DODGE: Tilden!

HALIE'S VOICE: That's the kind of statement that leads people right to the end of their rope.

DODGE: Tilden!

HALIE'S VOICE: It's no wonder people turn to Christ!

DODGE: TILDEN!!

HALIE'S VOICE: It's no wonder the messengers of God's word are shouted down in public places!

DODGE: TILDEN!!!!

DODGE *goes into a violent, spasmodic coughing attack as* TILDEN *enters from stage left, his arms loaded with fresh ears of corn.* TILDEN *is* DODGE'S *oldest son, late forties, wears heavy construction boots, covered with mud, dark green work pants, a plaid shirt and a faded brown windbreaker. He has a butch haircut, wet from the rain. Something about him is profoundly burned out and displaced. He stops center stage with the ears of corn in his arms and just stares at* DODGE *until he slowly finishes his coughing attack.* DODGE *looks up at him slowly. He stares at the corn. Long pause as they watch each other.*

HALIE'S VOICE: Dodge, if you don't take that pill nobody's going to force you.

The two men ignore the voice.

DODGE: *(to* TILDEN*)* Where'd you get that?

TILDEN: Picked it.

DODGE: You picked all that?

TILDEN *nods*.

DODGE: You expecting company?

TILDEN: No.

DODGE: Where'd you pick it from?

TILDEN: Right out back.

DODGE: Out back where!

TILDEN: Right out in back.

DODGE: There's nothing out there!

TILDEN: There's corn.

DODGE: There hasn't been corn out there since about nineteen thirty-five! That's the last time I planted corn out there!

TILDEN: It's out there now.

DODGE: (*yelling at stairs*) Halie!

HALIE'S VOICE: Yes dear!

DODGE: Tilden's brought a whole bunch of corn in here! There's no corn out in back is there?

TILDEN: (*to himself*) There's tons of corn.

HALIE'S VOICE: Not that I know of!

DODGE: That's what I thought.

HALIE'S VOICE: Not since about nineteen thirty-five!

DODGE: (*to* TILDEN) That's right. Nineteen thirty-five.

TILDEN: It's out there now.

DODGE: You go and take that corn back to wherever you got it from!

TILDEN: (*After pause, staring at* DODGE) It's picked. I picked it all in the rain. Once it's picked you can't put it back.

DODGE: I haven't had trouble with neighbors here for fifty-seven years. I don't even know who the neighbors are! And I don't wanna know! Now go put that corn back where it came from!

TILDEN *stares at* DODGE *then walks slowly over to him and dumps all the corn on* DODGE'S *lap and steps back.* DODGE *stares at the corn then back to* TILDEN. *Long pause.*

DODGE: Are you having trouble here, Tilden? Are you in some kind of trouble?

TILDEN: I'm not in any trouble.

DODGE: You can tell me if you are. I'm still your father.

TILDEN: I know you're still my father.

DODGE: I know you had a little trouble back in New Mexico. That's why you came out here.

TILDEN: I never had any trouble.

DODGE: Tilden, your mother told me all about it.

TILDEN: What'd she tell you?

TILDEN *pulls some chewing tobacco out of his jacket and bites off a plug.*

DODGE: I don't have to repeat what she told me! She told me all about it!

TILDEN: Can I bring my chair in from the kitchen?

DODGE: What?

TILDEN: Can I bring my chair in from the kitchen?

DODGE: Sure. Bring your chair in.

TILDEN *exits left.* DODGE *pushes all the corn off his lap onto the floor. . . .*

Where did the corn come from? Why does Tilden bring it in? Why does he drop it on Dodge's lap? What was the "trouble" in New Mexico? We will never receive overt answers to these questions. *Buried Child* is a play that radiates implication and never becomes explicit. It creates the impression of a theme not by rational plot development or logical moral positioning, but by a pattern of seeming non sequiturs, abrupt transitions, and bizarre, enigmatic actions.

There was, we find out, a baby that was killed many years ago and buried by Dodge out in back; this is the "buried child" of the title, a metaphorical fertilizer for Tilden's corn and a symbolic seminalization for mid-America, which the play gives us to understand was established by acts of murder and built by successive cover-ups. A series of demented children—there is also a crazed amputee, Bradley, and Tilden's shell-shocked and psychotic son, Vince—uncover the family's horrific past in the play's ambiguous (but curiously cathartic) conclusion.

Shepard plays upon our natural fascination with—and fear of—the unexpected and the unusual. The contrast between Dodge's violent spasm of coughing and Tilden's silent, corn-laden entrance exemplifies the theatricality of Shepard's technique: it is a wholly unforgettable — if inexplicable — moment of theatre. So also is Tilden's act of throwing the corn on Dodge's lap. The repetition of lines

TILDEN: Can I bring my chair in from the kitchen?
DODGE: What?
TILDEN: Can I bring my chair in from the kitchen?

seems at first a simple mimicry of humdrum conversation; as part of an overall pattern of dialogue, however, it enhances rhythms of uncertainty and confusion: unanswered questions about the possibilities of communication between these characters in their insistent attempts to get through to . . . something.

Shepard's suprarealism, with its highly theatrical use of rhythms and juxtapositions, creates an electrified surface intensity around an obscure center. Similar techniques are discernible in the recent plays of British authors Harold Pinter (*The Caretaker, The Homecoming, Betrayal*) and Simon Gray (*Butley, Otherwise Engaged, The Common Pursuit, Close of Play*), as well as in the plays of American authors Edward Albee (*Who's Afraid of Virginia Woolf?, Tiny Alice, The Lady from Dubuque*) and David Mamet (*Sexual Perversity in Chicago, American Buffalo, Glengarry Glen Ross, Speed-the-Plow,* and *Oleanna*).

ANTIREALISM

Realism and naturalism were not the only new movements to make themselves strongly felt in the modern theatre. A counterforce, equally powerful, was to emerge.

First manifest in the movement known as symbolism, this counterforce evolved and expanded into what we shall call antirealistic theatre, which moved across Europe and quickly began contesting the advances of realism virtually step by step.

The Symbolist Rebellion

The symbolist movement began in Paris during the 1880s as a joint venture of artists, playwrights, essayists, critics, sculptors, and poets. If realism was the art of depicting reality as ordinary men and women might see it, symbolism would explore — by means of images and metaphors — the *inner* realities that cannot be directly or literally perceived. "Symbolic" characters, therefore, would not represent real human beings, but would symbolize philosophical ideals, or warring internal forces in the human (or the artist's) soul.

Symbolism had another goal as well: to crush what its adherents deemed to be a spiritually bankrupt realism and to replace it with traditional aesthetic values — poetry, imagery, novelty, fantasy, extravagance, profundity, audacity, charm, and superhuman magnitude. United in their hatred for literal detail and for all that they considered mundane or ordinary, the symbolists demanded abstraction, enlargement, and innovation; the symbolist spirit soared in poetic encapsulations, outsized dramatic presences, fantastical visual effects, shocking structural departures, and grandiloquent speech. Purity of vision, rather than accuracy of observation, was the symbolists' aim, and self-conscious creative innovation was to be their primary accomplishment.

The first symbolist theatre, founded in 1890 by Parisian poet Paul Fort, was intended as a direct attack on the naturalistic Théâtre Libre of André Antoine, founded three years earlier. Fort's theatre, the Théâtre d'Art, was proposed as "a theatre for Symbolist poets only, where every production would cause a battle." In some ways Antoine's and Fort's theatres had much in common: both were amateur, both gained considerable notoriety, each served as a center for a "school" of artistic ideology that attracted as much attention and controversy as any of its theatrical offerings.

But the two theatres were openly, deliberately, at war. While Antoine was presenting premieres of naturalistic and realistic dramas by August Strindberg, Emile Zola, and Hen-

This 1990 production of George Bernard Shaw's 1903 play, Man and Superman, *employs costumes and props of Shaw's time, but has a thoroughly modern (or post-modern) spirit. Directed by Martin Benson and designed by Cliff Faulkner (scenery) and Shigeru Yaji (costumes) at the South Coast Repertory Theatre. (Photo: Christopher Gross.)*

rik Ibsen, Fort presented the staged poems and poetic plays of both contemporary and earlier writers such as the French Arthur Rimbaud (1854–1891) and Paul Verlaine (1844–1896), the Belgian Maurice Maeterlinck (1862–1949), and the American Edgar Allan Poe (1809–1849). Whereas Antoine would go to great lengths to create realistic scenery for his plays (for example, he procured sides of real beef and hung them on real meathooks for his presentation of *The Butchers*), Fort would prevail upon leading impressionist easel painters, including Pierre Bonnard, Mau-

rice Denis, and Odilon Redon, to dress his stylized stage. Silver angels, translucent veils, and sheets of crumpled wrapping paper were among the decors that backed the symbolist works at the Théâtre d'Art.

Fort's theatre created an immediate sensation in Paris. With the stunning success, in 1890, of *The Intruder,* a mysterious and poetic fantasy by Maeterlinck, the antirealist movement was fully engaged and, as Fort recalled in his memoirs, "the cries and applause of the students, poets, and artists overwhelmed the huge disapproval of the bourgeoisie."

REALISM AS BLINDNESS: CRAIG'S VIEW

Realism is a vulgar means of expression bestowed upon the blind. Thus we have the clear-sighted singing: 'Beauty is Truth, Truth Beauty—that is all ye know on earth, and all ye need to know.' The blind are heard croaking: 'Beauty is Realism, Realism Beauty—that is all I know on earth, and all I care to know—don't 'ya know!' The difference is all a matter of love. He who loves the earth sees beauty everywhere: he is a god transforming by knowledge the incomplete into the complete. He can heal the lame and the sick, can blow courage into the weary, and he can even learn how to make the blind see. The power has always been possessed by the artist, who, in my opinion, rules the earth. . . .

The limited section of playgoers who love beauty and detest Realism is a small minority of about six million souls. They are scattered here and there over the earth. They seldom, if ever, go to the modern theatre. That is why I love them, and intend to unite them.

Gordon Craig

The movement spread quickly as authors and designers alike awakened to the possibilities of a theatre wholly freed from the constraints of verisimilitude. Realism, more and more critics concluded, would never raise the commonplace to the level of art; it would only drag art down into the muck of the mundane. It ran counter to all that the theatre had stood for in the past; it throttled the potential of artistic creativity. Soon such naturalistic and realistic authors as Ibsen, Strindberg, Gerhart Hauptmann, and George Bernard Shaw came under the symbolist influence and abandoned their social preoccupations and environmental exactitude to seek new languages and more universal themes. As an added element, at about this time the research done by Sigmund Freud was being published and discussed, and his theories concerning dream images and the worlds of the Unconscious provided new source material for the stage.

By the turn of the century, the counterforce of theatrical stylization set in motion by the symbolists was established on all fronts; indeed, the half decade on either side of 1900 represents one of the richest periods of experimentation in the history of dramatic writing. Out of that decade came Hauptmann's archetypal fairy tale *The Sunken Bell* (Germany, 1896), Alfred Jarry's outrageously cartoonish and scatological *Ubu Roi* (France, 1898), Ibsen's haunting ode to individualism *When We Dead Awaken* (Norway, 1899), Strindberg's metaphoric and imagistic *The Dream Play* (Sweden, 1902), William Butler Yeats's evocative poetic fable *Cathleen ni Houlihan* (Ireland, 1903), Shaw's philosophical allegory *Man and Superman* (England, 1903), and James Barrie's whimsical, buoyant fantasy *Peter Pan* (England, 1904). Almost every dramatic innovation that has followed since that time has been at least in part prefigured by one or more of these seminal works for the nonrealist theatre.

The realist-versus-symbolist confrontation affected every aspect of theatre production. Symbolist-inspired directors and designers, side by side with the playwrights, were drastically altering the arts of staging and decor to accommodate the new dramaturgies that surged into the theatre. Realist directors like Antoine and Stanislavski suddenly found themselves challenged by scores of adversaries and renegades: a school of symbolist and poetic directors rose in France, and a former disciple of Stanislavski, the "constructivist" Vsevolod Meyerhold, broke with the Russian master to create a nonrealist "biomechanical" style of acting and directing in sharp contrast to that established at the Moscow Art Theatre; by 1904, Stanislavski himself was producing the impressionistic plays of Maurice Maeterlinck at the MAT. With the advent of electrical stage lighting, opportunities for stylizing were vastly expanded: the new technology enabled the modern director to create vivid stage effects, starkly unrealistic in appearance, through the judicious use of spotlighting, shadowing, and shading. Technology, plus trends in post-impressionist art that were well established in Europe by 1900, led to scenery and costume designs that departed radically from realism. Exoticism, fantasy, sheer sensual delight, symbolic meaning, and aesthetic purity became the prime objectives of designers who joined the antirealist rebellion.

In some respects, the symbolist aim succeeded perhaps beyond the dreams of its originators. Paul Fort's art theatre, although it lasted but a year, now has spiritual descendants in every city in the Western world where theatre is performed.

The Era of "Isms"

The symbolist movement itself was short-lived, at least under that name. "Symbolism," after all, was coined primarily as a direct contradiction of "realism," and movements named for their oppositional qualities—called for what they are not—are quickly seen as artistically limited, as critiques of art rather than as art itself.

Within months of the symbolist advances, therefore, symbolism *as a movement* was deserted by founders and followers alike. Where did they go? Off to found newer movements: the avant-garde, futurism, dada, idealism, aestheticism, impressionism, expressionism, constructivism, surrealism, formalism, theatricalism, and perhaps a hundred other isms now lost to time.

The first third of this century, indeed, was an era of theatrical isms, an era rich with continued experimentation by movements self-consciously seeking to redefine theatrical art. "Ism" theatres sprang up like mushrooms, each with its own fully articulated credo and manifesto, each promising a better art—if

not, indeed, a better world. It was a vibrant era for the theatre, for out of this welter of isms the aesthetics of dramatic art took on a new social and political significance in the cultural capitals of Europe and America: a successful play was not merely a play, but rather signified a *cause;* and behind that cause was a body of zealous supporters and adherents who shared a deep aesthetic commitment.

Nothing quite like that ism spirit exists today, for we have lost the social involvement that can turn an aesthetic movement into a profound collective belief. But the experiments and discoveries of those early days of this century and the nonrealistic spirit of symbolism itself survive and flourish under a variety of formats: ritual theatre, poetic theatre, holy theatre, theatre of cruelty, existentialist theatre, art theatre, avant-garde theatre, theatre of the absurd, and theatre of alienation. These present-day groupings, unlike the isms, are critic-defined rather than artist-defined; indeed, most theatre artists today reject any "grouping" nomenclature whatever. However, the formats these groupings pursue can be shown to reflect the general approach to structure, style, and experimentation that began with the symbolists in the late nineteenth century.

ANTIREALISTIC THEATRE

We have chosen the rather loose term "antirealistic theatre" or, occasionally, the "stylized theatre" to embrace the entire spectrum of nonrealistic modern theatre, which, although disparate in its individual manifestations, exhibits a universal insistence on *consciously stylizing reality* into larger-than-life theatrical experience. Any theatre mode in any era, of course, has its distinctive style, but in past eras that style was always largely *imposed* by current convention and technological limitations. Modern dramatists, by contrast, have consciously *selected and created* styles to satisfy

James Barrie's Peter Pan *features the famous flying young man, Peter, who symbolizes eternal youth. The role is usually played by a female actress. The play is most widely known today through a musical adaptation, here staged on Broadway in a revival starring Sandy Duncan as Peter. (Photo: Martha Swope and Associates.)*

their aesthetic theories, their social principles, or simply their desire for novelty and innovation.

Antirealistic theatre attempts to create new theatrical formats, not merely to enhance the portrayal of human existence but also to disclose fundamental patterns underlying that existence: patterns of perception, patterns of association, patterns of personal and environmental interaction.

The styles employed by this modern theatre come from anywhere and everywhere: from the past, from exotic cultures, and from present and futuristic technologies. The mod-

ern theatre artist has an unprecedented reservoir of sources to draw upon and is generally unconstrained in their application by political edict, religious prohibition, or mandated artistic tradition. The modern stylized theatre is undoubtedly the freest in history: neither the dramatist, the director, the actor, nor the designer is limited in his or her efforts save by the universal factors of physical resources and individual imagination. Virtually anything may be put upon a stage, and in the twentieth century it seems that virtually everything has been.

Antirealistic theatre does not altogether dispense with reality but wields it in often unexpected ways and freely enhances it with symbol and metaphor, striving to elucidate by parable and allegory, to deconstruct and reconstruct by language and scenery and lighting. Further, it makes explicit use of the theatre's very theatricality, frequently reminding its audience, directly or indirectly, that they are watching a performance, not an episode in somebody's daily life. Stylization inevitably reaches for universality. It tends to treat problems of psychology as problems of philosophy and problems in human relations as problems of the human condition. Stylization reaches for patterns, not particulars; it explores abstractions and aims for sharp thematic focus and bold intellectual impact.

In the stylized theatre, characters usually represent more than individual persons or personality types. Like the medieval allegories, modern stylized plays often involve characters who represent forces of nature, moral positions, human instincts, and the like — entities such as death, fate, idealism, the life force, the earth mother, the tyrant father, and the prodigal son. And the conflicts associated with these forces, unlike the conflicts of realism, are not responsive to any human agency: they are, more often than not, represented as permanent discords inherent in the human condition. The stylized theatre resonates with tension and human frustration in the face of irreconcilable demands.

But that is not to say that the antirealistic theatre is necessarily grim: quite to the contrary, it often uses whimsy and mordant wit as its dominant mode. Although the themes of the antirealistic theatre are anxious ones — for example, the alienation of humanity, the futility of communication, the loss of innocence, the intransigence of despair — it is not on the whole a theatre of pessimism or of nihilistic outrage. Indeed, the glory of the stylized theatre is that, at its best, it refuses to be swamped by its themes; it transcends frustration; it is the victory of poetry over aliena-

Irene Worth, as Winnie in Beckett's Happy Days, *is buried up to her chin for the play's second act. New York Shakespeare Festival production, 1979. (Photo: George Joseph.)*

tion, comedy over noncommunication, and artistry over despair. The antirealistic theatre aims at lifting its audience, not saddling them; and if it proffers no solutions to life's inevitable discords, it can provide considerable lucidity concerning the totality of the human adventure.

Ten Stylizations

The diversity of stylized theatrical works precludes further generalization about their shared characteristics, but ten brief examples from plays written in the past ninety years will serve to establish the main lines of the antirealistic theatre.

Ubu (Geoff Hoyle, right) tweaks the nose of Mrs. Ubu (Joe Bellan) in a modern revision of Jarry's Ubu Roi, *entitled* Ubu Unchained, *and produced by the Eureka Theatre of San Francisco. "The power and importance of Jarry's grotesque couple lies . . . in the boldness and clarity with which they . . . embody the qualities which . . . epitomize . . . our century: greed, violence and stupidity, all expressed with charismatic self-satisfaction," says Oscar Eustis, dramaturge of the 1986 production. (Photo: Courtesy Eureka Theatre.)*

THE FRENCH AVANT-GARDE:
Ubu Roi

The opening of Alfred Jarry's *Ubu Roi* (*King Ubu*) at the Théâtre Nouveau in Paris, on December 11, 1896, was perhaps the most violent dramatic premiere in theatre history: the audience shouted, whistled, hooted, cheered, threw things, and shook their fists at the stage. Duels were fought after subsequent performances. The *avant-garde* was born.

The term *avant garde* comes from the military, where it refers to the advance battalion, or the vanguard, or the "shock troops" that initiate a major assault. In France, the term initially described the wave of French playwrights and directors who openly and boldly assaulted realism in the first four decades of the current century. Today, the term is used worldwide to describe any adventurous, experimental, and nontraditional artistic effort.

Jarry, a diminutive iconoclast ("eccentric to the point of mania and lucid to the point of hallucination," says Roger Shattuck), unleashed his radical shock troops from the moment the curtain rose. Jarry had called for an outrageously antirealistic stage—painted scenery depicting a bed, a bare tree at its foot, palm trees, a coiled boa constrictor around one of them, a gallows with a skeleton hanging from it, and snow, falling. Characters entered through a painted fireplace. Costumes, in Jarry's words, were "divorced as far as possible from [realistic] color or chronology." And the title character stepped forward to begin the play with a word that quickly became immortal: *"Merdre!"* or *"Shitr!"*

This, *"le mot d'Ubu"* ("Ubu's word"), occasioned the scandal more than anything else, for while Ibsen had broken barriers of propriety in subject matter, no one had tested the language barriers of the Victorian age. Vulgar epithets, common enough in Aristophanes and Shakespeare, had been pruned from the theatre in the Royal era and abolished entirely in the lofty spirit of romanticism; far from trying to sneak them back in, Jarry simply threw them up, schoolboy-like, in the face of the astonished audience. The added "r" in *"merdre,"* far from "cleansing" the offending obscenity, only called more attention to it and to its deliberate intrusion onto the Parisian stage.

Ubu Roi was, in fact, a schoolboy play; Jarry wrote the first version at the age of fifteen as a satire of his high school physics teacher. Jarry was only twenty-three years old when the play astounded its Parisian audiences, and the juvenile aspects of the play's origins were everywhere evident in the finished product, which proved to be Jarry's sole masterwork.

Ubu Roi is a savage and often ludicrous satire on the theme of power, in which Father (later King) Ubu—a fat, foul-mouthed, venal, amoral, and pompous Polish assassin—proves one of the stage's greatest creations. The play sprawls; its thirty-three scenes are often just crude skits, barely linked by plot, but the interplay of farce and violence is inspired, as in the famous eating scene:

Father Ubu, Mother Ubu, Captain Bordure and his followers.

MOTHER UBU: Good day, gentlemen; we've been anxiously awaiting you.

CAPTAIN BORDURE: Good day, madam. Where's Father Ubu?

FATHER UBU: Here I am, here I am! Good lord, by my green candle, I'm fat enough, aren't I?

CAPTAIN BORDURE: Good day, Father Ubu. Sit down boys. (*They all sit.*)

FATHER UBU: Oof, a little more, and I'd have bust my chair.

CAPTAIN BORDURE: Well, Mother Ubu! What have you got that's good today?

MOTHER UBU: Here's the menu.

FATHER UBU: Oh! That interests me.

MOTHER UBU: Polish soup, roast ram, veal, chicken, chopped dog's liver, turkey's ass, charlotte russe . . .

FATHER UBU: Hey, that's plenty, I should think. You mean there's more?

MOTHER UBU: (*continuing*) Frozen pudding, salad, fruits, dessert, boiled beef, Jerusalem artichokes, cauliflower à la shitr.

FATHER UBU: Hey! Do you think I'm the Emperor of China, to give all that away?

MOTHER UBU: Don't listen to him, he's feeble-minded.

FATHER UBU: Ah! I'll sharpen my teeth on your shanks.

MOTHER UBU: Try this instead, Father Ubu. Here's the Polish soup.

FATHER UBU: Crap, is that lousy!

CAPTAIN BORDURE: Hmm — it isn't very good, at that.

MOTHER UBU: What do you want, you bunch of crooks!

FATHER UBU (*striking his forehead*): Wait, I've got an idea. I'll be right back. (*He leaves.*)

MOTHER UBU: Let's try the veal now, gentlemen.

CAPTAIN BORDURE: It's very good — I'm through.

MOTHER UBU: To the turkey's ass, next.

CAPTAIN BORDURE: Delicious, delicious! Long live Mother Ubu!

ALL: Long live Mother Ubu!

FATHER UBU (*returning*): And you will soon be shouting long live Father Ubu. (*He has a toilet brush in his hand, and he throws it on the festive board.*)

MOTHER UBU: Miserable creature, what are you up to now?

FATHER UBU: Try a little. (*Several try it, and fall, poisoned.*) Mother Ubu, pass me the roast ram chops, so that I can serve them.

MOTHER UBU: Here they are.

FATHER UBU: Everyone out! Captain Bordure, I want to talk to you.

THE OTHERS: But we haven't eaten yet.

FATHER UBU: What's that, you haven't eaten yet? Out, out, everyone out! Stay here, Bordure. (*Nobody moves.*) You haven't gone yet? By my green candle, I'll give you your ram chops. (*He begins to throw them.*)

ALL: Oh! Ouch! Help! Woe! Help! Misery! I'm dead!

FATHER UBU: Shitr, shitr, shitr! Outside! I want my way!

ALL: Everyone for himself! Miserable Father Ubu! Traitor! Meanie!

FATHER UBU: Ah! They've gone. I can breathe again — but I've had a rotten dinner. Come on, Bordure.

They go out with Mother Ubu.

The elements of deliberate scatology, toilet humor, juvenile satire, and a full-stage food fight make clear that *Ubu Roi* is a precursor of American teen films such as *Animal House;* it is a little more difficult to see the play as a precursor of a serious art and literary movement like surrealism, but such is the case. *Surrealism,* an invented word that means "beyond realism" or "superrealism," was officially inaugurated by André Breton in 1924 but can be said to date from this play — which, its advocates claim, reaches a superior level of reality by tracing the unconscious processes of the mind rather than the literal depictions of observable life.

EXPRESSIONISM:
The Hairy Ape

Of all the isms, expressionism is the one that has given rise to the most significant body of modern theatre, probably because of its broad definition and its seeming alliance with expressionism in the visual arts. The theatrical expressionism that was much in vogue in Germany during the first decades of the century (particularly in the 1920s) featured shocking and gutty dialogue, boldly exaggerated scenery, piercing sounds, bright lights, an abundance of primary colors, a not very subtle use of symbols, and a structure of short, stark, jabbing scenes that built to a powerful (and usually deafening) climax.

In America, Eugene O'Neill came under the influence of the expressionists after earlier ventures into naturalism, and in the 1920s

Eugene O'Neill's The Hairy Ape *in its original New York production by the Provincetown Playhouse. The setting is of the opening of Scene Three. (Photo: Courtesy Library of the Performing Arts, Lincoln Center, New York.)*

O'Neill wrote a series of explosive plays concerning human nature in an industrial landscape. *The Hairy Ape,* produced in 1921, is almost a textbook case of expressionist writing. Although this play seems clumsy, transparent, and naively ineffective today, it well illustrates the extreme stylization popular with "ism" writers. It is a one-act play featuring eight scenes. Its workingman–hero Yank meets and is rebuffed by the genteel daughter of a captain of industry. Enraged, Yank becomes violent and eventually crazed; he dies at play's end in the monkey cage of a zoo. Scene Three illustrates the tenor of the writing:

The stokehold. In the rear, the dimly outlined bulks of the furnaces and boilers. High overhead one hanging electric bulb sheds just enough light through the murky air laden with coal dust to pile up masses of shadows everywhere. A line of men, stripped to the waist, is before the furnace doors. They bend over, looking neither to right nor left, handling their shovels as if they were part of their bodies, with a strange, awkward, swinging rhythm. They use the shovels to throw open the furnace doors. Then from these fiery round holes in the black a flood of terrific light and heat pours full upon the men who are outlined in silhouette in the crouching, inhuman attitudes of chained gorillas. The men shovel with a rhythmic motion, swinging as on a pivot from the coal which lies in heaps on the floor behind to hurl it into the flaming mouths before them. There is a tumult of noise — the brazen clang of the furnace doors as they are flung open or slammed shut, the grating, teeth-gritting grind of steel against steel, of crunching coal. This clash of sounds stuns one's ears with its rending dissonance. But there is order in it, rhythm, a mechanical regulated recurrence, a tempo. And rising above all, making the air hum with the quiver of liberated energy, the roar of leaping flames in the furnaces, the monotonous throbbing beat of the engines.

O'NEILL'S EXPRESSIONISM

In the scene [in *The Hairy Ape*] where the bell rings for the stokers to go on duty, you remember that they all stand up, come to attention, then go out in a lockstep file. Some people think even that is an actual custom aboard ship! But it is only symbolic of the regimentation of men who are the slaves of machinery. In a larger sense, it applies to all of us, because we all are more or less the slaves of convention, or of discipline, or of a rigid formula of some sort.

The whole play is expressionistic. The coal shoveling in the furnace room, for instance. Stokers do not really shovel coal that way. But it is done in the play in order to contribute to the rhythm. For rhythm is a powerful factor in making anything expressive. You can actually produce and control emotions by that means alone.

Eugene O'Neill

As the curtain rises, the furnace doors are shut. The men are taking a breathing spell. One or two are arranging the coal behind them, pulling it into more accessible heaps. The others can be dimly made out leaning on their shovels in relaxed attitudes of exhaustion.

PADDY: (*from somewhere in the line—plaintively*) Yerra, will this divil's own watch nivir end? Me back is broke. I'm destroyed entirely.

YANK: (*from the center of the line—with exuberant scorn*) Aw, yuh make me sick! Lie down and croak, why don't yuh? Always beefin', dat's you! Say, dis is a cinch! Dis was made for me! It's my meat, get me! (*A whistle is blown—a thin, shrill note from somewhere overhead in the darkness.* YANK *curses without resentment.*) Dere's de damn engineer crackin' de whip. He tinks we're loafin'.

PADDY: (*vindictively*) God stiffen him!

YANK: (*in an exultant tone of command*) Come on, youse guys! Git into de game! She's gettin' hungry! Pile some grub in her. Trow it into her belly! Come on now, all of youse! Open her up! (*At this last all the men, who have followed his movements of getting into position, throw open their furnace doors with a deafening clang. The fiery light floods over their shoulders as they bend round for the coal. Rivulets of sooty sweat have traced maps on their backs. The enlarged muscles form bunches of high light and shadow.*)

YANK: (*chanting a count as he shovels without seeming effort*) One—two—tree—(*His voice rising exultantly in the joy of battle*) Dat's de stuff! Let her have it! All togedder now! Sling it into her! Let her ride! Shoot de piece now! Call de toin on her! Drive her into it! Feel her move. Watch her smoke! Speed, dat's her middle name! Give her coal, youse guys! Coal, dat's her booze! Drink it up, baby! Let's see yuh sprint! Dig in and gain a lap! Dere she go-o-es. (*This last in the chanting formula of the galley gods at the six-day bike race. He slams his furnace door shut. The others do likewise with as much unison as their wearied bodies will permit. The effect is of one fiery eye after another being blotted out with a series of accompanying bangs.*)

PADDY: (*groaning*) Me back is broke. I'm bate out—bate—(*There is a pause. Then the inexorable whistle sounds again from the dim regions above the electric light. There is a growl of cursing rage from all sides.*)

YANK: (*shaking his fist upward—contemptuously*) Take it easy dere, you! Who d'yuh tink's runnin' dis game, me or you? When I git ready, we move. Not before! When I git ready, get me!

VOICES: (*approvingly*) That's the stuff!
Yank tal him, py golly!
Yank ain't affeerd.
Goot poy, Yank!
Give him hell!
Tell 'im 'e's a bloody swine!
Bloody slave-driver!

YANK: (*contemptuously*) He ain't got no noive. He's yellow, get me? All de engineers is yellow. Dey got streaks a mile wide. Aw, to hell wit him! Let's move, youse guys. We had a rest. Come on, she needs it! Give her pep! It ain't for him. Him and his whistle, dey don't belong. But we belong, see! We gotter feed de baby! Come on! (*He turns and flings his furnace door open. They all follow his lead. At this instant the* SECOND *and* FOURTH ENGINEERS *enter from the darkness on the left with* MILDRED *between them. She starts, turns paler, her pose is crumbling, she shivers with fright in spite of the blazing heat, but forces herself to leave the* ENGINEERS *and take a few steps nearer the men. She is right behind* YANK. *All this happens quickly while the men have their backs turned.*)

YANK: Come on, youse guys! (*He is turning to get coal when the whistle sounds again in a peremptory, irritating note. This drives* YANK *into a sudden fury. While the other men have turned full around and stopped dumfounded by the spectacle of* MILDRED *standing there in her white dress,* YANK *does not turn far enough to see her. Besides, his head is thrown back, he blinks upward through the murk trying to find the owner of the whistle, he brandishes his shovel murderously over his head in one hand, pounding on his chest, gorilla-like, with the other, shouting.*) Toin off dat whistle! Come down outa dere, yuh yellow, brass-buttoned, Belfast bum, yuh! Come down and I'll knock yer brains out! Yuh lousy, stinkin', yellow mut of a Catholic-moiderin' bastard! Come down and I'll moider yuh! Pullin' dat whistle on me, huh? I'll show yuh! I'll crash yer skull in! I'll drive yer teet' down yer troat! I'll slam yer nose trou de back to yer head! I'll cut yer guts out for a nickel, yuh lousy boob, yuh dirty, crummy, muck-eatin' son of a— (*Suddenly he becomes conscious of all the other men staring at something directly behind his back. He whirls defensively with a snarling, murderous growl, crouching to spring, his lips drawn back over his teeth, his small eyes gleaming ferociously. He sees* MILDRED, *like a white apparition in the full light from the open furnace doors. He glares into her eyes, turned to stone. As for her, during his speech she has listened, paralyzed with horror, terror, her whole personality crushed, beaten in, collapsed, by the terrific impact of this unknown, abysmal brutality, naked and shameless. As she looks at his gorilla face, as his eyes bore into hers, she utters a low, choking cry and shrinks away from him, putting both hands up before her eyes to shut out the sight of his face, to protect her own. This startles* YANK *to a reaction. His mouth falls open, his eyes grow bewildered.*)

MILDRED: (*about to faint—to the* ENGINEERS, *who now have her one by each arm—whimperingly*) Take me away! Oh, the filthy beast! (*She faints. They carry her quickly back, disappearing in the darkness at the left, rear. An iron door clangs shut. Rage and bewildered fury rush back on* YANK. *He feels himself insulted in some unknown fashion in the very heart of his pride. He roars.*) God damn yuh! (*And hurls his shovel after them at the door which has just closed.*

It hits the steel bulkhead with a clang and falls clattering on the steel floor. From overhead the whistle sounds again in a long, angry, insistent command.)

Curtain

O'Neill's forceful combination of visual and auditory effects lends this expressionistic play a crude, almost superhuman power. The use of silhouette in the staging and lighting, the "masses of shadows everywhere," the "tumult of noise," the "monotonous throbbing heat of the engines," the "fiery light," the "rivulets of sooty sweat," the massed chanting and the movements in unison, the "peremptory, irritating note" of the "inexorable whistle," the shouting of curses and bold ejaculations, the animal imagery, and the "horror, terror . . . of . . . unknown, abysmal brutality, naked and shameless," are all typical of the extreme stylization of early-twentieth-century expressionism. The scene also demonstrates how O'Neill and his followers in the American theatre turned away from realism and romanticism in their effort to arrive at a direct presentation of social ideology and cultural criticism.

THEATRICALISM:
Six Characters in Search of an Author

First produced in 1921, *Six Characters in Search of an Author* expresses from its famous title onward a "theatricalist" motif in which the theatre itself becomes part of the content of play production, not merely the vehicle. "All the world's a stage," said Shakespeare; but in this play Luigi Pirandello explores how the stage is also a world — and how the stage and the world, illusion and reality, relate to each other. In this still stunning play, a family of dramatic "characters" — a father, his stepdaughter, a mother, her children — appear as if by magic on the stage of a provincial theatre where a new play by Pirandello is being rehearsed: the "characters," claiming they have an unfinished play in them, beg the director to stage their lives in order that they may bring a satisfactory climax to their "drama." This fantasy treats the audience to continuingly shifting perceptions, for clearly a "playwithin-the-play" is involved, but which is the real play and which the real life? There are actors playing actors, actors playing "characters," and actors playing actors-playing"characters"; there are also scenes when the actors playing "characters" are making fun of the actors playing actors-playing-"characters." It is no wonder that most audiences give up trying to untangle the planes of reality Pirandello proposes in this play; they are simply too difficult to comprehend except as a dazzle of suggestive theatricality.

Pirandello contrasts the passionate story of the "characters" — whose "drama" concerns a broken family, adultery, and a suggestion of incest — with the artifice of the stage and its simulations; in the course of this exposition

---

PIRANDELLO: THE PLANE OF REALITY TRANSFORMED

A stage which accommodates the fantastical reality of these six characters is not, itself, a fixed or immutable space, nor are the events of the play preconceived in a fixed formula. On the contrary, everything in this play is created freshly as it happens; it is fluid, it is improvised. As the story and the characters take shape, so the stage itself evolves, and the plane of reality is organically transformed.

Luigi Pirandello

Pirandello's performers discuss the theatricality of life, the life of theatricality, and the eternal confusions between appearance and reality:

THE FATHER: What I'm inviting you to do is to quit this foolish playing at art — this acting and pretending — and seriously answer my question: WHO ARE YOU?

THE DIRECTOR: (*amazed but irritated, to his actors*) What extraordinary impudence! This so-called character wants to know who I am?

THE FATHER: (*with calm dignity*) Signore, a character may always ask a "man" who he is. For a character has a true life, defined by his characteristics — he is always, at the least, a "somebody." But a man — now, don't take this personally — A man is generalized beyond identity — he's a nobody!

THE DIRECTOR: Ah, but me, me — I am the Director! The Producer! You understand?

THE FATHER: Signore — Think of how you used to feel about yourself, long ago, all the illusions you used to have about the world, and about your place in it: those illusions were real for you then, they were *quite* real — But now, with hindsight, they prove to be nothing, they are nothing to you now but an embarrassment. Well, signore, that is what your present reality is today — just a set of illusions that you will discard tomorrow. Can't you feel it? I'm not speaking of the planks of this stage we stand on, I'm speaking of the very earth under our feet. It's sinking under you — by tomorrow, today's entire reality will have become just one more illusion. You see?

THE DIRECTOR: (*confused but amazed*) Well? So what? What does all that prove?

THE FATHER: Ah, nothing, signore. Only to show that if, beyond our illusions (*indicating the other characters*), we have no ultimate reality, so your reality as well — your reality that touches and feels and breathes today — will be unmasked tomorrow as nothing but yesterday's illusion!

These lines illustrate Pirandello's use of paradox, irony, and the theatre as metaphor to create a whimsical drama about human identity and human destiny. By contrasting the passion of his "characters" and the frequent frivolity of his "actors," Pirandello establishes a provocative juxtaposition of human behavior and its theatricalization — and the whole fantastical style is nothing but an exploitation of the theatrical format itself.

THEATRE OF CRUELTY:
Jet of Blood

Antonin Artaud (1896–1948) is one of drama's greatest revolutionaries, although his importance lies more in his ideas and influence than in his actual theatrical achievements. A stage and film actor in Paris during the 1920s, he founded the Théâtre Alfred Jarry in 1926, producing, among other works, Strindberg's surrealist *A Dream Play* and, in 1935, an adaptation of Shelley's dramatic poem, *The Cenci*. His essays, profoundly influential in the theatre today, were collected and published in 1938 in a book entitled *The Theatre and Its Double*.

The theatre envisaged by Artaud was a self-declared "theatre of cruelty," for, in his words, "Without an element of cruelty at the root of every performance, the theatre is not possible." The "cruel" theatre would flourish, Artaud predicted, by "providing the spectator with the true sources of his dreams, in which his taste for crime, his erotic obsessions, his savagery, his illusions, his utopian ideals, even his cannibalism, would surge forth."

In Artaud's vision, ordinary plays were to be abolished; there should be, in his words,

The six characters from Luigi Pirandello's Six Characters in Search of an Author *(1921), in William Ball's production at American Conservatory Theatre. The six characters come from a world of fantasy, but as this production photograph well illustrates, their dramatic intensity gives them the appearance of a superior reality. (Photo: William Ganslen, ACT.)*

"no more masterpieces." In place of written plays there should be

> cries, groans, apparitions, surprises, theatricalities of all kinds, magic beauty of costumes taken from certain ritual models; resplendent lighting, the incantation of beautiful voices, the charms of harmony, rare notes of music, colors of objects, physical rhythm of movements whose crescendo and decrescendo will accord exactly with the pulsation of familiar movements, concrete appearances of new and surprising objects, masks, effigies yards high, sudden changes of light, the physical action of light which arouses sensations of heat and cold ... evocative gestures, emotive or arbitrary attitudes, excited pounding out of rhythms and sounds ... [and] all the abortive attitudes, all the lapses of mind and tongue, by which are revealed what might be called the impotences of speech.

Language in Artaud's theatre was an impotent force, drowned out by the more "sensational" (as in sensory) aspects of sonic vibrations and visual extravagance continuously assaulting all the senses. But this was not to be simply a theatre of stage effects; it was, for Artaud, a theatre of profound meaning:

> Even light can have a precise intellectual meaning, light in waves, in sheets, in fusillades of fiery arrows. ... paroxysms will suddenly burst forth, will fire up like fires in different spots. ... the varied lighting of a performance will fall upon the public as much as upon the actors—and to the several simultaneous actions or several phases of an identical action in which the characters, swarming over each other like bees, will endure all the onslaughts of the situations and the external assaults of the tempestuous elements.

In a famous metaphor, Artaud compared the theatre to the great medieval plague, noting that both plague and theatre had the capacity to liberate human possibilities and illuminate the human potential:

> The theatre is like the plague ... because like the plague it is the revelation, the bringing forth, the exteriorization of a depth of latent cruelty by means of which all the perverse possibilities of the mind, whether of an individual or a people, are localized ...
>
> In the theatre as in the plague there is a kind of strange sun, a light of abnormal intensity by which it seems that the difficult and even the impossible suddenly become our normal element.
>
> One cannot imagine, save in an atmosphere of carnage, torture, and bloodshed, all the magnificent Fables which recount to the multitudes the first sexual division and the first carnage of essences that appeared in creation. The theatre, like the plague, is in the image of this carnage and this essential separation. It releases conflicts, disengages powers, liberates possibilities, and if these possibilities and these powers are dark, it is the fault not of the plague nor of the theatre, but of life.

Artaud's ideas were radical and his essays were incendiary; his power to shock and inspire are undiminished today, and many contemporary theatre artists claim an Artaudian heritage. It is not at all clear, however, what final form the "theatre of cruelty" should actually take in performance, and it is readily apparent even to the casual reader that the theatre Artaud speaks of is much easier to realize on paper than on an actual stage. Artaud's own productions were in fact failures; he was formally "expelled" from the surrealist movement, and he spent most of his later life abroad in mental institutions. His one published play, *Jet of Blood* (1925), illustrates both the radically antirealistic nature of his dramaturgy and the difficulties that would be encountered in its production. This is the opening of the play:

THE YOUNG MAN: I love you, and everything is beautiful.

THE YOUNG GIRL: (*with a strong tremolo in her voice*) You love me, and everything is beautiful.

THE YOUNG MAN: (*in a very deep voice*) I love you, and everything is beautiful.

THE YOUNG GIRL: (*in an even deeper voice than his*) You love me, and everything is beautiful.

THE YOUNG MAN: (*leaving her abruptly*) I love you. (*Pause*) Turn around and face me.

THE YOUNG GIRL: (*she turns to face him*) There!

THE YOUNG MAN: (*in a shrill and exalted voice*) I love you, I am big, I am shining, I am full, I am solid.

THE YOUNG GIRL: (*in the same shrill tone*) We love each other.

THE YOUNG MAN: We are intense. Ah, how well ordered this world is!

A pause. Something that sounds like an immense wheel turning and blowing out air is heard. A hurricane separates the two. At this moment two stars crash into each other, and we see a number of live pieces of human bodies falling down: hands, feet, scalps, masks, collonnades, porches, temples, and alembics, which, however, fall more and more slowly, as if they were falling in a vacuum. Three scorpions fall down, one after the other, and finally a frog and a beetle, which sets itself down with a maddening, vomit-inducing slowness . . .

Enter a knight of the Middle Ages in an enormous suit of armor, followed by a nurse holding her breasts in both hands and puffing and wheezing because they are both very swollen.

Artaud's apocalyptic vision has stimulated many subsequent theatre directors, including Jean Louis Barrault and Roger Blin in France, Peter Brook in England, Jerzy Grotowski in Poland, and André Gregory in America; his influence can also be seen in the plays of Jean Genet and the productions of Robert Wilson. His notion of a theatre of cruelty, while not fully realized on stage in his lifetime, has been more closely approached by each of these artists and may still be achieved.

PHILOSOPHICAL MELODRAMA:
No Exit

No Exit is one of the most compelling short plays ever written. In this one-act fantasy written in 1944, Jean-Paul Sartre, the well-known French existentialist philosopher, establishes a unique "Hell," which is a room without windows or mirrors. Into it come three people, lately deceased, all condemned to this nether world because of their earthly sins. The three are brilliantly ill matched: Garcin, the sole man, tends toward homosexuality; so does Inez, one of the two women. Estelle, the final occupant of this bizarre inferno, tends toward heterosexual nymphomania: she pursues Garcin, Garcin pursues his fellow spirit Inez, and Inez pursues the beautiful Estelle in a triangle of misdirected affection that, one presumes, will continue maddeningly through all eternity. The infinite bleakness of this play's fantastical situation and the numbing futility of each character's aspirations provoke Garcin to beg for some good old-fashioned torture—but nothing quite so simple is forthcoming. Instead, he is forced to conclude: "Hell is other people." And the play ends with a curtain line that is characteristic of the modern stylized theatre:

GARCIN: Well, well, let's get on with it.

This line suggests that although the play concludes, the situation continues, eternally, behind the drawn curtain.

No Exit is a classic dramatic statement of existentialism, of which Sartre was this century's leading exponent. Remove the fantastical elements—that this is Hell and the characters are ghosts—and we have Sartre's vision of human interaction: every individual forever seeks affirmation and self-realization in the eyes of the Other. Each character in the play carries with him or her a baggage of guilt and expectation, each seeks from another some certification of final personal worth, and each is endlessly thwarted in this quest. We are all condemned to revolve around each other in frustratingly incomplete accord, suggests Sartre; we are all forced to reckon with the impossibility of finding meaning out of the unrelated events that constitute life.

One can accept or reject Sartre's view—which is perhaps more than usually pessimis-

EXISTENTIALISM, ABSURDISM, AND WORLD WAR II

Both Sartre's existentialism and Camus's philosophy of the absurd were forged largely in the outrages of World War II, when both men were leading figures in the French Resistance movement. A hellish world that affords "no exit," and in which human activity is as meaningless as Sisyphus' torment, seems perfectly credible during such desperate times, times of national occupation and genocidal slaughter. After the war, Jean-Paul Sartre, who was France's foremost exponent of existentialism and one of that country's leading dramatists in the 1940s and 1950s, spoke eloquently of his first experience as playwright and director, which occurred when he was a prisoner of war:

> My first experience in the theatre was especially fortunate. When I was a prisoner in Germany in 1940, I wrote, staged and acted in a Christmas play which, while pulling the wool over the eyes of the German censor by means of simple symbols, was addressed to my fellow prisoners. This drama, biblical in appearance only, was written and put on by a prisoner, was acted by prisoners in scenery painted by prisoners; it was aimed exclusively at prisoners (so much so that I have never since then permitted it to be staged or

even printed) and it addressed them on the subject of their concerns as prisoners. No doubt it was neither a good play nor well acted: the work of an amateur, the critics would say, a product of special circumstances. Nevertheless, on this occasion, as I addressed my comrades across the footlights, speaking to them of their state as prisoners, when I suddenly saw them so remarkably silent and attentive, I realized what theatre ought to be—a great collective, religious phenomenon.

> To be sure, I was, in this case, favored by special circumstances; it does not happen every day that your public is drawn together by one great common interest, a great loss or a great hope. As a rule, an audience is made up of the most diverse elements: a big business man sits beside a traveling salesman or a professor, a man next to a woman, and each is subject to his own particular preoccupations. Yet this situation is a challenge to the playwright: he must create his public, he must fuse all the disparate elements in the auditorium into a single unity by awakening in the recesses of their spirits the things which all men of a given epoch and community care about.

> Quoted in *Theatre Arts*

---

tic for having been written during the Nazi Occupation of Sartre's Paris—but there can be little dispute over the assertion that his technique for dramatically stylizing it is quite brilliant. The fantastical Hell, an amusing "valet" who brings each character onto the stage, and the highly contrived assemblage of mismatched characters all serve to focus the intellectual argument precisely. Sartre's characters are philosophically representative rather than psychologically whole; there is no intention on Sartre's part to portray individual people with interesting idiosyncracies, and there is no feeling on our part that the characters have a personal life beyond what we see in the

play. Biographical character analysis would be useless for an actor assigned to play one of these roles, and the interlock of psychological motivation, even in this sexually charged atmosphere, is deliberately ignored by the author. What Sartre presents instead is a general understanding of human affairs: a philosophy of interpersonal relations.

THEATRE OF THE ABSURD:
Waiting for Godot

The name *theatre of the absurd* has been applied by critics to a grouping of plays that share certain common structures and styles and are tied together by a common philosophical thread: the theory of the absurd as formulated by French essayist and playwright Albert Camus. Camus likened the human condition to that of the mythological Corinthian king Sisyphus, who because of his cruelty was condemned forever to roll a stone up a hill in Hades only to have it roll down again upon nearing the top. Camus saw the modern individual as similarly engaged in an eternally futile task, the absurdity of searching for some meaning or purpose or order in human life. To Camus, the immutable irrationality of the universe is what makes this task absurd. On the one hand, human beings yearn for a "lost" unity and lasting truth; on the other hand, the world can only be seen as irrecoverably fragmented — chaotic, unsummable, permanently unorganized, and permanently unorganizable.

The plays that constitute the theatre of the absurd are obsessed with the futility of all action and the pointlessness of all direction. These themes are developed theatrically through a deliberate and self-conscious flaunting of the "absurd" — in the sense of the ridiculous. Going beyond the use of symbols and the fantasy and poetry of other nonrealists, the absurdists have distinguished themselves by

---

ALBEE ON THE ABSURD

As I get it, The Theatre of the Absurd is an absorption-in-art of certain existentialist and post-existentialist philosophical concepts having to do, in the main, with man's attempts to make sense for himself out of his senseless position in a world which makes no sense — which makes no sense because the moral, religious, political, and social structures man has erected to 'illusion' himself have collapsed.

Edward Albee

---

creating clocks that clang incessantly, characters that eat pap in ashcans, corpses that grow by the minute, and personal interactions that are belligerently noncredible.

The theatre of the absurd can be said to include mid-twentieth-century works by Jean Genet (French), Eugène Ionesco (Romanian), Friedrich Duerrenmatt (Swiss), Arthur Adamov (Russian), Slawomir Mrozek (Polish), Harold Pinter (English), Edward Albee (American), Fernando Arrabal (Spanish), and the Irish poet, playwright, and novelist Samuel Beckett. And although Paris is the center of this theatre — so much so that the works of Ionesco, Adamov, Arrabal, and Beckett are all written in French rather than in their native tongues — its influence is felt worldwide.

Samuel Beckett, the unquestioned leader of the absurdist writers, eschews all realism, romanticism, and rationalism to create works that are relentlessly unenlightening, that are indeed committed to a final obscurity. "Art has nothing to do with clarity, does not dabble in the clear, and does not make clear," argues Beckett in one of his earliest works, and his theatre is based on the thesis that man is and will remain ignorant regarding all matters of importance.

Born in Dublin in 1906, Beckett emigrated in 1928 to Paris, where he joined a literary circle centered on another Irish emigré, James Joyce. Beckett's life before World War II was an artistic vagabondage, during which he wrote several poems, short stories, and a novel; following the war and his seclusion in the south of France during the Occupation, he produced the masterworks for which he is justly famous: the novels *Molloy, Moran Dies,* and *The Unnamable,* and the plays *Waiting for Godot* and *Endgame.* By the time of his death in 1989, Beckett had received the Nobel Prize for Literature, and his works had become the subject of literally hundreds of critical books and essays. It was *Godot* that first brought Beckett to worldwide attention: the play's premiere in Paris in 1953 occasioned a great stir among French authors and critics, and its sub-

A photograph of the original production of Waiting for Godot *at the Théâtre Babylone in Paris, 1953. In front of neutral backdrop and barren tree, Estragon (barefooted) and Vladimir doff their hats to listen for ticking of Pozzo's pocket watch—but all they hear is Pozzo's heartbeat. (Photo: Photo Pic.)*

The American Repertory Theatre 1984 production of Samuel Beckett's Endgame, *directed by JoAnne Akalaitis, caused an enormous scandal: Akalaitis had chosen to set the play in an abandoned subway station, and Beckett responded with a letter fiercely objecting to what he considered a violation of the author's specific staging instructions. The ensuing debate, though inconclusive, crystallized arguments that had been waged for half a century about the roles of directors and designers: are they implementors of playwrights' visions or free and independent creative artists? (Photo: Richard Feldman.)*

sequent openings in London and New York had the same effect there.

Waiting for Godot is a parable without message. On a small mound at the base of a tree, beside a country road, two elderly men in bowler hats wait for a "Mr. Godot" with whom they have presumably made an appointment. They believe that when Godot comes they will be "saved"; however, they are not at all certain that Godot has agreed to meet with them, or if this is the right place or the right day, or whether they will even recognize him if he comes. During each of the two acts, which seem to be set in late afternoon on two successive days (although nobody can be sure of that), the men are visited by passersby — first by two men calling themselves Pozzo and Lucky, subsequently by a young boy who tells them that Mr. Godot "cannot come today but surely tomorrow." The two old men continue to wait as the curtain falls. Although there is substantial reference in the play to Christian symbols and beliefs, it is not clear whether these imply positive or negative associations. The only development in the play is that the characters seem to undergo a certain loss of adeptness while the setting blossoms in rebirth (the tree sprouts leaves between the acts).

What Beckett has drawn here is clearly a paradigm of the human condition: an ongoing life cycle of vegetation serving as background to human decay, hope, and ignorance. Beckett's tone is whimsical: the characters play

Bertolt Brecht's most popular play, in his own time and ours, was one of his first:
The Threepenny Opera *(1927), adapted from an eighteenth-century English play*
(John Gay's The Beggar's Opera*), with new music by Kurt Weill.* Threepenny *was*
a giant popular success in pre-Nazi Berlin, and its Greenwich Village revival with
Lotte Lenya was a major factor in beginning New York City's off-Broadway move-
ment in the 1950s. An ironic and satiric romance about thieves, whores, beggars,
and the London police, the "opera" established Brecht's reputation as an iconoclastic
dramatist. Here directed by equally iconoclastic director Richard Foreman (the wire
strung across the stage is a Foreman motif) for the New York Shakespeare Festival
production at Lincoln Center. Raul Julia plays the head gangster, Macheath ("Mack
the Knife"). (Photo: George Joseph.)

enchanting word games with each other, they amuse each other with songs, accounts of dreams, exercises, and vaudevillian antics, and in general they make the best of a basically hopeless situation. Beckett's paradigm affords a field day for critical investigators. *Waiting for Godot* has already generated a veritable library of brilliantly evocative discussions, and few plays from any era have been so variously analyzed, interpreted, and explored for symbolic meaning and content. Owing largely to the international critical acceptance of this play and its eventual public success, not only absurdist drama but also the whole of modern stylized theatre was able to move out of the esoteric "art theatre" of the world capitals and onto the stages of popular theatres everywhere.

THEATRE OF ALIENATION:
The Good Woman of Sezuan

Contrasting vividly with the theatre of the absurd is the theatre of alienation, or of distancing. Whereas the hermetic, self-contained absurdist plays highlight the essential futility of human endeavors, the sprawling, socially engaged "epic" theatre of alienation concentrates on humanity's potential for growth and society's capacity to effect change.

The guiding genius of the theatre of alienation was Bertolt Brecht (1896–1956): theorist, dramatist, and director. No single individual has had a greater impact on post–World War II theatre than Brecht. This impact has been felt in two ways. First, Brecht introduced theatre practices that are, at least on the surface, utterly at variance with those in use since the time of Aristotle; second, his accomplishments invigorated the theatre with an abrasive humanism that reawakened its sense of social responsibility and its awareness of the capacity of theatre to mold public issues and events.

Brecht was born in Germany in 1898 and emerged from World War I a dedicated Marxist and pacifist. Using poems, songs, and eventually the theatre to promote his ideals following the German defeat, Brecht vividly portrayed his country during the Weimar Republic as caught in the grips of four giant vises: the military, capitalism, industrialization, and imperialism. His *Rise and Fall of the City of Mahagonny,* for example, an "epic opera" of 1930, proved an immensely popular blending of satire and propaganda, music and expressionist theatricality, social idealism and lyric poetry; it was produced all over Germany and throughout most of Europe in the early 1930s as a depiction of a rapacious international capitalism evolving toward fascism.

Brecht was forced to flee his country upon Hitler's accession to the chancellorship. Thereafter he moved about Europe for a time and then, for much of the 1940s, settled in America. Following World War II he returned in triumph to Berlin, where the East German government established for him the Berliner Ensemble Theatre; there Brecht was allowed to consolidate his theories in a body of productions developed out of his earlier plays and the pieces he had written while in exile.

Brecht's theatre draws upon a potpourri of theatrical conventions, some derived from the ancients, some from Eastern drama, and some from the German expressionist movement in which Brecht himself played a part in his early years. Masks, songs, verse, exotic settings, satire, and direct rhetorical address are fundamental conventions that Brecht adopted from other theatre forms. In addition, he developed many conventions of his own: lantern-slide projections with printed "captions," asides and invocations directed to the audience to encourage them to develop an objective point of view, and a variety of procedures aimed at demystifying theatrical techniques (for example, lowering the lights so that the pipes and wires would be displayed) became the characteristics of Brecht's theatre.

He deplored the use of sentimentality and the notion of audience empathy for characters and attempted instead to create a performance style that was openly "didactic": the actor was asked to alienate himself, or distance himself, from the character he played—to "demonstrate" his character rather than to embody that character in a realistic manner. In Brecht's view the ideal actor was one who could establish a *critical objectivity* toward his or her character that would make clear the character's social function and political commitment. In attempting to repudiate the "magic" of the theatre, he demanded that it be made to seem nothing more than a place for workers to present a meaningful "parable" of life, and he in no way wished to disguise the fact that the stage personnel—actors and stagehands—

were merely workers who were engaged in doing a job. In every way possible, Brecht attempted to prevent the audience from becoming swept up in an emotional, sentimental bath of feelings: his goal was to keep the audience "alienated" or "distanced" from the literal events depicted by the play so they would be free to concentrate on the larger social and political issues that the play generated and reflected. Brecht considered this theatre to be an "epic" one because it attempted, around the framework of a parable or archetypal event, to create a whole new perspective on human history and to indicate the direction that political dialogue should take to foster social betterment.

Brecht's theories were to have a staggering impact on the modern theatre. In his wholesale renunciation of Aristotelian catharsis, which depends on audience empathy with a noble character, and his denial of Stanislavski's basic principles concerning the aims of acting, Brecht provided a new dramaturgy that encouraged playwrights, directors, and designers to tackle social issues directly rather than through the implications of contrived dramatic situations. Combining the technologies and aesthetics of other media — the lecture hall, the slide show, the public meeting, the cinema, the cabaret, the rehearsal — Brecht fashioned a vastly expanded arena for his *dialectics:* his social arguments that sought to engender truth through the confrontation of conflicting interests. These ideas were played out, in Brecht's own works and in countless other works inspired by him, with a bold theatricality, an open-handed dealing with the audience, a proletarian vigor, and a stridently entertaining, intelligently satirical, and charmingly bawdy theatre. This theatre has proven even more popular in the 1970s and 1980s than it was in Brecht's day, because since then the world seems to have grown even more fragmented, more individualistic, and more suspicious of collective emotions and sentimentality.

No play better illustrates Brecht's dramatic theory and method than *The Good Woman of Sezuan* (1943). This play, set in western China (of which Brecht knew virtually nothing — thus adding to the "distancing" of the story) — concerns a kindhearted prostitute, Shen Te, who is astounded to receive a gift of money from three itinerant gods. Elated by her good fortune, Shen Te uses the money to start a tobacco business. She is, however, quickly beset by petty officials seeking to impose local regulations, self-proclaimed creditors demanding payment, and a host of hangers-on who simply prey upon her good nature. At the point of financial ruin, Shen Te leaves her tobacco shop to enlist the aid of her male cousin Shui Ta, who strides imperiously into the tobacco shop and routs the predators, making it safe for Shen Te to return. But the predators come back, and Shen Te again has to call on the tyrannical Shui Ta to save her. A simple story — but Brecht's stroke of genius is to make Shui Ta and Shen Te the same character: Shui Ta is simply Shen Te in disguise! The aim of the play is not to show that there are kindhearted people and tyrannical people, but that a person can choose to be one or the other. What kind of society is it, Brecht asks, that forces us to make this sort of choice?

Brecht is no mere propagandist, and his epic theatre is not one of simple messages or easy conclusions. At the end of *The Good Woman of Sezuan,* Shen Te asks the gods for help, but they simply float off into the air reciting inane platitudes as the curtain falls. The gods do not have the answer — so the audience must provide it. In the play's epilogue, a character comes forward and addresses us:

Hey, honorable folks, don't be dismayed
That we can't seem to end this play!
   You've stayed
To see our shining, all-concluding moral,
And what we've given you has been this
   bitter quarrel.
We know, we know — we're angry too,
To see the curtain down and everything
   askew.

We'd love to see you stand and cheer —
and say
How wonderful you find our charming
play!
But we won't put our heads into the sand.
We know your wish is ever our command,
We know you ask for *more:* a firm
conclusion
To this alarming more-than-mass
confusion.
But what is it? Who knows? Not all your
cash
Could buy your way — or ours — from this
mishmash.
Do we need heroes? Dreams? New Gods?
Or None?
Well, tell us — else we're hopelessly
undone.
The only thing that we can think to say
Is simply that it's *you* must end this play.
Tell us how our own good woman of
Sezuan
Can come to a good ending — if she can!
Honorable folks: you search, and we will
trust
That you will find the way. You must,
must, must!

Brecht's parables epitomize the conflicts between social classes; they do not presume to solve these conflicts. Indeed, the social problems he addresses are not to be solved on the stage but in the world itself: the audience must find the appropriate balance between morality and greed, between individualism and social responsibility. Brecht's plays reenact the basic intellectual dichotomy posed by Marx's dialectical materialism; thus they are, in a sense, Marxist plays, but they certainly are not Leninist, much less Stalinist. They radiate a faith in the human potential. Yet while they are both socially engaged and theatrically eclectic — qualities not particularly noticeable in the theatre of the absurd — they still resound with the fundamental human uncertainty that pervades all of modern stylized theatre.

COMEDY OF CONTEMPORARY MANNERS:
Bedroom Farce

Comedy has always been one of the greatest staples of the theatre; since the days of Aristophanes in ancient Greece and Plautus in Rome, comedians have entertained the public with puns, antics, light-hearted social commentaries, and a host of other amusing reflections on the human struggle. It is an axiom of the theatre that "comedy is serious business," and the true comedian is understood to be as inspired an artist as any who labors under the lights. Yet comedy is rarely accorded its fair share of academic consideration, partly because comedy tends to be topical and therefore less than universal and partly because the very thing that makes comedy popular — its accessibility — also makes it relatively simple, and academicians adore complexity. But simple does not mean simple-minded, and the relative scarcity of fine comic plays originating in any generation attests to the enormous talent it takes to write, direct, and act comedically.

In America, Neil Simon has for two decades exhibited enormous talent and success as a writer of light comedy for the stage (and film); in England, Alan Ayckbourn has demonstrated a comparable skill at the form. Ayckbourn's *Bedroom Farce* was first produced in 1975 by the Library Theatre in Scarborough, England, with which Ayckbourn is associated; the play was subsequently produced by the National Theatre in London in 1977 and came to Broadway and various other American cities shortly thereafter.

Like all of Ayckbourn's works, *Bedroom Farce* is an ingenious comedy of current manners, novel in its dramatic structure and reasonably true to life in its concerns. The setting for *Bedroom Farce* is three bedrooms, all in view simultaneously; the characters consist of four couples who, for reasons cleverly worked out in the plot, find themselves in one bedroom after another by turns. While the innuendos of this play are highly sexual, the action consists primarily of animated verbal

The opening scene from Alan Ayckbourn's Bedroom Farce, *The National Theatre, London, 1977. (Photo: Morris Newcombe.)*

exchanges and comic business and pratfalls; thus does the play live up to the farcical structure promised by its title.

The opening scene of *Bedroom Farce,* an exchange of dialogue between Ernest and Delia, the oldest couple in the play, typifies the witty and very British repartee mastered by Ayckbourn. The scene takes place in that bedroom which is described as a "large Victorian" room "in need of redecoration":

... DELIA *sits in her bedroom at her dressing table mirror. She is going out. She is in her slip and finishing her make-up. An elaborate operation.* ERNEST *wanders in. Birdlike, bumbling,*

nearly sixty. He is in evening dress. He stares at DELIA. *They are obviously going to be late but* ERNEST *has learnt that impatience gets him nowhere.*

ERNEST: Have you got much further to go?

DELIA: (*without turning*) Not long now.

ERNEST: Good. Good show. (*He walks out humming restlessly.*) No, that is definitely a damp patch, you know.

DELIA: Mmm?

ERNEST: A damp patch. Definitely. It's getting in from somewhere. I've just been standing on the spare bed in there feeling the ceiling. The verdict is, very very damp.

DELIA: Oh dear.

ERNEST: Yes. Which only goes to confirm my suspicion that those chaps we had crawling about the roof for six months didn't know their job. (*He leans out of the window backwards.*)

DELIA: What are you doing?

ERNEST: I'm trying to catch a glimpse of the repointing. It's seeping in from somewhere.

DELIA: You'll fall out in a minute.

ERNEST: No. You can't see a thing. That gutterwork's obscuring the whole. . . . Good lord. That needs a spot of attention. It's hanging off at one end. Good lord.

DELIA: Darling, you're in my light.

ERNEST: There's a whole chunk of guttering here hanging on by a screw. (*He comes in.*) Hadn't noticed that before.

DELIA: Oh, did I tell you. Susannah phoned this afternoon.

ERNEST: (*thoughtful*) Did he? Did he indeed.

DELIA: No, not he. Susannah.

ERNEST: Who?

DELIA: Susannah.

ERNEST: Oh, Susannah. Jolly good. Very worrying that guttering, you know. One light to medium monsoon, we'll have a waterfall in the dining room.

DELIA: She sounded very agitated.

ERNEST: Oh yes.

DELIA: Things are not good between her and Trevor.

ERNEST: Ah. It's twenty past, you know.

DELIA: All right, all right.

ERNEST: We're booked for eight o'clock.

DELIA: They'll hold the table.

ERNEST: They might not.

DELIA: Of course they will.

ERNEST: You never know. Not these days.

DELIA: They'll hold the table for us. We're regulars. We go there every year.

ERNEST: Oh, well. It's your anniversary.

DELIA: And yours.

ERNEST: True, true. I think I should have given these shoes another polish.

DELIA: Well, go and do it.

ERNEST: No, it doesn't matter. Nobody'll notice.

DELIA: It would appear that things between Susannah and Trevor are coming to a head.

ERNEST: Ah.

DELIA: He was always a difficult boy. I sometimes think if you hadn't ignored him quite as much—

ERNEST: I did?

DELIA: Of course you did. You hardly said a word to him all the time he was growing up.

ERNEST: I seem to remember chatting away to him for hours.

DELIA: Well. Chatting. I meant conversation. Conversation about important things. A father should converse with his son. About things that matter deeply.

ERNEST: Doesn't really leave them much to talk about then, does it?

DELIA: And that if I may say so is typical. No. Let's admit it. We weren't good parents. You did nothing and I tried to make up for it, and that's why he's like he is today. I mean if he'd had a stable childhood, he'd never have completely lost his sense of proportion and married Susannah. I mean, I sometimes feel on the rare occasions one does see them together that she's not really— awful thing to say but—not really resilient enough for Trevor. He wants somebody more phlegmatic. That Jan girl for instance would have been ideal. Do you remember her?

ERNEST: Jan? Jan? Jan?

DELIA: Nice little thing. Beautifully normal. She came to tea, do you remember? You got on very well with her.

ERNEST: Oh yes. She was jolly, wasn't she? She was very interested in my stamps. What happened to her?

DELIA: Oh, she married—someone else, I think. She still writes occasionally.

ERNEST: I must say I preferred her to Susannah. Never really hit it off with her, I'm afraid.

DELIA: Well, she's a very complex sort of girl, isn't she? Hasn't really made up her mind. About herself. I mean, I think a woman sooner or later has simply got to make up her mind about herself. I mean, even if she's someone like Carolyn—you know, Mrs. Brightman's Carolyn—who looks at herself and says, right, I'm a lump I'm going to be a lump but then at least everyone can accept her as a lump. So much simpler.

ERNEST: I think he should have married this other one.

DELIA: Jan? I don't think she was that keen.

ERNEST: She was altogether much jollier.

DELIA: Well, we're saddled with Susannah as a daughter-in-law—at least temporarily. We'd better make the best of it—I think I've put these eyes on crooked—we'd better make the best of it.

ERNEST: It's their bed. They can lie on it.

DELIA: Yes. I think that's one of the problems.

ERNEST: Eh?

DELIA: B—E—D.

ERNEST: B—E—D? Bed?

DELIA: Enough said.

ERNEST: Good lord. How do you know?

DELIA: One reads between the lines, darling. I've had a little look around their house. You can tell a great deal from people's bedrooms.

ERNEST: Can you? Good heavens. (*He looks about.*)

DELIA: If you know what to look for. Now then. Do I wear what I wore when I went to the Reynolds or shall I wear the stripy thing that you loathe.

ERNEST: I'd wear the Reynolds thing.

DELIA: Or there's the little grey.

ERNEST: Oh.

DELIA: Or the blue.

ERNEST: Ah.

DELIA: No, that isn't pressed. You decide, darling. Stripy or the other one.

ERNEST: Er . . .

DELIA: Or the grey.

ERNEST: Er . . .

DELIA: Right I've decided, it's the other one. Good. Now, in the spare wardrobe in Trevor's old room on the top shelf, there's a little black handbag. Could you fetch me that? . . .

(DELIA *goes into the bathroom*)

ERNEST: Little black handbag, right. (*Looking round*) I don't think you can tell very much from this bedroom. Except the roof's leaking from somewhere.

There is nothing obscure or difficult in *Bedroom Farce,* which stands out in the contemporary theatre mainly for its capacity to entertain, to titillate, and to dazzle with cleverness. Indeed, Ayckbourn makes clear his purely comedic intentions in the selection of his title, which suggests an even more frivolous diversion than Ayckbourn actually provides. For what the author has created in *Bedroom Farce* is, ultimately, something more than just another series of hijinks and dramatic clichés: it is a wry combination of social satire, middle-class insights, and boisterous good fun. The modern stylization can be seen in the intricacy of the plot design, which is echoed if not exceeded in Ayckbourn's other plays (*Absurd Person Singular* takes place, successively, in the kitchens of three married couples; *The Norman Conquests* consists of three interlocking plays, occurring simultaneously, involving the same cast of characters in three parts of the same house) and reflects a skill at construction that borders on pure genius. This kind of craftsmanship alone would suffice to elevate any comedy far beyond the usual level of tele-

vision skit or sitcom: in Ayckbourn's case, it enables his stage works to reach the heights of inspired farce.

THE CASE STUDY:
Wings

Wings, by American author Arthur Kopit (previously known for his intriguingly titled *Oh Dad, Poor Dad, Mama's Hung You in the Closet and I'm Feeling So Sad*), was originally written as a play for radio. It was subsequently revised for the stage and was presented first in 1968 at the Yale Repertory Theatre in New

Constance Cummings as Mrs. Stilson, in original production of Wings *by the Yale Repertory Theatre, directed by John Madden. Cummings is attended by Marianne Owen as Amy. (Photo: Eugene Cook.)*

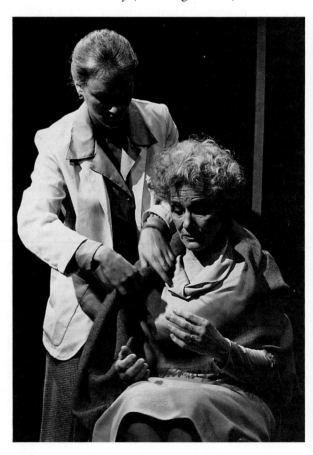

Haven, Connecticut, whence it eventually moved to Broadway for a limited run. In 1992, a musical version of the play was staged at the Goodman Studio Theatre in Chicago, bringing Kopit's intriguing work to new audiences.

The play is one of a growing number of dramatic works that present "case studies" of individuals in medical distress: other recent plays with similar themes include Bernard Pomerance's *The Elephant Man* (American, 1979), dealing with extreme disfigurement; Albert Innaurato's *The Transfiguration of Benno Blimpie* (American, 1978), dealing with obesity; Peter Shaffer's *Equus* (British, 1973), dealing with schizophrenic behavior; and Brian Clark's *Whose Life Is It Anyway?* (British, 1978), dealing with total paralysis. Medical issues are not the dominant concern of these plays, of course, but in each case a medical problem furnishes a perspective for the playwright's philosophical investigations.

Wings takes place in a setting that is nothing but "a system of black scrim panels that can move silently and easily, creating the impression of featureless, labyrinthine corridors." The setting, therefore, represents both a hospital and the inside of a patient's mind — the patient being a Mrs. Stilson, former aviatrix, now a victim of brain stroke. Mrs. Stilson sits in a chair downstage of the panels, and what we in the audience see and hear is a confusion of images, sounds, words, and illusions that represent Mrs. Stilson's "inner self," where "time and space are without definition," and "information is coming in too scrambled and too fast to be properly decoded." "Were her head a pinball game," Kopit says, "It would register TILT."

Kopit achieves this scrambled effect through a brilliant dramaturgical design whereby the information conveyed on stage assumes the form it would take in the perceptions of the stroke victim herself: in other words, by his stylization of the dramatic dialogue and imagery, Kopit gives his audience the opportunity not merely to observe stroke, but also to experience it. The first scene, entitled "Catastrophe," illustrates his technique:

IMAGES	SOUNDS OUTSIDE HERSELF	MRS. STILSON'S VOICE
	(SOUNDS live or on tape, altered or unadorned)	(VOICE live or on tape, altered or unadorned)
Mostly, it is whiteness. Dazzling, blinding.	Of wind.	*Oh my God oh my God oh my God —*
	Of someone breathing with effort, unevenly.	*— trees clouds houses mostly planes flashing past, images without words, utter disarray disbelief, never seen this kind of thing before!*
	Of something ripping, like a sheet.	
Occasionally, there are brief rhombs of color, explosions of color, the color red being dominant.	Of something flapping, the sound suggestive of an old screen door perhaps, or a sheet or sail in the wind. It is a rapid fibrillation. And it is used mostly to mark transitions. It can seem ominous or not.	*Where am I? How'd I get here?*
The mirrors, of course, reflect infinitely. Sense of endless space, endless corridors.	Of a woman's scream (though this sound should be altered by filters so it resembles other things, such as sirens).	*My leg (What's my leg?) feels wet arms . . . wet too, belly same chin nose everything (Where are they taking me?) something sticky (What has happened to my plane?) feel something sticky.*
	Of random noises recorded in a busy city hospital, then al-	

IMAGES	SOUNDS OUTSIDE HERSELF	MRS. STILSON'S VOICE

IMAGES

Nothing seen that is not a fragment. Every aspect of her world has been shattered.

Utter isolation.

In this vast whiteness, like apparitions, partial glimpses of doctors and nurses can be seen. They appear and disappear like a pulse. They are never in one place for long.

The mirrors multiply their incomprehensibility.

Sometimes the dark panels are opaque, sometimes transparent. Always, they convey a sense of layers, multiplicity, separation. Sense constantly of doors opening, closing, opening, closing.

Fragments of hospital equipment appear out of nowhere and disappear just as suddenly. Glimpse always too brief to enable us to identify what this equipment is, or what its purpose.

Mrs. Stilson's movements seem random. She is a person wandering through space, lost.

Finally, Mrs. Stilson is led by attendants downstage, to a chair. Then left alone.

SOUNDS OUTSIDE HERSELF

tered so as to be only minimally recognizable.
Of a car's engine at full speed.
Of a siren (altered to resemble a woman screaming).
Of an airplane coming closer, thundering overhead, then zooming off into silence.
Of random crowd noises, the crowd greatly agitated. In the crowd, people can be heard calling for help, a doctor, an ambulance. But all the sounds are garbled.

Of people whispering.
Of many people asking questions simultaneously, no question comprehensible.
Of doors opening, closing, opening, closing.
Of someone breathing oxygen through a mask.
VOICES: (garbled) Just relax. / No one's going to hurt you. / Can you hear us? / Be careful! / You're hurting her! / No, we're not. / Don't lift her, leave her where she is! / Someone call an ambulance! / I don't think she can hear.

MALE VOICE: Have you any idea—

OTHER VOICES: (garbled) Do you know your name? / Do you know where you are? / What year is this? / If I say the tiger has been killed by the lion, which animal is dead?

A hospital paging system heard.
Equipment being moved through stone corridors, vast vaulting space. Endless echoing.

MRS. STILSON'S VOICE

Doors! Too many doors!

Must have . . . fallen cannot . . . move at all sky . . . (Gliding!) dark cannot . . . talk (Feel as if I'm gliding!).

Yes, feels cool, nice . . . Yes, this is the life all right!
My plane! What has happened to my plane!

Help . . .

— all around faces of which nothing known no sense ever all wiped out blank like ice I think saw it once flying over something some place all was white sky and sea clouds ice almost crashed couldn't tell where I was heading right side up topsy-turvy under over I was flying actually if I can I do yes do recall was upside down can you believe it almost scraped my head on the ice caps couldn't tell which way was up wasn't even dizzy strange things happen to me that they do!

What's my name? I don't know my name!

Where's my arm? I don't have an arm!

What's an arm?

AB-ABC-ABC123DE451212 what? 123—12345678972357 better yes no problem I'm okay soon be out soon be over storm . . . will pass I'm sure. Always has.

By an ingenious combination of voices, non-verbal sounds, colors, and movements with an intricate interplay of actors, hospital equipment, and panels, Kopit captures the intellectual dislocation caused by brain trauma and compels his audience to partake of the victim's fear, bewilderment, and sense of helplessness. *Wings* is a disturbing play, but it is also extremely thought-provoking. Beyond the purely medical issues, it explores a whole range of philosophical and epistemological questions: What is communication? What is emotional support? What is learning? What are words and what are they worth? Finally, the play is inspiring as a portrait of a human being whose struggle to control her inner world has intense meaning for every sensitive person.

THE MUSICAL:
Sweeney Todd

Sweeney Todd is one of those works that must be classed as an American Broadway musical, for it boasts a theatrical format that is quintessentially American: bold, lavish, and spectacular. At the same time, it differs radically from most American musicals of the past in that it incorporates strains from both the epic theatre of Bertolt Brecht and the early expressionist theatre of Eugene O'Neill.

Musical plays are customarily "authored" by a triumvirate, with one person writing the spoken dialogue, or book, a second person writing the lyrics, a third writing the music. Two writers collaborated in the creation of *Sweeney Todd:* Hugh Wheeler wrote the book, and Stephen Sondheim wrote the music and lyrics. Sondheim, clearly the leading figure in this collaboration (which also included director Harold Prince), has played a major role in the creation of an impressive number of American musicals of the 1950s, 1960s, and 1970s, including *West Side Story, Gypsy, Follies, Company,* and *A Little Night Music* (see Chapter 8).

Sweeney Todd is based on a contemporary British version, by author Christopher Bond, of a nineteenth-century English melodrama.

It tells the story of the "Demon Barber of Fleet Street," who decides to wreak revenge upon a corrupt English judiciary by butchering his customers and, with the help of his landlady, Mrs. Lovett, grinding their corpses to make salable meat pies. That this grisly tale should serve as the basis of an American musical is in itself a startling idea, but the concoction of songs and staging effects created by Sondheim, Wheeler, and Prince has added to the sensation by virtually redefining the musical form.

The original staging of *Sweeney Todd* was something only the Broadway theatre could finance or accommodate. Onto the stage of the cavernous Uris Theatre, designer Eugene Lee brought a gigantic, real nineteenth-century factory that had been found abandoned in Rhode Island. This structure was painstakingly disassembled at its original site and just as painstakingly reassembled in the theatre. The desired effect was not realism, for *Sweeney Todd* is not set in a factory. Instead, the old building, complete with its steel girders, ancient windows and skylights, catwalks and pulleys, and broken-down machinery, served as a surround for the action, a symbol indicative of a certain social atmosphere: the op-

Angela Lansbury and Len Cariou sing a duet in Broadway production of Sweeney Todd, *directed by Hal Prince. (Photo: Martha Swope and Associates.)*

The original Broadway stage setting for Sweeney Todd, *designed by Eugene Lee, featured an entirely reconstructed factory, within which a cube represented Mrs. Lovett's meat shop and Sweeney's barber shop above. In background is painted drop of the London harbor used in play's opening scenes; pulleys and catwalks abound as industrial set dressing. Len Cariou is barber in this photograph of Broadway production. (Photo: Martha Swope and Associates.)*

pression of industrial London and the grimy sordidness that is the economic and moral background for the play's action. The action itself takes place, for the most part, in a setting that represents Todd's and his landlady's London quarters. Expressionist effects, such as a cruelly piercing factory whistle that sounds at the play's moments of crisis, punctuate the action; and the songs, often as not, are addressed directly to the audience in pure Brechtian fashion.

It is clear that *Sweeney Todd* has opened up the possibility of a reinvigoration of the American Broadway musical, partly by infusing that form with current intellectual and aesthetic developments in the theatre, partly by reasserting traditional elements of melodrama and grand opera from the nineteenth-century romantic theatre, and partly by dint of the sheer creative genius of its artistic collaborators.

The theatre of today exists on stage, not in the pages of this or any other book.

The theatre of today is being performed right now, in the multimillion-dollar theatres of the great cities of the world as well as on the simpler stages of schools and communities, dinner theatres and nightclubs, roadhouses and experimental theatre clubs everywhere.

The theatre of today is all around us, simply waiting to be discovered, seen, heard, felt, and experienced. The easiest and best way to apprehend its fundamental impulse is to go out and see for oneself.

We cannot evaluate our current theatre with the same objectivity as we do that of the past—even the recent past. Theatre is a business as well as an art, and the flurry of promotion, publicity, and puffery that surrounds each current theatrical success makes a cool perspective difficult. While poets and painters are often ignored in their own time, the opposite is more often true of theatre artists: they are frequently lionized in their own time, only to be forgotten just a few years later. A permanent place in the repertory of world theatre is the achievement of very few indeed. Among the playwrights once deemed equal to Shakespeare or better are such now-dimly re-

CHAPTER **8**

THEATRE TODAY

membered figures as John Fletcher, Joseph Addison, Edward George Bulwer-Lytton, August Friedrich Ferdinand von Kotzebue, Eugène Brieux, and Maxwell Anderson. Which of our present-day writers and actors and other theatre artists will achieve more than ephemeral glory? Which, if any, will leave a mark on future generations? No one can answer either question for sure. But there are some directions in today's theatre that show signs of becoming established, and these are worthy of examination.

THE MODERN AND
THE POSTMODERN

From a practical point of view—that is, from the standpoint of theatre practice, as opposed to theory—the theatre is, and probably will always be, a somewhat conservative institution. Almost certainly, theatre companies the world over will continue to present a large number of plays from past eras, including the "modern" one, and will "conserve" many of the theatre's traditional, if not indeed hoary, ways of working. In fact, virtually all of the plays mentioned in the previous chapters are being performed somewhere in the world today, while you read these pages, and the vigorous debates among today's actors and directors often repeat, almost verbatim, dialogues current in the days of Aristophanes, Shakespeare, and Stanislavski.

Yet, as we move into the last few years and months of the twentieth century and begin to address ourselves to the challenges of the third millennium, a new era seems to be, in William Butler Yeats's remarkable metaphor, "slouching towards Bethlehem to be born." The modern theatre—with both its realistic and non-realistic strains—is more and more perceived as a winding-down period in theatrical history. And an era of so-called postmodernism is perhaps finally beginning to emerge.

One must be somewhat guarded in using this terminology; broad declarations about the present time are notoriously outmoded by the next moon's rising, and dated appellations such as *modern* and *postmodern* can hardly be expected to have much currency in succeeding generations. Still, major identifiable shifts in thinking have dominated intellectual discussion and artistic creativity since the mid-1970s. These shifts seem to constitute a clear transition from the modernism that has flourished since 1875.

Modernism

Modernism defined itself, at the end of the nineteenth century, with its complete break from the past and its freedom to redefine convention. Whether naturalistic, realistic, symbolist, or surrealist, playwrights of the modern era have not felt it necessary to recapitulate works of earlier eras: there has been little or no conscious "renaissance" (rebirth) of classic theory or practice in the modernist plays of Ibsen, Chekhov, Shaw, Pirandello, Brecht, or Beckett, and there has been a consequent revulsion toward rules of art, categorizations of genre, and codifications of "well-made" artistic structures.

What *is* common to the modernist spirit, in all its varied forms, is its phenomenal energy for creative exploration, driven by a powerful sense of optimism for the human (and the social) potential. "It's true, it's true, you love me so," sings Winnie at the end of Beckett's *Happy Days;* and Brecht urges us on, at the end of *The Good Woman of Sezuan,* with a beacon of hope: "We will trust/ That you will find the way! You must! You must! You must!"

Modernism may be celebrated as bringing with it the first great epoch of artistic freedom. What is more, this freedom was successfully enhanced, and expanded, by each new generation. Ibsen's austere and unflinching portrayals of Victorian oppression, Chekhov's complex, gentle dramas of human weakness and courage—these works were strange fare

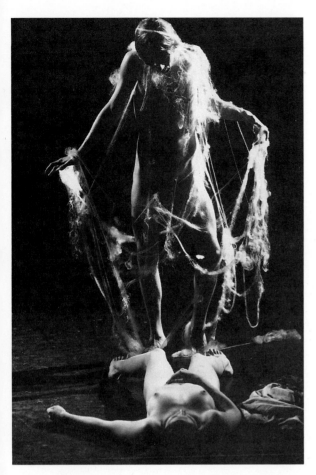

The Company Theatre of Los Angeles was only one of many theatre companies in the 1960s and 1970s experimenting with total nudity and participatory improvisation on stage. This original production, entitled The Emergence, *was one of the finest and most visually eloquent productions of the turbulent times.*

indeed for audiences accustomed to "storm and stress" romanticism and sensationalism. However, they rang of truth in their times, and in that way they brought significant change to the theatre and to modern culture. They also broke the political and aesthetic constraints under which playwrights had labored for centuries. In their wake came the growing public acceptance of Shaw's neo-Marxist sermonizing, Pirandello's paradoxical metatheatrics, O'Neill's brooding introspection, Sartre's existential pessimism, and Beck-

ett's wry absurdism; each artist successively broadening the palette of the theatre in what seems now to have been a steady evolutionary process.

The End of Modernism?

But modernism — with its confident optimism and cultural autonomy — seemed to become curiously irrelevant in the violent social decade starting in the late 1960s. In the ten years following Martin Luther King's assassination, a defining moment in American history, political and racial riots erupted here and abroad. Confrontations among the superpowers increased and intensified in the Third World, notably in Vietnam, Central America, and Africa. A series of political crises in the United States culminated in the forced resignation of a sitting president and vice-president. And the civilized world suddenly rediscovered, and began for the first time to confront, a list of past and present horrors: the Nazi Holocaust, the massacres of Native Americans, the formidable hidden oppression of women and minorities, the vast destruction of the planet's resources. Suddenly (or so it seemed), the potential for world-threatening disasters — nuclear Armageddon, unrestrained pollution, political chaos, environmental collapse — came to the attention of a seemingly helpless populace. Alluring but dangerous drugs proliferated. Crime and terrorism grew exponentially. Famine ravaged populations. Empires began to crumble. And an unknown, sex-linked disease arose from nowhere and began to decimate societies and redefine the pragmatics of lovemaking.

The arts first responded to these social changes with an artistic freedom that was truly frightening in its extremity — nowhere more so than in the theatre, where Dionysian ecstasy returned to the stage with force almost equal to that of the *dithyrambos*. As play-licensing laws fell in England and legal censorship became locally unenforceable in America, bold profanity, total nudity, open copulation, and direct political accusation—all unknown on the legitimate stage since ancient times—became almost commonplace. Plays popular in America in the 1960s and 1970s included one accusing the president (Lyndon Johnson) of murder, one accusing a past Pope (Pius XII) of genocide, one featuring a farm boy copulating with his pig, one showing a scene of mass masturbation, and one concluding with the audience undressing and marching out into the streets. *O, Calcutta!,* a smarmy, juvenile, all-nude review, played to record box-office receipts in major theatre capitals, including New York's Broadway. Theatre audiences the world over found themselves physically assaulted, hurtled about, handed lit "joints" (of marijuana), and, in at least one case, urinated and defecated upon. In some plays, actors engaged in sexual activity with each other and, in others, with members of the audience. These and other extreme behaviors had become part of the license claimed by a theatre purportedly trying to make itself heard above the societal din of war and corruption. Or were its adherents only clamoring for personal attention? In any event, it was a decade (or more) of this sort of dramaturgical violence and abandon that brought the age of "modernism" to a crisis, if not to a conclusion.

THE CRISIS OF TODAY'S THEATRE

By the late 1970s, this mood of violence was largely spent. The novelty of stage sex and profanity had mostly passed, and the latent voyeurism of the audience had been more than satisfied; an increasingly serious and sober public began demanding a more intelligent and focused response to major issues than the theatre was providing. And by the mid-1980s the AIDS crisis had largely eradicated the public's flirtation with unbridled sex as a cure for social ills ("make love, not war"

was replaced with the cry for "safe sex"). Moreover, many artists and critics were beginning to examine the hidden prejudices and privileges that continued to undermine even modernism's putative freedom and fairness.

The fears and confusion of the contemporary age had once again brought the theatre to the fore: as an arena where thoughts, fashions, feelings, morals, and aesthetics could be brought together to bring lucidity and structure to the problems that beset us. Theatre, which brings individual problems to collective attention and collective problems to individual attention, seemed a natural forum to rethink and restudy the crises in contemporary life.

While generalizations about an era wholly upon us and, indeed, just in its early stages, must be tentative, there are clearly three major movements—or themes—in the current theatre: the theatre of the age we increasingly call "postmodern." We might think of these as a theatre of *revival,* a theatre of *postmodern experiment,* and an *open theatre.* (Because these terms are not at all in general use, let us use the indefinite article "a"—rather than the definite "the"—in discussing them.)

A Theatre of Revival

The copulations, masturbations, and urinations of some of the more extreme theatrical experiments of the 1960s and 1970s did not transpire without the expected backlash—indeed, it could be argued that they were created so as to provoke such a backlash. That backlash still continues, leading to fierce battles in the 1990s between artists and the National Endowment for the Arts (NEA), the United States government agency established to "protect" the arts. "What is art?" is now a hot topic for newspaper editorials and presidential debates, as well as on the floor of the U.S. Senate.

The theatre of the past, including the theatre of the "modern" past, has consequently enjoyed an astonishing revival—not only by those revolted at what they considered the excesses of the 1960s, but also by those who were reminded, by the anarchic violence of late modernist art, of the sublime harmonies created by artists of an earlier age. Shakespearean festivals are only one visible national indication of a theatre of revival: at last count, there were 78 theatre companies, in almost every state in the United States, partly or wholly devoted to producing the works of England's great dramatist. Romanticism is also on the theatre of revival's program: the elaborate stage versions of nineteenth-century romantic novels—*Nicholas Nickleby, Les Misérables,* and *The Phantom of the Opera*—will be seen, literally, by hundreds of millions of theatregoers all over the world by the end of the 1990s. And the restagings of great modern plays, both realistic and otherwise, and of American musicals from the "golden era" of the 1940s, 1950s, and 1960s, constitute, at any given time, roughly half to two-thirds of the offerings along New York's famous Broadway and in America's community and academic theatres. New plays aping these modernist classics—serious dramas as well as comedies—might in any year make up another quarter of the bill.

The theatre of revival—including new plays mimicking those earlier forms—has a broad appeal; for most audiences, such a theatre is familiar, entertaining, and aesthetically satisfying. It is also a theatre capable of addressing, in some complexity, the serious and tangible problems facing humanity around the world. It is even a theatre capable of offering, if not solutions, at least political lucidity and intellectual focus. In avoiding show-offy formalistic innovation (art for art's sake) and gratuitous eroticism and scatology, the theatre of revival is not merely a theatre of nostalgia, but also a forum for insight, information, ideas, empathy, catharsis, wit, rapture, virtuosity, and laugh-till-you-cry humor. Though easily derided by avant-gardists, such a traditional (or derrière-garde) theatre needs no

Romanticism is in full sway in this stage adaptation, reviving Bram Stoker's gothic novel Dracula. *This Broadway production, starring Frank Langella as the fifteenth-century Transylvanian vampire, featured horrifically luscious scenery and costumes by noted artist Edward Gorey. (Photo: Martha Swope and Associates.)*

apologists: it is a vital, vibrant, thriving glory of the current stage.

But it is also no longer at the "cutting edge" of theatrical innovation and creativity.

A Theatre of Postmodern Experiment

The notion of a postmodern era is not as historically centered as the name suggests. As the term has developed since the 1970s, *postmodernism* indicates a way of thinking, or even of nonthinking, more than it defines a particular period in time.

The postmodern defies complete analysis—because postmodernism literally defies (repudiates) the act of analyzing. The post-

Cliff Faulkner's lighthearted and very postmodern setting for Shaw's Man and Superman *at South Coast Repertory Theatre in 1990 freely juxtaposes classical, Renaissance and contemporary elements. Production was directed by Martin Benson with costumes by Shigeru Yaji. (Photo: Christopher Gross.)*

modern approach essentially dismisses logic and cause-and-effect determinism, replacing both with more random associations and reflections. These reflections are of two sorts: self-reflections, where a work of art pays homage to itself, and reflections of the past, where the art pays homage to past texts and models.

One may see postmodernism, therefore, in the repeated and repainted images by Andy Warhol (of Campbell soup cans, headshots of Marilyn Monroe, and so on), which emphasize the artist's redefining a commercial product as an independent work of "art." One may see it also in Philip Johnson's AT&T building in New York (1984), with its neo-Renaissance facade and "Chippendale highboy" roofline. Whereas modernism repudiated the past, post-

modernism gaily embraces it, "quotes" it, and even recycles it.

A postmodernist work of art, therefore, is not about "something" so much as it is about itself. About "art."

Also, a postmodern work might also be said to "deconstruct" itself, so as to make us think about *ourselves*. Indeed, it is about *us* as well as it is about art. How do *we* view art? Are there any hidden assumptions about "what art is" that exclude us from enjoying it? Or that "privileges" other audiences? Inasmuch as a postmodern work is self-referential (refers to itself), it also contains its own critique; it parodies itself; it throws us back, sometimes in amusement and sometimes in irritation, upon our own thoughts.

Douglas-Scott Goheen's set for Much Ado About Nothing *intermixes outdoors and indoors, putting chandeliers in the "forest" and placing "real" birch trees in front of replicated photos of more birches. The set gives a sense of location, but also, in postmodernist fashion, suggests its own "setting" on the stage. At Theatre 40 in Beverly Hills, California, 1991. (Photo by the designer.)*

The contemporary sunglasses provide a startling contrast to the eighteenth-century dresses and ladies' parasol in this 1991 Alabama Shakespeare Festival production of Richard Brinsley Sheridan's The Rivals. *Costumes by Alan Armstrong; Monica Bell and Suzanne Irving are the performers. (Photo: Scarsbrook/ASF).*

Postmodern artists—and postmodern critics—are as deeply concerned with the social orders from which art springs, with the *processes* of creating art, and with the open or hidden assumptions that inform art as with the art *products* themselves.

Such definitions of the postmodern are admittedly complex, probably humorous (if not bewildering) to a first-time reader, and themselves subject to parody: which is itself a postmodern approach!

In theatre, which is a practical art, the notion of postmodernism may be concretely understood. Postmodern drama springs directly from the antirealistic theatre; but unlike most antirealistic theatres, it has little, if any, of the modernist's aesthetic or social optimism. Whereas the symbolists and surrealists were working to reveal inner truths, a "higher order" of reality, and where the Brechtian epic theatre was struggling to change (or save) the world and to create a higher level of society, none of these goals is deemed within the reach of the postmodernist—who presupposes no higher levels of reality or social or-

der. Because there is no higher reality to symbolize, the postmodernist abjures symbols (the postmodern is the art, one critic suggests, of the *métaphore manquée,* or missing metaphor). Because social progress is impossible (and social decline is probably inevitable), the postmodernist can only contemplate the future warily, if at all.

The postmodern writer, or director, therefore, is more likely to explore the *discontinuity* of observable reality and information, rather than attempt to find any integrated synthesis or meaning. Postmodern art celebrates the apparent randomness of arbitrary juxtaposition. Students of the postmodern find its salient features, for example, in the action painting of Jackson Pollock, whose paint was randomly dripped from buckets with holes in their bottoms; in break dancing, which is improvised, haphazard, and disjunctive; and in the music (or, as some say, cacophony) of the late John Cage, which consists of apparently indiscriminate sounds, few of which come from conventional "musical" instruments. Broadcast video, with its night and day agglomeration of new dramatic fragments, intermixed with commercials, promos, newsbreaks, announcements, station identifications, and old film clips, is a perfectly postmodern creation, made all the more discontinuous by picture-in-picture technology that permits the viewing of two agglomerations simultaneously and by remote-control devices permitting the viewer to shuttle between forty-odd channels at lightning speed.

The first great postmodern theatre (although its creators refused to call it "theatre") was the short-lived arts phenomenon called Dada, which flourished in the years immediately following World War I. Dada was begun in 1916 at the Cabaret Voltaire, in Zurich, Switzerland. As Mel Gordon describes it, Dada was a "chaotic mix of balalaika music, Wedekind poems, dance numbers, cabaret singing, recitations from Voltaire, and shouting in a kaleidoscopic environment of paintings. . . . Sound poems followed . . . with crazed piano playing and anti-war diatribes . . . [and] chance poetry," the latter created by poet Tristan Tzara, who pulled words at random out of a hat. Writing manifestos that declared themselves "anti-art," the Dadaists—as they came to be called (the name was chosen at random from an unabridged dictionary)— found themselves the artistic darlings of Berlin and Paris in the early 1920s. The movement clearly stimulated some of the experimentalism of the theatre of the absurd, which was its longer-lasting successor, and has, in many respects, been reborn in theatres around the world in the current genre of "performance art" (discussed more fully later in the chapter).

The postmodernism of the current theatre stems from both of the main nonrealistic strains of late modernism: the theatre of the absurd and the theatre of alienation.

It is the very late plays of Samuel Beckett that many feel best exemplify the pessimism and flight from meaning characteristic of the postmodern. For while he was always a proponent of meaninglessness, the stirring vitality of his 1961 *Happy Days* had turned, by the 1980s, to a grim despair, if not a complete nihilism. In his very short play, *Rockabye* (1981), Beckett's sole visible character is an old lady, with "huge eyes in white expressionless face." On a totally dark stage, she rocks alone, dimly lit in a rocking chair; during the play she says but one word (it is "More") in what is apparently a beyond-the-grave dialogue with her prerecorded voice. The play ends with the voice saying:

> rock her off
> stop her eyes
> fuck life
> stop her eyes
> rock her off
> rock her off

And the rocking stops as the lights fade out.

If Beckett's theatre stimulates the intellectual pessimism of the postmodern, Brecht's

stimulates its parodic and self-referential delight and the theatre's self-deconstruction as it throws issues back to the audience.

Neo-Brechtian authors like Heiner Müller (German), David Henry Hwang (American), Tom Stoppard (English), and Jean Genet (French), plus directors like Ariane Mnouchkine (French), Peter Brook (English), Jerzy Grotowski (Polish), and JoAnne Akalaitis (American), have ransacked the world's cultural history (and, in Grotowski's case, its cultural prehistory) to create contemporary theatre works that make bold associations between ancient models and current icons. Brecht's notion (and he did not, of course, invent it) of calling attention to the theatre itself, and to the means of production, has become almost a cliché of the contemporary theatre: in Robert Schenkkan's Pulitzer Prize-winning *The Kentucky Cycle,* for example, each act begins with the cast coming out to announce its subtitle (and theme); each act ends with the actors picking up their props and leaving the stage; brief interludes are enlivened by members of the cast who gloss the action by singing a relevant song.

It is this post-Brechtian direction—a theatre which, in order to refocus the audience's attention on social issues and values, calls attention to itself and deconstructs and parodies itself—that has led to, in the present day, a newly *open* theatre.

An Open Theatre

As much as we can be sure of anything, we can be sure that the theatre of the twenty-first century will be open to an infinitely wider range of interests, cultures, and individuals than was any period in the theatre's past history.

The deconstruction of the theatre promoted by its most stellar luminaries—Beckett and Brecht among them—made us painfully conscious of the theatre's failure to truly reflect the humanity inside us and the society around us. For most of us in the 1990s, the notion of an all-white, all-male, blank-verse-spouting acting company holding "a mirror up to nature" now seems impossibly limited (if not ludicrous) and makes us look back with some dismay at the theatre of the Shakespearean era, which employed such companies, and also at the so-called modern theatre, which in many respects only reformatted its putatively repudiated ancestors in this regard. How can an exclusively white male company wholly mirror the concerns of nonwhites and non-males? How many hidden assumptions infiltrate our minds when we find persons of color invariably portrayed as servants, exotics, or "noble" savages and when we see women routinely depicted as brainless playthings, saintly mothers, or simpering helpmeets?

A brilliantly innovative American company named The Open Theatre was created by Joseph Chaikin in 1963 and for a decade combined social improvisation with Brechtian techniques to develop a series of plays in which performers glided into and out of the characters they sometimes played (they also played scenery and props; more often they played themselves) and used story and character merely as vehicles for direct interactions with audiences. Their plays, including Megan Terry's *Viet Rock,* Susan Yankowitz's *Terminal,* and the company-authored *Mutation Show,* were continually evolving workshop performances that addressed immediate audience concerns. The company toured Europe — but also toured prisons. They made fraternal and sororal alliances with the New Lafayette Theatre in Harlem, the Teatro Campesino in California, and the Women's Collective Theatre. The Open Theatre ended its existence in 1973, but its influence has been extraordinary, and its name might very well be lent to the much larger "opening" of the contemporary stage.

For today's newest and most provocative theatre is truly open, or at least opening, to voices heretofore shut out, or severely limited, in the largely Western, white, and male-

Beth Henley's Abundance *is the story of two women who come to Wyoming to marry the strangers who have sent off for them by mail order. From the South Coast Repertory Theatre world premiere, with O'Lan Jones and Belita Moreno, 1989; the play subsequently enjoyed a run at the Manhattan Theatre Club (1991). (Photo: Ron Stone.)*

dominated theatre of yesterday, even of "modern" yesterday. And that opening is occurring on all levels: gender, race, physical condition, and sexual preference.

A Theatre By and About Women

Women, who — save for insignificant exceptions — were utterly unrepresented in the theatre until the seventeenth century and who from then until the 1950s have been largely relegated to acting and costume construction, are now a major force in playwriting, designing, directing, producing, and technical theatre. Three different American women (Beth Henley, Marsha Norman, Wendy Wasserstein) won Pulitzer Prizes for playwriting during the

1980s, and many critics accord Jane Wagner and Tina Howe similar stature; in England, no dramatic writer of the 1990s is more respected than Caryl Churchill. Women directors are making substantial inroads in the New York theatre, on and off Broadway, and are increasingly assuming artistic directorships at major American repertory companies: fully one-third of the 200-plus regional theatres have recently been headed by women, including JoAnne Akalaitis at the New York Public Theatre, Zelda Fitchandler at The (New York) Acting Company, Libby Appel at the Indianapolis Repertory Theatre, Sharon Ott at the Berkeley Repertory Theatre, Irene Lewis at Baltimore's Center Stage, Josephine Abady at the Cleveland Playhouse, Carey Perloff at the (San Francisco) American Conservatory Theatre, Emily Mann at the (Princeton) McCarter Center, Bonnie Monte at the New Jersey Shakespeare Festival, Mary Robinson at the Philadelphia Drama Guild, and Lynne Meadow at the Manhattan Theatre Club. This is an astounding record of achievement in a field where, until two decades ago, women were all but invisible.

Meanwhile, over one hundred separate feminist theatre groups—groups of women pre-

August Wilson's Fences *is set in front of the ramshackle home of its fallen hero, a onetime ballplayer in the Negro Leagues and a victim to American racism and low self-esteem—the two obviously not unrelated. The play won both the Tony Award and the Pulitzer Prize in 1987. Alabama Shakespeare Festival production, 1991.*

senting plays by, about, and for women—have been founded in the United States since 1970. The goal of each is to present plays concerning such issues as sex-role stereotyping, abortion, pregnancy, motherhood, rape, mothers and daughters, lesbianism, domestic violence, historically important women, battered women, and women in prison. "The content of almost all feminist drama," says Elizabeth J. Natalle, "comes out of the personal lives of the theatre group members. Feminist theatre groups write their own drama, and the reality they depict comes from their own experience."[1] And from the experience not only of the actors, but of the audience as well, Natalle explains: "In feminist theatre the audience is more than just a passive body viewing the action on stage. . . . Audience members [play] an active role in the creation of a total theatre experience." Natalle goes on to show how, in a play about rape, for example, the audience is invited "to stop the play at any moment and give witness to their own rapes, both literal and metaphoric."

A Theatre of Color

It is a typically postmodern phenomenon that the leading American playwright of the late 1980s and early 1990s has been, without doubt, the African American August Wilson, whose *Ma Rainey's Black Bottom, Fences, The Piano Lesson, Joe Turner's Come and Gone* and *Two Trains Running* are among the most powerful and evocative dramas of our times, concerning, as they do, an entire twentieth-century history of black America. But Wilson's plays have also been commercial "hits," playing to huge "crossover audiences" of blacks, whites, and members of all races, both on Broadway and in various American re-

Langston Hughes's Mule Bone, *written with Zora Neale Hurston in the "Harlem Renaissance" of the 1930s, did not make it to the Broadway stage until 1990, when the Lincoln Center Theatre company brought it to exuberant stage life. (Photo: Brigitte Lacombe.)*

gional theatres; Wilson is certainly the most honored playwright of recent years (see discussion of American playwrights later in this chapter), yet he is but one of a number of minority voices that are surfacing in the theatre of the 1990s and beyond.

African-American Theatre An African-American theatre, which had intermittent successes in the earlier years of this century (Langston Hughes's *Mulatto* in the 1930s and Lorraine Hansberry's *A Raisin in the Sun* in the late 1950s), became a revolutionary force on the American stage with Amiri Baraka (then LeRoi Jones) in the early 1960s. With his boldly defiant plays *Dutchman* and *The Toilet,* Baraka confronted American rac-

[1]Elizabeth J. Natalle, *Feminist Theatre: A Study in Persuasion* (New York: Scarecrow Press, 1985), 21. I am also indebted to this work for the list of subjects covered in feminist theatre.

ism head on and did not shrink from its potentially violent ramifications, to which American society seemed to be potentially subject. In light of the 1965 Watts riots, Baraka's voice proved prophetic; in light of the 1992 Los Angeles uprisings, we can understand how the problems he revealed have still not been solved.

The Negro Ensemble Company, which was created by Douglas Turner Ward, and the New Lafayette Theatre in Harlem, with Ed Bullins as chief playwright-in-residence, soon followed Baraka's successes, inching the African-American experience into the global arts marketplace. In 1970, Charles Gordone's *No Place To Be Somebody*, produced by Joseph Papp at the New York Public Theatre, won the Pulitzer Prize for Drama, at once putting black and minority playwrights into the American forefront. Black authors achieving national success in subsequent years included Lonne Elder III (*Ceremonies in Dark Old Men*), Adrienne Kennedy (*Funnyhouse of a Negro*), and Ntozake Shange (*For Colored Girls Who Have Considered Suicide/When the Rainbow is Enuf*). Meanwhile, in Africa, a theatre of color reached another milestone when Ni-

African-American playwright Suzan-Lori Parks won a slot at the 1992 Humana New Play Festival at the Actors Theatre of Louisville, where her Devotees in the Garden of Love *was well received. Esther Scott (left) and Margarette Robinson are the actors. (Photo: Richard C. Trigg.)*

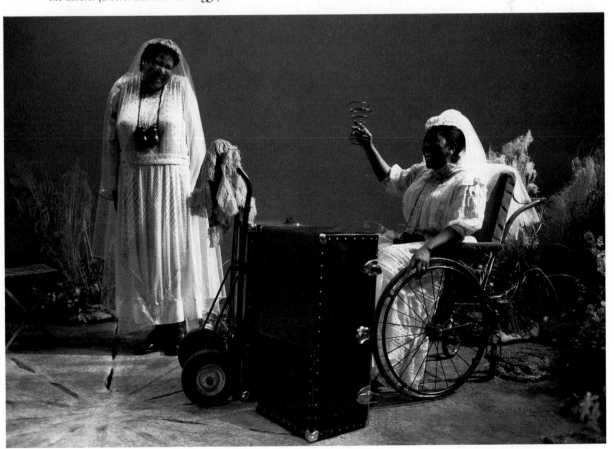

George C. Wolfe's Jelly's Last Jam *brilliantly pairs the "black musical" entertainment format with a serious and avant-garde exploration of African-American life. The play portrays the life and times of Creole jazz composer/performer Jelly Roll Morton. The staging, which is by Wolfe, employs both traditional musical comedy elements and neo-Brechtian stylizations. (Photo: Martha Swope Associates/William Gibson.)*

gerian dramatist Wole Soyinka received the Nobel Prize for Literature in 1986.

On Broadway, the 1970s inaugurated an era of lavishly produced black musicals, that, by the 1990s, included *Purlie, Bubbling Brown Sugar, The Wiz, Ain't Misbehavin', Sophisticated Ladies, Dreamgirls, Timbuktu, Once on This Island,* and *Five Guys Named Moe;* at many times during these years, African-American performers have constituted up to a third of the theatre artists on Broadway. And a merger of the Broadway black musical and more serious African-American theatre was achieved in 1992, with the audacious and remarkable *Jelly's Last Jam,* an exuberant but critical view of the life and career of Jelly Roll Morton, created by the brilliant writer-director, George C. Wolfe, author of the previously well-regarded *The Colored Museum.* With *Jelly's Last Jam,* Wolfe managed to captivate a near-universal audience: black and white, commercial and sophisticated, Broadway and avant-garde.

Many other colors, and other cultural voices, were raised in the postmodernist and experimental theatre of the 1980s and 1990s.

Hispanic Theatre A Spanish-speaking theatre has existed in North America since the late sixteenth century; indeed, the first play ever staged in what is now the United States was *Los moros y los cristianos* at the San Juan Pueblo outside of Santa Fe, then part of Mexico. By the mid-nineteenth century, serious and talented professional Mexican touring companies had established residence in Los Angeles and San Francisco and were touring to Texas, Arizona, and New Mexico by the century's end. On the East Coast at that time, Hispanic theatre—largely imported from Spain and Cuba—had established permanent beachheads in New York and Tampa, with stable Spanish-language companies presenting the classical plays of Calderón de la Barca and Lope de Vega, mixed with melodramas and *zarzuelas*—light operettas. Spanish-speaking theatre of this time largely served a community function, preserving traditional Hispanic culture in Anglo-dominated environments. With the founding of the Teatro Campesino by Luis Valdez in 1965, however, a contemporary Chicano theatre, with a powerful creative and political thrust, burst into prominence in California and ultimately won national acclaim. Valdez, a Mexican American, created his *Teatro* with and for migrant farmworkers in California. "In a Mexican way," wrote Valdez in 1966, "we have discovered what Brecht is all about. If you want unbourgeois theatre, find unbourgeois people to do it." Valdez's short, didactic *actos* of the farmworker's situation have been performed—in English and Spanish—on farms, in city squares, and, eventually, in theatres all over California, and on national and European tours as well; his full-length plays, *Zoot Suit* and *I Don't Have to Show You No Stinking Badges,* have played to major metropolitan audiences; and his film, *La Bamba,* has brought his Teatro to international acclaim (and some financial stability). "Our theatre work is simple, direct, complex

El Teatro Campesino in one of its early, highly political performances. The stage is one that can quickly be set up in a dining or meeting hall.

and profound, but it works. In the heart, *el corazon,* of a way of life," Valdez explains.

East-West Theatre The Eastern voice was epitomized in the American drama during the late 1980s by David Henry Hwang, whose *M. Butterfly* strikingly reinterpreted the "Madame Butterfly" myth, effectively exploding (if not completely displacing) the narrow and deprecatory "Orientalism" with which Occidental man stereotypes and misperceives Asian culture as the "Other." Hwang's incorporation of Peking Opera technique into Western drama draws on a tradition that predates postmodernism—Ezra Pound, Bertolt Brecht, W. S. Gilbert, and Antonin Artaud all drew heavily on Asian dramatic styles in their antinaturalistic works of the modernist period—but Hwang, who is of Asian (Chinese) background himself (see discussion later in this chapter), incorporates true Asian performers along with Western ones in this deliberately confrontational play, which poses East against West (and maleness against femaleness) in a continually informing, contin-

Man of the Flesh, *by Octavio Solis, was directed by Jose Cruz Gonzalez at the*
South Coast Repertory Theatre, where Gonzales heads the Hispanic Playwrights
Workshop. (Photo: Christopher Gross.)

ually surprising way. Hwang's play truly brought postmodernism into the American theatre mainstream—as a certified Broadway "hit" spectacle.

In the same way as Hwang, French director Ariane Mnouchkine introduces Japanese Kabuki technique to her production of Shakespeare's *Richard II* and Indian Kathakali technique to her *Twelfth Night,* thereby setting each play's Western orientation in bold relief and universalizing many of the play's themes. Peter Brook's *Mahabharata,* employing an international cast—and performing in Paris and Los Angeles, in French and in English—avoids any hint of "quaintness" or "artsy-craftsy" patronization of this great Sanskrit epic, but presents it with its origins and contemporary realization precisely juxtaposed. Jerzy Grotowski trains an international group of performers in prehistoric "performance" techniques drawn from around the world, to create an "objective drama" that seeks to dissolve the unconsciously applied linguistic and cultural codes that separate human beings from their true biological (and, some might say, spiritual) selves. (Wilson, Wolfe, Hwang, Mnouchkine, Brook, and Grotowski are each discussed more fully later in this chapter.)

Theatre of Difference

Nor are gender and ethnicity the only bases for the new voices that have entered the mainstream of postmodern theatre. The issue of sexual preference had been buried deeply in the closet during most of the theatre's history, and as late as 1958 the representation of homosexuality was actually illegal in England and widely (if not legally) suppressed in America. The sexual preference that "dared not speak its name" came to the stage in those eras only through authors' implications and audiences' inferences, and gay playwrights such as Tennessee Williams, Gertrude Stein,

In M. Butterfly, *David Henry Hwang creatively explores Eastern and Western cultural relations and theatrical traditions. Chinese Opera alternates with American realism and the arias of Puccini in this fascinating drama. The Broadway production was directed by John Dexter, with John Lithgow (left) and B. D. Wong. (Photo: Martha Swope and Associates.)*

Edward Albee, William Inge, and Gore Vidal were forced to speak—at certain critical moments in their work—only by innuendo and through oblique code words. Gay and lesbian life—and gay/lesbian issues—were first directly treated as serious dramatic subjects in the late 1960s, particularly by Mart Crowley in his groundbreaking comedy *Boys in the Band* (1968). Since that time, sexual-prefer-

Peter Brook's Mahabharata *is an adaptation of the Sanskrit (India) classic, performed in Paris (in French) and subsequently Los Angeles (in English) with a multicultural cast. The play is divided into three parts and lasts all day. (Photo: Gilles Abegg.)*

ence issues have become principal or secondary topics in literally hundreds of plays, including mainstream Broadway musicals (*La Cage Aux Folles, Falsettos, Aspects of Love*), popular comedies (*Norman, Is That You?*), and serious dramas (*Bent, Equus, M. Butterfly*). In the 1980s, in the wake of a new and terrible illness, a growing genre of AIDS plays (*The Normal Heart, As Is*) addressed the tragic human consequences of this disease, so particularly wrenching to the art and theatre world. And in 1992, Tony Kushner's extraordinary "gay fantasia on national themes," entitled *Angels in America,* proved one of the most celebrated stage productions of the decade in both England and the United States. Sexual preference has emerged, in the 1990s, as a defining issue for many theatre groups, theatre festivals, and theatre publications, each seeking to examine the political, cultural, and aesthetic implications of gay- and lesbian-themed drama.

Persons differently abled are also represented in new theatre companies created specifically for these voices and for expanding audiences. Theatre By The Blind, in New York, employs sightless actors for all of its productions, and the National Theatre of the Deaf is only one of three American companies (Deaf West and the Fairmount Theater of the Deaf are the other two) that create theatre of and for the hearing-impaired, employing ASL (American Sign Language) as the primary verbal dramatic medium. With Mark Medoff's *Children of a Lesser God,* the hearing-impaired found a mainstream audience, and a number of hearing-impaired actors and actresses found national recognition.

Nontraditional Casting

Across the country, multicultural and cross-gender casting in the classics—once thought of as daring—has become routine, and the casting of differently abled actors in "nondisadvantaged" roles has become equally accepted. African Americans playing roles once "reserved" for whites, and women cast in roles initially "written for" men, have become commonplace. The New York Shakespeare Festival has employed blind interracial casting for years: Morgan Freeman played their most recent Petruchio, and Denzel Washington their most recent Richard III. Both Paris and New York saw female King Lears in the early 1990s, in celebrated productions, and female Hamlets have become almost as customary as male ones in cities at the theatre's cutting edge. At the Los Angeles Mark Taper Forum in 1992, Cassius in *Julius Caesar* was played by an African American, Casca by a woman, and Flavius and Marullus were renamed "Flavia" and "Marulla" to accommodate the actresses who performed them; these practices no longer even raise eyebrows, much less audience objection.

The racial diversification of the American theatre in the current era is not merely anecdotal; it can be measured by powerful statistics: in 1990–91, actors of color received more than 21 percent of the roles in America's regional professional theatre, almost double what had been the case only four years earlier, and probably twenty times what it was twenty years ago. Nontraditional and cross-gendered casting may first have surfaced as a novelty;

Theatre By The Blind's production of Lanford Wilson's Talley and Son. *From left: Susan Stevens, George Ashiotis, and Xenophon Thophall; the latter two are legally blind. Directed in New York City by Isaac Schambelain, TBTB's artistic director. (Photo: Martha Swope and Associates/Carol Rosegg.)*

The casting of Mark Medoff's play Children of a Lesser God *presents special problems, for the play concerns deaf people. Here, in Gordon Davidson's production at the Mark Taper Forum, deaf actress Phyllis Frelich has been cast in the lead opposite John Rubenstein, who learned sign language during rehearsals. Actress Frelich actually inspired the writing of the play, which eventually moved to Broadway. (Photo: Courtesy the Mark Taper Forum.)*

today, however, these practices boldly and routinely serve to echo the needs and interests of increasingly broadly based and multicultural artistic communities of artists and audiences.

Indeed, multiculturalism now reaches to the very center of world theatre. The experiments of Brook and Grotowski are among the most admired and most imitated in theatre capitals here and abroad. The theatres of Africa, South America, and the East have become principal topics in widely read international theatre publications, such as *Performing Arts Journal* and *The Drama Review*. The "canon" of past dramatic works is being exhumed and expanded — to "discover" women and minority voices that had been suppressed or ignored in the past: revivals today are likely to focus on recently unheralded female authors like Aphra Behn (one of the most prolific Restoration dramatists), Alice Brown, Rachel Crothers, Susan Glaspell, and Zoe Atkins and to demonstrate how women and minorities have often been neglected and marginalized in past cultural undertakings.

Theatres devoted to the exploration of minority voices are but one way to expand the canon with new works. Theatre companies such as the St. Louis Black Repertory Company, the Penumbra Theatre of St. Paul, the New Federal Theatre of New York, the Crossroads Theatre Company of New Brunswick (New Jersey), the Mixed Blood Theatre of Minneapolis, the Latino Chicago Theatre, the Teatro Campesino, the Traveling Jewish Theatre, the East West Players, the INTAR Hispanic American Arts Center in New York, Jomandi Productions of Atlanta, the National Jewish Theatre, the New Federal Theatre (New York), the Pan Asian Repertory Theatre, and Repertorio Español are only a few of the professional theatre companies seeking to make minority voices competitive in the American theatre world. And for each professional company, there are a dozen amateur and university companies now forming. It is abundantly clear, as we head into the new millennium,

The Mark Taper Forum Theatre's 1991 Julius Caesar, *directed by Oskar Eustis, amply illustrates the company's racially diversified casting. (Photo: Jay Thompson.)*

that the theatre will never again revert to the protected confines of a privileged elite. Nor can it live successfully in social isolation in some "underprivileged" ghetto. Ghettoization, at the top or bottom, simply has no place in the postmodern culture. One of the great achievements of the current era has been the relentless (if incomplete) democratization of art and the multiplicity (if not the integration) of struggling, and often competing, voices.

The theatre of today might, in fact, be entering its greatest phase. Certainly, in terms of sheer quantity, there is *more* theatre now than at any time in the past, and there is more interest in theatre. It is odd to think it was only a few decades ago, when developments in cinema and television were much before the public eye, that it became fashionable to consider the theatre a dying art form, a "fabulous invalid" doomed by its technological backwardness and the yoke of tradition. Theatre has not just survived, but it has also thrived. The box-office income just for the Broadway production of *Miss Saigon* during 1992 exceeded the home-ticket income for the New York Yankees and Mets *combined* during the same year. The number of professional plays mounted in the United States every year is vastly greater than the number of professional films made for cinema and television combined, and the number of amateur theatrical events simply boggles the imagination. Nor is all this limited to the "major" theatrical venues: most large cities in the United States and Canada—those with a population of a quarter million or more—have at least one *professional* theatre, plus at least half a dozen amateur, college, or community theatres. European, South American, and Asian cities are the same; most European countries enjoy a wide range of publicly supported national and municipal theatres, plus, in most cases, commercial theatres and cabaret theatres as well. The Eastern World is no less theatrically active: one expert maintains that there "are more different types of theatre being performed simultaneously in Tokyo than in any other city in the world." The theatre has more than challenged the great boom of electronic media; it has triumphed. And its triumphs are there to be experienced on any given night of the theatrical season.

WHERE IT'S HAPPENING

The current theatre happens all over the world: in rural villages, summer resorts, exurban dinner theatres, festival towns, classrooms, prisons, and civil auditoriums; atop mobile street trestles; within ancient palaces; aboard ocean liners—even, in the case of one recent Russian production, inside an interurban railway car.

But mostly the current theatre is "celebrated" in the cities—in the traditionally great theatrical capitals such as New York, Moscow,

London, Paris, Vienna, Tokyo, and Berlin, as well as in cities of more modest theatrical repute, such as Kyoto, Zurich, Hamburg, Edinburgh, Buenos Aires, Helsinki, Mexico City, Cracow, Chicago, San Francisco, Seattle, Minneapolis, New Haven, Louisville, Los Angeles, Hartford, Boston, and Washington, D.C.

In the United States, New York City is without question the center of the nation's theatrical activity. Every year it is the site of more performances, more openings, more revivals, more tours, and more dramatic criticism than any half-dozen other American cities put together. Theatrically, it is the showcase of the nation. In the minds of many Americans, the "Big Apple" is *the* place to experience theatre; thus the New York theatre is a prime tourist attraction and a major factor in the city's economy. In the minds of theatre artists—actors, directors, playwrights, and designers—New York is the town where the standards are the highest, the challenge is the greatest, and the rewards are the most magnificent. "Will it play in Peoria?" may be the big question in the minds of film and television producers, but "Will it make it in New York?" remains a cardinal issue in the rarefied world of American professional theatre. Thus the reality of New York is surrounded by a fantasy of New York, and in a "business" as laced with fantasy as is the theatre, New York commands a strategic importance of incomprehensible value in the theatrical world.

Broadway

Broadway is the longest street in Manhattan, slicing diagonally down the entire length of the island; the world knows it, however, mainly for its cluster of thirty-some theatres congregated in the dozen blocks north of Times Square, at 42nd Street. This has been the "Great White Way" of the American theatre since the first years of the century: the place where Eugene O'Neill, Arthur Miller,

Tennessee Williams, William Inge, and Edward Albee all saw their masterpieces first produced; where memories of George M. Cohan, Ethel Merman, Mary Martin, and Barbara Streisand — "Broadway Babies" all — sang and danced; and where John Barrymore, Marlon Brando, Helen Hayes, Ingrid Bergman, Shirley Booth, Audrey Hepburn, Henry Fonda, Alfred Lunt, Lynn Fontanne, and thousands of others acted their way into America's hearts — and, most of them, into Hollywood's films.

But these romantic memories must be set aside with the explosive urban scene that Broadway is today. There is precious little that is sentimental or glamorous about Times Square now: it's the home of sex shops, crack houses, porno movie theatres, tourist emporia, videogame parlors, and even more raucously sleazy enterprises, which vie with each other, and with the Broadway theatres, for each passerby's attention. Urban redevelopment, currently in progress, has promised to tame this raffish district of its bawdier ways, but Broadway will clearly remain a glitzy, sleazy, alluringly dangerous locale for years to come. Broadway's lure is its dazzling visual and social excitement; its heady mix of bright lights and famed celebrities; its trend-setting fashions, big-buck entertainments, and high-toned Tony Awards. The stakes are higher on Broadway than anywhere else, and the money is dicier: the gross annual Broadway box-office "take" comes in at close to $300,000,000 for the twelve or fourteen city blocks, which is not the income of an invalid, fabulous or otherwise. If you make it here, as the song says, you make it anywhere, and the energy that this lyric connotes — and attracts — makes the Broadway district unforgettably fascinating.

The very popular "TKTS booth" in New York's Duffy Square (Broadway at 47th Street — the heart of the New York theatre district) sells unsold tickets at a 25 percent or 50 percent discount for most Broadway and off-Broadway shows on the afternoon of the performance only. An always-changing sign indicates what shows are available each day. Additional TKTS booths (with shorter lines but further from the theatres) are in the World Trade Center (downtown Manhattan) and in Brooklyn. Other cities in the United States (Chicago, Los Angeles) and abroad (London) have set up similar operations.

It has been a long time, however, since Broadway passed as a district known for its intellectual or artistic innovation, and few of the theatre's brilliant achievements find their first staging here. Rather, the Broadway theatre has become the place of origin only for spectacular musicals, the occasional new comedy (usually by Neil Simon) or comedy review (such as *Catskills on Broadway*), or the star-heavy revival of an American classic (such as Jessica Lange and Alec Baldwin in the 1992 version of Williams's *Streetcar Named Desire*). The serious new plays coming to Broadway in the 1990s are, almost without exception, works that garnered their first rave reviews and standing ovations at one of America's many regional theatres, such as the Seattle Repertory Theatre (Wendy Wasserstein's *The Heidi Chronicles*; Herb Gardner's *Conversations With My Father*), South Coast (California) Repertory Theatre (Craig Lucas's *Prelude to a Kiss*), the Yale Repertory Theatre (August Wilson's *Fences, Two Trains Running*), or the

Waiting for standing-room tickets to a hit Broadway musical, crowds line up in fabled Shubert Alley and gaze at theatre posters adorning wall.

Crazy For You *is only one of several Broadway musicals set right on Broadway that are mining the venerable vein of show business nostalgia. This 1992 adaptation of an older Gershwin show is set in the 1930s, in front of the "Zangler Follies," an obvious reference to the famous Ziegfeld show whose motto was "Glorifying the American girl." Here, with the chorus of "Zangler girls" is Harry Groener as Bobby. (Photo: Joan Marcus.)*

THE BROADWAY MUSICAL: A GOLDEN AGE

The Broadway musical, or musical comedy as it used to be called, is often described as America's greatest contribution to the theatre; certainly the hundreds of musical plays that have flourished on Broadway since the 1900 production of *Floradora* have included America's most spectacular stagings and most lucrative commercial successes. Some have also been considered works of true dramatic art.

The musical—a dramatic play with an integrated musical score, often lavishly produced, whose characters both sing and dance—has been a feature of the American stage at least since 1866, when *The Black Crook* was staged at Niblo's Garden in New York City. English imports, including Leslie Stuart's *Floradora* and the operettas of Gilbert and Sullivan (*The Pirates of Penzance, The Mikado,* etc.), as well as light operas from the European continent (Victor Herbert's *Naughty Marietta,* Franz Lehar's *The Merry Widow*) competed with the American product in the years prior to World War I. After that war, however, a particularly American style of musical theatre emerged, and from then until the 1960s Broadway artists created, and all America enjoyed, a virtual golden age of musicals.

There were two distinct phases of this golden age. In the first, "musical comedy" reigned. George Gershwin's *Lady Be Good, Strike Up the Band, Girl Crazy,* and *Of Thee I Sing*; Vincent Youman's *No, No, Nanette*; Jerome Kern's *Sunny*; Cole Porter's *Anything Goes;* and a series of musical comedies by Richard Rogers (music) and Lorenz Hart (lyrics), including *A Connecticut Yankee, On Your Toes,* and *Babes in Arms,* employed strictly comedic plots and characters, invariably on a trivial theme, all to be enlivened by lots of singing and dancing, much usually incidental to the play. A growing seriousness, however, plus an increasing integration of plot and musical treatment, enabled the musical form to gain stature and importance. *Of Thee I Sing* received the 1931 Pulitzer Prize, as much for its political satire as its entertaining cleverness; and Jerome Kern's "Ol' Man River" from *Showboat* became one of the great pieces of acted (as opposed to merely sung) vocal literature in the twentieth century—as did George Gershwin's entire score from the folk opera *Porgy and Bess* (1935).

The second phase of the Golden Age is usually dated from Rodgers and Hart's brilliant *Pal Joey* (1939), adapted from some grimly ironic stories by John O'Hara and featuring an amoral gigolo and his often unsavory companions in a musical pastiche of the contemporary urban nightclub scene. Tame by today's standards, *Joey* shocked prewar audiences with its blithely suggestive lyrics about sexual infidelity and shady business ethics and with a show-stopping song belted out by an intellectual stripteaser—who sang out her thoughts while doing her act. Many serious musicals followed, straining the word "comedy" out of the musical's nomenclature. *Lady in the Dark* (1941), with a book by dramatist Moss Hart and with music by Kurt Weill (the Bertolt Brecht colleague who, like Brecht, had fled to America from Nazi rule in Germany) concerned itself with psychoanalysis and dream analysis. *Oklahoma!* (1943), with music by Richard Rodgers and lyrics by Oscar Hammerstein II, dealt with social and sexual tensions in the opening of the western states; the musical featured brilliantly integrated dance choreography by Agnes de Mille and treated its historical subject with romantic passion and a new level of social intensity.

During the late 1940s and 1950s, Broadway musicals dominated the commercial American theatre. Rodgers and Hammerstein followed *Oklahoma!* with one success after another: *Carousel, South Pacific, The King and I,* and *The Sound of Music,* all marked with some social (even intercultural) conflict, richly romantic settings and songs, beautiful solo numbers and love duets, and thrilling choral, choreographic, and orchestral ensembles. Frank Loesser's *Guys and Dolls,* based on the idiosyncratic stories of Damon Runyon, also proved immensely popular, as did Cole Porter's *Kiss Me Kate,* based on Shakespeare's

Taming of the Shrew, and Irving Berlin's *Annie Get Your Gun,* based on the life of American folk heroine Annie Oakley. Leonard Bernstein, one of America's leading orchestral conductors and composers, also left a considerable mark on the musical's golden age with his *On the Town* and *West Side Story.* Alan Jay Lerner (book and lyrics) and Frederick Loewe (music) first successfully collaborated with the fantasy *Brigadoon,* about a mythical Scottish village, and then with their brilliant musical revision of Shaw's *Pygmalion,* which they called *My Fair Lady.*

The Broadway musical during its golden age was broadly influential. Plays ran not for weeks or months, but for years; for the first time, theatre tickets were sold up to six months in advance, and business travelers returning from New York City were expected to provide a full report on "the new musical in town." Touring companies brought the best musicals to the countryside: first-class national tours, with the Broadway stars, and, subsequently, "bus and truck" tours with less well known performers—nonetheless advertising "straight from Broadway!" Perhaps most Americans in these years first experienced live theatre in the form of a road version of a Broadway musical. Songs from the musicals routinely made the "hit parade" (forerunner of the "top ten" or "top forty" listings of today); films of the musical plays were widely popular; and, for a couple of decades, it seemed as if everyone in America was whistling the latest creation from the tunesmiths of Shubert Alley. Performers made famous by the musicals they starred in—performers such as Mary Martin, Alfred Drake, Ethel Merman, Julie Andrews, Rex Harrison, Yul Brynner, Carol Channing, John Raitt—became national celebrities and the pioneer performers on America's new entertainment medium, television. It is certain that the theatre has never played such a central role in American popular culture before; it is questionable if it ever shall again.

Musical drama has continued to develop in the decades since the 1970s, but it is rarely a "Broadway" creation any more and is no longer dominated by American artists; there can be little doubt but that the golden age has fragmented into more sporadic and diverse efforts. Stephen Sondheim is clearly the reigning genius in today's American musical theatre, and his work gets special discussion in this chapter. There have also been some outstanding individual American musicals in the past twenty years: Marvin Hamlisch's *A Chorus Line,* James Lapine and William Finn's *Falsettos,* and George C. Wolfe's *Jelly's Last Jam,* among several others. But the most successful musicals running on Broadway in the 1980s and 1990s have, so far, tended to be revivals from the earlier era (Jerry Zaks's production of *Guys and Dolls* and Ken Ludwig's revision of the Gershwins' *Girl Crazy*—retitled *Crazy for You*—were the runaway hits of 1992), and the spectacular British musicals of Andrew Lloyd Webber (*Jesus Christ Superstar, Evita, Cats, Starlight Express, Phantom of the Opera, Aspects of Love*), plus the French-British musicals of Alain Boublil and Claude-Michel Schönberg (*Les Misérables, Miss Saigon*). Broadway has also seen Polish (*Metro*), South African (*Sarafina*), and various Asian musicals in recent years. American musicals will undoubtedly flourish in the future, but they must now compete on an increasingly international scene.

One of the best Broadway musicals of the 1980s was Tommy Tune's great staging of Grand Hotel, *set in pre-Nazi Germany. The influence of Bertolt Brecht is clear. (Photo: Martha Swope and Associates.)*

The Buddy Holly Story, *a foot-stomping Broadway revue of rock-and-roller Buddy Holly's life and music, was in fact an English import. Paul Hipp, shown here, played Buddy on both sides of the Atlantic. (Photo: Martha Swope and Associates.)*

Goodman Theatre in Chicago (David Mamet's *Glengarry Glen Ross,* Frank Galati's adaptation of John Steinbeck's *The Grapes of Wrath*). Or the play might be a transfer from England, such as Peter Shaffer's *Lettice and Lovage* or *The Buddy Holly Story.* The latter production proved a special embarrassment for the American theatre, because the subject was strictly American rock and roll music. For new drama, Broadway has become the nation's second stage, not its first.

It is quite clear why this is so. Broadway is America's premier *commercial* theatre, and plays mounted there must pay their costs, and make their profits, mainly from box-office income. But the costs of producing on Broadway have grown astronomically over the past two decades. City real estate values, the escalating payroll demands in a labor-intensive, highly unionized business, and the huge ex-

penses of New York advertising have priced even the simplest Broadway production well into seven figures. But the chances of recouping those costs (not to mention making a profit) are, if anything, more slender than ever, particularly with a "straight" (that is, nonmusical) play. Despite ticket prices that in 1992 ascended to upwards of $50 a ticket for straight dramas, and (in some cases) $100 for musicals, most new productions on Broadway are, in fact, financial failures. Increasingly, therefore, Broadway producers await the new plays whose worth is first "proven" in the subsidized European (chiefly English) theatre, or on the not-for-profit American regional stage. Only the star-studded revival, or new musical, is likely to be "bankable" and offer sufficient opportunity for commercial success in these financially difficult times. And Broadway, once the flagship of the American theatre, is now mainly its museum.

Off-Broadway and Off-Off-Broadway

Not all of New York theatre is performed within the geographical and commercial confines of the Broadway district: distinctly non-Broadway theatres have operated in the nation's largest city for many decades. The symbolic centrality of Broadway, however, is so strong that these theatres are named not for what they are, but for what they are not: they are the *off-Broadway* theatres. "Off-Broadway" is a term that came into theatrical parlance during the 1950s. It refers to professional theatres operating on significantly reduced budgets. They are found primarily in Greenwich Village, in the area south of Houston Street ("SoHo"), and on the upper East and West sides of Manhattan. A few houses in the Broadway geographical area itself fall into this category, but only because they operate under off-Broadway financing structures. Yet another category of theatre is known as *off-off-Broadway,* a term dating from the 1960s.

David Margulies's Sight Unseen *portrays an idealistic young Jewish art student who, over the years, becomes a celebrity. The witty, disturbing play was first seen at the South Coast Repertory Theatre in 1991 (pictured here); it went on to a very successful off-Broadway run at the Manhattan Theatre Club the following year. (Photo: Christopher Gross.)*

This category consists of semiprofessional or wholly amateur theatres that are located throughout the metropolitan area, often in church basements, YMCAs, coffeehouses, and converted studios or garages.

The off-Broadway and off-off-Broadway theatres generate a great deal of fertile and vigorous activity; leaner and less costly than the Broadway stage, they attract specialized cadres of devotees, some of whom would never allow themselves to be seen in a Broadway house. Much of the original creative work in the American theatre since World War II has been done in these theatres, and their generally low ticket prices have lured successive generations of theatre audiences their way to see original works before they are show-cased to the Broadway masses, works still raw with creative energy and radiating the excitement of their ongoing development.

In composite, Broadway and non-Broadway theatres provide almost every conceivable opportunity for theatrical exploration and achievement. Between them, they present in season about fifty professional and one hundred amateur productions *each night;* they also mount close to a thousand new productions each year. Their offerings are a great conglomeration of original scripts, classical revivals, opulent musicals, provocative imports, and a basic collection of workmanlike thrillers, reviews, comedies, and holdover dramas. What is more, thanks to extensive press coverage in the national media—weekly news magazines, monthly journals of opinion, television talk shows and specials, and the annual televising of the "Tony" awards ceremonies—the New York theatrical season does not long remain a strictly local phenomenon: it becomes a centerpiece of American cultural activity, and before long the world is privy to its innovations, its successes, its radical ideas, its catastrophes, and its gossip.

The Nonprofit Professional Theatre

But the nonprofit professional theatre is where, in the last decades of the twentieth century, America's theatre is truly happening.

The nonprofit theatre, often called the "regional" or "resident" theatre (because the theatres generally are in "regions" outside of New York, with "resident" staffs and at least some resident company members), is a phenomenon of the last third of the century, an outpouring of theatrical activity that at first diversified the American theatre and has since improved it.

Nonprofit means noncommercial; the nonprofit theatres have in common at least one funding source other than the box office: either government grants, foundation or corporate support, private donations, or a combination of these. The nonprofit designation is a legal one: the theatre has no owners, makes no profit, and is exempt from most taxes—and donors to the theatre receive tax deductions for their gifts. But, although noncommercial, these are professional theatres in every sense, employing professional artists, often exclusively, at every level. There were no such theatres at the end of World War II. There are over two hundred today, and they exist in virtually every major city in America—including New York City. They produce over a thousand productions each year, giving tens of thousands of performances, and provide Americans in every part of the country an opportunity to see professional theatre, often at its best.

The American Repertory Theatre often presents conventional plays in unconventional ways, as with Anne Bogart's 1990 production of George S. Kaufman's and Moss Hart's classic American comedy, You Can't Take It With You. *Dispensing with the traditional realistic scenery provides fresh and ironic focus on the hidden assumptions of the characters—and of the writers. (Photo: Richard Feldman.)*

Nonprofit theatres vary enormously in character: some concentrate on classics, some on the contemporary international repertoire, others on new American plays. Some operate on tiny stages with tiny budgets and, while engaging professional artists, reduce costs by negotiating salary waivers with the professional unions. Other theatres operate several stages simultaneously and are enormous operations: the New York Shakespeare Festival has an annual budget of more than ten million dollars and often has its productions running all over the city.

Some of the most distinguished of the nonprofit theatre companies in recent years are described in the following paragraphs.

Boston *The American Repertory Theatre,* actually in Cambridge, was founded by Robert Brustein in 1980. Taking some of his colleagues from the Yale Repertory Theatre (discussed later) when he left, Brustein created his award-winning ART in Harvard University's Loeb Drama Center; the company also operates a smaller theatre facility nearby. The ART has been one of America's most experimental companies since its founding and has been known particularly for giving free rein to many of the most experimental directors working in the United States—including Andrei Serban, Peter Sellars, Adrian Hall, Jonathan Miller, Anne Bogart, Susan Sontag, Des McAnuff, Jo-Anne Akalaitis, and Robert Wilson. ART won the 1986 Tony Award for its history of groundbreaking, controversial productions, including, in the late 1980s and early 1990s, JoAnne Akalaitis's revisionist version of Samuel Beckett's *Endgame* (which created a storm of controversy when the author protested—and threatened to disallow—the production concept); Andrei Serban's stunningly updated classics—Shakespeare's *Twelfth Night* and Molière's *The Miser;* Adrian Hall's *King Lear;* and Robert Wilson's visually magnificent performance pieces: an adaptation of Euripides' *Alcestis* (including

some new material from the German postmodernist Heiner Müller); Henrik Ibsen's *When We Dead Awaken;* and several fragments of Wilson's own opus (still unproduced in its totality), *The CIVIL warS.*

Chicago *The Goodman Theatre,* which won the 1992 Tony Award for regional companies, is Chicago's oldest and largest nonprofit theatre. Originally founded in 1925 by the Chicago Art Institute, it operates two theatres in a building adjacent to the

The Steppenwolf Theatre Company is known for intense acting performances. Here Danny Glover (left) and Francis Guinan enjoy a nervous laugh prior to breaking into a shattering battle in a 1986 production of Athol Fugard's A Lesson from Aloes. *(Photo: Lisa Ebright.)*

famous museum and also produces plays elsewhere in the city. The theatre is known for its production of new plays, particularly those of Chicago native David Mamet, who has been an in-residence playwright and whose award-winning *American Buffalo, Glengarry Glen Ross,* and *A Life of the Theatre* were first seen there. The Goodman also premiered David Rabe's *Hurlyburly,* which went on to a major Broadway success, and Scott McPherson's *Marvin's Room,* which was reprised off-Broadway to win the 1992 Drama Desk Award for outstanding new play.

After more than twenty years in a small (211 seat) North Chicago theatre facility, the exceptionally vigorous *Steppenwolf Theatre Company* moved, in the early 1990s, into a 510-seat mainstage theatre closer to the center of town. A collective theatre (seven of the nine founding members remain with the company today), Steppenwolf is known internationally for its intense naturalistic acting and has pioneered in what is frequently called a new "Chicago style" of fervently emotional performances. The actors Gary Sinese, Joan Allen, and John Malkovich are among Steppenwolf's major talents; the Frank Galati adaptation of John Steinbeck's *The Grapes of Wrath,* premiering at Steppenwolf, received the 1990 Tony Award upon its Broadway transfer.

Louisville   *Actors Theatre of Louisville,* founded in 1964, came to national prominence under the artistic leadership of Jon Jory. The ATL national recognition has come from its annual Humana Festival of new plays, in which five to ten new plays are produced simultaneously, attracting an audience of theatre critics from all over the country. Many of these plays, including *The Gin Game, Getting Out, Crimes of the Heart, Agnes of God, Extremities, Talking With,* and *Execution of Justice* have enjoyed long subsequent lifetimes in the national repertory, and José Rivera's 1992 *Marisol* has enjoyed subsequent success in New York, Chicago,

San Diego, and other regional theatres. Meanwhile, since 1986, an annual ATL "Classics in Context" festival has brought the Moscow Art Theatre, the Berliner Ensemble, and members of Milan's Teatro Piccolo to Louisville, where these artists collaborate with the resident company to reexplore classic theatre works, and historically important acting theories and practices, in the context of contemporary American thinking and culture. The ATL is one of the first American companies to attempt this infusion of scholarship with theatre production, which is more usually observed in the European government-subsidized theatre.

Los Angeles   *The Mark Taper Forum* was founded in 1967 by Gordon Davidson, who continues to serve as artistic director. The Forum is celebrated primarily for its production of new American plays, many of which have subsequently received national recognition. These include George C. Wolfe's *Jelly's Last Jam,* Robert Schenkkan's Pulitzer Prize-winning *The Kentucky Cycle* (first created in workshop form at the Taper, then expanded to its present length at Seattle's Intiman Theatre), Mark Medoff's *Children of a Lesser God,* Luis Valdez's *Zoot Suit,* Marsha Norman's *Getting Out,* Michael Christopher's *The Shadow Box,* and Daniel Berrigan's *The Trial of the Catonsville Nine;* these works constitute a remarkable diversity of authorial interests and backgrounds. Located in America's film and television capital, the Taper occasionally attracts internationally prominent actors for its productions, including Jack Lemmon and Walter Matthau, who costarred in Sean O'Casey's *Juno and the Paycock,* as well as well-known

The Guthrie Theatre has specialized in evocative productions of great classic plays. This is the chorus in Garland Wright's 1992 production of the "Clytemnestra Plays," a massive compilation of works by the three great Greek tragedians on the Oresteian theme. (Photo: Courtesy the Guthrie Theatre, Minneapolis.)

television stars available during the spring-time hiatus between TV seasons: in 1992, Kelsey Grammer played the title role in the Taper's *Richard II*.

And, forty-five miles south of Los Angeles, the *South Coast Repertory* Theatre vies for attention with its only slightly older rival (the Taper) to the North. SCR was founded by David Emmes and Martin Benson, who are still the company's artistic co-directors, as an amateur touring company in 1964; the then-tiny group enjoyed its first "permanent" home a year later in a small abandoned boat-repair shop in Newport Beach and now occupies its own sumptuous, two-stage facility in Costa Mesa. SCR's success story has been built on excellent productions, a devotion to community relations, and, above all, a superb knack at finding (or commissioning) outstanding new plays. Craig Lucas's *Prelude to A Kiss*, commissioned by SCR, went on to become a Broadway success. The company's record for sending new plays to New York expanded mightily in the 1991–92 season, when New York producers mounted no less than three SCR-premiered American plays: Howard Korder's *Search and Destroy*, Donald Margulies's *Sight Unseen*, and Richard Greenberg's *The Extra Man*. South Coast was awarded the Tony for regional theatres in 1988.

Minneapolis *The Guthrie Theatre*, founded by the celebrated English director Tyrone Guthrie in 1963, has gained a distinguished record of classical theatre productions under a variety of managements. Nationally noted early productions included Aeschylus' *Oresteia*, directed by Guthrie in 1967, and Shakespeare's *The Tempest* and *A Midsummer Night's Dream*, directed by the company's second artistic director, the Romanian Liviu Ciulei, in the early 1980s. The Guthrie's newest artistic director, Garland Wright, has recently overseen a successful $25 million endowment drive and has created a perma-

nent acting company, permitting the compilation of elaborately coordinated and epic-scale productions of Shakespeare's interrelated histories (*Richard II, Henry IV,* etc.) and the various Clytemnestra plays written by the three ancient Greek tragedians. "We at the Guthrie firmly commit our efforts to artistic excellence at every level, to

The Guthrie Theatre's 1990 production of Richard II, *directed by Garland Wright. (Photo: Michael Daniel.)*

the greatest plays of the world repertoire, to the actor as the central communicator of the ideas and the poetry within those plays, and to the imagination and its transforming power," says Wright.

New Haven   The *Long Wharf Theatre*, founded in 1965, has become widely known for its fine, sensitive productions of midcentury American and English classics, often staged by Long Wharf's artistic director Arvin Brown. Several of these have subsequently moved to New York, including outstanding presentations of Arthur Miller's *A View from the Bridge,* Eugene O'Neill's *Long Day's Journey into Night,* Simon Gray's *Quartermain's Terms,* and Rod Serling's *Requiem for a Heavyweight.*

Yale Repertory Theatre was founded in 1966 by Robert Brustein as an adjunct to the Yale University School of Drama. New Haven is fortunate to have two world-class professional theatres; YRT is generally more adventurous than the Long Wharf and became known, when Lloyd Richards assumed the artistic leadership in 1979, as the first American home of the widely celebrated plays of South African Athol Fugard

The Long Wharf Theatre in New Haven enjoys the services of leading American actors. Filmgoers should recognize Richard Dreyfus (center) and John Lithgow (bottom), with Richard Proval (left) and Daniel Keyes in the 1984 Long Wharf Requiem for a Heavyweight, *which subsequently transferred to Broadway. (Photo: Gerry Goodstein.)*

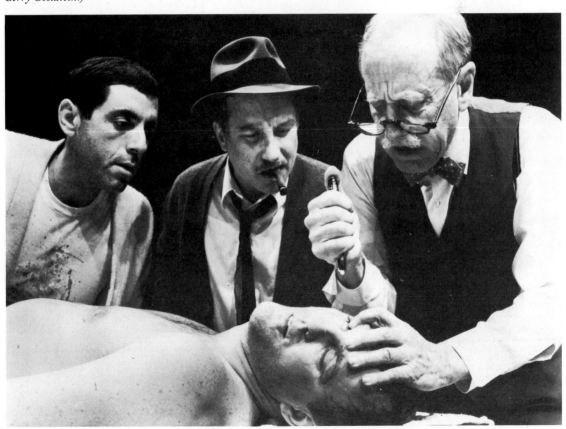

(*A Lesson from Aloes, Master Harold . . . And the Boys, The Road to Mecca*), Nigerian Wole Soyinka (*A Play of Giants*) and American playwright August Wilson (*Ma Rainey's Black Bottom, Fences, The Piano Lesson, Joe Turner's Come and Gone,* and *Two Trains Running*.) YRT also produces a wide variety of classics, invariably in unconventional ways, and a winter festival (called Winterfest) of new and recent works for the theatre. In 1991–92, Stan Wojewodski, Jr., took over the helm as the YRT's third artistic director, stating as his goal the creation of "a theatre always teeming with ideas, the ripest and readiest of which can then be born to the public view."

The New York Shakespeare Festival has pioneered in nontraditional casting, to the extent that they are creating a new tradition — perhaps the term "nontraditional" will soon be obsolete. Tracey Ullman is Katherine to Morgan Freeman's Petruchio in this 1990 production of Shakespeare's The Taming of the Shrew. *(Photo: George Joseph.)*

New York *The New York Shakespeare Festival* was founded by Joseph Papp in 1954 with the goal of presenting free Shakespeare productions on trestles in Central Park; by the time Papp died in 1991, the company was operating six performance spaces in its downtown Public Theatre, plus the huge outdoor Delacorte Theatre in Central Park. NYSF has also toured plays around the city and managed full-scale Broadway transfers of several of its successful productions, including *A Chorus Line, The Pirates of Penzance, The Mystery of Edwin Drood, That Championship Season, Much Ado About Nothing,* and *Plenty.* Indeed, the festival has unquestionably been the most important single American theatre-producing agency since the 1970s. It has spawned, in addition to transferred-to-Broadway successes, a wide variety of new plays, including David Rabe's *The Basic Training of Pavlo Hummel,* Reinaldo Povod's *Cuba and His Teddy Bear,* Eric Bogosian's *Talk Radio,* and Ntosake Shange's *For Colored Girls Who Have Considered Suicide/When the Rainbow is Enuf,* as well as novel or experimental stagings, such as Gerald Freedman's stunning "Chaplinesque" production of *The Taming of the Shrew* and the John Guare-Mel Shapiro musical version of *Two Gentlemen of Verona;* Richard Foreman's "post-Brechtian" production of *The Threepenny Opera,* starring Raul Julia as Macheath; a well-received *Hamlet,* directed by, and starring, Kevin Kline; the late A. J. Antoon's opulent productions of *A Midsummer Night's Dream* (set in Brazil) and *The Taming of the Shrew* (with Morgan Freeman as Petruchio and Tracey Ullman as Kate), and a thrilling 1992 version of *'Tis Pity She's a Whore,* directed by JoAnne Akalaitis and starring Val Kilmer. Despite its commercial successes, the Festival retains its goal of producing high-quality professional productions for a broadly based public audience, and it continues to present its outdoor summer productions, often employing major stars, with no admission charge. The company is also extraordinarily devoted to interracial and cross-gender casting and to the representation of the widest possible variety of ethnic, racial, and "different" voices. Shortly following Papp's death, one of its leading experimental directors, Jo-Anne Akalaitis, was appointed artistic director of the company, with George C. Wolfe (an African American; discussed later in the chapter) and David Greenspan (a performance artist and playwright with an interest in gay/lesbian and gender themes) as associate directors. In 1993, George Wolfe became sole artistic director.

Seattle There are a great many important professional theatres in Seattle, including the Intiman (which created the first full-

Eric Bogosian wrote and starred in Talk Radio, *produced here by the New York Shakespeare Festival at its downtown Public Theatre. The play is a searing, scathing study of an embittered radio host, at war with the world—and with himself. (Photo: George Joseph.)*

length production of the 1992 Pulitzer Prize–winning *The Kentucky Cycle*), the avant-garde Empty Space (a theatre of "offbeat eclecticism," which is "devoted to the exploration of cutting-edge works and unusual classics"), and A Contemporary Theatre, focusing on playwrights; but the theatre with the largest national reputation is undoubtedly the *Seattle Repertory Theatre,* whose productions of Bill Irwin's *Largely New York,* Wendy Wasserstein's *The Heidi Chronicles,* and Herb Gardner's *Conversations with My Father,* (the latter two directed by Seattle Rep's artistic director, Daniel Sullivan) went on to notable Broadway successes, and, in the case of *Heidi,* the Pulitzer Prize and the Tony Award for best new American drama. In 1991–92, the Seattle Rep joined with New York's Circle Repertory Theatre to create the premiere of Lanford Wilson's *Redwood Curtain* before the New York "re-opening." The Seattle Rep is also one of the growing number of American theatres that employs a resident acting company for an entire season, thus permitting actors to enjoy relatively long-term employment in the same city.

San Francisco The American Conservatory Theatre was founded as a touring company by William Ball in 1965 and settled in San Francisco shortly thereafter; from the beginning, it set a high standard for brilliantly staged and performed revivals of theatre classics, and for the integration of teaching (through its conservatory) and actual performing. This true "conservatory theatre" also won great admiration for its adoption of a true rotating repertory schedule, where many different plays would alternate in a night-by-night schedule, permitting visitors to San Francisco to see up to half a dozen plays at the same theatre in the space of a week's visit. Sagging income and political infighting, however, plus the resignation of Mr. Ball from the theatre's management in

1986 (he died in 1991), and then the devastating earthquake of 1989, which closed the company's principal theatre facility, have all set ACT scrambling in recent years. Undaunted, the theatre's new director, Carey Perloff, is patiently and vigorously rebuilding the company and its facilities and conservatory to what one hopes will again be world-class levels.

Washington The *Arena Stage* was founded by Zelda Fitchandler in 1950; Ms. Fitchandler served as producing director through the 1990–91 season, when, following her resignation, Douglas C. Wager took over the Arena's helm. The Arena retains the novelty of its name, with in-the-round staging (the audience seated on all four sides of the stage) for its primary performance space, "the arena." But the company has also added three non-arena performance facilities to supplement its primary one. The Arena has had a long history of success; as the leading theatre in the national capital it has lived up to its particular challenge with a series of outstanding classical and new productions. These include the world or American premieres of several important plays such as William Sackler's *The Great White Hope,* Christopher Durang's *A History of the American Film,* Michael Weller's *Moonchildren,* and Dario Fo's *Accidental Death of an Anarchist.* The Arena has increasingly been dedicated to echoing the racial and ethnic mix of its hometown and proudly emphasizes its "longstanding commitment to encourage participation by people of color in every aspect of the theatre's life. . . . We seek to create a vibrant emotional and intellectual theatrical landscape that, through storytelling, probes the infinite mystery of the human experience."

This is merely a sampling of important American nonprofit theatres; many others are equally distinctive. The Alliance Theatre of Atlanta, the La Jolla Playhouse, the Alley Theatre of Houston, the Center Theatre of Baltimore, the Wisdom Bridge Theatre of Chicago, the Milwaukee Repertory Theatre, the Denver Theatre Center, the Berkeley Repertory Theatre, the Indiana Repertory Theatre, the Missouri Repertory Theatre, the Philadelphia Drama Guild, and the Alabama Shakespeare Festival are all notable theatre companies that have created excellent productions over the years for their communities and have had substantial influence in the theatre world well beyond their local confines. The Goodspeed Opera House in East Haddam, Connecticut, has pioneered in the production of American musicals (they created the original *Annie*) and particularly the revival of several rarely produced American musicals, including *No, No, Nanette, Very Good Eddie, Fanny,* and a 1991 two-piano revival of Frank Loesser's great *Most Happy Fella,* which, like many of the Goodspeed revivals, went on to great success on Broadway. And there are other nonprofit theatres with focused repertoires — such as the Teatro Campesino, Pan Asian Repertory Theatre, Mixed Blood Theatre Company, National Jewish Theatre, Crossroads Theatre Company, and St. Louis Black Repertory Company, all mentioned earlier — that provide, throughout America's many regions, an extraordinary variety of theatrical art, involvement, and excitement.

The nonprofit professional theatre, which was a "movement" during the 1960s and 1970s has become, quite simply, America's theatre: it is the theatre where America's plays are first shaped and first exposed to the American audience. More and more, the national press is attuned to the major theatre happenings in the nonprofit sector; more and more the Broadway audience, while admiring the latest "hit," is aware that they are seeing that hit's second, third, or fourth production. National theatre prizes, once awarded only for New York productions, are now seized by the-

atres around the country; world-renowned actors, once seen live only on the Broadway stages and on tour, are appearing in the country's two hundred nonprofit regional theatres.

Most important: for the first time in America's history, the vast majority of individuals throughout the country can see first-class professional theatre created in or near their hometowns, and professional theatre artists can live in virtually any major city in the country — not only in New York.

Shakespeare Festivals

In the heyday of Broadway there was also "summer stock," a network of theatres, mainly located in resort areas through the mountains of the Northeast, which provided summer entertainment for tourists and assorted local folks. This "straw hat circuit," as it was called, produced recent and not-so-recent Broadway shows, mainly comedies, with a mix of professional theatre artists from New York and young theatrical hopefuls from around the country; it was both America's vacation theatre and professional training ground.

Summer stock is mostly gone today, but in its place has arisen another phenomenon that, like summer stock, is unique to the United States. This is the collection of Shakespeare festivals, which since 1935 has grown to include almost every state in the nation. The year 1935 marks the founding of the Oregon Shakespeare Festival, now the grandparent of such festivals. Beginning with a three-night run in an abandoned outdoor amphitheater, the Oregon festival now operates a year-round schedule in three theatres, absolutely dominating the small rural town of Ashland, which it calls home.

Characteristic of Ashland and all Shakespeare festivals is a series of summer Shakespearean productions, usually performed outdoors, often supplemented with other plays and sometimes additional indoor stagings. In their varied repertoire the Shakespeare festi-

American summer festivals often offer "Shakespeare under the Stars," as in this 1988 outdoor staging of A Midsummer Night's Dream *at the Colorado Shakespeare Festival. The (literally) moonlit scenery is by Douglas-Scott Goheen, as is the photograph.*

vals are like Shakespeare's own company, the King's Men, which performed plays of many authors, both at the outdoor Globe and the indoor Blackfriars. A number of American Shakespeare festivals are professional, at least in part: these include the Oregon, Alabama, New Jersey, California, San Diego (Old Globe), and New York Shakespeare festivals. Other distinctive festivals, most of which engage professional artists in key positions, include the Utah, Colorado, Illinois, Texas, Idaho, Virginia, and Santa Cruz Shakespeare festivals.

Shakespeare festivals are a wonderful bridge between amateur and fully professional the-atre; most engage, as the old summer stock companies did, a combination of professional artists and advanced students in professional training programs. The repertoire of these theatres is much more varied and serious than is that of the summer stock theatre, however, and the level of theatrical excellence is often outstanding. Many of the Shakespeare festivals, indeed, are moving into fully professional status during the 1990s and are expanding their facilities, their seasons, and their repertoires. In combination, these festivals provide a unique and immensely valuable network of artistic activity and training possibilities for the American theatre.

Summer and Dinner Theatres

There remain, in the United States, some notable professional summer theatres without the word *Shakespeare* in their names. The Williamstown Theatre Festival in Massachusetts is probably the best of these. Founded in 1955 by the charismatic and flamboyant Nikos Psacharopoulos, the WTF has been led, since Psacharopoulos's death in 1989, by his longtime colleague Peter Hunt, who has continued and expanded on the Williamstown tradition of mounting elegant productions, of both new plays and revered world classics, in this beautiful Berkshire Village. Williamstown employs many of New York's best known actors, designers, and directors, eager to leave the stifling city in July and August and spend their month or two in the country, playing Chekhov, Brecht, O'Neill, and Tennessee Williams. The Berkshire Theatre festival in nearby Stockbridge is also a highly accomplished professional summer theatre in this culturally rich area, just two or three hours' north of New York (visitors to the Berkshires can also drop in at Tanglewood to see the Boston Symphony Orchestra playing in shirtsleeves). Several other summer companies in New England and the Mid-Atlantic states have become equally distinguished: theatres such as the Barter Theatre of Abingdon, Virginia (the nation's oldest, founded in 1933); the Theatre at Monmouth (Maine); the Gloucester (Massachusetts) Stage Company (headed by noted playwright Israel Horovitz); and the American Theatre Works (run by author-director Jill Charles, in Dorset, Vermont). These companies and others like them can provide outstanding professional (or semiprofessional) theatre in attractive summer vacation environments, appealing to tourists and local residents alike.

Dinner theatres, which operate year round, were broadly introduced to suburban America in the 1970s, offering a "night on the town" package of dinner and a play in the same facility. The novelty of dinner theatre has worn thin, however, and the acceptable repertory for such packaging — light comedies, mystery melodramas, and pared-down productions of golden-age Broadway musicals — was quickly exhausted; dinner theatre seems to be a declining art in the 1990s. Never high in its artistic aspirations (the format virtually excludes adventurous dramaturgy, challenging themes, or even elaborate staging), dinner theatre has played important roles in bringing the theatre to those otherwise unacquainted with it and in providing employment (and training) to thousands of theatre artists each year.

Amateur Theatre: Academic and Community

Finally, there is an active amateur theatre in America, sometimes operating in conjunction with educational programs.

There are more than one thousand Departments of Drama (or Theatre) offering degrees in the United States, and perhaps an equal number of educational institutions also put on plays or give classes in the various dramatic arts. This is not unique to America. Stage performances in schools have been used worldwide since the Renaissance, not only for the purpose of teaching and exploring dramatic literature (arguably the most important single literary form in history) but also for teaching foreign languages, human behavior, and cultural history, as well as the more personal skills of speech, social development, and self-presentation. For these reasons the putting on of "school plays" has long been a curricular or extracurricular activity, and in the United States this has become a major enterprise. Long before the development of the nonprofit professional theatre, American universities were providing audiences around the country with the masterworks of the international dramatic repertory, as well as the more serious new works of the American stage. The founding of the Yale Drama Department (now the

Yale School of Drama) in 1923 signaled the beginning of a new commitment on the part of American higher education: to assume not merely the role of theatre producer, but also that of theatre trainer. Today, the vast majority of American professional theatre artists receive their training in American college and university departments devoted, in whole or in part, to that purpose. As a result, the academic and professional theatres have often grown closer together, with many artists working interchangeably in both kinds of institution. For this reason, the performances at many university theatres often reach extremely sophisticated levels of excellence in many areas and are, on occasion, equal or superior to

professional productions of the same dramatic material.

Community theatres are amateur groups who put on plays for their own enjoyment and for the entertainment or edification of their community. There are occasions when these theatres, too, reach levels of excellence; some community theatres acquire substantial funding, handsome facilities, and large subscription audiences. One should always remember that many of the world's great theatres, including Stanislavski's Moscow Art Theatre and Antoine's Théâtre Libre, began, essentially, as community theatres run by amateurs. One should also remember that the word "amateur" means "lover" and that the artist who creates

University theatres have as their mission the training of young theatre artists — and also the exploration of important dramatic works that may appear to have little commercial or popular potential. This University of California, Irvine, production of Heiner Müller's Hamletmachine *was directed by Keith Fowler and designed by Douglas-Scott Goheen (scenery) and Elizabeth Novak (costumes); the postmodern approach shows Shakespeare, in a picture on the back wall, glaring at the actors who dare to adapt his work. (Photo: Philip Channing.)*

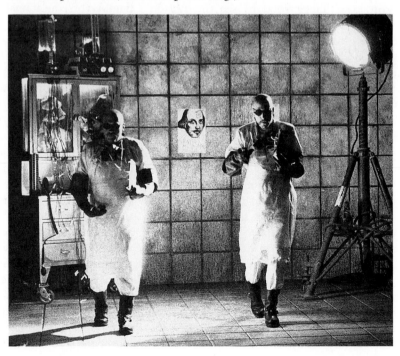

theatre out of love rather than commercial expedience may in fact be headed for the highest levels of art, not necessarily the lowest. The community theatre has, then, a noble calling: it is the theatre a community makes out of itself and for itself, and it can therefore tell us a lot about who we are and what we want.

Current Theatre in Europe

European theatre has always exerted a keen influence on America — indeed, until well into this century, our theatre was always an import or an imitation of the European — and that influence is no less important today. There has also been, particularly since the 1970s, a reciprocal influence of American theatre in Europe.

The European theatre is organized quite differently from our own. It is, first of all, highly institutionalized, with state-supported and city-supported theatres the norm rather than the exception. Germany, for example, has more than 200 government-subsidized professional theatres. Finland, whose population is smaller than Philadelphia's, has thirty-five state and city theatres. In most European countries, theatres are as routinely financed by public monies as libraries are in America. These theatres engage artists on annual contracts (unlike show-by-show contracts common in America) and enjoy the luxuries of long rehearsal periods, long-lasting collaborations, and a deeply developed sense of artistic ensemble. Drawbacks of state support include the intransigent threat of bureaucratic meddling and the imposition — or threatened imposition — of political control over the artistic product; artistic stagnation and complacency are also dangers. However, the generously funded public theatres of Europe are spared a great many financial worries and, when strongly motivated, can undertake the production of a wide variety of classics and experimental plays without an overreliance on box-

The experimental KOM theatre in Helsinki has helped to make the Finnish theatre one of the most vibrant in Europe. This 1983 production is an adaptation of Russian author Mikhail Bulgakov's novel, The Master and Margarita. *At the time it was produced, Bulgakov still could not be produced in what was then the Soviet Union. (Photo: Rauno Träskelin.)*

office success or the distractions of fundraising.

The best European theatre productions are seen increasingly in the United States. International festivals, which have been common in Europe for decades, are growing in popularity in America, particularly since the extraordinarily successful Olympics Theatre Festival in Los Angeles in 1984. Chicago, Denver, Baltimore, New York, and Los Angeles have become sites of international theatre festivals, some recurring; and international tours and theatre exchanges, fostered by the International Theatre Institute and various governments, are greatly on the increase throughout the country.

It is possible that nothing could prove more valuable for the world today than such theatre exchanges, for drama's capacity to serve as a vehicle for international communication — a communication that goes beyond mere rhetoric — is one of culture's greatest potential gifts to humanity. Drama's syntheses of meaning and aesthetics, of intellect and emotions, can coalesce disparate cultures into common understandings; it can transcend ideologies and make antagonists partners, strangers friends. As drama once served to unite the thirteen tribes of ancient Greece, so it may serve in the coming decades to unite a world too often fractured by prejudice and divided by ignorance. The theatre's virtue is to explore the fullest potential of humankind and to lay before us all the universality of the worldwide human experience: human hopes, fears, feelings, and compassion for the living. Nothing could be more vital in the establishment of a true world peace than a shared, cross-cultural awareness of what it means to be human on this planet.

Jean Genet's The Blacks *was one of the first plays to treat the oppression and exploitation of Africans and their descendants. This French play was given a German staging by Peter Stein in 1983; the production emphasizes the international political reality of contemporary Africa and its peoples. (Photo: Courtesy German Information Center.)*

A trip to a dramatic festival, either in the United States or abroad, is certainly the best way to sample the theatres of several other countries; in Europe the main international theatre festivals are in Avignon (France), Edinburgh (Scotland), Spoleto (Italy), and—although limited to German-language plays—Berlin (Germany). On the other hand, nothing can quite match a theatre tour abroad, where the adventurous theatregoer can see not only the dramatic productivity of a given culture, but also the "theatre scene" in its own setting. For such adventurers, we shall look at some possible destinations.

England The first and most rewarding stop for American students on a European theatre tour is likely to be England, first because the language is familiar, and second because the English theatre is currently one of the most vigorous in the world. Two subsidized companies are the focus of English theatrical activity: the National Theatre, operating three stages in a fabulous complex overlooking the River Thames on Shakespeare's Bankside, and the Royal Shakespeare Company, which operates theatres both in London (the Barbican) and in Shakespeare's natal town of Stratford-upon-Avon. Each of these companies has several plays in repertory at any given time; and in a week's visit, split between London and Stratford, it would be possible with adroit scheduling to view nearly a dozen different productions.

Commercial theatres in London also are active year round (although as in New York, the most active period is the "season" stretching from October through May), and many fine plays and productions may be seen at the theatres that line Shaftesbury Avenue in the West End, a district comparable to Broadway, and at "fringe" theatres, located elsewhere in the city, that correspond to our off-Broadway and off-off-Broadway ventures. Regional theatre, or "provincial theatre" as it is called in England, is as active there as in the United States, with publicly supported theatres in every major town performing plays in repertory or stock during the seasonal period. Indeed, the "provincial rep" of English towns is the traditional training ground for English actors, who are considered by many to be the most polished and versatile actors in the world.

So esteemed is England in the world of theatre—owing to the past contributions of Shakespeare, Marlowe, Garrick, and Shaw, as well as the splendid contemporary achievements of playwrights such as Tom Stoppard, Edward Bond, Harold Pinter, Simon Gray, Alan Ayckbourne, Pam Gems, Howard Brenton, David Hare, Caryl Churchill, Trevor Griffiths, and Peter Shaffer—that several American colleges have set up summer drama programs to allow their students to experience the riches of English theatre and scholarship at first hand. Flocks of Americans, students and tourists alike, de-

The Royal Shakespeare Theatre is famous for its namesake playwright, of course, but it produces contemporary plays as well. This 1991 production of Pam Gems's The Blue Angel *was directed by Trevor Nunn; Kelly Hunter and Philip Madoc are the actors. (Photo: Clive Barda.)*

The Comédie Française, founded in 1680, presents classic French plays in the traditional manner, but also experiments with contemporary stagings. Here, in a production of Molière's Don Juan, *the traditional chandeliers are used in a novel fashion to enhance a sense of decadence. (Photo: Courtesy French Cultural Services.)*

scend every year upon the meccas of London and Stratford and on the summer festivals of Chichester and Edinburgh.

France and Germany The countries that spawned the theatre of the absurd and the theatre of alienation, respectively, as well as the earlier symbolist and expressionist dramatic movements—France and Germany—remain active theatre centers today. Both countries provide a mix of traditional and strikingly original theatre.

French theatre, headquartered as always in Paris, maintains the traditional Royal theatre style in the Comédie Française, which continues to operate in the French capital much as it has since 1680. But newer state-supported provincial Parisian theatres, including the Théâtre National de Strasbourg, the Comédie de Caen, the National Popular Theatre (T.N.P.) at Villeurbanne, and the Theatre of East Paris (T.E.P.), have complemented the traditional Comédie Française in recent years, and a new "theatre on the hill" (the Théâtre National de la Colline) has taken up the task of presenting new French plays and translations of foreign plays not yet known in France. Another nationally subsidized theatre, the Bobigny MC93 (MC stands for "Maison de la Culture"), brings modern and postmodern performing artists from all over the world to this Paris suburb: artists like Robert Wilson, Peter Sellars, Heiner Müller, David Byrne, and the Kodo drummers of Japan. Meanwhile, two more independent companies—Ariane Mnouchkine's Théâtre de Soleil at the Cartoucherie in Vincennes and Peter Brook's Center of Theatre Research at the Bouffes du Nord in Paris—have created productions of world renown, which are discussed in more detail later in this chapter. French theatre is not noted only for productions, however: it has been

The contemporary German theatre is in part dedicated to an exhaustive re-examination of classic works, with an eye to the possibility of strikingly fresh and unorthodox new theatrical realizations. The result is often starkly, even shockingly, expressive. This production of Euripides' Medea treats the same scene depicted in Chapter 3 (p. 41), but with a clearly postmodern impact: Agave holds the head of her son, Pentheus, as a near-naked Cadmus writhes in agony. This Medea was directed by Michael Grüber as part of a multi-year "Antiquities Project," funded by the German Government at the Berlin Schaubühne. (Photo: Courtesy German Information Center.)

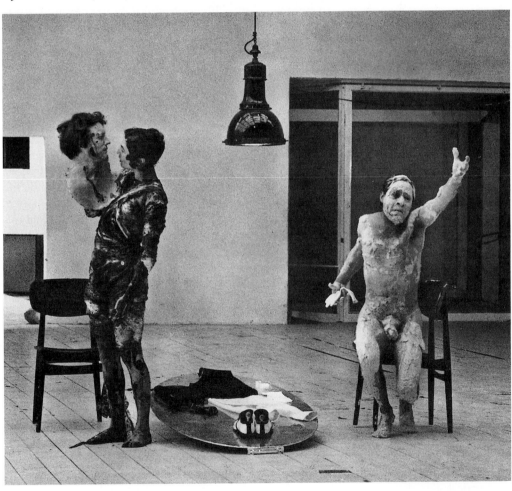

largely French intellectuals — Jean-Paul Sartre, Albert Camus, Roland Barthes, Claude Lévi-Strauss, Jacques Lacan, Jacques Derrida, Jean Baudrillard, and Hélène Cixous — who have been at the forefront first of existentialism (Sarte, Camus) and then of the critical theorizing (structuralism, post-structuralism, deconstruction, feminism) that characterizes all phases of the postmodern age — and the postmodern drama.

In Paris, comedies of the Broadway type (but entirely Gallic in flavor) are the basic fare at the commercial theatres along the boulevards; indeed, the term "boulevard theatre" in France signifies a light, diverting piece, invariably having to do with marital infidelity. More experimental works can be seen throughout the city and in the suburbs, where warehouses, parks, and abandoned factories are more likely to serve as dramatic venues than are traditional theatres. An annual summer theatre festival at the ancient city of Avignon, in the south of France, brings together the most significant of the avant-garde and popular productions of the preceding year and presents them in the spectacular setting of the former Papal Palace, offering visitors a unique opportunity to sample the entire range of contemporary French dramatic endeavor.

In contrast to France, Germany has no theatre capital; rather, it boasts a myriad of civic theatres — and every year one or more of them does something that causes a national sensation. In recent years, Hamburg, Berlin, Munich, Frankfurt, Cologne, Bochum, Rostock, and Bremen have all been sites of exciting theatrical activity. German theatre, adhering to none of the traditions of its past, is perhaps the most radically innovative in the Western world, particularly in the areas of directing and design; thus a visit to German theatre, particularly in a broad sampling, can be of inestimable value even to the theatre student who has no knowledge of the German language. Richly imaginative and frequently visually astonishing, the German theatre offers a wealth of fresh insights into the possibilities of theatrical aesthetics.

Current Theatre in the World

America, England, France, and Germany provide, in combination, a dazzling spectrum of contemporary theatre. But these countries hardly exhaust the theatre of the world today. The International Theatre Institute has official representation in 79 countries around the globe, each of which enjoys a remarkable theatrical history and an active and provocative current theatre. Plays have been staged in *Canada* since the beginning of the seventeenth century; today, theatre flourishes in every Canadian province, with the Stratford (Ontario) Festival Theatre and the Shaw Festival at Niagara-on-the-Lake having international prominence among the country's more than 220 professional theatre groups: Canada now enjoys a virtual flood of new Canadian playwrights, directors, and theatre critics who are developing global reputations.

The sturdy *Russian* theatre has survived revolution, war, purges, foreign occupation, and the astonishing recent political upheavals. Chekhov's three sisters still enchant sold-out houses at the Moscow Art Theatre, while fresh and innovative stagings continue to stimulate huge audiences in St. Petersburg, Moscow, and other cities across this broad land, rife with new artistic — as well as political — fervor. Former USSR-dependent states and nations have exploited their independence both onstage and off in these turbulent recent years. Reenergized theatre companies in *Lithuania, Poland, Hungary,* (ex-Soviet) *Georgia,* and the *Ukraine* are attracting international audiences at home and on international tours. It is hardly coincidental, moreover, that both Czechoslovakia and Hungary elected dissident (and previously jailed) playwrights — Vaclav Havel and Arpád Göncz respectively — as their presidents in the immediate post-Communist period or that the first president of the breakaway Republic of (ex-Soviet) Georgia was also that country's leading Shakespearean translator (Zviad Gamsakhurdia), for the theatre in Eastern Europe has been the primary locus of independent, dissident, and underground expression since the earliest days of the Cold War. When the "Velvet Revolution" in Czechoslovakia overthrew the Communist government in 1989, the revolution was headquartered in the basement of Havel's theatre in Prague. Nor is it entirely coincidental that the presiding Pope of this period is himself a former playwright; this is Karol Jozef Wojtyla (John Paul II), a Pole whose commitment to free social and artistic expression has proved seminal during this tumultuous era.

Nor is political-activist playwriting limited to Eastern Europe. Wole Soyinka (Akinwande Oluwole) of *Nigeria* has played an equally crucial role in the politics and theatre art of his country and the international scene; Soyinka, who like Havel and Göncz was jailed for his radical political activity, has helped shape his country's destiny since the mid-1960s. And no theatre has had more political impact in the world today than the Market Theatre of Johannesburg, *South Africa,* which has won its reputation not only for the outstanding quality of its productions, but also for its courageous and effective confrontation with that country's dying policy of racial apartheid: particularly in productions of Athol Fugard's *Sizwe Banzi is Dead, The Island, Master Harold . . . And the Boys, A Lesson from Aloes,* and Mbongeni Ngema's *Woza Albert!* and *Asinamali!* Productions of Fugard and Ngema, which have now toured and been restaged the world over, have proved crucial in shaping world opinion on this bitter issue.

Japanese theatre is internationally known for its magnificent traditional repertoire of classical Noh, the popular Kabuki, and the Bunraku (puppet) theatre, but *shingeki* ("new drama"), influenced by modernist European realism, has asserted itself since the beginning of the century; and an avant-garde, nonrealistic countermovement called post-*shingeki* has proven even more popular and intellectually exciting to the Japanese theatregoer since the early 1960s. Post-*shingeki*—explosive, violent, sexual, surreal, and often sadistic/masochistic—coalesces present-day Japan with its legendary and mythic past, and often features the meta-morphosis of modern characters into ancient gods. While it may be true that traditional rather than avant-garde theatre dominates most of Asia, partly because of political restraints (as in China and the two Koreas), the experimental work of many Japanese artists, such as Tadashi Suzuki (director of SCOT—the Suzuki Troupe of Toga), have proven influential in both staging and theatre training around the world.

Only our own cultural insularity lets us imagine ourselves at the center of the universe, the true and legitimate heirs of those who invented theatre; the truth is that theatre is happening throughout the known world and in forms so diverse as to defy accounting or assimilation. Every component of theatre—from architecture to acting, from dramaturgy to directing—is in the process of change, of learning, of rebelling from convention, of building anew. The theatre's diversity is its very life, and change is the foremost of its vital signs. We must not think to pin it down, but rather to seek it out, to produce it ourselves, and to participate in its growth.

WHAT'S HAPPENING?

No book can tell you what's happening—for by the time you read it in a book, it has already happened.

What we can do is list a few promising artists and artistic trends that should be at the forefront of theatrical life during the last years of the century. Even if the list is less than prophetic, it should give a general picture of the diversity of the theatre of our times and of the sorts of dramatic possibilities that theatre artists and enthusiasts are currently anticipating.

Martha Clarke and Dance-Theatre

Dance-theatre occupies a middle ground between plays and ballet; it is an impressionistic series of musical tableaux, based on a theme

The Garden of Earthly Delights, *a highly innovative dance-drama conceived and directed by Martha Clarke, is a brilliantly evocative staging — with music, mime, dance (on the ground and in the air), and stunning stage effects — of the great Hieronymous Bosch painting of the same name (c. 1510). Adam and Eve are seen here in the 1987 New York off-Broadway revival; lighting is by Paul Gallo, costumes by Jane Greenwood, and flying effects by Peter Foy. (Photo: Martha Swope Assoc./Carol Rosegg.)*

but lacking a conventional plot or set of characters. Martha Clarke, a veteran of the Pilobolus dance troupe, created two stunning dance-theatre pieces in the late 1980s: *The Garden of Earthly Delights,* based on a painting by Hieronymous Bosch, and *Vienna Lusthaus,* evoking the artistic and sexual ferment of Vienna at the time of Gustave Klimt. Clarke's pieces are in the tradition of surrealism and suggest the dream worlds of the later August Strindberg and Antonin Artaud; however, they are highly original in both conception and execution. Her more recent works

indicate an increased interest in social and political themes as well. *Miracolo d'Amore,* introduced at the Spoleto (South Carolina) festival in 1988, deals with sexual violence. *Endangered Species,* which premiered in Stockbridge (Massachusetts) in 1990, employs circus animals, a text from Walt Whitman, and eight actors to explore American Civil War themes in the context of comtemporary environmental issues. Clarke, who received a $285,000 MacArthur Foundation fellowship for her work in 1990, will surely prove a major force in dance-drama for years to come.

The One-Person Show

Although Chekhov wrote a short play for a single actor (*On the Harmfulness of Tobacco,* in which the character is a lecturer addressing his audience), it has only been in quite recent times that authors have seriously entertained the possibilities of full-length plays employing a single actor. Sometimes, these are little more than star vehicles or extended monologues, but some are serious attempts at serious drama and dramaturgy. Spalding Gray's impressionistic and autobiographical storytellings, seemingly casual ruminations that develop a subtly enchanting momentum, became avantgarde classics in the 1980s (*Swimming to Cambodia*) and early 1990s (*Monster in a Box*). Patrick Stewart's one-man presentation of Charles Dickens's *A Christmas Carol,* in which the celebrated Shakespearean actor (and "Star Trek" TV star) played all the roles, became a surprise Broadway success in 1991 and is certain to return in future years. Employing a more traditional dramaturgy, Jay Presson Allen, in the ineffably poignant *Tru,* depicts the late author-celebrity Truman Capote alone on stage, shuffling around his New York apartment and making wan jokes to the audience; as played by actor Robert Morse on Broadway (1990), the play probed deeply into serious issues of creativity and social alienation, particularly as Capote is shown against the backdrop of nighttime Manhattan: the thousand lit windows outside his apartment window representing the parties to which he's not invited. Loneliness is also the subtext of Allen's subsequent (coauthored) *The Big Love,* in which Tracey Ullman played Florence Aadland, the mother of Errol Flynn's mistress, and Willy Russell's fictional *Shirley Valentine* (1990), in which the sole character is presumed to be speaking to her kitchen wall (and, in the second act, to a rock on a Greek island); this play is a wonderful portrayal of an ordinary English woman's despair in a loveless marriage, made all the more touching by her isolation on stage. The American Place Theatre in New York has premiered both one-person recitals, such as *Calvin Trillin's Words, No Music,* featuring this wryly urbane and witty social commentator; and, in 1992, Roger Rosenblatt's capital-less *"and"* (with Ron Silver in the solo role), which subsequently moved to a theatre in Hollywood, California. The American Place also gave its stage to Eric Bogosian's intense performances — savage and comic by turns — of roles created by him in his solo piece, *Drinking in America,* which Bogosian subsequently followed with *Sex, Drugs, and Rock & Roll* (1991) and *Dog Show* (1992); these works have protrayed, with a penetrating and disturbing intensity, the miasma of homelessness, addiction, power-tripping, and urban destruction in the United States at the turn of the decade.

The most brilliant one-person experiment in recent stagings, however, has been Jane Wagner's wondrous *The Search for Signs of Intelligent Life in the Universe,* which Wagner wrote for her friend and colleague, the actress Lily Tomlin, who performed it to rapturous reviews in 1985. Like Bogosian, Wagner creates (and Tomlin performs) a remarkable variety of ragged urban characters, ranging across the breadth of American society: a bag woman, a jaded socialite, a cokehead, a radical feminist, and Agnus Angst, a teenage punk performance artist ("even as a fetus I had womb angst"). But unlike Bogosian's compilations of individual sketches, Wagner's characters interact with each other, and her play comes to a remarkable closure that brings together both characters and audience in a "goose bump" experience: a spirit of theatrical communion. Rarely have there been standing ovations in the recent theatre as spontaneous and warm-hearted as at this play — with its amazing solo performance. Indeed, it is such a *theatrical* piece of drama that its subsequent film version proved only the palest of imitations and failed to find an appreciable audience.

Jerzy Grotowski and Ritual Arts

The very ancient and the very new mix in the current work of Jerzy Grotowski (born 1933), who was first internationally heralded for his series of extraordinarily intense and highly disciplined performances at the Polish Laboratory Theatre in Wroclaw, where he served as founder-director during the late 1960s and early 1970s. Grotowski called this the "poor theatre" because it dispensed with "rich" elements of costume and scenery and focused directly on the deepest potential of the actor. Grotowski's stagings were preceded by rigorous and intensive training sessions and rehearsals for the actors — which went on for years. "No one since Stanislavski has investigated the nature of acting, its phenomenon, its meaning, the nature and science of its mental, physical, emotional process as deeply and completely as Grotowski," said Peter Brook, who invited Grotowski to lead workshops with the Royal Shakespeare Company in the 1960s. Grotowski abandoned his theatre company in the 1970s in order to explore human creativity outside the theatre or, as he called it, in the "para-theatre." His research led him to explore the creativity of performers in all parts of the world and to research the "theatre of sources," as he defined it, in varied rituals,

GROTOWSKI ON
THE PERFORMER

The Performer, with a capital letter, is a man of action. He is not a man who plays another. He is a dancer, a priest, a warrior: he is outside aesthetic genres. Ritual is performance, an accomplished action, an act. Degenerated ritual is a spectacle. I don't want to discover something new but something forgotten. Something which is so old that all distinctions between aesthetic genres are no longer of use.

Jerzy Grotowski

chants, and tribal dances from Asia, Africa, South America, and Native (Indian) America.

Grotowski's most recent creative phase is his study of "ritual art" and "objective drama," which are his terms for the "performative elements" common in prehistoric rituals around the world. Working with traditional specialists from Haiti, India, Bali, Japan, and elsewhere (but principally in non-Europeanized cultures), Grotowski and his assistants approach the possibility of developing an intercultural ensemble of performers, capable of recombining these performative fragments into whole artistic products. Working initially out of a barn on the campus of the University of California at Irvine, and now in a two-story farm building outside of Pontedera, Italy, Grotowski and his team seek to uncover and re-create the most ancient "roots of drama" and to train what he calls "Performer, with a capital letter."

Ariane Mnouchkine
and the Théâtre de Soleil

Mnouchkine's company astounded American audiences in its 1984 appearance at the Los Angeles Olympics with three Asian-inspired Shakespearean productions, particularly *Richard II,* utilizing quasi-Kabuki techniques, and *La Nuit des Rois (Twelfth Night),* which drew on Indian Kathakali dance patterns. But Mnouchkine and the Théâtre de Soleil (Theatre of the Sun) company she heads had been celebrated in Europe since the late 1960s for radically innovative stage productions created collaboratively by the entire theatrical ensemble. The notion of collaborative creation is itself radical, since it dispenses with the ordinary theatrical hierarchy and absolute separation of duties. In Mnouchkine's company, productions come out of improvisations, discussion, and group study; and all members of the group share the various responsibilities of research, scriptwriting, staging, interpretation, design, construction, and even house management. All company members in the Théâtre de Soleil are allocated the same salary—even Mnouchkine herself, who, perhaps alone among artistic directors, has worked to diminish the formal and merely hierarchal superiority of the director in the theatre. (Even today, Mnouchkine herself might be tearing the tickets at the door or clearing away paper plates at the theatre's buffet bar.)

After its initial success with Arnold Wesker's *The Kitchen,* the Théâtre de Soleil moved into a former munitions factory, the Cartoucherie, in the Paris suburb of Vincennes; there, influenced by the French student rebellions and other civil disorders of 1968, the company began to seek a new language of theatre, based in part on Artaudian freedom, in part on Brechtian political commitment, in part on collective improvisation, and in part on a new interculturalism, particularly in blending Eastern with Western performance traditions. The Théâtre de Soleil also stakes out new ground by working not on single plays, but on groupings of plays linked by time, theme, and methodology. A trilogy of such plays, individually entitled *1789, 1793,* and *The Golden Age,* were the principal result of the company's work in the decade of the 1970s; these company-improvised works, which were concerned with the French Revolution in the light of contemporary French history, proved immediate successes in France and, subsequently, abroad. The company's Kabuki-and Kathakali-inspired Shakespearean productions followed in the early 1980s; then, in the latter part of that decade, Mnouchkine began to mount a series of ancient Greek plays, collectively entitled *Les Atrides* (the house of Atreus), consisting of Euripides' *Iphigeneia at Aulis,* followed by the three plays of Aeschylus' *Oresteia.* By 1991, when the entire tetralogy had been assembled and staged, French audiences cheered and international critics raved. "You will be fortunate if you ever see a more exhilarating production of the first great tragedies in European drama," said the *New York Times.* This great compilation was presented in Montreal, Canada, and Brooklyn, New York, in 1992.

Mnouchkine's experiments are brilliantly realized — with a group of artists who, over the years, have developed and integrated truly extraordinary performance skills. Her work has redefined the potential of virtually every theatrical element, from stage movement (characters generally run onstage at full tilt) to staging (mostly full front, facing the audience) to music (live and virtually continuous performance employing more than 140 instruments from many different cultures) to play selection (trilogies and tetralogies) to a devoted intercultural approach to theatrical creativity and convention. The work is profound, yet it is also broadly entertaining; the Théâtre de Soleil is a popular, no less than an intellectual success, and its future work is awaited with the greatest anticipation.

Robert Wilson and Performance Art

The term "performance art," referring to a largely improvised, nondramatic performance by visual artists, came to prominence in the early 1970s. Performance art differs from theatre to the extent that it recognizes no conventions, ordinarily takes place in nontheatrical facilities (such as art galleries), and normally employs people without theatrical training (although not necessarily without theatrical gifts). Instead, performance art creates a series of visual happenings and audial rhythms, often interwoven with some sort of spoken narrative or dialogue. There is generally no plot, no characters (the performers play themselves), and frequently no perceptible theme. There is also little or no dramatic momentum: a provocative association of impressions, rather than suspense, building excitement, or catharsis, provides the aesthetic impact. Dada experiments in the early years of the century (see beginning of this chapter) were certainly forerunners of this provocative art form, which is a pure example of postmodernist ideas and aesthetics.

Lines between the arts are not absolute, however, and many theatre artists may also, in at least some of their work, be regarded as performance artists as well. Or vice versa. Since the early 1970s, Americans Richard Foreman and Robert Wilson have made significant contributions jointly in performance and theatre art. Wilson's achievement, particularly, has enjoyed a high visibility here and overseas.

Wilson, born in Texas, first came to prominence in Germany, where his highly original collages of poetic texts, recited against brilliantly evocative *tableaux vivants* ("living pictures"), gained substantial attention from enthusiasts of the avant-garde. The extraordinary length of these pieces, which Wilson both wrote and directed, earned him some early notoriety for that reason alone: *The Life and Times of Joseph Stalin* (1973) lasted twelve hours; *Ka Mountain* (1972) lasted twenty-three. Wilson was invited to create the central performance work of the 1984 Los Angeles Olympics Arts Festival, for which he composed *The CIVIL warS,* a massive piece which was rehearsed in segments, in several countries around the world; however, funds could not be raised for the ultimate performance, and by the late 1980s, only fragments of the work had been performed.

Wilson's work is not, strictly considered, performance art, for his pieces have a theme, are not improvised, and the performers usually (but not always) play some sort of character other than themselves. Nevertheless, his work is hard to categorize in other ways—incorporating, as it does, virtually all elements of performance and the arts, including dance, music, sculpture, video, painting, lighting, poetry, narrative, and human expressiveness. The sheer time duration of Wilson's work forces a reexamination of the nature of performance and the relationship of audience and art, meaning and aesthetics. Wilson's work makes us question the foundations of dramaturgy: why do we watch theatre? What are we looking for? What do we care about?

In 1986, Wilson forged a stronger link with drama, by freely adapting a script from the classical theatre repertory (Euripides' *Alcestis*) and by staging it in his own fashion at the American Repertory Theatre in Cambridge, Massachusetts. The result was a visually stunning theatre piece, magically provocative in its imagery, yet contained within the conventional framework of a three-hour performance, staged with professional actors in a normal proscenium theatre. Wilson followed this with a production of Heiner Müller's *Hamletmachine* at the same ART playhouse.

Wilson has turned increasingly to combining his unique aesthetic imagination with at least the rudiments of traditional playtexts, although his cutting, interpretation, and staging of these plays are strictly postmodern and revisionist. Overscale props, intermixing of humans and puppets, exotically nontraditional casting, ideographic and kinetic scenery, interposition of alternate text material, and extreme "slow motion" stage movements characterize Wilson's highly stylized stagings. "I

Robert Wilson is the director, John Conklin the costume designer, and both co-designed the scenery for this dreamlike American Repertory Theatre production of Ibsen's When We Dead Awaken *in 1991. (Photo: Richard Feldman.)*

hate ideas," Wilson states, "that's why my theatre is different, noninterpretive. Interpretation is for the audience."

Many of Wilson's recent works, like his initial ones, have premiered in Germany, where he receives more funding than in his native United States. In 1990 alone, Wilson premiered a *King Lear* in Frankfurt; Chekhov's *Swan Song* in Munich; an adaptation of Virginia Woolf's *Orlando* in Berlin; and a play of his own, *The Black Rider*, in Hamburg. In 1992 his Berlin production of Gertrude Stein's *Doctor Faustus Lights the Lights* received exceptional acclaim. Wilson does return home from time to time, however, and in 1991 he directed *When We Dead Awaken* (Ibsen) at the American Repertory Theatre in Cambridge and the Alley Theatre in Houston.

Stephen Sondheim and the Broadway Musical

No one has changed the face of the American musical more than Sondheim (born in 1930), whose first important work was the composition of lyrics for Leonard Bernstein's 1957 Broadway musical, *West Side Story*. After one more assignment as lyricist (for *Gypsy*), Sondheim turned composer as well, winning high praise and success for both words and music to the songs in the highly novel *A Funny Thing Happened on the Way to the Forum,* drawn from the Roman comedies of Plautus.

Since the 1970s, Sondheim and his collaborators have departed dramatically from the standard Broadway musical format, developing a style marked by a disturbing plot and highly sophisticated and adult lyrics, intricately rhymed and brilliantly integrated with an often-jarring atonal musical score. *Company, Follies,* and *A Little Night Music* established Sondheim's supremacy in the American musical form, and Sondheim has gone on to break new boundaries in subsequent works. His *Pacific Overtures* (1975) used Oriental music to trace the modern history of Japan–

"*The history of the world, my sweet/Is who gets eaten and who gets to eat!*" sings Len Cariou, as Sweeney, to Angela Landsbury, as Mrs. Lovett, in Stephen Sondheim's savagely amusing Broadway musical, Sweeney Todd. *Together, Sweeney and Mrs. Lovett make meat pies out of freshly murdered Londoners of all professions. "The trouble with poet/Is how do you know it/'s deceased? Try the priest!" offers Lovett. "Is that squire/On the fire?" asks Todd. "Mercy no sir," responds Lovett, "Look closer,/You'll notice it's grocer." Sondheim's brilliant, unexpected lyrics, perfectly matched to his innovative tunes, are among Broadway's finest creations. (Photo: Martha Swope and Associates.)*

United States relations, while his *Sweeney Todd* (1979) integrated Brechtian alienation techniques, Italian grand opera, English music hall, and Victorian melodrama, all in a morbid story of a barber's revenge—which takes the form of killing his customers and serving up their flesh in meat pies sold to the public. Conversely, *Sunday in the Park with George* (1984) is an elegant musical play about the pointillist painter, Georges Seurat; for this production Sondheim invented a "pointillist" style of music to echo Seurat's style.

Sondheim's most controversial new work is surely his *Assassins* (1991), which jumps through the centuries to tell the musical story of each presidential assassination and near assassina-

The characters of Sondheim's Sunday in the Park with George *pose as the famous painting by Georges Seurat, whose life this provocative musical dramatizes. South Coast Repertory Theatre production starring Harry Groener as Georges; directed by Barbara Damashek, with outstanding scenery, costumes, and lighting by Cliff Faulkner, Shigeru Yaji, and Tom Ruzika respectively. (Photo: Christopher Gross.)*

tion; its protagonists (if not its heroes) are John Wilkes Booth, Lee Harvey Oswald, Squeaky Fromme, and John Hinckley, among actual and would-be presidential killers. Sondheim's musical was so unconventional and, to some, so alarming that it did not open on Broadway after its limited run in an off-Broadway premiere; *Assassins* has reached a national audience only for its music and lyrics — via the issue of an original cast recording. A 1993 run in London, England, has been more successful, however.

Sondheim's sheer genius (he is also the fabricator of devilish crossword puzzles) and the creative extravagance of his collaborators, particularly director Hal Prince, has not only kept the Broadway musical alive during the 1980s, but has also provided what many say are its finest masterpieces and has certainly served to forecast what must be the vast potential, still unrealized, of this medium.

Peter Brook and Intercultural Theatre

No director has been more influential in the later half of the twentieth century, and none is more provocative in the current theatre than Peter Brook. Born in 1925, Brook began his directorial career as a teenager during World War II, startling English theatregoers with freshly conceived productions of Shakespeare, Marlowe, Sartre, and Cocteau; in 1945, at the age of twenty, he was engaged to direct at the Shakespeare Memorial Theatre at Stratford-upon-Avon and, shortly thereafter, at Covent Garden Opera House, the Metropolitan Opera in New York, and on Broadway. His 1955 *Hamlet* at Stratford, with Paul Scofield in the title role, toured to Moscow — the first English company playing there in the Soviet era. Brook's career went into its ascendancy, however, in 1962 when, as the codirector of the new Royal Shakespeare Company at Stratford, he staged *King Lear*, again with Scofield, in a production deeply influenced by the theatre of the absurd; Brook followed this two years later with the English-language premiere of Peter Weiss's *Marat/Sade*, a production influenced in part by the theatre of cruelty. These two productions enjoyed immense international success, both on world tours and in subsequently filmed versions. Brook's subsequent publication of *The Empty Space* in 1968 established his reputation not merely as a director but as a theorist as well: this long essay puts forth a brilliant analysis of modern drama, which Brook divides into "the deadly theatre, the holy theatre, and the rough theatre" (corresponding, more or less, to the conventional theatre, the theatre of Artaud, and the theatre of Brecht) and culminates with a manifesto on behalf of "the immediate theatre." To Brook, the immediate theatre is not something preplanned by the director, but instead is something developed through an entirely creative and improvisational process, "a harrowing collective experience" rather than a polite collaboration of craft experts. Brook then astonished the theatre world with his vigorously comic, penetrating, "immediate" production of *A Midsummer Night's Dream*, a production that — staged without sentimentality on a bare white set — combined circus techniques with uninhibited sexual farce and created amazingly fresh interactions between the play's well-known (and often shallowly understood) characters. The *Dream* captivated critics and audiences throughout Europe and America during the early 1970s and established Brook as one of the most creative and talented theorist/theatrical practitioners of all time.

Brook's current phase began in 1971, as he moved to Paris to create The International Center of Theatre Research. Using a company of actors from all parts of the world and performing in a dilapidated and clay-floored Parisian theatre (the Bouffes du Nord), as well as in various nontheatrical spaces in and out of Europe, Brook has produced a series of intercultural works of extraordinary interest, including *The Iks*, which is about a Northern Ugandan tribe, *The Conference of the Birds*, based on a twelfth-century Persian poem, Jarry's *Ubu*, Bizet's opera *Carmen*, a production of Shakespeare's *The Tempest*, and, most remarkably perhaps, *The Mahabharata*, which opened in Paris in 1986 and which Brook filmed for worldwide audiences in 1991. *The Mahabharata* is the national novel of India, ancient, archetypal, and immense (it is the longest single work of world literature). Brook has adapted it into a nine-hour play, staged with his cast of assorted Asian, American, African, and European actors; it was performed in a rock quarry outside of Avignon and on the clay stage of the Bouffes du Nord. Brook blends the text with a myriad of natural (but not naturalistic) elements: actors wade in pools and rivers of real water, trapped by circles of real fire; chariot wheels are mired in real mud; armies clash by torchlight; candles float in the pond. The multifaceted reality of this Indian epic directed by an Englishman in a French theatre with an international cast creates a universality to the production that leaves the audience fulfilled in ways previously unrealized in the theatre's history. Brook's notion of an "immediate" theatre is not something that will, in the coming decade, be limited merely to the pages of his book.

AMERICAN PLAYWRIGHTS

In the 1980s and 1990s, no playwrights have dominated the American theatre as forcefully as did Tennessee Williams and Arthur Miller in the 1940s and 1950s. In part, this is because of the decentralization of the American theatre, which has eliminated the absolute primacy of New York (and the total dominance of New York critics) as America's central locus of theatre production. Today, the new American drama is appearing simultaneously in Los Angeles, Seattle, San Diego, Louisville, Minneapolis, and dozens of other cities around the country. And no single observer, or critic,

Fire is a recurrent motif in Peter Brook's production of The Mahabharata. *Brook employs the natural elements more than most directors: the floor of his Théâtre de Bouffes du Nord is clay, the back wall is naturally aged concrete, and a pond of water occupies a considerable portion of the stage. This play, indeed, was originally staged in a rock quarry in southern France. Paris, 1986. (Photo: Gilles Abegg.)*

can hope to track the dozens of new playwrights emerging from the hundreds of theatres throughout the United States now dedicated—in whole or in part—to commissioning and presenting original dramas.

But it is rather to our benefit that, instead of one or two dominant voices, there are today *dozens* of American playwrights commanding national (and, sometimes, international) attention, both for their existing achievements and for their continuing potential in contemporary drama.

August Wilson

While none may dominate, one is clearly foremost: this is August Wilson, who in less than a decade has received five Tony award nominations and two Pulitzer Prizes and whose work continues to grow and deepen year by year. Wilson, born of an interracial couple in Pittsburgh in 1945, has not merely ascended to the highest rank of importance, but he has also helped to redefine the nature of American theatre.

A little-known poet in the 1970s, Wilson began his remarkable rise as a dramatist when he submitted a manuscript to the Eugene O'Neill Theatre Center in Waterford, Connecticut, in 1981. There it came to the attention of the Center's director, Lloyd Richards. Already a major figure in the American theatre (he had directed the major African-American play of the postwar era, Lorraine Hansberry's *A Raisin in the Sun,* in 1959), Richards quickly saw Wilson's writing potential; in the ensuing ten years (through 1991), he was to encourage and direct an astonishing series of five brilliant August Wilson plays: *Ma Rainey's Black Bottom, Fences, Joe Turner's Come and Gone, The Piano Lesson,* and *Two Trains Running.* Each of these works was first produced at the Yale Repertory Theatre (which Richards also headed at the time); each went on to regional theatre tours and prize-winning Broadway runs.

Together, Wilson's remarkable new canon of plays creates a decade-by-decade history of the lives, accomplishments, and struggles of ordinary twentieth-century African Americans: presenting a lively and evocative depiction of (largely) black home life within the context of a (largely) white political society. Wilson's dramaturgy takes many forms, from mainstream American realism (*Fences* is, in many ways, a black *Death of a Salesman*), to musical/dramatic/satiric commentary (*Ma Rainey,* the story of a black jazz singer), to profoundly emotive family dramas that draw deeply upon black American history and ancient African roots (*Piano Lesson* and *Joe Turner's Come and Gone,* which is Wilson's masterpiece, so far).

Wilson's commitment to explore African-American culture is both broadly political and deeply aesthetic, and he is not interested in synthesizing the races or glossing over cultural differences (and cultural glories). "I find in

August Wilson's delicate and imaginative The Piano Lesson *won the Pulitzer Prize for Drama in 1990. The world premiere, shown here, was at the Yale Repertory Theatre, directed by Lloyd Richards. The actors are Charles S. Dutton and Rocky Carroll. (Photo: Gerry Goodstein.)*

Willy Loman is bent low by his heavy bags in Arthur Miller's Death of a Salesman, *a masterpiece of mid-century (1949) American realism. Willy, a traveling salesman with failing prospects and unhelpful grown sons, has been beaten down by the unending struggle to make a living and be "well-liked"; with this play, Miller makes his case that such a "low man" is a modern tragic hero. Actor William Leach plays Willy in this superb 1991 Utah Shakespearean Festival production, directed by Eli Simon. Willy's classic pose is inspired by the original Broadway poster. (Photo: Jess Allen.)*

black life a very elegant kind of logical language, based on the logical order of things," he says. "There's the idea of metaphor. For instance, when one character in *The Piano Lesson* asks, 'What time does Berneice get home?' instead of getting a response like 'Berneice gets home at 5 o'clock,' you get: 'You up there asleep, Berneice leave out of here early in the morning, she out there in Squirrel Hill cleaning house for some big shot down there at the steel mill. They don't like you to come late. You come late they won't give you your carfare. What kind of business you got with Berneice?' When you ask a question, instead of getting an answer to the question, you get this guy's ideas, his opinions about everything, a little explanation. You get all these kinds of things just from one question." A poet still, Wilson blends drama with profound observation and abiding humanity.

Another Dozen

A remaining dozen American playwrights, here listed in the order of their birthdates (and thereby by the approximate duration of their writing careers), have at least two plays (and at most twenty-some) regularly represented on professional and academic stages around the country. At least another dozen playwrights could have been included, but this is a representative sample of the most highly regarded working dramatists in the United States today.

Arthur Miller (born 1915) Although he now claims to have abandoned Broadway, Miller continues to write plays of great merit. (It may of course be that Broadway has abandoned him.) Two new Miller plays debuting in the early 1990s have gained considerable attention. *The Ride Down Mount Morgan*, which premiered in London (England) in 1991, is a play that covers almost everything Miller had written about earlier—and then some. Although its principal plot concerns hospitalization and bigamy, the play manages to bring in the warring generations, pleasure, guilt, marriage, money, children, race, sex, death, business, Jewishness, non-Jewishness, socialism, Christianity, suicide, political and sexual betrayal, men versus women, humans versus animals, the Reagan-Bush administration versus Arthur Miller, and, almost as an afterthought, capital-T Truth, delivered in an exquisitely Millerish agony. "Only the truth is sacred, Leah" Miller's protagonist declares to one of his wives at play's end. And Mr. Miller's *The Last Yankee,* which premiered at the (off-Broadway) Manhattan Theatre Club in 1993, mines many of these same themes in a play also set, in part, in a hospital waiting room, where two middle-aged couples serve as Miller's exemplars of life in America's competitive society. If neither play is quite vintage Miller, both evidence the passionate and clearsighted intensity of America's most consistently political writer since World War II.

Neil Simon (born 1927) It can be argued that Neil Simon is not only America's most successful commercial playwright, but also the most successful playwright in the history of theatre. Initially a TV comic writer in the early 1950s, Simon spun off a phenomenal series of "hit" Broadway comedies in the following decades, including consistently revived works like *Barefoot in the Park, The Odd Couple, Plaza Suite, The Last of the Red Hot Lovers, The Sunshine Boys,* and *California Suite,* plus the books for musicals such as *Little Me, Sweet Charity* and *Promises, Promises.* In addition, Simon has written the scripts for dozens of films, some based on the plays, some not. Virtually all of his plays "work," in the sense that they make

Neil Simon's award-winning Lost in Yonkers *(1990) is one of his most serious and moving plays. Here Irene Worth (seated) plays an embittered Holocaust survivor, and Mercedes Reuhl plays her slightly retarded daughter. (Photo: Martha Swope and Associates.)*

the audience laugh, and they have made Simon enormously rich; yet in the late 1980s, Simon turned more serious and philosophical, and his deeply felt trilogy of autobiographical plays, *Brighton Beach Memoirs, Biloxi Blues,* and *Broadway Bound* have proved astute and compassionate works that have attracted a more sober appreciation of Simon's gifts. In the 1990s, Simon has both returned to broad comedy (with a bald farce called *Rumors*) and deepened his realistic investigations of family life, with *Lost in Yonkers* (which won the 1991 Pulitzer Prize) and *Jake's Women,* which treats the women in his life, and in his mind, simultaneously. *Jake's Women* is Simon's first unconventionally structured play and has received a rocky reception, but it indicates the writer's unflagging energy and creativity. Simon is a consummate New York playwright, whose work is also popular in dinner and community theatres; his work is rarely performed in regional theatres, however, and it is almost a mark of pride for regional theatres to say "we don't do Neil Simon" as a short-hand way of saying that they don't produce conventional, or commercial, or well-made comedies. Simon probably has more fans and more detractors than any other living playwright, but his early comedies are unmatchable in their craftsmanship and easygoing humor, and his recent work shows evidence of a deep and lasting theatrical achievement.

Edward Albee (born 1928) *The Zoo Story,* a one-act, two-character play set in New York's Central Park, brought Edward Albee to prominence in 1959. The play concerns a chance meeting between a married publisher (Peter) and a young drifter (Jerry), both male; at play's end Jerry impales himself on a knife he has given to Peter. The odd story, its electrifying dialogue, its gingerly oblique treatment of homosexuality, and, particularly, its initial pairing on a double bill with Samuel Beckett's *Krapp's Last*

Tape gave Albee immediate national attention that would be almost impossible to achieve today. And with his first full-length play, *Who's Afraid of Virginia Woolf?,* premiering on Broadway shortly thereafter, Albee quickly assumed the mantle of America's leading new playwright in the early 1960s. Subsequent Albee plays have had both great success—*A Delicate Balance* (what happens when a married couple mysteriously gets frightened and moves in with their best friends) and *Seascape* (what happens when a pair of lizards pop in on a married couple at the beach) won the Pulitzer Prizes in 1967 and 1975—and failure (*Tiny Alice* provoked outrage along with mild admiration; *The Man With Three Arms* was scathingly attacked by New York critics); but Albee's new plays, *Three Tall Women* (1991) and *Marriage Play* (1992), have enjoyed excellent receptions in Vienna and Houston (the Alley Theatre) in recent years, and Albee will surely have an impact on the theatre for a long time to come.

Lanford Wilson (1937) A pioneer playwright in the heady days of New York experimental theatre in the 1960s, Lanford Wilson's first plays, many produced at the Café La Mama and Caffe Cino theatre bars, included evocative and sometimes profound studies of male homosexuality (*The Madness of Lady Bright*), interracial marriage (*The Gingham Dog*), and small-town small-mindedness (*The Rimers of Eldritch*). Joining with director Marshall Mason and other Caffe Cino colleagues, Wilson helped create the Circle Repertory Theatre in New York, which produced his celebrated *The Hot l Baltimore,* about the comings and goings of a down-and-out hotel (the missing "e" in the title indicates the hotel's neon sign with one letter burnt out) and a series of emotionally affecting plays about the fictional midwestern Talley family: *The Fifth of July, Talley's Folly* (which won the 1980 Pulitzer Prize), and *A Tale Told.* In recent years the

Circle Repertory has coproduced Wilson's newer plays with regional theatres in different parts of the country, developing *Burn This* (1987, with John Malkovich) at the Los Angeles Mark Taper Forum before taking it to New York and its subsequent Broadway success, and *Redwood Curtain,* which premiered at the Seattle Repertory Theatre before transferring to New York in 1993. Wilson is a prolific playwright, with more than thirty published plays. His writing for the most part (*Burn This* is an exception) is gentle, poetic, natural, and wise; although he is dramaturgically innovative, his plays do not call attention to their structures or to the author's subtle sytlistic departures. Wilson is one of America's most classical native playwrights.

John Guare (born 1938) Going from graduate school (Yale) also into the Café La Mama–Caffe Cino avant-garde circle in the early 1960s, Guare became widely known with a series of mildly surrealistic and "wacky" plays, such as *Muzeeka* in 1968 and *The House of Blue Leaves* in 1970, laced with social and cultural satire. Guare continued to mine the same vein, securing a small but loyal New York audience through the 1970s and 1980s; in the 1990s, however, he again burst onto the national scene with the masterful satire, *Six Degrees of Separation,* which explores, and acidly reveals, racial stereotyping, contemporary parenting and misparenting, and the cultural dissonances in contemporary adult America. *Six Degrees,* which opened at Lincoln Center in 1990, was widely produced by America's regional theatres shortly thereafter. Guare's subsequent *Four Baboons Adoring the Sun,* an even more ambitious allegory, proved more controversial but equally provocative in its 1992 Lincoln Center debut.

Sam Shepard (born 1943) Also coming to prominence in the Caffe Cino–Café La Mama experimental theatre of New York in the 1960s, Sam Shepard then received great acclaim in the 1970s and 1980s with his successful full length plays *The Tooth of Crime, The Curse of the Starving Class, Buried Child* (which won the Pulitzer Prize), *True West, Fool for Love,* and *A Lie of the Mind.* Shepard's plays are virtual prose poems; the language is highly musical, and the subject matter, which is generally contemporary and American, suggests modern myth more than everyday reality. His plays, which invariably involve some violence, create arresting (and often inexplicable) images and tantalize the audience with moments of extreme surface realism that ultimately opens into something more abstract. His early plays are quite wildly surreal and dreamlike, but these qualities have diminished in his somewhat more realistic plays of the late 1980s. During this period Shepard has become additionally well known for his acting performances in films such as *The Right Stuff* and his own *Fool for Love,* but he continues to write for the theatre and scored a significant success in New York with his *States of Shock* in 1991.

David Mamet (born 1947) Known as a Chicago playwright because Chicago is his birthplace, his home, the setting of most of his plays, and the city where his plays have most often been premiered, David Mamet served for some time as an associate artistic director of Chicago's Goodman Theatre. Mamet's plays, like some of Shepard's, employ at least fragments of intensely realistic writing and feature rhythmic language patterns that, though brutal, may seem almost musical. Indeed, Mamet's dialogue is often strung out of mere fragments of language: the tortured syntax of everyday speech, rather than the turned phrases of eloquent discourse. Mamet's characters' talk is a series of frustrated stammerings, grunts, curses, repetitions, trail-offs, and the hemmings and hawings of nervous conversation; in all, there might not be but one or two complete

Sam Shepard's plays are immensely popular abroad as well as in the United States. This production of his True West *was staged by the Finnish National Theatre in Helsinki; virtually every country in Western Europe has seen a Shepard production in the past decade. (Photo: Johnny Korkman.)*

sentences in an entire Mamet play. *Sexual Perversity in Chicago* brought him immediate attention in 1974, and *A Life in the Theatre, American Buffalo, Glengarry Glen Ross,* and *Speed-the-Plow* (starring Madonna on Broadway) have solidified his reputation in the ensuing years. In the 1990s, Mamet (like Shepard) has turned much of his attention to the cinema (with screenplays such as *Hoffa, The Untouchables,* and *House of Games*), but in 1992 he returned to the theatre with the scorching play, *Oleanna,* a masterful and intense play about a charge of sexual (and academic) harassment brought

by a college student (female) against her professor (male). David Mamet will clearly continue to play a major role in the coming era of American theatre.

Marsha Norman (born 1947) National attention focused on Marsha Norman at the new play festival of the Actors Theatre of Louisville (Kentucky) in 1978 with her first play, *Getting Out:* a driving, biting study of a woman's release from prison — and her even more powerful subsequent "imprisonment" by the forces of economics, male chauvinism, and sexual harassment. Norman's subsequent play, 'night, Mother, a brutally sad depiction of a young woman's suicide and the helplessness of her mother to stop it, earned Norman the Putlizer Prize for Drama in 1983. Norman's subsequent play, Traveller in the Dark, failed to gain critical approval, however, and her career faltered for some time, until she wrote the book for the musical version of A Secret Garden, a major Broadway success of 1991. Norman is a strong, committed writer on social and feminist issues, as well as the creator of vivid stage characters and powerful dramatic emotions.

Wendy Wasserstein (born 1950) After graduating from Mount Holyoke College (B.A.) and City College of New York (M.A.),

Wendy Wasserstein wrote her first important play, Uncommon Women and Others, while a graduate student at the Yale Drama School (1976); since then she has been highly admired for her successful off-Broadway play, Isn't It Romantic?, and then The Heidi Chronicles, which was created in workshop format at the Seattle Repertory Theatre before opening on Broadway and capturing both the Tony Award and Pulitzer Prize for 1989. Wasserstein is deeply concerned with the situation of the American woman, particularly women who struggle with what they see as the dialectics of marriage and career, romance and political struggle, fiery activism and traditionally passive "feminine" roles. Wasserstein's characters mostly come from the upper-middle-class Jewish

David Mamet's Glengarry Glen Ross, *as directed by Gregory Mosher at the Goodman Theatre (Chicago) in 1984. This scene is set in a Chinese restaurant in Chicago—it could be right outside the theatre. (Photo: Brigitte Lacombe.)*

Marsha Norman's 'night, Mother *is one of the most searing, most touching depictions of the relations between a mother and a daughter ever written. The play is here shown in its 1986 production at the Alliance Theatre of Atlanta, Georgia.*

intelligentsia that the author springs from herself ("Heidi" is an academic and mildly feminist art historian), but her writing is universal and broadly probing. There are no easy answers in Wasserstein's work, but there is a deep level of investigation and a powerful dramatic momentum. Wasserstein's new play, *The Sisters Rosensweig*, explores some of her usual themes, and was, like *Heidi*, developed in a Seattle Repertory workshop in 1992, and opened on Broadway in 1993.

Beth Henley (born 1952) *Crimes of the Heart*, Beth Henley's first play, was awarded the Pulitzer Prize for Drama in 1981. Initially produced at the Actors Theatre of

Louisville new play festival before going to Broadway, *Crimes* is a wildly irreverent comedy about three young Mississippi sisters coming together at the joint crises of their individual lives; the play, while not directly feminist in its themes, was one of the first major mainstream American plays to focus primarily on women's problems and women's issues. Henley's more recent work has stayed true to this focus: *The Miss Firecracker Contest*, an off-Broadway success in 1984, is another Mississippi family drama in which two cousins vie for top prize in a beauty contest; and *Abundance*, which premiered at South Coast Repertory Theatre in California before moving to off-Broadway, is the story of two mail order brides in chauvinist nineteenth-century Wyoming. "Henley has an unmistakable talent for making human desperation seem funny, complex and unpredictable," said reviewer Robert Massa in the *Village Voice* of this work.

George C. Wolfe (born 1954)   Widespread attention came to George C. Wolfe with his satirical musical play, *The Colored Museum*, in 1986, and *Spunk*, a musical and dramatic adaptation of tales by Zora Neale Hurston, in 1989; both were initially produced at the Crossroads Theatre of New Brunswick, New Jersey, and subsequently at the Public Theatre in New York, where Wolfe became artistic director in 1993. Wolfe, a Kentucky-born African American, uses humor and music as wedges to explore deeply painful subjects; as a result, his plays are hilarious and unsettling—even scathing—at the same time. "Once we reach the desired altitude, the Captain will turn off the 'Fasten Your Shackle' sign," says the stewardess of the "Celebrity Slaveship" at the beginning of *The Colored Museum*. Wolfe's genius (he is also the director of his plays) is to skewer hoary clichés and persistent stereotypes of the "colored" world that emanate from both white and African-American subgroups—and at the same time to embed his societal critique of racism in a theatricality that is enthusiastic, accessible, and celebratory. With his *Jelly's Last Jam* in 1992, a Broadway musical about the African American jazz musician Jelly Roll Morton, Wolfe went mainstream—winning Tony nominations for both writing and directing and also winning a worldwide audience of admirers.

David Henry Hwang (born 1957)   Growing up in San Gabriel, California, Hwang began writing—"on a lark" he says—while a Stanford undergraduate; his first play, *FOB* ("Fresh Off the Boat") is a biting, honest, angry reaction to hidden (and not-so-hidden) American racism; it was first produced by the Stanford Asian-American Theatre Project. Subsequently, it was accepted and produced at the O'Neill Center in Connecticut and then at the New York Public Theatre in 1980, where it (and its leading actor) both won "Obie" (Off-Broadway) awards. Hwang's subsequent *M. Butterfly* (1988), his most celebrated work, explores the bizarre relationship between a French diplomat and his Chinese mistress: bizarre because the mistress is revealed, during the play, to be—unbeknownst to the diplomat—a man in disguise. Here, Hwang's subject is "Orientalism," or the ingrained sense of deprecation with which Western culture views the Asian East. Hwang, of Chinese heritage, brilliantly interweaves gritty Western realism with Asian theatre and Chinese Opera technique in these two works, lending them both current/political and timeless/mythic proportions; in *M. Butterfly* he inserts portions of the Puccini opera that gives the play its name, creating a wonderfully theatrical East-West confabulation. *M. Butterfly* won Hwang the Tony Award and international fame. His subsequent *1000 Airplanes on the Roof*, a "science-fiction music-drama" written in collaboration with composer Philip Glass and designer Jerome Sirlin, is a boldly imaginative fantasy monologue, with music and projections, that toured the world following its 1988 premiere in a Vienna airplane hangar. This work is not particularly concerned with East-West themes; Hwang clearly does not intend to be bound to ethnic subject matter in his future work.

CONCLUSIONS ON THE CURRENT THEATRE?

Can there be any conclusions concerning the current theatre? No, there cannot—simply because what is current is never concluded. The current theatre is in process; it is like a book we are just beginning. The plays and playwrights discussed in this chapter may not, in the end, be accorded very significant positions in our era of theatre; even the movements they now seem to represent may prove distinctly minor and transitory. We are not in a position even to hazard guesses at this point: we can only indicate certain directions in which to look for clues as to where the future will lead us.

Meanwhile the evidence, it should be clear, plays nightly on the stages of the theatre world. It is there to apprehend, there to enjoy, there to appreciate, and there, finally, to be refined by opinion and encapsulated into critical theory and aesthetic categorization—if that is our wish.

More than being a play, or a series of plays, or a spectrum of performances, the current theatre is a worldwide event, a *communication* between people and peoples that raises the level of human discourse and artistic appreciation wherever it takes place. The current theatre responds to the impulses of creativity and expression and to the demands of human contact and understanding. It synthesizes the impulses of authors and artists, actors and audiences, to foster a medium of focused interaction that incorporates the human experience and embodies each culture's aspirations and values. No final chapter can be written on this medium, no last analysis or concluding categorization. All that is certain is that the art, and the feeling, of theatrical life will endure.

It is eleven o'clock; the lights fade a final time, the curtain falls, the audience applauds, and the play is over. The actors go back to their dressing rooms, take off their make-up, and depart. The audience disperses into the night.

But the theatrical experience is not over; in important ways, it is just beginning.

A play does not begin and end its life on a stage. A play begins in the mind of its creator, and its final repository is in the minds and memories of its audiences. The stage is simply a focal point where the transmission takes place — in the form of communication we know as theatrical performance.

After the performance is over, the play's impact remains. It is something to think about, talk about, fantasize about, and live with for hours, days, and years to come. Some plays we remember all our lives: plays whose characters are as indelible in our memories as the real beings who populate our personal world, plays whose settings are more deeply experienced than are most of the locales of our growing up, and plays whose themes abide as major object lessons behind our decision making. Should we take up arms against a sea of troubles? Can we depend on the kindness of strangers? What's in a name? Shall we be as defiant as Prometheus, as deter-

CHAPTER **9**

THE CRITIC

The Humana New Play Festival at the Actors Theatre of Louisville generates a national gathering of
critics, who have a chance to review several important
new American plays from around the country in a
single long weekend. Shown here, Marisol, by José
Rivera, which was featured at the 1992 Humana
festival; critical response was so favorable that Rivera's
play was accepted for production by several other theatres around the country in 1993–94. (Photo:
Richard C. Trigg).

David Rabe's The Basic Training of Pavlo Hummel
was one of the first indictments of the Vietnam War
to appear in the American theatre. New York Shakespeare Festival, 1972. (Photo: George Joseph.)

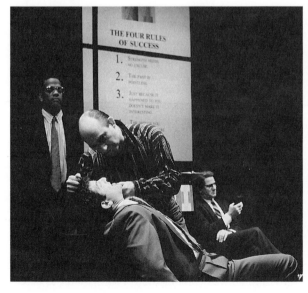

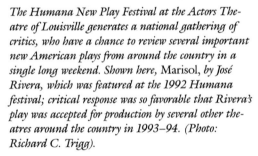

Howard Korder's Search and Destroy probes deeply
into the success orientation of American business, ex-
ploiting the duplicity and hypocrisy Korder finds on
our ethical fringe. Or is it at our core? This explosive
South Coast Repertory Theatre premiere led to a New
York production in 1991. (Photo: Christopher Gross.)

mined as Oedipus, as passionate as Romeo, as accepting as Winnie, as noble as Hecuba? What is Hecuba to us, or we to Hecuba? We talk about these matters with our friends.

And we also talk about the production, about the acting, the costumes, the scenery, the sound effects. Were we convinced? impressed? moved? transported? changed? Did the production hold our attention throughout? Did our involvement with the action increase during the play, or did we feel a letdown after the intermission? Did we accept the actors as the characters they were playing, or were we uncomfortably aware that they were simply "acting" their parts rather than embodying their roles?

The formalization of postplay thinking and conversation is known as dramatic criticism. When it is formalized into writing it can take many forms: production reviews in newspapers or periodicals, essays about plays or play productions written as academic assignments, commentaries in theatre programs or theatre journals, magazine feature articles on theatre artists, or scholarly articles or books on dramatic literature, history, or theory. All of these and more are in the realm of dramatic criticism, which is nothing other than an informed, articulate, and communicative response to what the critic has seen in the theatre or read in the theatre's vast literature.

CRITICAL PERSPECTIVES

What makes a play particularly successful? What gives a theatrical production significance and impact, and what makes it unforgettable? What should we be looking for when we read a play or see a dramatic production? We have, of course, complete freedom in making up our minds; for response, by definition, can never be dictated: the price of theatrical admission carries with it the privilege of thinking what we wish and responding as we will. But five perspectives can be partic-

---

IS IT ART . . . OR TRASH?

The theatre critic spends most of his time with trash. But the trash is as much a part of his subject as the non-trash. . . . Part of his function is to make sure that false messiahs and peddlers and charlatans are shown as such. Hope—non-delusionary, non-inflationary, non-self-aggrandizing hope—is the core of the critic's being: hope that good work will recurrently arrive, hope that (partly by identifying trash) he may help it to arrive, hope that he may have the excitement and privilege of helping to connect that good work with its audience.

Stanley Kauffman

---

ularly useful in helping us focus our response to any individual theatrical event. These perspectives relate to a play's social significance, its human or personal significance, its artistic quality, its theatrical expression, and its capacity to entertain.

A Play's Relation to Society

Theatre, as we have seen in the preceding pages, is always tied to its culture. Many theatres have been directly created or sustained by governments and ruling elites: the Greek theatre of the fifth century B.C. was a creation of the state; the medieval theatre was generated by the Church, the township, and the municipal craft guilds; and the Royal theatre was a direct extension of a monarchical reign. Even in modern times, government often serves as sponsor or cosponsor or silent benefactor of the theatre. But the intellectual ties between a theatre and its culture extend well beyond merely political concerns: thematically, the theatre has at one time or another served as an arena for the discussion of vir-

Theatre reflects and comments on our society, and good theatre does so without preaching or moralizing. The audience will draw its own conclusions, but the critical voice can help the audience do this; and it can also draw the attention of new audiences — of both readers and theatregoers — to the issues. AT LEFT — Luis Valdez's Zoot Suit, *a musical drama dealing with the cultural clashes in Los Angeles during the 1940s, drew serious public attention to continuing social problems in the 1970s in its 1978 Mark Taper Forum premiere. James Olmos plays "El Pachucho" against the newspaper headline. (Photo: Courtesy Mark Taper Forum.)* ABOVE — Athol Fugard's My Children! My Africa! *was a shattering study of South African* apartheid *that was heralded in its La Jolla Playhouse production in 1991. Sterling Macer Jr., Brock Peters, and Nancy Travis are the actors; Fugard directed. (Photo: Micha Langer.)*

tually every social issue imaginable. In modern times, for example, we have seen such issues as alcoholism, homosexuality, venereal disease, prostitution, public education, racial prejudice, capital punishment, thought control, prison reform, character assassination, civil equality, political corruption, and military excess examined repeatedly in theatrical productions, and from different points of view. The best of these productions have presented the issues in all their complexity and have proffered solutions not as dogma but as food for thought—for great theatre has never sought to purvey pure propaganda. The playwright is not necessarily brighter than the audience, nor even better informed: he and his fellows, however, may be able to focus public debate, stimulate dialogue, and turn public attention and compassion toward social injustices, inconsistencies, and irregularities. The theatre artist traditionally is something of a nonconformist; his point of view is generally to the left or right of the social mainstream, and his perspective is of necessity somewhat unusual. Therefore, the theatre is in a strong position to force and focus public confrontation with social issues, and at its best it succeeds in bringing the audience into touch with their own thoughts and feelings about those issues.

A Play's Relation to the Individual

The theatre is a highly personal art, in part because it stems from the unique (and often oblique) perspectives of the playwrights who initiate it and the theatre artists who execute it, and in part because its audiences all through history have decreed that it be so.

The greatest plays transcend the social and political to confront the hopes, concerns, and conflicts faced by all humankind: personal identity, courage, compassion, fantasy versus practicality, kindness versus self-serving, love versus exploitation, and the inescapable problems of growing up and growing old, of wasting and dying. These are some of the basic themes of the finest of plays and of our own stray thoughts as well: the best plays simply link up with our deepest musings and help us to put our random ideas into some sort of order or philosophy. The theatre is a medium in which we of the audience invariably see reflections of ourselves, and in the theatre's best achievements those reflections lead to certain discoveries and evaluations concerning our own individual personalities and perplexities.

A Play's Relation to Art

The theatre is an art of such distinctive form that even with the briefest exposure we can begin to develop certain aesthetic notions as to what that form should be. We quickly come to know—or think we know—honesty on stage, for without being experts we feel we can recognize false notes in acting, in playwriting, and even in design.

Beyond that, we can ask a number of questions of ourselves. Does the play excite our emotions? Does it stimulate the intellect? Does it surprise us? Does it thrill us? Does it seem complete and all of a piece? Are the characters credible? Are the actors convincing? enchanting? electrifying? Does the play seem alive or dead? Does it seem in any way original? Is it logically sound? Is the action purposeful, or is it gratuitous? Are we transported, or are we simply waiting for the final curtain? In the last analysis, does the play fit our idea of what a play should be—or, even better, does it force us, by its sheer luster and power, to rewrite our standards of theatre?

Aesthetic judgments of this sort are necessarily comparative, and they are subjective as well. What seems original to one member of the audience may be old hat to another; what seems an obvious gimmick to a veteran theatregoer can seem brilliantly innovative to a less jaded appetite. None of this should intimidate us. An audience does not bring absolute standards into the theatre—and certainly such standards as it brings are not shared absolutely. The theatrical response is a composite of many individual reactions. But each of us has an aesthetic sensibility and an aesthetic response. We appreciate colors, sights, sounds, words, actions, behaviors, and people that please us. We appreciate constructions that seem to us balanced, harmonic, expressive, and assured. We appreciate designs, ideas, and performances that exceed our expectations, that reveal patterns and viewpoints we didn't know existed. We take great pleasure in sensing underlying *structure:* a symphony of ideas, a sturdy architecture of integrated style and action.

A Play's Relation to Theatre

As we've already discussed, plays are not simply things that happen "in" the theatre, but they "are" theatre—which is to say that each play or play production redefines the theatre itself and makes us reconsider, at least to a certain extent, the value and possibilities of the theatre itself.

In some cases the playwright makes this reconsideration mandatory, by dealing with theatrical matters in the play itself. Some plays are set in theatres where plays are going on (Luigi Pirandello's *Six Characters in Search of an Author,* Michael Frayn's *Noises Off,* Richard Nelson's *Two Shakespearean Actors*); other plays are about actors (Jean Paul Sartre's *Kean*) or about dramatic characters (Tom Stoppard's *Rosencrantz and Guildenstern Are Dead*); still other plays contain plays within themselves (Anton Chekhov's *The Seagull,* William Shakespeare's *Hamlet*) or the rehearsals of such plays (Shakespeare's *A Midsummer Night's Dream,* Molière's *The Versailles Rehearsals,* Jean Anouilh's *The Rehearsal*). We use the term *metatheatre* or *metadrama* to describe those plays that specifically refer back to themselves in this manner, but in fact all plays and play productions can be analyzed and evaluated on the way they use the theatrical format

to best advantage and the way they make us rethink the nature of theatrical production.

For all plays stand within the spectrum of a history of theatre, and a history of theatrical convention (see Chapter 2). All plays and productions can be studied, often with illuminating results, from the perspective of how they adopt or reject prevailing theatrical conventions, how they fit into or deviate from prevailing dramatic genres, and how they echo various elements of past plays or productions—and what may be the theatrical effects, good and bad, of such historical resonances.

A Play as Entertainment

Finally, we look upon all theatre as entertainment.

Great theatre is never less than pleasing. Even tragedy delights. People go to see *Hamlet* not for purpose of self-flagellation or to wallow in despair, but to revel in the tragic form and to experience the liberating catharsis of the play's murderous finale. Hamlet himself knows the thrill of staged tragedy:

HAMLET: What players are they?
ROSENCRANTZ: Even those you were wont to take such delight in, the tragedians . . .

What is this entertainment value that all plays possess? Most obviously the word "entertainment" suggests "amusement," and so we think immediately of the hilarity of comedy and farce; indeed, most of the literature regarding theatrical entertainment concentrates on the pratfalls and gags that have been part of the comic theatre throughout its history. But entertainment goes far beyond humor. Another definition for "entertainment" is "that which holds the attention." This definition casts quite a bit more light on our question. It means that entertainment includes the enchantment of romance, which stimulates our curiosity about our own emotions and longings. It takes in the dazzle of brilliant debate, witty epigram, and biting repartee; the exotic appeal of the foreign and the grotesque; the beauty and grandeur of spectacle; the nuance and crescendo of a musical or rhythmic line. It accommodates suspense and adventure, the magic of sex appeal and the splendor of sheer talent. Finally, of course, it includes any form of drama that profoundly stirs our feelings and heightens our awareness of the human condition. It is no wonder that Hamlet delights in the performance of tragedians — and that we delight in *Hamlet* — for the concatenation of ideas, language, poetry, feelings, and actions that constitute great tragedy confers one of life's truly sublime entertainment experiences.

Indeed, the theatre is a veritable storehouse of pleasures, not only for the emotional, intellectual, spiritual, and aesthetic stimulation it provides, but also for its intrinsic social excitement. It is a favored public meeting place for people who care about each other — "two on the aisle" implies more than a choice seating location: it implies companionship in the best theatrical experience. For the theatre is a place to commune in an especially satisfying way with strangers. When in the course of a dramatic performance we are gripped by a staging of romantic passion, or stunned by a brilliantly articulated argument, or moved by an inexpressibly touching denouement, the thrill is enhanced a hundredfold by the certainty that we are not alone in these feelings, that possibly every member of the audience has been stirred to the same response. Theatre, in its essence, serves to rescue humankind from an intellectual and emotional aloneness; and therein lies its most profound "entertainment" value.

CRITICAL FOCUS

These five perspectives on the theatre experience — on its social, personal, artistic, theatrical, and entertainment values — are all implicit in the responses of any audience, regardless of its training or theatrical sophistication. These are the five angles from which we view and judge plays — and judge them we do, for our involvement with a play naturally generates a series of comparisons: the play vis-à-vis other plays, the play vis-à-vis our personal experiences, the play vis-à-vis other things we might have done that evening. Judging plays and performances, which has been done formally since ancient Greek times and continues today through the well-publicized Tony and Obie Awards, Pulitzer Prizes, and Critics Circle citations, is one of the fundamental aspects of theatrical participation — and yet it is a participation open to amateur and professional alike.

Professional Criticism

Professional criticism takes the basic form of production reviews and scholarly books and articles written, for the most part, by persons who specialize in this activity, often for an entire career.

Newspaper reviews of play productions are common throughout the theatre world; in-

---

A CRITIC'S TASTES

Somebody recently wrote one of my editors to the effect that I had no sense whatever of the tastes of my readers or the public at large. He was, unintentionally, paying me a great tribute which I can only hope I deserve. For it is extremely hard not to be influenced by the tastes of one's milieu; yet resisting them is precisely the critic's duty. It is only in being uncompromisingly himself that a critic performs a true service, and as a man of taste (not infallible taste, for there can be no such thing), goes down in history, or as a man of no taste, goes down the drain.

John Simon

CRITICAL PERVERSITY

The critical voice in its ever-changing moods sometimes effects reversals that seem exceptionally perverse. In an article entitled "The Curious Case of *Time* and Tennessee Williams," *Esquire* magazine demonstrated the way in which *Time* continued to accord the celebrated playwright negative notices right up to the moment it chose to call him America's greatest living dramatic author.

> The play [*A Streetcar Named Desire*] could stand more discipline; along with an absence of formulas there is sometimes an absence of form. And it could stand more variety: only the clash between Blanche and Stanley. . . gets real emotion and drama into the play.
> —December 15, 1947

> *Summer and Smoke* . . . is all too plainly— but not too happily—by the author of *The Glass Menagerie* and *A Streetcar Named Desire*. What stamps, and sometimes rubberstamps, it as his is the nature of the story and the style of the storytelling; far too often missing is the talent of the storyteller.
> —October 18, 1948

> [In] *The Rose Tattoo* . . . Williams has never seemed so blatantly himself. . . . often the play. . . is lush, garish, operatic, decadently primitive, a salt breeze in a swamp, a Banana Truck Named Desire.
> —February 12, 1951

> *Camino Real* is perhaps excessively pessimistic in reaction against Williams' previous *Rose Tattoo,* with its factitious "affirmation." But very excessive it is—and not only excessively black, but excessively purple. *Camino Real* lacks philosophic or dramatic progression (on that score, it might claim the dead-endness of a wasteland), but it also lacks all discipline and measure, so that the wasteland becomes a swamp. What makes the play ultimately unacceptable is not that it is often dull and even more often arty, but that it exposes decadence with decadent means.
> —March 30, 1953

> [T]he play [*Cat on a Hot Tin Roof*], closing on a lame, stagy note, lacks stature. Perhaps there is a little too much of everything: Williams is not only lavish of suffering, but voluble in articulating it. There might well be less emotionalism and should certainly be fewer words, particularly profane ones: the profanity often seems to relieve Williams' own feelings rather than his characters'. But more important, *Cat* never quite defines itself as chiefly a play about a marriage, about a family, or about a man. . . . it needs sharper form, greater unity, a sense of something far more deeply interfused.
> —April 4, 1955

> Unhappily, Williams' story [*Garden District*] dies with his telling it, for though he weaves a spell he cannot validate a vision. It matters less that noisomely misanthropic symbols keep recurring in his work than that they nowhere seem purgative.
> —January 20, 1958

deed, the box-office success of most theatres depends on receiving favorable press coverage. In the commercial Broadway theatre, favorable reviews—particularly from the influential *New York Times*—are all but absolutely necessary in order to guarantee a successful run. Where theatre audiences are generated by subscriptions and where institutional financing secures the production funds, newspaper reviews play a less crucial short-term role, but

they still bear weightily in a theatre's ultimate success or failure.

In New York, newspaper reviews have traditionally been written immediately following the opening-night performance and are published the following morning; actors and producers gather after opening night at Sardi's restaurant, in the Broadway theatre district, awaiting the first edition of the next morning's *Times* to see how their show fared with the

In *Period of Adjustment,* which opened last week at Miami's Coconut Grove Playhouse, Playwright Tennessee Williams repaired no cracking masonry in his familiar dramatic neighborhood, but at least he slapped on a coat of whitewash. Billed as a "Serious Comedy," *Period* sounds more like a mad Gothic anecdote.

—January 12, 1959

Sweet Bird of Youth . . . is very close to parody, but the wonder is that Williams should be so inept at imitating himself. The sex violence, the perfumed decay, the hacking domestic quarrels, the dirge of fear and self-pity, the characters who dangle in neurotic limbo—all are present—but only like so many dramatic dead cats on a cold tin roof.

—March 23, 1959

Many serious, liberal-minded intellectuals worry profoundly about the unattractive impression the U.S. often makes abroad, blaming everyone from unimaginative ambassadors to loud tourists with star-spangled sport shirts. But few would ever admit that some of their own heroes—for example, Playwright Tennessee Williams—can be the worst ambassadors of all. Last week two Williams plays, presented by a free-lance theatrical troupe called the New York Repertory Company (which claimed association with Manhattan's Actors Studio) had left a fairly indelible stain in Rio de Janeiro.

—September 1, 1961

Summer and Smoke. . . . Playwright Tennessee Williams often writes like an arrested adolescent who disarmingly imagines that he will attain stature if (as short boys are advised in Dixie) he loads enough manure in his shoes. In his most famous plays, he has hallucinated a vast but specious pageant of depravity in which fantasies of incest, cannibalism, murder, rape, sodomy and drug addiction constitute the canon of reality. . . . Nevertheless, the film conspicuously possesses Playwright Williams' characteristic virtue: a pathethic-romantic atmosphere that lingers from scene to scene like an ineffable sachet of self-pity.

—December 1, 1961

The fact is that Tennessee Williams . . . is a consummate master of theatre. His plays beat with the heart's blood of the drama: passion. He is the greatest U.S. playwright since Eugene O'Neill, and, barring the aged Sean O'Casey, the greatest living playwright anywhere. . . .Williams has peopled the U.S. stage with characters whose vibrantly durable presences stalk the corridors of a playgoer's memory: . . . Williams' dialogue sings with a lilting eloquence far from the drab, disjunctive patterns of everyday talk. And for monologues, the theatre has not seen his like since the god of playwrights, William Shakespeare.

—March 9, 1962

current critic. This is "instant criticism," and the journalist who tackles these assignments has to be very fluid at articulating his or her immediate impressions. Outside of New York, newspaper critics frequently take two or three days to review a production, allowing themselves the luxury of somewhat considered opinions and more polished essays. Some New York newspaper critics have recently begun to emulate this practice; while their reviews are still published the day after opening night, they have actually attended a preview performance two or three days earlier and have had the opportunity to write their review at some leisure.

Still, the journalist's review must be limited to a brief, immediate, reaction rather than to a detailed or exhaustive study. It provides a firsthand, audience-oriented response to the production, often vigorously and wittily expressed, and may serve as a useful consumer guide for the local theatregoing public. Writing skill rather than dramatic expertise is often the newspaper critic's principal job qualification, and at many smaller papers, staff reporters with little dramatic background are assigned to the theatre desk. But many fine newspaper critics throughout the years — New York's Walter Kerr and Boston's Elliot Norton, for example — have proven extremely subtle and skillful at transcending the limitations of their particular profession and have written highly intelligent dramatic criticism that remains pertinent long after its consumer-oriented function has run its course.

More scholarly critics, writing without the deadlines or strict column-inch (space) restrictions of journalists, are able to analyze plays and productions within detailed, comprehensive, and rigorously researched critical contexts. They are therefore able to understand and evaluate, in a more complex way, the achievements of playwrights and theatre artists, within any or all of the five perspectives we have discussed. Scholarly critics (and by *scholarly* we mean only "one who studies") seek to uncover hidden aspects of a play's structure, to analyze its deep relationships to social or philosophical issues, to probe its various meanings and dramatic possibilities, to define its place in cultural history, to amplify its resonance of earlier works of art, to shape its future theatrical presentations, and to theorize about larger issues of dramaturgy, art, and human understanding. Such criticism is itself a literary art, and the great examples of dramatic criticism have included brilliantly styled essays which have outlasted the theatrical works that were their presumed subjects: Aristotle, Goethe, Shaw, and Neitzsche are among the drama critics who, simply through their analyses of drama, have helped shape our vision of life itself.

The scholarly critic is ordinarily distinguished by his or her broad intellectual background and exhaustive research, and writes with a comprehensive knowledge of the specific subject — a knowledge that includes the work of all important previous scholars who have studied the same materials. The professional scholar is not content to repeat the opinions or discoveries of others, but seeks to make fresh insights from the body of literature (playtexts and productions, production records, previous scholarship) that constitutes the field of study. Scholarly critics tend to work within accepted methodologies, which develop and change rapidly in contemporary academic life. Traditional methodologies include historical and biographical approaches ("the man and his work"), thematic and rhetorical analyses, studies of character and plot, examinations of staging and theatrical styles, and detailed exegeses of meaning or *explication de texte*. More contemporary methodologies include systems and theories developed since the 1970s, particularly structuralist, semiotic, and deconstructive approaches; these bypass traditional questions of history, biography, character, theme, and meaning and focus instead on the internal relationships of various dramatic ingredients and their particular combination in a self-referential dramaturgic system. Contemporary methodologies, which draw heavily from the fields of philosophy, linguistics, anthropology, and critical theory, are intellectually demanding and difficult to master; they provide, however, stunning insights to those properly initiated.

Student Criticism

One does not expect of the beginning theatre student a thoroughly comprehensive background in the subject; indeed, a student writing a class paper is likely to be looking seriously at the subject for the first time in his or her life. Naturally, different standards apply.

Such beginning students will characteristically analyze plays from any of the five perspectives cited earlier, but without the need for a tremendously sophisticated or advanced methodology. Some simple but effective methodologies, for writing both class essays and production reviews for local or school newspapers, are provided in the appendix to this book.

WE ARE THE CRITICS

Whether we are professional writers, students, or just plain theatregoers, we are all the critics of the theatre. We the audience are a party to the theatrical experience, not a mere passive receptacle for its contrived effects. The theatre is a forum of *communication,* and communication demands *mutual* and *active* participation.

To be an *observant* critic, one need only go to the theatre with an open mind and sharply tuned senses. Unfettered thinking should be a part of every theatrical experience, and provocative discussion should be its aftermath.

To be an *informed* critic, one needs sufficient background to provide a context for opinion and evaluation. A play may be moving, but is it as moving as *The Three Sisters?* as passionate as *The Trojan Women?* as romantic as *Romeo and Juliet?* as funny as *The Bourgeois Gentleman?* as intriguing as *Happy Days?* An actor's voice may be thrillingly resonant, but how does it compare with the voice of Laurence Olivier? If our opinions are to have weight and distinction, they may do so only against a background of knowledge and experience. If we are going to place a performance on a scale of one to ten, our friends (or readers) must know just what is our "one" and what is our "ten."

To be a *sensitive* critic, one must be receptive to life and to artistic experience. The most sensitive criticism comes from a compassionate approach to life, to humankind, and to artistic expression; this approach elicits and provokes a *personalized* response to dramatic works. Sensitive criticism admits the critic's *needs:* it begins from the view that life is difficult and problematical and that relationships are demanding. The sensitive critic is quest-

ing, not smug; humane, not self-absorbed; eternally eager for personal discovery and the opportunity to share it. He recognizes that we are all groping in the dark, hoping to encounter helping hands along the way in the adventure of life — that this indeed is the hope of theatre artists too.

To be a *demanding* critic is to hold the theatre to the highest standards of which it is capable. For, paradoxically, in the theatre's capacity to entertain, to supply immediate gratification, lies the seed of its own destruction. As we have seen so often in the preceding pages, the theatre wants to be liked. It has tried from its very beginning to assimilate what is likeable in the other arts. Almost scavengerlike, it has appropriated for itself in every era the most popular music and dance forms, the most trendy arguments, vocabularies, philosophies, and fashions in dress. In the process, alas, it often panders to tastelessness and propagates the meanest and most shallow values of its time. And here the drama critic in each of us can play a crucial role. The very need of the theatre to please its patrons tends to beget a crass insecurity: a tendency to resort to simple sensationalism in exchange for immediate approval. Cogent, fair-minded, penetrating criticism keeps the theatre mindful of its own artistic ideals and its essential responsibility to communicate. It prevents the theatre from either selling out completely to the current whim or bolting the other way into a hopelessly abstract and arcane self-absorption.

To be an *articulate* critic is to express one's thoughts with precision, clarity, and grace. "I loved it" or "I hated it" is not criticism, but rather a crude expression of opinion and a wholly general opinion at that. Articulation means the careful building of ideas, through a presentation of evidence, logical argument, the use of helpful analogy and example, and a style of expression neither pedantically turgid nor idiosyncratically anarchic. Good criticism should be a pleasure to write, a pleasure to read; it should make us want to go deeper into the mysteries of the theatre and not suffocate us with the prejudices or egotistical displays of the critic.

In sum, the presence of a critical focus in the audience — observant, informed, sensitive, demanding, and articulate — keeps the theatre honest. It *inspires* the theatre to reach its highest goals. It ascribes *importance* to the theatrical act. It telegraphs the expectations of the audience to producer, playwright, director, and actor alike, saying "We are out here, we are watching, we are listening, we are hoping, we *care*: we want your best — and then we want you to be better yet." The theatre needs such demands from its audience. The theatre and its audience need to be worthy coparticipants in a collective experience that enlarges life as well as art.

If we are to be critics of the theatre, then, we must be knowledgeable, fair, and open-minded; receptive to stimulation and excitement; open to wisdom and love. We must also admit that we have human needs.

In exchange, the theatre must enable us to see ourselves in the characters of the drama and in the performers of the theatre. We must see our situations in the situations of plays, and our hopes and possibilities in the behavior staged before us. We must be drawn to understand the theatre from the *inside* and to participate in thought and emotion in a play's performance.

Thus do we become critics, audience, and participants in one. The theatre is then no longer simply a remote subject encountered in a book, or in a class, or in the entertainment columns of the world press; the theatre is part of us.

It is *our* theatre.

If you study theatre in an academic setting, sooner or later, you will probably be required to write a critical paper on a play (or plays) that you read or see. "Critical" is used here not in the everyday sense of "finding fault with," but in the scholarly sense of "examining closely."

Writing such a paper is, of course, a test of your perception, but it is also much more than that: it is an opportunity for you to organize and focus your thoughts, to investigate drama with a specific purpose, and to communicate your considered opinion to someone else. The act of writing is an act of clarification, for the author as well as for the reader. You will usually learn much more by writing a paper than by reading one.

You will also *remember* the subject of your paper long after the course is over. This is because the acts of researching a topic, and of organizing, clarifying, and writing up your ideas will make the subject an important part of your own life; and although you will ultimately "give" the paper to the instructor, the ideas in it will remain yours: they will represent your contribution to the literature of drama.

Your instructor will give you a specific assignment for your paper, often including its proper length and an acceptable range of top-

APPENDIX

WRITING ON THEATRE

295

ics. The instructor will also usually guide you on appropriate procedures, some of which may differ quite markedly from the suggestions that follow. Absent instructions to the contrary, however, the advice given here may serve as a general guide to the writing of an undergraduate paper.

YOUR PURPOSE

Your purpose in writing a paper is to demonstrate something to someone: to present a clear point of view about your topic that leads to some conclusions about it.

"Demonstration" involves more than merely citing facts or opinions: it requires the arrangement of these facts and opinions in a careful and persuasive way.

"Conclusions" are what the paper is finally all about; your paper should end by persuading its readers that your point of view is, if not the definitive truth, at least worthy of further consideration. A coherent set of conclusions is usually called your paper's "thesis" (which is not to be confused with a formal paper required for certain graduate degrees such as a master's thesis).

"Clear" is simply the quality of good writing, plus good rewriting. A clear paper requires a good structure and an uncluttered use of language. A good paper is clear; a fine paper is both clear and convincing; an excellent paper is clear, convincing, and original.

YOUR AUDIENCE

The actual readership of your paper is usually limited to your instructor (and perhaps a reader or teaching assistant); but you should remember that the assigned paper is an exercise, and, as with an acting exercise, you should write the paper "as if" the readership were a more general one, including your fellow theatre students, theatre students and teachers at other institutions, theatre artists,

and theatre enthusiasts in and out of the academic world.

Your assumption of a general audience will prevent your paper from becoming merely a letter to the instructor. At the same time, the assumption that your audience already possesses a basic theatre background means that you can use theatrical terms and cite major dramatists without detailed preamble. Your readers already know what a proscenium is and who Anton Chekhov is; you don't have to define the former or identify the latter unless it serves your purpose to do so. You can also assume that your readership is interested in the basic subject: you do not have to "sell them" on the notion that drama is a worthwhile artistic form.

YOUR WORKING METHOD

Generally, the writing of a paper consists of six steps: choosing a topic, conducting research, developing a thesis, organizing the argument, writing the draft, and revising the draft. In practice, these steps do not always proceed neatly or in this order: the topic is often chosen during the research phase, and the thesis is developed (and refined) continually throughout the process.

Choosing a Topic

Often, this is the most single difficult part of writing a paper; certainly it is the one most subject to procrastination and deferral. You have read or seen a play, but what then? What is there to say about it?

What you might not realize is that your reading or viewing of a play, even when shared with a class or an audience, is a unique experience. What you receive from a play is a combination of two things—the play and you—and the uniqueness of either your reading or viewing comes from your contribution to the experience: your social background, your personal preoccupations, your particular hopes and fears, your unique perspective on human behavior. Your individuality gives you a view of the play that no one else has: if you can develop that view in an intelligent manner, you already have begun the search for a topic without knowing it.

It might be best, in hunting for a topic, to discuss a play that interests you with fellow students. How do they see the play differently from you? What do you see (or focus on) that they don't? What important aspect of the play have they missed? What has the instructor missed? What has the director of the play, or the editor of the play anthology, missed?

There are six general topic approaches that you should consider as well; most good papers fall into one of these:

1. The contextual analysis. This sort of paper analyzes one or more plays according to their historical, social, and/or philosophical context: for example, *Hamlet* as a Renaissance tragedy; *Happy Days* as a masterpiece of the twentieth-century avant-garde. Such essays are often seen as the introductory matter in play anthologies or as director's or dramaturge's notes in production programs. Beware, however: this is ordinarily the *least* interesting sort of paper you can write, for unless the assignment is purely to create a "research paper" or unless you are particularly passionate about the specified context, you might try something a little more adventurous.

The contextual paper must be marked with thorough research, which includes at least one source of recent scholarship; you should be certain that you are at least aware of current thinking on your topic, even if you disagree with it. You should also try to focus the contextual approach toward some sort of conclusion and evaluation, so that something is finally demonstrated: it is not very interesting to say that *Hamlet* is a Renaissance tragedy, which we already know, but it might be important to understand why that does (or doesn't) make *Hamlet* a fine play, or why it does (or doesn't) make Hamlet revenge his father in Act V rather than in Act III.

2. The comparative analysis. Comparisons are the most basic building blocks of learning: if you can understand similarities and differences at the deepest levels, you can discover untold fields of wisdom. It was Newton's comparison of the fall of an apple and the motions of the planets that led to the theory of gravity and its consequent application to rocket travel, and it was Pasteur's comparison of the incidence of disease and the incidence of hygienic procedures that led to the discovery of bacterial infection and the development of rubber gloves. In the same way the study of literature is basically the study of similarities (which define genres and styles) and differences (which define creative departures and imaginative leaps).

Comparative papers might demonstrate the similarities and differences between two or more plays, authors, or between one or more plays and a nondramatic idea. Plays by Tennessee Williams and Arthur Miller could be compared, for example, or Aristophanes' attitudes toward war could be compared to the antiwar movement of ancient Athens.

The comparative paper is not, however, merely a mechanical listing of observed similarities and differences; your comparison should point up possible influences, conscious or unconscious; or, alternatively, it might demonstrate how both compared subjects were subject to the same influences. Mere coincidental similarities are of no importance—although if you probe deeply enough, you might find the coincidences are, in fact, not coincidences at all.

A comparison is worth investigating when you discover an interesting similarity. This can be as simple as recognizing that Williams and Miller are both midcentury American playwrights, that they both write a form of poetic realism, that they both have dealt with problems of modern urban life, that they both have written autobiographical plays dealing with themselves as young writers working in impersonal surroundings, and that they both had successful Broadway hits in the same decade. Or, more originally, perhaps you read Hamlet's

> And you, my sinews, be not instant old,
> But bear me stiffly up,

and it makes you think of the line from *Henry V*:

> Stiffen the sinews, summon up the blood.

What do stiff sinews have in common, and why did Shakespeare use the same expression in these two plays? Are there any other similarities between Prince Hamlet and King Henry? Entire books have been written stemming from what were initially curiosities like this one.

3. A problem investigation. Often you will read or see a play and, while liking it, find yourself bothered by something. Perhaps the story seems faulty, or the characters unlikeable, or you simply don't understand what the playwright was driving at. You ask one or two classmates, and they have the same problems with the play, although they, perhaps, are not so preoccupied with them as you. You may have found fertile ground for an investigation.

Why, for example, does Othello suspect Desdemona of unfaithfulness, when there literally has not been time for her to be alone with Cassio? Some eighteenth-century critics dismissed *Othello* out of hand because of this and similar problems; it might bother you too. You could actually work on this problem itself, for although you would certainly not be the first to do so, there is no definitive answer. But there are an infinite number of such problems in the world's dramatic literature to investigate; and while the answers are not, so to speak, in the back of the book (final answers simply don't exist for most literary problems), your work on the subject may prove illumi-

nating for both you and what will be your readership.

Problem investigations provide good opportunities for research into specialized critical literature; your reference librarian can help you find articles on your topic, and related ones, that will help guide you deeper and deeper into the subject.

4. An observed peculiarity in a play. "Tragedy in *Hamlet*" is probably not a very good title, but "Comedy in *Hamlet*" is better. Everyone knows that *Hamlet* is a tragedy, but there is also a peculiarly heavy dose of comedy in the play, right up to the last act, unlike *Macbeth, King Lear,* and even *Romeo and Juliet,* where the comedy is limited to the first half of the play or so. Why is this? Who does it do to the tragic conclusion of the play? Why might Shakespeare have written *Hamlet* this way? Was it a mistake? Why not?

5. A confrontation with higher authority. Ordinarily you will turn to critical literature for facts and for expert opinion on subjects that interest you, but there may also be times when you feel that experts, no matter how well recognized, are simply wrong in their opinions or evaluations. If you can back up an interesting though contrary point of view, you might have a chance at rewriting critical opinion. Of course this is a dangerous field; you will be matching wits with scholars of wide literary background and proven critical judgment; still, in the final analysis, the best opinion will out, and it might very well be yours. All opinions are ultimately reversed, refined, or revoked anyway; there is no reason not to try to "set the matter straight." A confrontational paper, if you have the heart for it, can draw from you your most dedicated research, persuasive writing, and passionate attention to detail; it can also give you a confidence in your ideas unattainable simply by quoting learned authority. It is certainly worth a try—when you find yourself in considered disagreement with a published expert.

6. A discovered pattern. Perhaps, through a series of comparisons, contextual analyses, and investigations into observed problems, you will discover some fundamental pattern of writing in an author (or directing in a director, or designing in a designer). This is not usually the sort of thing one finds in an undergraduate paper—rather it is more often the subject of a book-length Ph.D. dissertation—but it is the deepest goal of writing on the theatre or on any other scholarly subject. Discovering aesthetic or dramaturgical patterns in individual dramatic works not only makes clear the nature of the works considered, but also throws light on the art of theatre itself. Such discoveries require, of course, a very broad background in theatre studies, plus a sustained intellectual investigation; still, several such papers, on limited topics, are written by undergraduate students every year.

Limiting Your Topic

When you have made the initial choice of a topic, you should be careful to limit it to what you can realistically cover in the time allotted and what you can, in all good conscience, write about in the paper. To deal with more than one or two plays in a six-to-eight-page paper is probably a mistake, and such a paper should have, at the most, only one principal topic and no more than two or three subordinate ones.

Conducting Your Research

Having initially selected your topic (and remember, you will continually refine the topic as you work), reread everything that pertained to your having selected the topic in the first place, noting everything in your rereading that might pertain to the topic you have chosen. If the material that generated the topic is a play you have seen, get a copy of the play. (If it is an unpublished play, go to the theatre office, explain your purpose, and see if you can borrow a script copy.)

Make notes any way you choose, but be sure that they will be easily retrievable. Many students collect notes on handy 3- by 5-inch cards, which can then be arranged in any order you like; if you have access to a personal computer, there are appropriate programs for collecting and arranging material like this.

Understand your basic material in as much detail as possible. Look up words and references that you don't know, using historical dictionaries (such as the *Oxford English Dictionary*) and well-annotated editions (such as the Arden Shakespeare) where necessary to study the meanings of older words and obsolete allusions.

Then, expand your reading to include material that might be related: other plays by the same playwright(s), essays on the play(s) by the playwright(s), and essays on the play and related subjects by scholars, critics, and editors. Get help from the reference librarian at your school library to ferret out pertinent books and essays that will help you probe deeper into your analysis, investigation, and/or comparison. Write down important facts and interesting and/or well-expressed opinions of others, being careful to write down such opinions in their exact words, putting quotation marks around them. Such *citations,* as they are called, should be identified in your notes by their source (book or article and page reference) so that you don't have to hunt up that information all over again when writing your footnotes.

Research need not take place only in your school library, of course. There are specialized libraries containing theatre works, including one-of-a-kind production books and manuscripts, that might be useful; you may also wish to correspond with living authors, directors, designers, or actors if such communications could prove useful to the subject at hand. Seeing one or more of the plays under consideration and talking about it afterwards with the director or dramaturge could certainly prove an invaluable aid to your developing investigation.

Developing Your Thesis

Somewhere in this process—probably starting at the point where you initially selected the topic—you will be arriving at a conclusion about your research, in terms of both what it seems to indicate about the subject and why your conclusion might be important. Where does your research lead? What observations are you drawing from your study? Are the experts right? Have they missed something? Are they ignoring the most important part?

A thesis need not be earth-shattering (for example, "Shakespeare's plays were really written by Queen Elizabeth"), but it should have at least some element of surprise, some conclusion the average reader or viewer would not arrive at on his or her own. This will follow easily and naturally if you have responded to the play yourself, with your own unique set of attributes, and have not simply tried to "find" your thesis in existing essays.

Organizing Your Argument

All papers are organized in the form of an *argument,* which does not mean a quarrel, but rather a logical series of suppositions, elaborations, demonstrations, proofs, and conclusions that argues your position coherently, perhaps even convincingly. Some form of outline is usually helpful in creating this organization. Perhaps the outline will have an order something like this, which includes some headings that may usually be omitted for student papers (and are so identified) but that are fundamental to advanced critical writing:

 I. Initial statement of the topic (problem, peculiarity, subjects of comparison).
   A. Major questions posed by topic.

   B. Indications of why these questions have attracted your attention.
 II. General review of earlier scholarly attempts to deal with the topic (ordinarily omitted in undergraduate paper).
III. General review of the limitation of these earlier scholarly attempts (ordinarily omitted in undergraduate paper).
IV. Presentation of specific material to be critically considered.
   A. Citations of primary materials (the texts considered).
   B. Citations of secondary analyses (historical sources, critical interpretations, reference materials).
 V. Drawing of proofs and conclusions.
VI. Final statement of thesis.

The outline, bald as it is, provides a starting point for arranging your paper and presenting your ideas as a structured argument rather than as a random collection of unrelated notions that, however brilliant, can never lead to new discoveries.

When the outline is done, you can rearrange your notes according to the outline's structure—which will be your paper's structure as well.

Writing Your First Draft

The first draft is more than a fleshing out of the outline: it is the test of your ability to articulate, on paper, what is by now buzzing about in your head and organized in your outline.

Writing is a skill, and you learn it from the time you begin to speak and understand English. There are literally hundreds of ways of saying the same thing, each with its own slight variation:

These are the times that try men's souls.
These times are trying to men.
Men have a trying time of it these days.

Men's souls are sorely tried by modern times.

These are trying times to the soul of man.

And so forth. All of these sentences have probably been uttered at one time or another, but only Tom Paine's, the one at the top, has entered the history books.

No essay is going to teach you to be a good writer, but the advice from here is that the more strongly you want to demonstrate something, the more cogently and persuasively you will write. Good writing is not an end in itself; good writing serves your argument, your thesis, your point of view. If you want to develop your writing, write essays (or letters) trying to explain to somebody else something that is important to you; if what you're trying to explain is the subject of your paper, you are in good shape for this assignment.

A well-written paper is always divided into paragraphs, each having its own central point — usually broached in the opening sentence, sometimes called a "topic sentence." Look at the first sentence of the paragraph above, or of this one. The remainder of the paragraph develops and explains the topic idea; and when the author thinks the idea is satisfactorily expressed and communicated, the paragraph is brought to a close, often with a slight shift in tone that signals closure and gives the reader a little breathing space. Such as "entered the history books," two paragraphs above. Or such as this short sentence fragment.

You should cite all quoted material inside quotation marks, always, and you should identify all quoted material by author and published source. This is for two reasons: (1) you don't want to be accused of stealing another author's direct ideas, which is a serious academic crime (plagiarism), and (2) you want to direct the reader to the original author, who probably has more to say on the subject. Your instructor might have specific instructions on footnoting; if not, you can follow any of several standard formats, such as those used in any scholarly journal or textbook. Footnotes should always include page references, except for well-known classic plays from which lines can usually be cited, directly in the text of your paper, by act, scene, and line reference (an initial footnote should identify the edition used).

When should you cite an outside authority? There are basically four situations where this is useful: (1) where you want to establish a standard critical opinion on something that provides a background to your argument, (2) where you want to state facts you haven't directly uncovered yourself, (3) where you want to disagree with the outside authority, and (4) where you want to support your first steps toward your conclusion. It is in number 4 where you must be careful, because you cannot use an outside authority to state your conclusion or even to support your final finding. The final finding must be yours alone: if you are going to end up at the same place as a leading critic, then why should I read *your* essay?

Rewriting the Paper

Rewriting does *not* mean turning all the simple words into fancy ones or turning to the thesaurus. Indeed, you should think of rewriting not as a fancying up but as a paring down. Read each sentence — aloud if that helps — and ask yourself: "Am I saying that as clearly as possible?" "Am I being persuasive or am I just filling in blanks?"

You should know that authors rewrite everything, and rewrite many times. Leo Tolstoy wrote out the 1,800 pages of *War and Peace* seven times — in longhand. (Actually, his wife did most of the writing out.) And he was a professional writer with great experience at the time. I've written this section five times — at least. So you mustn't be embarrassed to rewrite, nor be so cocky as to think you've said things perfectly the first time around. "These times are sure trying for men's souls." It's okay, but don't you think you could make it better?

Word-processing computer software has enormously eased the technical burden of rewriting in the past decade; if you have not already done so, and if you expect to do a substantial amount of paper writing in the next few years, you should certainly consider buying or gaining access to a personal computer. Most writers who have made the switch from typewriters to computers will never go back.

SOME FINAL THOUGHTS

Writing a paper is a creative task, not a duty. (Answering essay questions on exams, by contrast, is pretty much a duty.) You choose the topic, you choose the method of investigation, you dig into the material and into the relevant research field as deeply as you have time and inclination. Perspicacity, organizational skill, writing ability, and stick-to-it-iveness are all required, but so is imagination and originality. Fine papers explore new ground, and you can always be sure that if you really dig into yourself, as well as into the material at hand, you will be very much on that new ground. Nobody else could ever go precisely where you go; that is a fundamental principle. Consequently, the potential results, for someone interested in pursuing scholarship, are quite substantial. You really can uncover things your instructors haven't and that the world of outside experts hasn't. Undergraduate essays, particularly those that thoroughly and creatively address specific comparisons, problems, patterns, or peculiarities, are published in scholarly literature each year; the present author's writing career began with just such an undergraduate paper. And, apart from publication, the excitement of treading where no scholar or critic has ever tread before may prove to be one of the highlights of your many years of higher education.

GLOSSARY

Terms within the definitions which are themselves defined in this glossary are in *italic*.

absurd The notion that the world is meaningless. Derives from an essay, "The Myth of Sisyphus," by Albert Camus, which suggests that man has an unquenchable desire to understand, but that the world is eternally unknowable: the resulting conflict puts man in an "absurd" position, like Sisyphus, who, according to Greek myth, was condemned for eternity to push a rock up a mountain, only to have it always fall down to the other side. The philosophical term gave the name to a principal postwar dramatic genre: theatre of the absurd.

act (verb) To perform in a play. (noun) A division of a play. Acts in modern plays are bounded by an intermission or by the beginning or end of the play on each side. Full-length modern plays are customarily divided into two acts, sometimes three. Roman, Elizabethan, and neoclassic plays were usually printed in five acts, but these were not necessarily divided by intermissions, only stage clearings.

ad lib A line improvised by an actor during a performance, usually because the actor has forgotten his or her line or because there has been an accident on stage. Sometimes an author directs the actors to ad lib, as in crowd scenes where individual words could not be distinguished by the audience.

aesthetic distance The theoretical separation between the created artifice of a play and the "real life" that the play appears to represent.

agon Action, in Greek. Refers to the major struggles and interactions of Greek tragedies. The root word of our "agony."

alienation effect A technique by which the actor deliberately presents rather than represents his or her character and "illustrates" the character without trying to embody the role fully, as naturalistic acting technique demands. This may be accomplished by "stepping out of character"—as to sing a song or to address the audience directly—and by developing a highly objective and "didactic" mode of expression. Developed by German playwright Bertolt Brecht (1898–1956). The actor is alienated from the role ("estranged" and "distanced" are perhaps better terms—all translations of the German word *verfremdungs*) in order to make the audience more directly aware of current political issues. Highly influential today, particularly in Europe.

amphitheatre In Rome, a large elliptical outdoor theatre, originally used for gladiatorial contests. Today the term is often used to designate a large outdoor theatre of any type.

anagnorisis Recognition, in Greek. Aristotle claimed every fine tragedy had a recognition scene, in which the *protagonist* discovered either some fact unknown to him or her or some moral flaw in his or her character. Scholars disagree as to which of these precise meanings Aristotle had in mind. See *hamartia.*

Apollonian That which is beautiful, wise, and serene, in the theories of Friedrich Nieztsche, who believed drama sprang from the junction of Apollonian and *Dionysian* forces in Greek culture.

apron That part of the stage in front of the *proscenium;* the forwardmost portion of the stage. Used extensively in the English Restoration period, from whence the term comes. Today, usually called the *forestage.*

arena stage A stage with the audience arranged on all sides. Also known as "theatre-in-the-round." A famous such stage is in Washington, D.C. (The Arena Stage). The term is Latin (where it means "sand") and originally referred to the dirt circle in the midst of an *amphitheatre.*

arras A curtain, often at the rear of the stage. Polonius is stabbed hiding behind one in Shakespeare's *Hamlet.*

aside A short line in a play delivered directly to the audience; by dramatic convention, the other characters on stage are presumed not to hear it. Popular in Shakespeare and in the Restoration, the aside has made a comeback in recent years and is used to good effect, in conjunction with the longer *direct address,* by contemporary American playwrights such as Lanford Wilson and Neil Simon.

audition The process whereby actors are seen and heard by directors or casting directors during the casting of a play or a season of plays. Actors can audition both by presenting rehearsed monologues or scenes or by reading from the text of the play being presented.

avant-garde The "advance-guard" of an army goes beyond the front lines to break new ground; in theatre, the avant-garde are those theatre artists who abandon the conventional models and create works that are in the forefront of new theatrical movements and styles. The term has had wide currency in the twentieth-century theatre, particularly in France.

backstage The offstage area that is hidden from the audience. Used for scenery storage, for actors preparing to make entrances, and for stage technicians running the show. "Backstage plays," such as *The Torchbearers* and *Noises Off,* "turn the set around" and exploit the furious backstage activity that takes place during a play production.

beat The smallest unit of action in a scene, according to acting theorist and teacher, Konstantin Stanislavski (1863–1938).

biomechanics An experimental acting system, characterized by expressive physicalization and bold gesticulation, developed by Russian play director Vsevolod Meyerhold in the 1920s.

blackout The sudden extinguishing of all stage lights, leaving the theatre in blackness. As contrasted to a fadeout, which is a gradual fading of the lights.

blackout sketch In *vaudeville* and vaudeville-inspired plays: a short farcical scene, culminating in a punch line that is followed by a blackout.

blocking The specific staging of a play's movements, ordinarily by the director. "Blocking" refers to the precise indications of where actors are to move, moment by moment, during the performance. Often this is worked out ("blocked out") on graph paper by the director beforehand.

book In a musical play, the actual dialogue text, apart from the music and song lyrics.

border A piece of flat scenery, often black velour but sometimes a *flat,* which is placed horizontally above the set, usually to *mask* the lighting instruments. Often used with side *wings,* in which combination the scenery system is known as "wing and border."

box set A stage set consisting of hard scenic pieces representing the walls and ceiling of a room, with one wall left out for the audience to peer into. Developed in the nineteenth century and still very much in use in realistic plays.

Broadway The major commercial theatre district in New York, bordered by Broadway and Eighth Avenue; 44th Street and 52nd Street.

burlesque Literally, a parody or mockery, from an Italian amusement form. Today used to imply broad, coarse humor in farce, particularly in parodies and vaudeville-type presentations.

business The minute physical behavior of the actor, as in fiddling with a tie, sipping a drink, drumming the fingers, lighting a cigarette, and so forth. Sometimes this is controlled to a high degree by the actor and/or the director for precise dramatic effect; at other times the business is improvised in order to convey a naturalistic versimilitude.

callback After initial auditions, the director or casting director will "call back" for additional readings those actors who seem most promising; this is the "callback audition," of which there may be many. Rules of the actors' unions require payment to actors for callbacks after a certain minimum number have been held.

caricature A character portrayed very broadly and in a stereotypical fashion. Ordinarily objectionable in realistic dramas. See *character*.

catharsis In Aristotle, the "purging" or "cleansing" of terror and pity which the audience develops during the climax of a *tragedy*.

character A "person" in a play, as performed by an actor. Hamlet, Oedipus, and Willy Loman are "characters." Characters may or may not be based on real people.

character actor An actor particularly noted for playing roles with pronounced characteristics, such as old age, a comical appearance, a foreign accent, etc.

chorus (1) In classic Greek plays, an ensemble of characters representing the general public of the play, such as the women of Argos or the elders of Thebes. Originally, the chorus numbered fifty; Aeschylus is said to have reduced it to twelve, and Sophocles to have increased it to fifteen. More recent playwrights, including Shakespeare and Jean Anouilh, have occasionally employed a single actor (or small group of actors) as "Chorus," to provide narration between the scenes. (2) In musical plays, an ensemble of characters who sing and/or dance together (in contrast to soloists who sing and/or dance independently).

classical drama Technically, plays from classical Greece or Rome. Now used frequently (if incorrectly) to refer to masterpieces of the early and late Renaissance (Elizabethan, Jacobean, French neoclassical, etc.).

climax The point of highest tension in a play, when the conflicts of the play are at their fullest expression.

comedy Popularly, a funny play; classically, a play that ends happily; metaphorically, a play with some humor that celebrates the eternal ironies of human existence ("divine comedy").

comedy of humours In Elizabethan England, a comedy based on character types, which in turn were thought to be based on chemical imbalances in the bodily fluids. An imbalance of blood made one character "sanguine," an imbalance of bile made another "bilious," and an imbalance of phlegm made another "phlegmatic," for example. Ben Jonson's *Every Man in His Humour* (1598) is the exemplar of this type of play.

comedy of manners A comedy that exploits the foibles and follies of contemporary social behavior. The comedy of manners perhaps originated with Molière's *The Precious Ladies* (1658) and reached its peak shortly thereafter with the playwrights of the English Restoration (1660–1700), particularly William Congreve and William Wycherly.

comic relief In a tragedy, a short comic scene that releases some of the built-up tension of the play—giving the audience a momentary "relief" before the tension mounts higher. The "porter scene" in Shakespeare's *Macbeth* is an often-cited example; following the murder of Duncan, a porter jocularly addresses the audience as to the effect of drinking on sexual behavior. In the best tragedies, comic relief also provides an ironic counterpoint to the tragic action.

commedia dell'arte A form of largely improvised, masked street theatre that began in northern Italy in the late sixteenth century and still can be seen today. The principal characters—Arlecchino, Pantalone, Columbine, Dottore, and Scapino among them—appear over and over in literally thousands of commedia stories.

constructivism A twentieth-century design style, marked by large structural pieces and abstract, geometric regularity, which flourished in Europe, particularly in Russia after the Revolution.

continental seating An arrangement of audience seating without a center aisle.

convention A theatrical custom that the audience accepts without thinking, such as "when the curtain comes down, the play is over." Each period develops its own dramatic conventions, which playwrights may either accept or violate.

cue The last word of one speech, which then becomes the "cue" for the following speech. Actors are frequently admonished to speak "on cue" or to "pick up their cues," both of which mean to begin speaking precisely at the moment the other actor finishes.

cycle plays In medieval England, a series of *mystery plays* that, performed in series, relate the story of religion, from the *Creation of the Universe* to *Adam and Eve* to *The Crucifixion* to *Doomsday*. The York cycle includes forty-eight such plays.

cyclorama In a proscenium theatre, a large piece of curved scenery that wraps around the rear of the stage and is illuminated to resemble the sky or to serve as an abstract neutral background. Usually made of fabric stretched between curved pipes; sometimes made permanently with concrete and plaster.

denouement The final scene or scenes in a play, devoted to tying up the loose ends after the climax (although the word originally meant "the untying").

deus ex machina In Greek tragedies, the resolution of the plot by the device of a god (*deus*) arriving onstage by means of a crane (*machina*) and solving all the characters' problems. Today, any such contrived play ending, such as the discovery of a will. Considered clumsy by Aristotle and virtually all succeeding critics; occasionally used ironically in the modern theatre, as by Bertolt Brecht in *The Threepenny Opera*.

dialogue The speeches—delivered to each other—of the characters in a play. Contrasted to *monologue*.

diction One of the six important features of a drama, according to Aristotle, who meant by the term the intelligence and appropriateness of the play's speeches. Today refers primarily to the actor's need for articulate speech and clear pronunciation.

didactic drama Drama dedicated to teaching lessons or provoking intellectual debate beyond the confines of the play. The dramatic form espoused by Bertolt Brecht. See *alienation effect*.

dimmer In lighting, the electrical device, technically known as a potentiometer, which regulates the current passing through the bulb filaments and, thereby, the amount of light emitted from the lighting instruments.

dim out To fade the lights gradually to blackness.

Dionysia, or *Great Dionysia* or *City Dionysia*. The week-long Athenian springtime festival in honor of Dionysus, which was, after 534 B.C., the major play-producing festival of the Greek year.

Dionysian Passionate revelry, uninhibited pleasure-seeking. The opposite of *Apollonian*, according to Nieztsche, who considered drama a merger of these two primary impulses in the Greek character.

Dionysus The Greek god of drama; also the god of drinking and fertility. *Bacchus* in Rome.

direct address A character's speech delivered directly to the audience. Common in Greek Old Comedy (see *parabasis*), in Shakespeare (see *soliloquy*), in *epic theatre,* and in some otherwise realistic modern plays (such as Neil Simon's *Broadway Bound*).

discovery A character who appears on stage without making an entrance, as when a curtain opens. Ferdinand and Miranda are "discovered" playing chess in Shakespeare's *The Tempest* when Prospero pulls away a curtain that had been hiding them from view.

dithyramb A Greek religious rite in which a chorus of fifty men, dressed in goatskins, chanted and danced; the precursor, according to Aristotle, of Greek tragedy.

documentary drama Drama that presents historical facts in a nonfictionalized, or only slightly fictionalized, manner.

domestic tragedy A tragedy about ordinary people at home.

double (1) An actor who plays more than one role is said to "double" in the second and following roles. Ordinarily the actor will seek, through a costume change, to disguise the fact of the doubling; occasionally, however, a production with a *theatricalist* staging may make it clear that the actor doubles in many roles. (2) To Antonin Artaud, the life that drama reflects, as discussed in his book, *The Theatre and Its Double*. See *theatre of cruelty*.

downstage That part of the stage closest to the audience. The term derives from the eighteenth century, when the stage was *raked* so that the front part was literally below the back (or *upstage*) portion.

drama The art of the theatre. Plays, playmaking, and the whole body of literature of and for the stage.

dramatic Plays, scenes, and events that are high in conflict and believability and that would command attention if staged in the theatre.

dramatic irony The situation when the audience knows something the characters don't, as in Shakespeare's *Macbeth* when King Duncan remarks on his inability to judge character — while warmly greeting the man (Macbeth) we already know plans to assassinate him.

dramaturge A specialist on dramatic construction and the body of dramatic literature; a scientist of the art of drama. Dramaturges are frequently engaged by professional and academic theatres to assist in choosing and analyzing plays, develop production concepts, research topics pertinent to historic period or play production style, and write program essays. The dramaturge has been a mainstay of the German theatre since the eighteenth century and is becoming increasingly popular in the English-speaking world; sometimes identified by the German spelling *dramaturg*.

dramaturgy The science of drama; the art of play construction. Sometimes used to refer to play structure itself.

dress rehearsal A rehearsal, perhaps one of several, in full costume; usually also with full scenery, properties, lighting, sound, and technical effects. Ordinarily the last rehearsal(s) prior to the first actual performance before an outside audience.

drop A flat piece of scenery hung from the *fly gallery*, which can "drop" into place by a *flying system*.

eccyclema (also *ekkyklema*). A Greek stage machine, possibly a rolling platform that could be pushed through a stage door. Often used to

bear corpses, as in Aeschylus' *Libation Bearers*, when the bodies of Aegisthus and Clytemnestra are so displayed.

empathy Audience identification with dramatic characters and their consequent shared feelings with the plights and fortunes of those characters. One of the principal effects of good drama.

ensemble Literally, the group of actors (and sometimes directors and designers) who put a play together; metaphorically, the rapport and shared sense of purpose that bind such a group into a unified artistic entity.

environmental theatre Plays produced not on a conventional stage, but in an area where the actors and the audience are intermixed in the same "environment" and where there is no precise line distinguishing stage space from audience space.

epic theatre As popularized by Bertolt Brecht, a style of theatre where the play presents a series of semi-isolated episodes, intermixed with songs and other forms of *direct address,* all leading to a general moral conclusion or set of integrated moral questions. Brecht's *Mother Courage* is a celebrated example. See also *alienation*.

epilogue In Greek tragedy, a short concluding scene of certain plays, generally involving a substantial shift of tone or a *deus ex machina*. Today, a concluding scene set substantially beyond the time frame of the rest of the play, in which characters, now somewhat older, reflect on the preceding events.

existential drama A play based on the philosophical notions of existentialism, particularly as developed by Jean-Paul Sartre (1905–80). Existentialism, basically, preaches that "you are your acts, and nothing else," and that people must be held fully accountable for their own behavior. *No Exit* contains Sartre's most concise expression of this idea.

exodos In Greek tragedy, the departure of the chorus at the end of the play.

exposition In play construction, the conveyance, through dialogue, of story events that have occurred before the play begins. The difficulty in writing effective expository dialogue is in making such discussions of the past appear to be natural and uncontrived.

expressionism An artistic style that greatly exaggerates perceived reality in order to express inner truths directly. Popular mainly in Germany between the world wars, expressionism in the theatre is notable for its gutty dialogue, piercing sounds, bright lighting and coloring, bold scenery, and shocking, vivid imagery.

farce Highly comic, light-hearted, gleefully contrived drama, usually involving stock situations (such as mistaken identity or discovered lovers' trysts), punctuated with broad physical stunts and pratfalls.

flat Fabric, stretched over a wooden frame and painted, often to resemble a wall or portion of a wall. A traditional staple of stage scenery, particularly in the realistic theatre, since it is exceptionally lightweight, may be combined with other flats in various ways, and may be repainted and reused many times over several years.

fly (verb) To raise a piece of scenery (or an actor) out of sight, by a system of ropes and/or wires. Used in the theatre at least since ancient Greek times (see *deus ex machina*).

fly gallery The operating area for flying scenery, where fly ropes are tied off (on a pinrail) or where ropes in a counterweight system are clamped in a fixed position.

flying system The specific mechanics of flying scenery, usually either rope pulleys or, more commonly, a counterweight system. Electric motorized systems are sometimes used.

footlights In a proscenium theatre, a row of lights across the front of the stage, used to light the actors' faces from below and to add light and color to the setting. Used universally in previous centuries, but employed only on special occasions today.

forestage A modern term for *apron*. The small portion of the stage forward of the *proscenium*.

full house All audience seats are filled. See *house*.

genre Literally, "kind" (French). A term used in dramatic theory to signify a distinctive class or category of play, such as tragedy, comedy, farce, etc.

greenroom A room near the stage where actors may sit comfortably before and after the show, or during scenes in which they do not appear. This room is traditionally painted green; the custom arose in England, where the color was thought to be soothing.

gridiron The open framework well above the stage, where the pulleys of the *flying system* are

anchored. The "grid," as it is usually called, should be at least three times as high as the *proscenium* and should have at least six to ten feet of clearance above it, so as to permit technicians to walk freely about.

ground plan A schematic drawing of the stage setting, as seen from above, indicating the location of stage scenery pieces and furniture on (and sometimes above) the floor. A vital working document for directors in rehearsal, as well as technicians in the installation of scenery.

ground row A low horizontal piece of stage scenery, often used to hide lighting instruments and to indicate a horizon. Originally the term was used for the low-lying lighting instruments themselves.

hamartia In Aristotle, the "tragic flaw" of the *protagonist*. Scholars differ as to whether Aristotle was referring primarily to a character's ignorance of certain facts or to a character's moral defect.

Hellenistic theatre Ancient Greek theatre during the fourth and third centuries B.C. The surviving stone theatres of Athens and Epidaurus date from the Hellenistic period, which began well after the great fifth-century tragedies and comedies were written. The Hellenistic period did produce an important form of comedy (*New Comedy*), however, and Alexandrian scholars during this period collected, edited, and preserved the masterpieces of the Golden Age.

high comedy A comedy of verbal wit and visual elegance, usually peopled with upper-class characters. The Restoration comedies of William Congreve and the Victorian comedies of Oscar Wilde are often cited as examples.

himation The gown-like basic costume of the Greek tragic actor.

house The audience portion of the theatre building.

house out In lighting, a direction to take the lights out in the audience portion of the theatre.

hubris In Greek, an excess of pride. The most common character defect (one interpretation of the Greek *hamartia*) of the *protagonist* in Greek tragedy. "Pride goeth before a fall" is an Elizabethan expression of this foundation of tragedy.

improvisation Dialogue and/or stage business invented by the actor, often during the performance itself. Some plays are wholly improvised, even to the extent that the audience may suggest situations that the actors must then create. More often, improvisation is used to "fill in the gaps" between more traditionally memorized and rehearsed scenes.

inciting action In play construction, the single action that initiates the major conflict of the play.

ingenue The young, pretty, and innocent girl role in certain plays; also used to denote an actress capable of playing such roles.

interlude A scene or staged event in a play not specifically tied to the plot. Also, in medieval England, a short moral play, usually comic, that could be presented at a court banquet amidst other activities.

intermission (in England, *interval*). A pause in the action, marked by a fall of the curtain or a fade-out of the stage lights, during which the audience may leave their seats for a short time, usually ten or fifteen minutes. Intermissions divide the play into separate *acts*.

Kabuki One of the national theatres of Japan. Dating from the sixteenth century, the Kabuki features magnificent flowing costumes; highly stylized scenery, acting, and make-up; and elaborately styled choreography.

lazzo A physical joke, refined into traditional business and inserted into a play, in the *commedia dell'arte*. "Eating the fly" is a famous *lazzo*.

Lenaea The winter dramatic festival in ancient Athens. Because there were fewer foreigners in town in the winter, comedies that might embarrass the Athenians were often performed at this festival rather than at the springtime *Dionysia*.

liturgical drama Dramatic material that was written into the official Catholic church liturgy and was staged as part of regular church services in the medieval period, mainly in the tenth through twelfth centuries.

low comedy Comic actions based on broad physical humor, scatology, crude punning, and the argumentative behavior of ignorant and lower-class characters. Despite the pejorative connotation of its name, low comedy can be inspired, as in the "mechanicals" scenes of Shakespeare's *A Midsummer Night's Dream*. Good plays, such as this one, can mix low comedy with high comedy in a highly sophisticated pattern.

mask (noun) A covering of the face, used conventionally by actors in many periods, including Greek, Roman, *commedia dell'arte*. Also used in other sorts of plays for certain occasions, such as the masked balls in Shakespeare's *Romeo and Juliet* and *Much Ado About Nothing*. Also, a symbol of the theatre; particularly the two classic masks of Comedy and Tragedy. (verb) To hide backstage storage or activity by placing, in front of it, neutrally-colored *flats* or drapery (which then become "masking pieces").

masque A minor dramatic form combining dance, music, a short allegorical text, and elegant scenery and costuming; often presented at court, as in the royal masques written by Ben Jonson, with scenery designed by Inigo Jones, during the Stuart era (early seventeenth century).

melodrama Originally a term for musical theatre, by the nineteenth century this became the designation of a suspenseful, plot-oriented drama featuring all-good heroes, all-bad villains, simplistic dialogue, soaring moral conclusions, and bravura acting.

metaphor A literary term designating a figure of speech that implies a comparison or identity of one thing with something else. It permits concise communication of a complex idea by use of associative imagery, as with Shakespeare's "morn in russet mantle clad."

metatheatre Literally, "beyond theatre"; plays or theatrical acts that are self-consciously theatrical; that refer back to the art of the theatre and call attention to their own theatricality. Developed by many authors, including Shakespeare (in plays-within-plays in *Hamlet* and *A Midsummer Night's Dream*) and particularly by the twentieth-century Italian playwright Luigi Pirandello (*Six Characters in Search of an Author, Tonight We Improvise*), thus leading to the term "Pirandellian" (meaning "metatheatrical"). See *play-within-the-play*.

mime A stylized art of acting without words. Probably derived from the *commedia dell'arte*, mime was revived in France during the mid-twentieth century and is now popular again in the theatre and in street performances in Europe and in the United States. Mime performers traditionally employ white-face make-up to stylize and exaggerate their features and expressions.

mise-en-scène The staging of a play; literally, the "putting [a play] into the scenery."

modern classic A term used to designate a play of the past hundred years that has nonetheless passed the test of time and seems as if it will last into the century or centuries beyond, such as the major works of Chekhov, Shaw, and Samuel Beckett. See *classical drama.*

monologue A long unbroken speech in a play, often delivered directly to the audience (when it is more technically called a *soliloquy*).

morality play An allegorical medieval play form, in which the characters represent abstractions (Good Deeds, Death, etc.) and the overall impact of the play is moral instruction. *Everyman* (fifteenth century) is the most famous of these plays in English; the name of the author is not known.

motivation That which can be construed to have determined a person's (or character's) behavior. Since *Stanislavski,* actors have been encouraged to study the possible motivations of their characters' actions. See *objective.*

musical A generic name for a play with a large number of songs, particularly when there is also dancing and/or a chorus.

mystery play A term describing medieval plays that developed from *liturgical drama* and treated biblical stories and themes. Unlike liturgical dramas, which were in Latin, mystery plays are in the vernacular (English, French, German, Italian, Spanish, and Russian versions exist) and were staged outside of the church. The exact origin and original meaning of the term is unclear. See *cycle play.*

naturalism An extreme form of realism. Its proponents, active in the late nineteenth and early twentieth century, sought to dispense with all theatrical convention in the search for complete verisimilitude to life: a "slice of life," as the naturalists would say. Probably attainable only in theory, naturalism has nonetheless had a major impact on the theatrical arts, particularly on film acting and film writing.

neoclassicism Literally, "new classicism," or a renewed interest in the literary and artistic theories of ancient Greece and Rome and an attempt to reformulate them for the current day. A dominant force in seventeenth-century France, neoclassicism promoted restrained passion, balance, artistic consistency, and formalism in all art forms; it reached its dramatic pinnacle with the tragedies of Jean Racine.

Noh drama The classical dance-drama of Japan. Performed on a bare wooden stage of fixed construction and dimension and accompanied by traditional music, the Noh is the aristocratic forebear of the more popular *Kabuki* and remains generally unchanged since its fourteenth-century beginnings.

objective The basic "goal" of a character. Also called "intention" or "victory." Since *Stanislavski,* the actor has been urged to discover his or her characters' objectives and, by way of "living the life of his/her character," to pursue that character's objective during the course of the play.

off-Broadway The New York professional theatre located outside the *Broadway* district; principally in Greenwich Village and around the upper East and West sides. Developed in the 1950s, when it was considered highly experimental, the off-Broadway theatre is now more of a scaled-down version of the Broadway theatre, featuring musicals and commercial revivals as much as (or more than) original works.

off-off-Broadway A term designating certain theatre activity in New York City, usually nonprofessional (although with professional artists involved) and usually experimental and avant-garde in nature. Developed in the 1970s as a supplement to the commercialism of both Broadway and, increasingly, off-Broadway.

open the house A direction to admit the audience. See *house.*

orchestra (1) In the ancient Greek or Roman theatre, the circular (in Rome, semicircular) ground-level acting area in front of the stagehouse, or *skene.* It was used primarily by the chorus. (2) In modern theatre buildings, the main ground-level section of the audience, which usually slopes upward at the rear. Distinct from the mezzanine and balconies and ordinarily containing the more expensive seats.

parabasis A "coming-forward" of a character in Old Greek Comedy, who then gives a *direct address* to the audience in the middle of the play. In Aristophanes, the parabasis is often given in the author's name and may have been spoken by Aristophanes himself. The parabasis was often unrelated to the plot and dealt with the author's immediate political or social concerns.

parados In the ancient Greek theatre, one of two passageways between the stagehouse (*skene*) and the audience area (*theatron*), employed primarily for the entrance and exit of the chorus.

parody Dramatic material that makes fun of a

dramatic genre or mode or of specific literary works. A form of theatre that is often highly entertaining but that rarely has lasting value.

pathos Passion, in Greek; also suffering. The word refers to the depths of feeling evoked by tragedy; it is at the root of our words "sympathy" and "empathy," which also describe the effect of drama on audience emotions.

peripetia (in the Anglicized form, *peripety*). The reversal of the protagonist's fortunes that, according to Aristotle, is part of the climax of a tragedy.

pièce-bien-fait See *well-made play.*

play-within-the-play A play that is "presented" by characters who are already in a play; as "The Murder of Gonzago," which is presented by "players" in *Hamlet.* Many plays are in part about actors and plays and contain such plays-within-plays; these include Chekhov's *The Seagull,* Anouilh's *The Rehearsal,* and Shakespeare's *A Midsummer Night's Dream* and *The Taming of the Shrew.*

plot The events of the play, expressed as a series of linked dramatic actions. More generally, and in common terms, the story of the play. The most important aspect of play construction, according to Aristotle.

practical In stage terminology, a property that actually works on stage the way it does in life. For example, a "practical" stove, in a stage setting, is one on which the characters can actually cook. A "nonpractical" stove, by contrast, is something that only looks like a stove (and may in fact be a stove without insides).

problem play A realistic play that deals, often narrowly, with a specific social problem. George Bernard Shaw's *Mrs. Warren's Profession,* for example, is virtually a dramatic tract on prostitution; Henri Becque's *The Vultures* deals quite single-mindedly with the need for husbands to write wills that protect their widows from unscrupulous lawyers. The term was most popular around the beginning of the present century; today it is mostly descriptive of certain movies for television.

producer (1) In America, the person responsible for assembling the ingredients of a play production: financing, staff, theatre, publicity, and management. Not ordinarily involved in the day-to-day artistic direction of the production, the American producer nonetheless controls the artistic process through his or her authority over personnel selection and budgeting. (2) In the English theatre, the term refers to what Americans call the director.

prologue In Greek tragedy, a speech or brief scene preceding the entrance of the chorus and the main action of the play, usually spoken by a god or gods. Subsequently, the term has referred to a speech or brief scene that introduces the play, as by an actor in certain Elizabethan plays (often called the *chorus*) and in the Restoration. Rarely used in the modern theatre.

properties, or *props* The furniture and handheld objects (*hand props*) used in play productions. These are often real items (chairs, telephones, books, etc.) that can be purchased, rented, borrowed, or brought up from theatre storage; they may also, particularly in period or stylized plays, be designed and built in a property shop.

proscenium The arch separating the audience area from the main stage area, in a theatre so designed. The term derives from the Roman playhouse, in which the proscenium (literally, *pro skene* or "in front of the stage") was the facing wall of the stage. Modern thrust and arena stages have no proscenium.

proscenium theatre A theatre equipped with a proscenium. First popular in the late seventeenth century, and reaching its apogee in the late nineteenth and early twentieth centuries. Still the basic theatre architecture of America's Broadway and of major European theatre companies.

protagonist In Greek tragedy, and subsequently in any drama, the principal character. Often opposed by an *antagonist.*

raked stage A sloped stage, angled so that the rear (*upstage*) area is higher than the forward (*downstage*) area. Standard theatre architecture in the seventeenth century; often used today in scene design, but rarely in a theatre's permanent architecture.

realism The general principle that the stage should portray, in a reasonable facsimile, ordinary people in ordinary circumstances, and that actors should behave, as much as possible, as real people do in life. While there are roots that go back to Euripides, realism developed as a conscious movement as a striking contrast to the florid romanticism that swept the European theatre in the mid-nineteenth century. See also *naturalism,* which is an extreme version of realism.

recognition See *anagnorisis.*

rehearsal The gathering of actors and director to put a play into production; the period in which the director stages the play and the actors develop and repeat their dialogue and actions. Etymologically, a "reharrowing," or repeated digging into. In French, the comparable term is "repetition."

repertory The plays a theatre company produces. A company's current repertory consists of those plays available for production at any time.

Restoration In England, the period following the restoration of the monarchy in 1660. In the theatre, the period is particularly noted for witty and salacious comedies, through to William Congreve's brilliant *The Way of the World* in 1700.

rising action In dramatic structure, the escalating conflict; events and actions that follow the inciting action.

ritual A traditional cultural practice, usually religious, involving precise movements, music, spoken text, and/or gestures, that serves to communicate with deities. Often incorporated into plays, either as conventions of the theatre or as specific dramatized actions.

romanticism A nineteenth-century European movement away from neoclassic formalism and toward outsized passions, exotic and grotesque stories, florid writing, and all-encompassing world views. Supplanted in the late century by *realism,* romanticism survives today primarily in grand opera.

rotating repertory The scheduling of a series of plays in nightly rotation. This is customary in most European theatres and in many American Shakespeare festivals; it is otherwise rare in America. See *repertory.*

satire A play or other literary work that ridicules social follies, beliefs, religions, or human vices, almost always in a lighthearted vein. Not usually a lasting theatre form, as summed up by dramatist George S. Kaufmann's classic definition: "Satire is what closes on Saturday night."

satyr A mythological Greek creature, half man and half goat, who attended Dionysus and represented male sexuality and drunken revelry. Satyrs served as the *chorus* of the *satyr play.*

satyr play The fourth play in a Greek *tetralogy.* Satyr plays were short bawdy farces that parodied the events of the tragedies that preceded them.

scene (1) The period of a stage time, now usually marked either by the rise or fall of a curtain, or the raising and lowering of lights, but in the past often marked simply by a stage clearing, where the stage represents a single space over a continuous period of time. Often the subdivision of an *act.* (2) The locale where the events of the play are presumed to take place, as represented by scenery. As "the scene is the Parson's living room. . . ." (3) Of scenery, as "scene design."

scenery The physical constructions that provide the specific acting environment for a play and that often indicate, by representation, the locale where a scene is set. The physical setting for a scene or play.

scenography Scene design, particularly as it fits into the moving pattern of a play or series of plays. Scene design in four dimensions (three physical dimensions plus time).

scrim A theatrical fabric woven so finely that when lit from the front it appears opaque, and when lit from behind it becomes transparent. Often used for surprise effects or to create a mysterious mood.

script A play's text as used in and prior to play production, usually in manuscript or typescript rather than in a published version.

semiotics The study of signs, as they may be perceived in literary works, including plays. A contemporary tool of dramaturgical analysis, which offers the possibility of identifying all the ingredients of drama (staging as well as language) and determining the precise conjunctions between them.

setting or *set.* The fixed (stable) stage scenery.

skene The Greek stagehouse (and root word of our "scene"). The skene evolved from a small changing room behind the *orchestra* to a larger structure with a raised stage and a back wall during the Greek period.

slapstick Literally, a prop bat made up of two hinged sticks that slap sharply together when the bat is used to hit someone; a staple gag of the *commedia dell'arte.* More generally, any sort of very broad physical stage humor.

slice-of-life Pure naturalism: stage action that merely represents an ordinary and arbitrary "slice" of the daily activity of the people portrayed.

soliloquy A monologue delivered by a single actor with no one else onstage. Sometimes played as the character "thinking aloud" and sometimes as a seeming dialogue with the (silent) audience.

spine In Stanislavski, the through-line of a character's actions in a play.

stage business See *business*.

stage directions Scene descriptions, blocking instructions, and general directorial comments written, usually by the playwright, in the script.

stage left Left, from the actor's point of view.

stage right Right, from the actor's point of view.

Stanislavski, Konstantin The great Russian director, acting teacher, and acting theorist (1863–1938) whose most noted dictum was "live the life of your character on the stage."

stichomythia In Greek plays, dialogue that is an alternation of speeches, each a single line of verse. Also seen in Shakespeare and in many later playwrights.

stock character A character recognizable mainly for his or her conformity to a standard ("stock") dramatic stereotype: the wily servant, the braggart soldier, the innocent virgin, etc. Most date from at least Roman times.

stock situation One of a number of basic plot situations, such as the lover hiding in the closet, twins mistaken for each other, etc., which, like stock characters, have been used in the theatre since Plautus and before.

style The specific manner in which a play is shaped, as determined by its genre, its historical period, the sort of impact the director wishes to convey to the audience, and the skill of the artists involved. The term generally refers to these aspects inasmuch as they differ from naturalism, although it could also be said that naturalism, too, is a style.

stylize To deliberately shape a play (or a setting, or a costume, etc.) in a specifically non-naturalistic manner.

subplot A secondary plot in a play, usually related to the main plot by play's end. The Gloucester plot in *King Lear* and the Laertes plot in *Hamlet* are examples.

subtext In Stanislavski, the deeper and usually unexpressed "real" meanings of a character's spoken lines. Of particular importance in the acting of realistic plays, such as those of Chekhov, where the action is often as much between the lines as in them.

superobjective In Stanislavski, the character's long-range *objective*, pursued throughout the play.

surrealism An art movement of the early twentieth century, in which the artist sought to go beyond realism into super-realism (of which surrealism is a contraction).

symbolism The first major antirealistic movement in the arts and in the theatre; emphasizing the symbolic nature of theatrical presentation and the abstract possibilities of drama. Flourished as a significant movement from the late nineteenth century to the early twentieth, when it broke into various submovements: expressionism, surrealism, theatricalism, etc.

tableau A "frozen moment" onstage, with the actors immobile. Usually employed at the end of a scene, as the curtain falls or the lights dim.

teaser A neutral front *border* specifically used to hide lighting instruments.

tetralogy Four plays performed together in sequence. In ancient Greek theatre, this was the basic pattern for the tragic playwrights, who presented a *trilogy* of tragedies, followed by a *satyr play*.

text A playscript. Sometimes used to indicate the spoken words of the play only, as apart from the stage directions and other material in the script.

theatre-in-the-round See *arena stage*.

theatre of cruelty A notion of theatre developed by the French theorist, Antonin Artaud (1896–1948). Artaud's goal was to employ language more for its sound than for its meaning and to create a shocking stream of sensations rather than a coherent plot and cast of characters. Although Artaud's practical achievement was slight, his theories have proven extraordinarily influential.

theatre of the absurd See *absurd*.

theatre of alienation See *alienation, epic theatre*.

theatrical Something that "works" in the theatre; a play that is highly entertaining, showy, and marked by virtuoso skills. Generally not used to describe naturalistic plays or performances and occasionally pejorative when so used.

theatricalist A style of contemporary theatre that boldly exploits the theatre itself and that calls attention to the theatrical contexts of the play being performed. Often used to describe plays about the theatre that employ *plays-within-the-play.*

thespian Actor. After Thespis, the first Greek actor.

tormentor In a proscenium theatre, one of two large vertical flats, painted black or a neutral color, placed at the far downstage left and right of the stage to *mask* the area between the proscenium and the first piece of stage scenery.

tragedy The word comes from the Greek "goat song" and originally meant a serious play. Refined by Greek playwrights (Thespis being the first) and subsequently the philosopher Aristotle into the most celebrated of dramatic genres: a play that treats, at the most uncompromising level, human suffering. The reason for the name is unclear; a goat may have been the prize, and/or the chorus may have worn goatskins.

tragic flaw See *hamartia.*

tragicomedy A play that begins as a tragedy, but includes comic elements and ends happily. A popular genre in the eighteenth century, but rarely employed, at least under that name, in the modern theatre.

traveler A curtain that, instead of flying out (see *fly*), moves horizontally and is usually opened by dividing from the center outward.

trilogy Three plays performed in sequence. The basic pattern of ancient Greek tragedies, of which one—Aeschylus' *The Oresteia* (*Agamemnon, The Libation Bearers,* and *The Eumenides*)—is still extant.

trope A written text, usually in dialogue form, incorporated into the Catholic Church service. In the tenth century A.D. these became the first *liturgical dramas.*

unities The unity of place, unity of time, and unity of action were the three "unities" that neoclassic critics of the seventeenth century claimed to derive from Aristotle; plays said to "observe the unities" were required to take place in one locale, to have a duration of no more than one day (in an extreme interpretation, in no more time than the duration of the play itself), and could concern themselves with no more than one single action. Aristotle made no such demands on playwrights, however, and very few authors have ever been able to make such observances with success.

unit set A set that, by the moving on or off of a few simple pieces and perhaps with a change of lights, can represent all the scenes from a play. A fluid and economical staging device; particularly useful for Shakespeare.

upstage (noun) In a *proscenium theatre,* that part of the stage farthest from the audience; the rear of the stage. So called because it was in fact raised ("up") in the days of the *raked stage.* (verb) To stand upstage of another actor. Often considered rude, inasmuch as it forces the downstage actor to face upstage (and away from the audience) in order to look at the actor to whom he/she is supposed to be speaking. Figuratively, the term may be used to describe any sort of acting behavior that calls unwarranted attention to the "upstaging" actor and away from the "upstaged" one.

vaudeville A stage variety show, with singing, dancing, comedy skits, and animal acts; highly popular in America from the late 1880s to the 1930s, when it lost out to the competition from movies, radio, and subsequently television.

well-made play In the nineteenth century, a superbly plotted play, particularly by such gifted French playwrights as Eugène Scribe and Victorien Sardou. Today, generally used pejoratively, as to describe a play that has a workable plot but shallow characterization and trivial ideas.

West End The commercial theatre district of London, England.

wings In a proscenium theatre, the vertical pieces of scenery to the left and right of the stage, usually parallel with the footlights.

This bibliography first lists works of general scope and then cites studies particularly pertinent to discussions in this book.

SELECT
BIBLIOGRAPHY

HISTORICAL SURVEYS OF THEATRE AND DRAMA

Brockett, Oscar G. *History of the Theatre.* 6th ed. Boston: Allyn & Bacon, 1991.

Duerr, Edwin. *The Length and Depth of Acting.* New York: Holt, Rinehart & Winston, 1962.

Dukore, Bernard F., ed. *Dramatic Theory and Criticism: Greeks to Grotowski.* New York: Holt, Rinehart & Winston, 1974.

Gassner, John. *Masters of the Drama.* 3d ed. New York: Dover, 1954.

Hartnoll, Phyllis, ed. *The Oxford Companion to the Theatre.* 4th ed. New York: Oxford University Press, 1983.

Hill, Errol. *The Theatre of Black Americans.* New York: Applause Books, 1987.

Kanellos, Nicolás, ed. *Hispanic Theatre in the United States.* Houston: Arte Público Press, 1984.

_____. *Mexican American Theater: Legacy and Reality.* Pittsburgh: Latin American Literary Review Press, 1987.

Leacroft, Richard and Helen. *Theatre and Playhouse.* London: Methuen, 1984.

Nagler, Alois M. *Sources of Theatrical History.* New York: Dover, 1952.

Nicoll, Allardyce. *World Drama from Aeschylus to Anouilh.* Rev. ed. London: Harrap, 1976.

Pottlitzer, Joanne. *Hispanic Theater in the United States and Puerto Rico.* New York: Ford Foundation, 1988.

The Revels History of Drama in English. 8 vols. London: Methuen, 1975–1983.

Sanders, Leslie C. *The Development of Black Theater in America.* Baton Rouge: Louisiana State University Press, 1988.

GENERAL STUDIES OF THEATRE AND DRAMA

Barry, Jackson G. *Dramatic Structure: The Shaping of Experience.* Berkeley: University of California Press, 1970.

Beckerman, Bernard. *Dynamics of Drama: Theory and Method of Analysis.* New York: Knopf, 1970.

———. *Theatrical Presentation: Performer, Audience, and Act,* ed. by Gloria Brim Beckerman and William Coco. New York: Routledge, 1990.

Bentley, Eric. *The Life of the Drama.* New York: Antheneum, 1964.

Chinoy, Helen, and Jenkins, Linda, eds. *Women in American Theatre.* New York: Crown, 1981.

Esslin, Martin. *An Anatomy of Drama.* New York: Hill & Wang, 1976.

Fergusson, Francis. *The Idea of a Theater.* Princeton, N.J.: Princeton University Press, 1949.

Granville-Barker, Harley. *On Dramatic Method.* New York: Hill & Wang, 1956.

Hayman, Ronald. *How to Read a Play.* New York: Grove Press, 1977.

Heffner, Hubert. *The Nature of Drama.* Boston: Houghton Mifflin, 1959.

Kilgore, Emile S., ed. *Contemporary Plays by Women.* Englewood Cliffs, N.J.: Prentice-Hall, 1991.

Styan, J. L. *The Elements of Drama.* New York: Cambridge University Press, 1960.

———. *Drama, Stage, and Audience.* New York: Cambridge University Press, 1975.

SPECIALIZED STUDIES

Greek and Roman Theatre

The oldest extant archeological remains of Greek theatres date from a century following the classical period; therefore, all reconstructions of earlier times are based solely on fragmentary written evidence and stylized vase paintings, which themselves are often of later periods as well. The existence of a raised stage as part of the *skene* is disputed, as is the shape of the stage. Peter Arnott and Clifford Ashby survey the controversies in detail.

Arnott, Peter D. *Greek Scenic Conventions in the Fifth Century, B.C.* New York: Oxford University Press, 1962.

———. *Public and Performance in the Greek Theatre.* New York: Routledge, 1989.

———. *The Ancient Greek and Roman Theatre.* 2d ed. Princeton, N.J.: Princeton University Press, 1961.

Ashby, Clifford. "The Case for the Rectangular/Trapezoidal Orchestra," *Theatre Research International* 13:1 (Spring 1988), 1–20.

———. "The Siting of Greek Theatres," *Theatre Research International* 16:3 (Autumn 1991), 181–201.

———. "Where Was the Altar?" *Theatre Survey* 32:1 (May 1991), 3–21.

Burkert, Walter. *Greek Religion.* Oxford: Basil Blackwell, 1985.

———. "Greek Tragedy and Sacrificial Ritual," *Greek, Roman and Byzantine Studies* 7 (1966), 87–121.

Butler, James H. *The Theatre and Drama of Greece and Rome.* San Francisco: Chandler, 1972.

Else, Gerald F. *The Origin and Early Form of Greek Tragedy.* Cambridge, Mass.: Harvard University Press, 1965.

Flickinger, Roy C. *The Greek Theatre and Its Drama.* 4th ed. Chicago: University of Chicago Press, 1960.

Kitto, H. D. F. *Greek Tragedy.* 3d ed. London: Methuen, 1961.

Padel, Ruth. "Making Space Speak," in John Winkler and Froma I. Zeitlin, eds., *Nothing to Do With Dionysos?* Princeton, N.J.: Princeton University Press, 1990.

Pickard-Cambridge, A. W. *Dithyramb, Tragedy, and Comedy.* 2d ed., rev. by T. B. L. Webster. Oxford: Clarendon Press, 1962.

———. *The Dramatic Festivals of Athens.* 2d ed., rev. by John Gould and D. M. Lewis. Oxford: Clarendon Press, 1968.

Taplin, Oliver. *Greek Tragedy in Action.* Berkeley: University of California Press, 1978.

———. *The Stagecraft of Aeschylus.* New York: Oxford University Press, 1977.

Toepfer, Karl. *Theatre, Aristocracy, and Pornocracy: The Orgy Calculus.* New York: PAJ Publications, 1991.

Winnington-Ingram, R. P., "The Origins of Tragedy," in P. E. Easterling and B. M. W. Knox, eds., *The Cambridge History of Classical Literature.* Vol. 1, *Greek Literature,* pp. 258–63. Cambridge: Cambridge University Press, 1985.

Zimmerman, Bernhard. *Greek Tragedy: An Introduction.* Trans. by Thomas Marier. Baltimore: Johns Hopkins Press, 1991.

The Medieval Theatre

"Perhaps the most difficult period of Western theatrical history," according to historian Dunbar Ogden in *Theatre Survey,* May 1978. The idea of processional staging of the cycle plays has come under strong attack, primarily from Nelson, Tydeman, and Nagler, all of whom favor the position that the procession was of *tableaux vivants* only, with the full performance held either indoors (Nelson) or at the last station. Our reconstruction, however, is consistent with the available records from the period, which have only recently been published in full (Johnston and Rogerson); and the traditional view, which we espouse, is still widely supported, as, for example, by Clifford Davidson: "The evidence of the records . . . does appear to prove conclusively that the Corpus Christi play was performed at various stations through the city. . . . While it remains an attractive theory to suggest that the pageants grew out of tableaux vivants, . . . we can no longer seriously defend, I believe, Alan H. Nelson's revisionist theories about the staging of the York cycle indoors." (*Comparative Drama,* Spring 1980, pp. 79–80.)

Chambers, E. K. *The Medieval Stage.* 2 vols. Oxford: Clarendon Press, 1903.

Collier, Richard J. *Poetry and Drama in the York Corpus Christi Play.* New York: Archon, 1978.

Haridison, O. B. *Christian Rite and Christian Drama in the Middle Ages: Essays in the Origin and Early History of Modern Drama.* Baltimore: Johns Hopkins Press, 1965.

Johnston, Alexandra F., and Rogerson, Margaret. *Records of Early English Drama: York.* Toronto: University of Toronto Press, 1979.

Kolve, V. A. *The Play Called Corpus Christi.* Stanford, Calif.: Stanford University Press, 1966.

Nagler, A. M. *The Medieval Religious Stage: Shapes and Phantoms.* New Haven, Conn.: Yale University Press, 1976.

Nelson, Alan H. *The Medieval English Stage: Corpus Christi Pageants and Plays.* Chicago: University of Chicago Press, 1974.

Nicoll, Allardyce. *Masks, Mimes, and Miracles.* New York: Harcourt Brace, 1931.

Southern, Richard. *The Medieval Theatre in the Round.* London: Faber & Faber, 1957.

Tydeman, W. *The Theatre in the Middle Ages.* New York: Cambridge University Press, 1979.

Wickham, Glynne. *Early English Stages, 1300–1660.* 2 vols. New York: Columbia University Press, 1959.

———. *The Medieval Theatre.* London: St. Martin's Press, 1974.

Woolf, Rosemary. *The English Mystery Play.* Berkeley: University of California Press, 1972.

The Shakespearean Theatre

The literature on Shakespeare is voluminous, and the attempts to reconstruct a Shakespearean theatre have yielded varied interpretations. Our reconstruction is based largely on the original evidence, and particularly Hodges's reading of it; nothing uncovered in the recent excavations (reported in Gurr and Orrell) changes the speculations presented in the drawings in this chapter. The list below is highly selective, and includes some recent titles of considerable interest.

Adams, John. *The Globe Playhouse: Its Design and Equipment.* 2d ed. New York: Barnes & Noble, 1961.

Baldwin, T. W. *The Organization and Personnel of the Shakespearean Company.* Princeton, N.J.: Princeton University Press, 1927.

Beckerman, Bernard. *Shakespeare at the Globe, 1599–1609.* New York: Macmillan, 1962.

Bentley, Gerald E. *The Profession of Dramatist in Shakespeare's Time, 1590–1642.* Princeton, NJ: Princeton University Press, 1971.

———. *The Jacobean and Caroline Stage.* 8 vols. New York: Oxford University Press, 1941–68.

Chambers, E. K. *The Elizabethan Stage.* 4 vols. London: Oxford University Press, 1923.

Dash, Irene G. *Wooing, Wedding and Power: Women in Shakespeare's Plays.* New York: Columbia University Press, 1981.

David, Richard. *Shakespeare in the Theatre.* New York: Cambridge University Press, 1978.

Gurr, Andrew, "A First Doorway into the Globe," *Shakespeare Quarterly,* Spring 1990, 95–100.

Harbage, Alfred. *Shakespeare's Audience.* New York: Columbia University Press, 1941.

Hildy, Franklin, J., ed. *New Issues in the Reconstruction of Shakespeare's Theatre.* New York: Peter Lang, 1990.

Hodges, C. Walter. *The Globe Restored.* 2d ed. New York: Oxford University Press, 1968.

———. *Shakespeare's Second Globe.* New York: Oxford University Press, 1973.

Hotson, Leslie. *Shakespeare's Wooden O.* New York: Macmillan, 1960.

Kahn, Coppélia. *Man's Estate: Masculine Identity in Shakespeare.* Berkeley: University of California Press, 1981.

Mann, David. *The Elizabethan Player.* New York: Routledge, 1991.

Nagler, A. M. *Shakespeare's Stage.* New Haven, Conn.: Yale University Press, 1958.

Neely, Carol T. *Broken Nuptials in Shakespeare's Plays.* New Haven: Yale University Press, 1985.

Orrell, John, and Gurr, Andrew. "What the Rose Can Tell Us," *Antiquity,* 63 (1989), 421–29.

Southern, Richard. *The Staging of Plays Before Shakespeare.* New York: Theatre Arts Books, 1973.

Speaight, Robert. *Shakespeare on the Stage.* New York: William Collins Sons, 1972.

Thompson, Ann. "The Warrent of Womanhood: Shakespeare and Feminist Criticism," in Graham Holderness, ed., *The Shakespeare Myth.* Manchester, England: Manchester University Press, 1988.

The Royal Theatre

Deierkauf-Holsboer, Wilma. *Histoire de la Mise-en-scène dans le Théâtre Française à Paris de 1600 à 1673.* Paris: Nizet, 1960.

Holland, Peter. *The Ornament of Action: Text and Performance in Restoration Comedy.* New York: Cambridge University Press, 1979.

Lancaster, H. C. *A History of French Dramatic Literature in the Seventeenth Century.* 5 vols. Baltimore: Johns Hopkins Press, 1929–42.

Lawrenson, T. E. *The French Stage in the XVIIth Century.* Manchester: Manchester University Press, 1957.

McBride, Robert. *Aspects of 17th Century French Drama and Thought*. Totowa, N.J.: Rowman & Littlefield, 1980.

Nicoll, Allardyce. *History of English Drama, 1660–1900*. 6 vols. London: Cambridge University Press, 1955–59.

Wiley, W. L. *The Early Public Theatre in France*. Cambridge, Mass.: Harvard University Press, 1960.

The Modern and Postmodern Theatre

Antoine, André. *Memories of the Théâtre Libre*. Trans. by Marvin Carlson. Coral Gables, Fla.: University of Miami Press, 1964.

Artaud, Antonin. *The Theatre and Its Double*. Trans. by Mary C. Richards. New York: Grove Press, 1958.

Bentley, Eric. *The Playwright as Thinker*. New York: Reynal, 1946.

Bigsby, C. W. E. *A Critical Introduction to Twentieth-Century American Drama*. 3 vols. Cambridge: Cambridge University Press, 1985.

Birringer, Johannes H. *Theatre, Theory, Postmodernism*. Bloomington: Indiana University Press, 1991.

Bordman, Gerald. *American Musical Theatre*. New York: Oxford University Press, 1978.

Bradby, David. *Modern French Drama 1940–1980*. Cambridge: Cambridge University Press, 1984.

Brecht, Bertolt. *Brecht on Theatre*. Trans. by John Willett. New York: Hill & Wang, 1965.

Brook, Peter. *The Empty Space*. New York: Atheneum, 1968.

Brown-Guillory, Elizabeth. *Their Place on the Stage: Black Women Playwrights in America*. New York: Greenwood Press, 1988.

Brustein, Robert. *The Theatre of Revolt: An Approach to Modern Drama*. Boston: Little, Brown, 1964.

Craig, Edward Gordon. *On the Art of the Theatre*. 2d ed. Boston: Small, Maynard, 1924.

Croyden, Margeret. *Lunatics, Lovers and Poets: The Contemporary Experimental Theatre*. New York: McGraw-Hill, 1974.

de Jongh, Nicholas. *Not in Front of the Audience: Homosexuality on Stage*. London: Routledge, 1992.

Derrida, Jacques. "The Theatre of Cruelty and the Closure of Representation." In *Writing and Difference*, trans. Alan Bass. Chicago: University of Chicago Press, 1978.

Esslin, Martin. *Brecht: The Man and His Work*. New York: Doubleday, 1960.

———. *The Theatre of the Absurd*. Rev. ed. New York: Doubleday, 1969.

Gaggi, Silvio. *Modern/Postmodern*. Philadelphia: University of Pennsylvania Press, 1989.

Gassner, John. *Form and Idea in the Modern Theatre*. New York: Holt, Rinehart & Winston, 1956.

Gordon, Mel. *Dada Performance*. New York: PAJ Publications, 1987.

Guicharnaud, Jacques. *Modern French Theatre from Giraudoux to Beckett*. New Haven, Conn.: Yale University Press, 1961.

Grotowski, Jerzy. *Towards a Poor Theatre*. New York: Simon & Schuster, 1968.

Houghton, Norris. *Moscow Rehearsals*. New York: Harcourt Brace, 1936.

Innes, Christopher. *Modern German Drama: A Study in Form*. New York: Cambridge University Press, 1979.

Kerensky, Oleg. *The New British Drama: Fourteen Playwrights Since Osborne and Pinter*. New York: Taplinger, 1979.

Kerr, Walter. *Journey to the Center of the Theatre*. New York: Knopf, 1979.

Kirby, Michael, ed. *The New Theatre: Performance Documentation*. New York: New York University Press, 1974. Photos and texts of major experimental theatres in Poland, Belgium, France, Brazil, Italy, Japan, United States, England in the late 1960s/early 1970s: Grotowski (*Apocalpysis cum figuris*), Mnouchkine (*1789*).

Marranca, Bonnie, and Dasgupta, Gautam. *American Playwrights: A Critical Survey*. New York: Drama Book Specialists, 1981.

Marranca, Bonnie, and Dasgupta, Gautam, eds. *Interculturalism and Performance*. New York: PAJ Publications, 1991.

Matlaw, Myron. *Modern World Drama: An Encyclopedia*. New York: E. P. Dutton, 1972.

Natalle, Elizabeth, J. *Feminist Theatre: A Study in Persuasion*. Metuchen, N.J.: Scarecrow Press, 1985.

Roose-Evans, James. *Experimental Theatre: From Stanislavski to Peter Brook*. New York: Universe Books, 1984.

———. *Experimental Theatre: From Stanislavski to Today*. Rev. ed. New York: Universe Books, 1973.

Seltzer, Daniel, ed. *The Modern Theatre: Readings and Documents*. Boston: Little, Brown, 1967.

Shaw, George Bernard. *The Quintessence of Ibsenism*. London: Constable, 1913.

Trachtenberg, Stanley, ed. *The Postmodern Moment*. Westport, Conn.: Greenwood Press, 1985.

Vanden Heuvel, Michael. *Performing Drama/Dramatizing Performance*. Ann Arbor: University of Michigan Press, 1991.

Völker, Klaus. *Brecht: A Biography*. New York: Seabury Press, 1978.

Wellwarth, George E. *The Theatre of Protest and Paradox*. New York: New York University Press, 1964.

Willett, John. *The Theatre of Bertolt Brecht*. New York: New Directions, 1959.

Williams, Mance. *Black Theatre in the 1960s and 1970s*. Westport, Conn.: Greenwood Press, 1985.

Ziegler, Joseph. *Regional Theatre*. New York: Da Capo Press, 1973.

Acting and Directing

Barish, Jonas. *The Anti-Theatrical Prejudice*. Berkeley: University of California Press, 1981.

Barrault, Jean-Louis. *Reflections on the Theatre*. London: Salisbury Square, 1951.

Benedetti, Robert L. *The Actor at Work*. 3d ed. Englewood Cliffs, N.J.: Prentice-Hall, 1981.

Berry, Cecily. *Voice and the Actor*. London: Harrap, 1973.

Boleslavski, Richard. *Acting: The First Six Lessons*. New York: Theatre Arts Books, 1933.

Brook, Peter. *The Shifting Point*. New York: Harper & Row, 1987.

Chaikin, Joseph. *The Presence of the Actor*. New York: Atheneum, 1972.

Chekhov, Michael. *To the Actor*. New York: Harper & Row, 1953.

Cohen, Robert. *Acting Power*. Palo Alto, Calif.: Mayfield, 1978.

———. *Acting Professionally*. 4th ed. Mountain View, Calif.: Mayfield, 1990.

———, and Harrop, John. *Creative Play Direction*. 2nd ed. Englewood Cliffs, N.J.: Prentice-Hall, 1984.

Cole, Toby, and Chinoy, Helen K., eds. *Actors on Acting*. Rev. ed. New York: Crown, 1970.

———. *Directors on Directing*. Rev. ed. Indianapolis: Bobbs-Merrill, 1963.

Dean, Alexander. *Fundamentals of Play Directing*. 4th ed., rev. by Lawrence Carra. New York: Holt, Rinehart & Winston, 1980.

Diderot, Denis. "The Paradox of Acting," in William Archer, *Masks or Faces?* New York: Hill & Wang, 1957.

Felsenstein, Walter. *The Music Theatre of Walter Felsenstein*. New York: W. W. Norton, 1975.

Goldman, Michael. *The Actor's Freedom*. New York: Viking, 1975.

Guthrie, Tyrone. *Tyrone Guthrie on Acting*. New York: Viking, 1971.

Hagen, Uta. *Respect for Acting*. New York: Macmillan, 1973.

Hodge, Francis. *Play Directing: Analysis, Communication, and Style*. Englewood Cliffs, N.J.: Prentice-Hall, 1971.

King, Nancy. *Theatre Movement: The Actor and His Space*. New York: DBS Publications, 1972.

Lewis, Robert. *Method or Madness*. London: Heinemann, 1960.

———. *Advice to the Players*. New York: Harper & Row, 1980.

Linklatter, Kristin. *Freeing the Natural Voice*. New York: DBS Publications, 1976.

Marowitz, Charles. *The Act of Being: Toward A New Theory of Acting*. New York: Taplinger, 1978.

McGaw, Charles J. *Acting Is Believing*. 4th ed. New York: Holt, Rinehart & Winston, 1980.

Penrod, James. *Movement for the Performing Artist*. Palo Alto, Calif.: Mayfield, 1974.

Roach, Joseph R. *The Player's Passion: Studies in the Science of Acting*. Newark: University of Delaware Press, 1985.

Spolin, Viola. *Improvisation for the Theatre*. Evanston, Ill.: Northwestern University Press, 1963.

Stanislavski, Konstantin. *An Actor Prepares*. Trans. by Elizabeth Reynolds Hapgood. New York: Theatre Arts Books, 1936.

Wills, J. Robert, ed. *The Director in a Changing Theatre*. Palo Alto, Calif.: Mayfield, 1976.

Design

American Theatre Planning Board. *Theatre Check List: A Guide to the Planning and Construction of Proscenium and Open Stage Theatres*. Middletown, Conn.: Wesleyan University Press, 1969.

Aronson, Arnold. *American Set Design*. New York: Theatre Communications Group, 1985.

Bablet, Denis. *Revolutions of Stage Design in the Twentieth Century*. New York: L. Amiel, 1976.

Bay, Howard. *Stage Design*. New York: DBS Publications, 1974.

Barton, Lucy. *Historic Costume for the Stage*. Boston: Baker's Plays, 1935.

Bellman, Willard F. *Scenography and Stage Technology: An Introduction*. New York: Harper & Row, 1977.

Bergman, Gosta M. *Lighting in the Theatre*. Totowa, N.J.: Rowman & Littlefield, 1977.

Burdick, Elizabeth B., et al., eds. *Contemporary Stage Design*. Middletown, Conn.: Wesleyan University Press, 1975.

Burris-Meyer, Harold, and Cole, Edward C. *Scenery for the Theatre*. 2d rev. ed. Boston: Little, Brown, 1972.

Corson, Richard. *Stage Make-up*. 5th ed. New York: Appleton-Century-Crofts, 1975.

Izenour, George C. *Theatre Design*. New York: McGraw-Hill, 1977.

Jones, Robert Edmund. *The Dramatic Imagination*. New York: Meredith, 1941.

Mielziner, Jo. *Designing for the Theatre*. New York: Atheneum, 1965.

Motley. *Designing and Making Stage Costumes*. London: Studio Vista, 1964.

———. *Theatre Props*. New York: DBS Publications, 1976.

Oenslager, Donald. *Stage Design: Four Centuries of Scenic Invention*. New York: Viking, 1975.

Pilbrow, Richard. *Stage Lighting*. New York: DBS Publications, 1979.

Russell, Douglas. *Stage Costume Design*. New York: Appleton-Century-Crofts, 1973.

TEXT CREDITS

Page 74 From *Strasberg at the Actors Studio* by Robert Hethman. Copyright © 1965.

Page 94 From *Dirty Linen* by Tom Stoppard and *Silence* by Harold Pinter reprinted by permission of Grove Press, Inc., and Faber and Faber Ltd. Copyright © 1969 by Harold Pinter and 1976 by Tom Stoppard.

Page 120 From *The Dramatic Imagination* by Robert Edmund Jones. Reprinted with the permission of the publishers, Theatre Arts Books, 29 West 35 Street, New York, New York 10001.

Page 139 From *Designing and Making Stage Costumes* by Motley. Copyright © 1964 by Elizabeth Montgomery, Sophie Devine and Margaret Harris. Reprinted by permission of Eatson-Guptill Publications.

Page 160 From *The Empty Space* by Peter Brook by permission of Atheneum Publishers, Inc.

Page 183 From *Buried Child* by Sam Shepard by permission of Urizen Books, Inc. Copyright © 1979 by Sam Shepard.

Page 188 From Edward Gordon Craig's *On the Art of the Theatre*. Reprinted with the permission of the publishers, Theatre Arts Books, 29 West 35 Street, New York, New York, 10001.

Page 193 *Ubu Roi* from Michael Benedikt and George Wellwarth's *Modern French Theatre*. Reprinted by permission of Georges Borchardt, Inc.

Page 200 *Jet of Blood* from Michael Benedikt and George Wellwarth's *Modern French Theatre*. Reprinted by permission of Georges Borchardt, Inc.

Page 202 Selection by Jean-Paul Sartre from *Theatre Arts,* July 1946. Reprinted by permission of Mrs. W. A. Bradley.

Page 210 "Bedroom Farce" from *Absurd Person Singular* by Alan Ayckbourne reprinted by permission of Grove Press, Inc., and Chatto and Windus. Copyright © 1975 by Alan Ayckbourn.

Page 213 "Castrophe" from *Wings* by Arthur Kopit. Copyright © 1978 by Arthur Kopit. Reprinted by permission of Hill and Wang (a division of Farrer, Straus & Giroux, Inc.).

INDEX

Quem Queritis, 136

Rabe, David
  The Basic Training of Pavlo
    Hummel, 284*f*
  Hurlyburly, 246
A Raisin in the Sun, 228
Raphael, 130
Realism, 178–81, 188*q*
Rehearsing, 12, 26–28, 78–81
Reilly, Claudia, *Astronauts*, 105*f*
Requiem for a Heavyweight, 249*f*
Resonance, 69
Return to the Forbidden Planet,
  costumes for, 144*f*
Reviews, newspaper, 289–92
Revival, theatre of, 220–21
Richard, Lloyd, 249
Richard II, 248*f*
Ride Down Mount Morgan,
  274–75
Rimbaud, Arthur, 187
Rise and Fall of the City of
  Mahagonny, 43*f*, 207
Ritual art, 265–66
The Rivals, 224*f*
Rivera, José, *Marisol*, 246, 284*f*
The Robbers, 177
Robinson, Mary, 227
Rockabye, 225
Romanticism, 177–78, 221*f*
Romeo and Juliet
  casting of, 164
  genre of, 32
  stageability of, 95
Rosenblatt, Roger, *"and"*, 265
Rostand, Edmond de, *Cyrano*
  de Bergerac, 147*f*
Routine, in acting, 77–84
Royal Shakespeare Company
  (England), 259
Rumors, 38*f*
Running, 12
Russell, Willy, *Shirley Valentine*,
  265
Russia, current theatre in, 262

St. Louis Black Repertory
  Company, 253
Salvini, Tommaso, 68
San Francisco, nonprofit theatre in,
  252
Sangallo, Aristotile da, 118
Sardou, Victorien, 42
Sartre, Jean-Paul, *No Exit*, 201–2

Sato, Shozo, *Kabuki Medea*, 138*f*
Scene design, 117–30
Schary, Dore, *Sunrise at*
  Campobello, 54
Schenkkan, Robert, *The Kentucky*
  Cycle, 31*f*, 32, 165*f*, 225
Schiller, Friedrich, *The Robbers*, 177
Schnitzler, Arthur, 182
The School for Scandal, 152*f*
Scofield, Paul, 166
Scribe, Eugéne, 42
Scrim, 127
Scripted play, 26–28
Search and Destroy, 22*f*, 284*f*
Search for Signs of Intelligent Life in
  the Universe, 82*f*, 265
Seascape, 276
Seating, 49
Seattle, nonprofit theatre in,
  251–52
Seattle Repertory Theatre, 252
Serban, Andrei, 245
Serling, Rod, *Requiem for a*
  Heavyweight, 249*f*
Serlio, Sebastiano, 118, 130
Servandoni, Jean-Nicholas, 123
Set piece, 126–27
Sexual preference, and theatre of
  difference, 233–34
Shaffer, Peter, *Equus*, 54, 92, 213
Shakespeare, William
  comedies of, 35
  Cymbeline, 167*f*
  dark comedies of, 37
  on genres, 33*q*
  Hamlet, 33*q*, 71*f*, 122*f*
  Henry IV, 36*f*, 63*f*
  Henry V, 51–52
  history plays of, 36
  Julius Caesar, 32*f*, 62*f*, 126*f*,
    235, 236*f*
  King Lear, 36–37, 44*f*, 132*f*,
    166
  Macbeth, 29, 52, 53
  A Midsummer Night's Dream,
    30, 113*f*, 120*f*, 254*f*, 271
  Much Ado About Nothing, 223*f*
  Richard II, 248*f*
  Romeo and Juliet, 32, 95, 164
  The Taming of the Shrew, 250*f*
  Twelfth Night, 80*f*, 159*f*, 163*f*
  Two Gentlemen of Verona, 136*f*
Shakespeare festivals, 253–54
Shakespearean era, staging of, 158
Shange, Ntozake, *For Colored Girls*

Who Have Considered Suicide
  When the Rainbow is Enuf,
  229
Shattuck, Roger, 193
Shaw, George Bernard, 97, 179
  Androcles and the Lion, 169*f*
  Back to Methuselah, 32
  Man and Superman, 187*f*, 188,
    222*f*
  on Sardou, 42
Shaw Festival (Canada), 262
Shepard, Sam, 277
  Buried Child, 182–86
  A Lie of the Mind, 142*f*
  True West, 278*f*
Sheridan, Richard Brinsley
  The Rivals, 224*f*
  The School for Scandal, 152*f*
Shingeki, 263
Shirley Valentine, 265
Shubert Alley, 239*f*
Sight Unseen, 243*f*
Silence, 94
Sills, Paul, 11
Simon, John, 289*q*
Simon, Neil, 209, 275–76
  Broadway Bound, 76*f*
  Jake's Women, 103*f*, 276
  Rumors, 38*f*
Situational intentions, in acting, 75
Six Characters in Search of an
  Author, 198–99
Society, play's relation to, 285–87
Solis, Octavio, *Man of the Flesh*,
  232*f*
Solon, 19
Sondheim, Stephen, 269–70
  Pacific Overtures, 269
  Sunday in the Park with George,
    269, 270*f*
  Sweeney Todd, 120, 215–16, 269*f*
Song of Singapore, 21*f*
Sound, 8–9, 128, 144–45
South Africa, current theatre in,
  27, 263
South Coast Repertory theatre
  (SCR), 248, 270*f*
Soyinka, Wole, 263
Speakability, in playwriting, 93, 95
Spectacle, 45–46
Stage design, 108–9, 111–12, 113*f*
Stage fright, 58
Stage machinery, 128
Stage manager, 12–13, 150
Stageability, in playwriting, 95